CW01604188

WELCOME

The greatest films ever? Yeah, sure, that won't be any problem at all...

Oh, the rows. The endless debates, the constant bickering. The former friendships now destroyed. You really won't believe the trouble we went to in putting together this list of the greatest films of all time.

Naturally, everyone on the team's choices differed wildly and what you have in your hands is our noble attempt at compromise (while trying desperately to ignore the constant, growing, unspoken threat of violence that began to permeate the office...).

Still, the final 100 we settled on isn't half bad. Suffice to say, every film present here is worthy of your attention and would look handsome sitting on your shelves. So enjoy. And, yes, feel free to send your thoughts, queries, disputes and – hey – copious buckets of praise to the usual address...

Aubrey

Aubrey Ganguly, Editor-in-Chief

CONTENTS

EXCLUSIVE TO WHSmith

100

GOLDFINGER

Bigger thrills, better spills and Pussy Galore... Bond finds its blockbuster formula.

Here's a poser. If so many fine books have been made into lame films, why is it that, paradoxically, so many lame books have become fine films? Is it because, when the source material is so unsacred filmmakers feel free to cannibalise to their heart's content, using only the bits that suit the screen?

The audience is made to laugh, gasp, grin and gawp... but rarely think

If that is the case, then it's no wonder James Bond is so popular. Because, let's be honest, Ian Fleming's secret agent series is amongst the most stupid ever to be put on paper. Even if you put the old-school snobbery, casual racism and adolescent misogyny down to more 'innocent' times, you're still left with trite, inconsistent characters, clumsy coincidence-laden plots and a lack of common sense that would shame the Cat in the Hat. Even Fleming himself admitted, "If one has a grain of intelligence, it is difficult to go on being serious about a character like James Bond."

Take *Goldfinger* for example. The original novel has the titular baddie purchase a bomb from an American airbase (as you do), intending to blow open the security doors of Fort Knox (again, as you do) and carry out an impossibly large tonnage of gold (as you, er, couldn't actually physically do). Meanwhile Bond simply bumps into Goldfinger in a handy plot coincidence before ruining his nefarious plans, primarily by using his superhuman virility to convert a wayward lesbian into a socially conscious, man-hungry sex kitten. Although, apparently, she was asking for it...

And yet, in what folks once referred to as the magic of the silver screen, what we end up with from this rag-tag of colonial public schoolboy wish fulfilment is one of the most thrilling films of the '60s. A silly, funny, excellent escapade that cemented the foundations of one of the most popular franchises in movie history and practically invented the blockbuster as we know it. So where did it all go right?

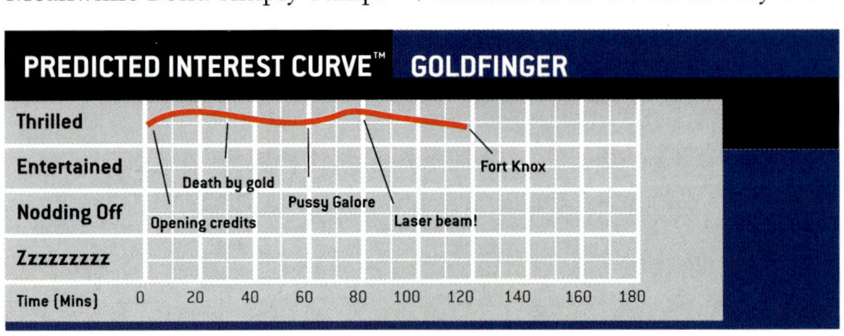

Some of the credit has to go to screenwriters Richard Maibaum and former Oscar winner Paul Dehn, who took all the best bits from the book (the Aston Martin, Pussy Galore, Oddjob) and filtered out the least logical segments. Now, Bond and Goldfinger don't meet by chance but purpose. And Goldfinger's plot is only to irradiate the gold in Fort Knox, making it unusable and his own stockpile more valuable. Peter Hunt's editing style helps too, all frantic cuts and frenzied action that doesn't give the audience too much time to think about remaining plot gaps.

Then there's the appeal of Connery, who was mutating through the role into the world's most desired man.

"Sean really was a very sexy man," observed Hunt. "There are very few film stars who had that sort of quality. He could virtually

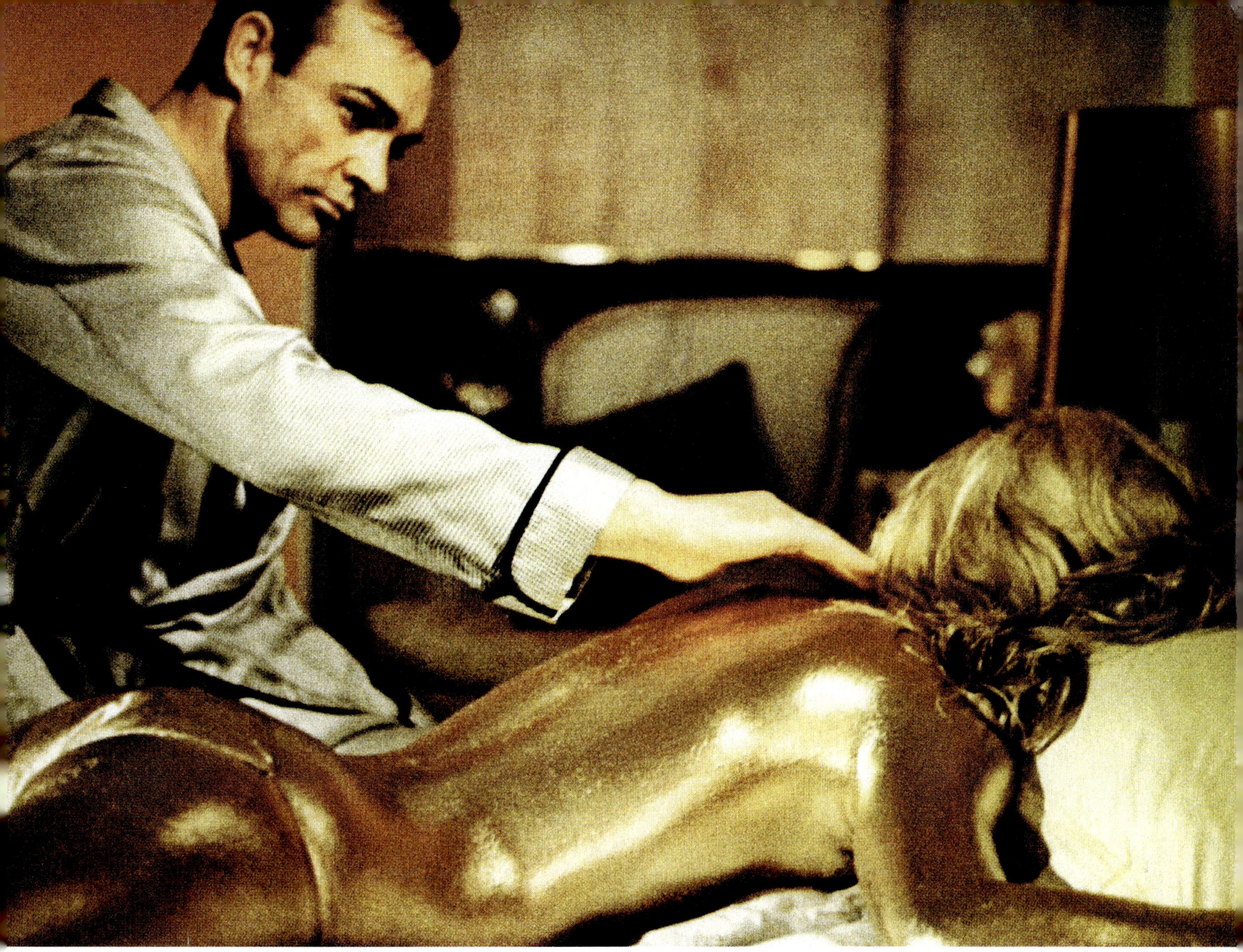

walk into a room and fuck anybody." Certainly the sexual tension on screen between Connery and Honor Blackman is so palpable as to make a mockery of her character's supposed distaste for him. "Sean's the sexiest man I've ever met," sighed Blackman in numerous interviews later.

But perhaps the defining feature of *Goldfinger* – and every successful Bond since – was director Guy Hamilton's philosophy that "the important thing is for everyone – the audience and James Bond – to have a lot of fun." As Hamilton admitted, "If you believe a man can steal all the gold in the world, monkeys can fly. So you've got to take it all with a pinch of salt. My approach to the audience was, 'We're going to take you to wonderful places, we're going to show you beautiful girls, we're going to have some suspense and we're going to have some laughs. So let's enjoy it!'"

Hence the dazzling pre-credits sequence, a mini-adventure where Bond (with the aid of a fake seagull) infiltrates and destroys some installation possibly in South America (actually an oil refinery in England) before electrocuting an unfortunate assailant.

"Positively shocking," tuts Bond as we enter the opening credits – shimmering images projected on the nubile Margaret Nolan as John Barry and Shirley Bassey conspire to knock our socks off with the standard-setting theme tune.

From then until 100-odd minutes later (*Goldfinger* was one of the last Bond films to clock in at under two hours) there's really no let up, with iconic moment following iconic moment: the tuxedo-concealing wetsuit; the gold-painted Shirley Eaton; the bowler-hatted menace of Oddjob; the golf scene; the ejector seat in the Aston Martin; the almost-genital destroying laser beam; the beyond-belief cheek of naming a character Pussy Galore; the climactic battle at Fort Knox. The audience is made to laugh, gasp, grin and gawp... but rarely think. And, ultimately, this is how Bond achieves world domination. By offering pure escapism. And all the safari-suited Roger Moores in the world can't stop him.

Aubrey Ganguly

NEED TO KNOW

Year 1964
Running time 108 mins
Director Guy Hamilton
Stars Sean Connery, Gert Fröbe, Honor Blackman, Harold Sakata, Shirley Eaton
Buy it on Region 2
Tagline "James Bond back in action!"
Best line "No Mr Bond, I expect you to die!" – Goldfinger
Critic's view "*Goldfinger* really is a dazzling object lesson in the principle that nothing succeeds like excess." – Monthly Film Bulletin
Best watched when... Your tuxedo is at the dry cleaners.

99

THREE KINGS

David O Russell and George Clooney kick up a desert storm...

Troy Barlow (Mark Wahlberg), in the opening scene of *Three Kings*, asks, "Are we shooting?" If this is a sly, potentially smug in-joke – yes, the cameras are rolling – it's immediately undercut when he trains his rifle on the waving Iraqi soldier, fires, hits. He runs up to find a man his own age, choking on his own blood, having been shot in the throat. While dumbass American grunts take photos of the dying enemy soldier, Troy contemplates what he's done.

It's fearless in presenting the politics of the war and the human cost of America's actions

Then, bam, we're away into the celebrations that mark the end of the first Gulf War: Troy dancing to a raucous track by Rare Earth; Frat House japes under canvas with illicit booze; desperate shagging in the comms room between a cynical reporter and Special Forces Major Archie Gates (George Clooney). Soon, Gates, Troy, Chief Elgin (Ice Cube) and hick private Conrad Vig (Spike Jonze, then a video director who was editing his breakthrough film, *Being John Malkovich*) are united by a map discovered in the arse of an Iraqi prisoner: a route to a cache of Kuwaiti gold pilfered by Saddam Hussein. They're ready to steal it back...

So it's *Kelly's Heroes* in the Gulf. But where Clint Eastwood's picture was an unevenly enjoyable caper that treated the Second World War as a giant playground (never mind the Holocaust), *Three Kings* engages with its time and place. Only the second film (after *Courage Under Fire*) to tackle Gulf War I, it's fearless in presenting the politics of the war and the human cost of America's actions.

Audiences who had no idea about the aftermath of the conflict – when US troops, under orders after the truce with Saddam Hussein, had to stand by and watch as Iraqi soldiers slaughtered their own people – were presented the truth in stark terms. As Gates puts it, "Bush told the people to rise up against Saddam. They thought they'd have our support. They don't. Now they're getting slaughtered." In contrast, the first film to tackle the Vietnam War was John Wayne's jingoistic, heroically dull *The Green Berets*. Even *The Deer Hunter* and *Apocalypse Now* (both on this list) explored 'Nam as an American tragedy.

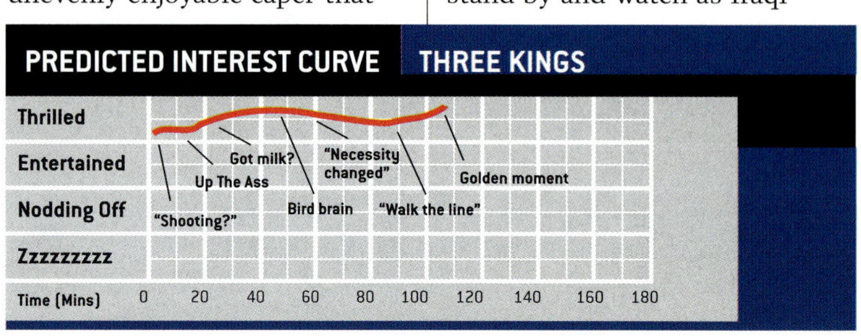

It's ironic, given the protests against Gulf War II (of which Clooney was a vocal opponent), that *Three Kings* could be said to argue that the US should have deposed of Saddam back in 1991. Certainly it damns the policy of leaving the Iraqi people, as a rebel leader puts it, "twisting in the wind".

It's also clear on the real motives for kicking Saddam out of Kuwait: not an altruistic action to save the beleaguered sheikdom, but a bid to secure

oil supplies. "They say you exorcised the ghosts of Vietnam with a clear moral imperative," Nora Dunn's reporter says to jubilant soldiers, while the film goes on to show how bogus her assertion is. Particularly in the quite brilliant scene when Barlow is tortured by an Iraqi soldier (Saïd Taghmaoui), whose life in many ways reflects his own. Forced to choke on oil after hearing how US bombs killed Saïd's child, Barlow's horror mirrors that of the audience, dealing with a situation that couldn't be any further from cut and dried.

Three Kings, however, is much more than simply a sermon on US foreign policy, thanks to both Russell's writing, layering his message on to an original heist script called *Spoils Of War* by John Ridley, and the performances. Wahlberg shows how intense a presence he can be when working with a director he clicks with; ditto Ice Cube. As Gates, Clooney holds the film's potent moral conscience in his eyes. Tom Cruise and Nicolas Cage both came close to signing up for the role, while Mel Gibson, Warren Beatty, Kevin Costner and John Travolta were all considered.

However Clooney, not quite on the A-list at that point, fought hard to secure the part, and then fought publicly on-set with Russell over his poor treatment of an extra. Russell apparently found the Arizona desert shoot a considerable step-up from his indie comedies *Spanking The Monkey* and *Flirting With Disaster*.

NEED TO KNOW

Year 1999
Running time 114 mins
Director David O Russell
Stars George Clooney, Mark Wahlberg, Ice Cube, Spike Jonze, Saïd Taghmaoui
Buy it on Region 2
Tagline "In a war without heroes they are kings."
Best line "Walter, just stand outside so Chief can translate my Iraqi ass map... okay?" – Troy Barlow
Critic's view "Impudently comic, stylistically aggressive and, finally, very thoughtful." – *Variety*
Best watched when... America is waging war with somewhere. So pretty much any time really...

You know Clooney's performance is great because you can't imagine anyone else half as effective in the role. And the star-director friction didn't detract from the end result. Russell's DoP, Newton Thomas Sigel, created a stark, desaturated look to match the mood of the piece, and the bullet-in-the-gut scene was so realistic people believed a mischief-making Russell when he claimed they'd used a real cadaver for the shot.

"I hope the film will last as a portrait of a very strange, morally complicated and morally compromised war," says Russell on his DVD commentary. It's *M*A*S*H* for the 21st century: hilarious and still frighteningly relevant.
Nev Pierce

98

CASABLANCA

Bogart and Bergman strike sparks in one of Hollywood's Golden Age greats.

Casablanca, with more than 60 years gone by since it was made, should be a tricky film to judge. One of the most famous films ever seared onto celluloid, there should be no way to dig past its iconic status for a clear-eyed squint at the movie itself. You should be blinded by the countless parodies, replica posters and bad impressionists muttering "Play it again, Sam!" through clenched lips (a line never actually spoken in the film). It should be impossible to appreciate the movie any more.

It could be argued that Rick redefined celluloid heroes

But somehow, *Casablanca* manages to rise above all that gubbins. Indeed, plonk yourself down to watch Michael Curtiz's studio-set potboiler now and you're immediately struck by its freshness. Forget the stagey awkwardness of lame '40s melodrama: there's an icy, modern snap to *Casablanca's* dialogue that jolts your head back. "I don't mind a parasite. I object to a cut-rate one," Bogart's Rick snarls to Peter Lorre's doomed wheeler-dealer Ugarte, before sauntering off for a quick verbal duel with a German officer. Asked if he can picture the Nazis in Paris, London or maybe New York, Rick quips, "Well there are certain sections of New York, Major, that I wouldn't advise you to try to invade..."

It could be argued that Rick Blaine redefined celluloid heroes. As snug in a dinner jacket as he is in a trenchcoat, here's a man with a hard outer shell who's still not afraid to expose his feelings when his long-lost love turns up on Moroccan shores hitched to another fella. A savvy blend of toughness and wit, style and substance, romance and cynicism, it's a role you can't imagine anyone other than Humphrey Bogart playing. Neither could producer Hal B Wallis. Legend has it that Ronald Reagan and George Raft were considered before studio second-stringer Bogart got his shot, but that's largely Holly-myth. Wallis owned the rights, and said in a memo to studio head Jack Warner, "Bogart is ideal for *Casablanca*, and it is being written for him."

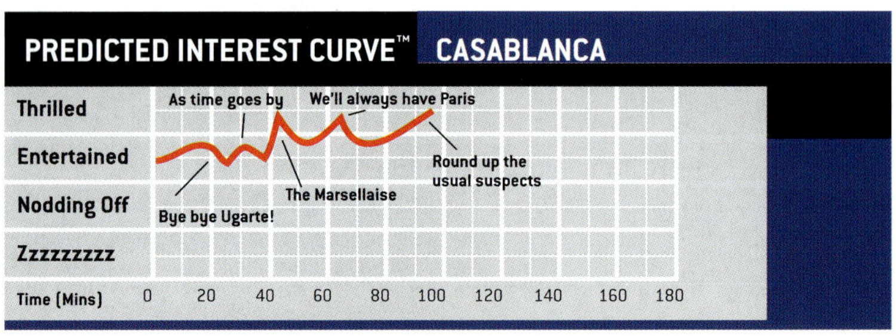

But even if that bit of planning was always in place, it's alarming how much of the rest of the film was made up on the hoof. Murray Burnett and Joan Alison's source play, *Everyone Comes To Rick's*, suffered so much script surgery, director Michael Curtiz wasn't even sure how the film was going to end when he started shooting. When Ingrid Bergman demanded to know whether her torn-between-two-lovers character, Ilsa, was supposed to end up with Rick or her husband, Victor Laszlo, Curtiz just shrugged and told her, "Play it in between".

Casablanca is always thought of as a love story. And yes, the plot pivots on Ilsa's unexpected arrival, jolting Rick out of his

apathetic cynicism. Their doomed romance, with its flashbacks to happier times in Paris, is still one of cinema's finest, with an uplifting self-sacrifice at its core that blinds you to the fact that Ilsa is a cipher whose fate is not self-determined, but decided by the two men she loves.

But love isn't everything in the film. It's also a passionate anti-Nazi declaration – that line about the Germans invading New York must have had a very different ring when *Casablanca* was released three years into the Second World War – and a noiry tale of corrupt officials and double dealing. Most surprising, however, is the fact that it's also a wise-cracking buddy picture, the friendship between Rick and French Vichy police captain Renault (Claude Rains) keeps the movie ticking along. A mismatched pair of anti-heroes, the hard-bitten gunrunner-turned-casino owner and the lecherous self-centred bent copper, they not only constitute the film's only unbroken relationship but get to split all the best lines between them.

Rick's contributions to the movie dictionary of quotations are well documented (from "Here's looking at you, kid" to "This is the beginning of a beautiful friendship"), but just take a look at some of Renault's corkers: "We haven't quite decided yet whether he committed suicide or died trying to escape"; "How extravagant you are, throwing away women like that. Some day they may be scarce"; and the immortal "Round up the usual suspects!" are all delivered with biting elegance. Small wonder then that the studio toyed with adding a scene – after the Germans invaded Casablanca shortly before the film's release – where Rick and Renault prepare to go into battle with a platoon of the Free French. Unfortunately it was never shot.

All too often 'classics' can leave you riddled with disappointment. *Casablanca* never does and never will. Possibly the best film to ever come out of Golden Age Hollywood's studio system, you can't claim to love a movie unless you've seen it. Watch it or you'll regret it.

Ceri Thomas

NEED TO KNOW

Year 1942
Running time 102 mins
Director Michael Curtiz
Stars Humphrey Bogart, Ingrid Bergman, Paul Henreid, Claude Rains, Conrad Veidt
Buy it on Region 1 SE
Tagline "They had a date with fate in Casablanca!"
Best line "Of all the gin joints in all the towns in all the world, she walks into mine." – Rick Blaine
Critic's view "Bogart is more at ease as the bitter and cynical operator of a joint than as a lover." – *Variety*
Best watched when You need a movie to both make your girlfriend cry and for your gran to get all misty-eyed over.

97

TRAINSPOTTING

Ewan McGregor's lust for life powers Danny Boyle's generation-defining junkie drama...

Born in the thrusting throes of Britpop, *Trainspotting* was the cultural calling card and Ewan McGregor – skinny, skinheaded and glowering out of dayglo orange – the posterboy for Cool Britannia. Blair strolled into Number 10, Noel and Damon twatted it out at the top of the charts and Danny Boyle's ferocious follow-up to *Shallow Grave* spoke for a generation who felt disenfranchised, embracing its cheery nihilism in the wake of the Tories. Here was a cocky, style-to-spare shot of Brit grit that faced up to Hollywood on its own terms: the British are coming, the British are coming... to kick your head in.

Well, that proved to be so much hype and hot air, as privatised railways, cluster-bombed Iraqis and a liar's glazed grin curdled our belief in New Labour. And British film took a tabloid tumble, too, when the hallowed trinity of Boyle, screenwriter John Hodge and producer Andrew Macdonald chose *A Life Less Ordinary* (by no means a terrible film; just a stretch of goodwill to truly like). But *Trainspotting* still stands as a captivating capsule of a time, place and attitude. Viewers who crave a 'British *Fight Club*', tap up your vein and mainline this: one of the best movies ever made about being young and alone.

If you crave a British Fight Club, tap your vein and mainline this

A star was born in the scabrous adaptation of Irvine Welsh's 'unfilmable' novel, a youth icon to jostle with and overthrow James Dean and Malcolm McDowell: a picture of cadaverous cool. On screen, McGregor was joyful, cheeky and frighteningly charismatic. Off screen, he clearly couldn't believe his luck. Whether swanning down the Cannes red carpet or getting lashed in interviews, he made being a movie star look like what it should be: fun. No British actor since has come close to McGregor's superstar blend of craft and charisma (Daniel Craig has the ability but not the evident joie de vivre that rewards crowds' adulation).

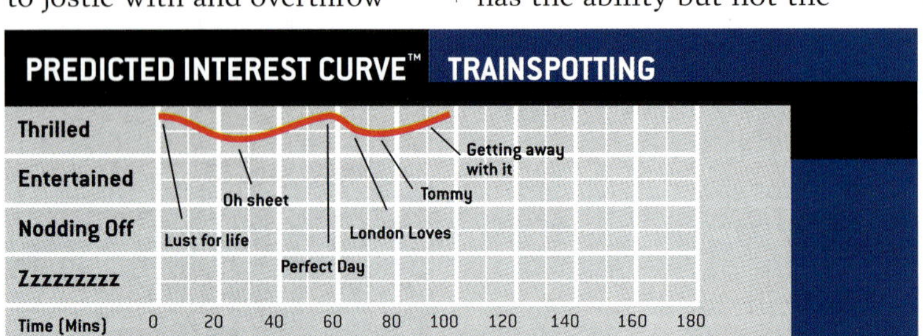

In the tradition of Connery and Caine, McGregor (who has suffered a similar critical snobbery to his predecessors; time will prove him a great actor) favoured instinct over intellect in his performance – he just had *it*, whether staring down from thousands of bedroom walls or beaming out TV soundbites about the controversy of making a movie that admitted drugs can be enjoyable. As his character Mark 'Rent Boy' Renton says, "People think it's all about misery and desperation and death and all that shit, which is not to be ignored, but what they forget is the pleasure of it. Otherwise we wouldn't do it. After all, we're not fucking stupid. At least, we're not that fucking stupid." It was time someone said it.

Which isn't to surrender to the argument that *Trainspotting* somehow glamorised skag. If watching the cold turkey

sequence didn't get smack romanticism out of your system, you were probably born cooking up. But compare *Trainspotting* to, say, *Requiem For A Dream* and it's a much less concerned, needy film, unafraid to let the audience draw its own conclusions and refusing to batter home a 'DRUGS ARE BAD' message. It's funny, reckless and full of cruel glee, stylistically indebted to Scorsese for sure, but taking a rare vision to blend the New York master's visual verve with material usually left to Ken Loach. Boyle even takes Robert Carlyle, from Loach's *Riff-Raff*, and reinvents him as startling Joe Pesci-eat-your-gob-out psycho Begbie.

Beyond the style, substance abuse and gleeful surrealism, it's a film about need and loneliness. The burnished, wittily edited set-pieces – the first detox, Archie Gemmill sex, Lou Reed overdose – lower the guard to a voiceover laden with self-loathing (Renton of his mates: "They reminded me so much of myself I could hardly bear to look at them").

There's camaraderie and elation and a connection when the friends score together. Take the tenderness when Ewen Bremner's Spud kisses Jonny Lee Miller's Sick Boy, and Peter Mullan's Mother Superior bites his cheek – like a father with a newborn child – after they all shoot-up. But it only lasts a little longer than the draining of a syringe. There are few scenes as desperate as the cot death, as Sick Boy sobs his guts out and Renton's fuck-it-all reaction is simply, "I'm cookin' up".

NEED TO KNOW

Year 1996
Running time 94 mins
Director Danny Boyle
Stars Ewan McGregor, Robert Carlyle, Ewen Bremner, Kelly Macdonald, Jonny Lee Miller
Buy it on Region 2 Definitive Edition
Tagline "Never let your friends tie you to the tracks."
Best line "Who needs reasons when you've got heroin?" – Renton
Critic's view "Scabrous, brutal and hip, *Trainspotting* is *A Clockwork Orange* for the '90s." – *Variety*
Best watched when... Considering whether you should just say no.

The story closes in on itself, a loop of Renton cleaning up but not getting out, until the final frames, which leave a tantalising question mark over the future of this smart but soured man (There is talk of adapting Welsh's sequel, *Porno*, but McGregor is reluctant, wisely, to do so. *The Two Jakes*, *The Phantom Menace*... It would be a mistake).

"Choose life. Choose a job. Choose a career. Choose a family. Choose a fucking big television..." It's an acrid high in the life of a low-life, who's now a totemic figure of dysfunction, an idol to the need to connect. Another hero striding mean streets, from *Rebel Without A Cause* to *A Clockwork Orange* – except this time, hey, it mattered, because someone was speaking for us.
Nev Pierce

96

STAND BY ME

Growing pains... Four boys journey into adulthood as they search for a dead body.

It's like stepping out into an August morning, eyes squinting in the sun

Two films into a burgeoning directorial career, Rob Reiner fancied a stretch. Sure, pomp-metal satire *This Is Spinal Tap* and teen romantic drama *The Sure Thing* had established him as an electrifying talent, but one doubter remained: himself. In his mind at least, he continued to dwell in the artistic shadow of his father Carl, a renowned director who acted as puppetmaster to a loose-limbed Steve Martin in the comic's earlier, funnier movies: *The Jerk, The Man With Two Brains, All Of Me*. Reiner Jnr needed to step into the light; he needed to make a film devoid of his father's fingerprints.

"I was looking to do something more dramatic, something different from the things I'd done in the past," he said. "But, at first, I wasn't sure *The Body* [*the title of Stephen King's source novella – Reiner changed it to escape the horror connotations*] was it. I loved the writing and the characters were well drawn, but I didn't understand what it was about. Then I realised it wasn't about the kids finding the dead body in the woods. It was about what happens to them en route."

Told through the misty eyes of Gordie LaChance (Richard Dreyfuss), a middle-aged writer whose gaze turns inward when he learns of the death of a childhood friend, *Stand By Me* unfurls as an 80-minute flashback. The time is the summer of 1959, as four 12-year-old boys haul ass over 30 miles of train track to eyeball a dead kid. To Chris (River Phoenix), Teddy (Corey Feldman) and Vern (Jerry O'Connell) it's a summer adventure, a chance to smoke, camp in the woods and cavort in fame's spotlight ("We'd even be on TV... we can be heroes!") when they find the corpse. To fragile, sensitive Gordie (Wil Wheaton), however, it's something more: an opportunity to stare death in the face in an effort to understand the senseless demise of his older brother (John Cusack).

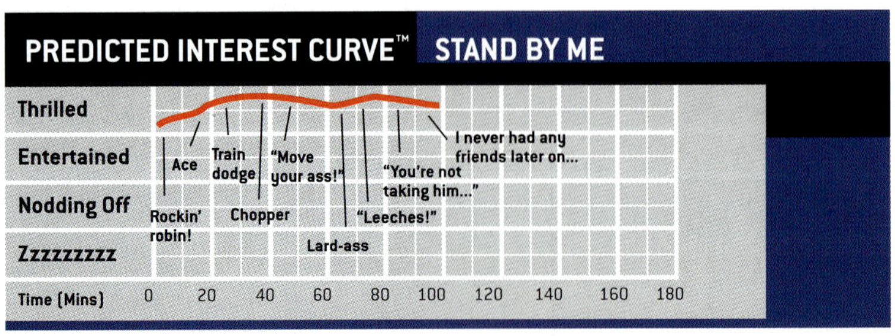

"Gordie is a boy who doesn't feel good about himself, who's looking for approval from his dad," Reiner explains. "These are feelings I had growing up."

Shot in Oregon, Maine and the Mount Shasta area of California in the summer of 1985, the production was blessed by 60 days of almost continuous sunshine. Grasping what he was given and adding to it by overlighting many of the scenes and utilising long lenses to give the action a shimmer-swelter heatwave quality, Reiner turned in a movie that looks like no other. Switch on *Stand By Me* and it's like stepping out into an August morning, eyes squinting as the white sun burns down from a cloudless sky. This is the summer that you remember from your own childhood – at least until Reiner "brought in every wind

machine in Hollywood" and darkened the lens to add a touch of pathetic fallacy to the discovery of the corpse. Of course, by this point the quest has become a full-blown obsession for Gordie, the earlier banter ("Did your mother ever have any kids that lived?"), affectionate put-downs ("pussy", "cock-knocker", "four-eyed pile of shit") and heart- racing set-pieces ("Traaaaaaaain!") replaced by tears, confessions and quiet introspection.

It's a mark of *Stand By Me*'s superlative quality that it shifts gears with never a clunk, racing through any adjective you care to throw at it – funny, touching, exhilarating, outrageous, horrifying, mournful – and back again with sublime ease, subliminal control.

Such assurance is rare in film as in any art form, and its presence here can be explained by one further virtue: honesty. The actors have it, two weeks of rehearsal time and a host of trust exercises allowing them to interact with thoughtless insouciance and genuine affection. The period design and wall-to-wall golden oldies soundtrack also have it, Reiner and King knowing exactly how 1959 (well, 1960 in King's case, but let's not be precious) looked and sounded as a 12-year-old boy. But most of all it's King and Reiner themselves who have it, each using the story's quest narrative as just a string on which to hang their own memories. Their own *lives*. And while it was a four-year-old King who saw a playpal hit by a train and who grew up to trade all the lingo and skin palms and swear-on pinkies and dish out "two for flinching" and watch friends dash across train trestles and long, long, long, all the while, to become a writer, it was Reiner who brought Gordie to the fore of the story and kissed the pain from his knitted brow. Watch the scene where Gordie backs away from the body and coughs up his grief to Chris ("My dad said it, I'm no good")... and then consider that Reiner wrote it, tears oozing down his cheeks as he fumbled the words on to the page. *Stand By Me* is the finest coming-of-age movie in US cinema, but it's the rite of passage occurring beind the camera that makes it so damn special.

Jamie Graham

NEED TO KNOW

Year 1986
Running time 85 mins
Director Rob Reiner
Stars Wil Wheaton, River Phoenix, Corey Feldman, Jerry O'Connell, Kiefer Sutherland
Buy it on Region 1 Deluxe Edition
Tagline "If I could only have one food for the rest of my life? That's easy. Pez, cherry-flavoured Pez."
Best line "Suck my fat one, you cheap dime-store hood." – Gordie
Critic's view "*Stand By Me* is the funniest and most intelligent teen picture for adults in years." – *NME*
Best watched when... You've just cleared out the loft and found your old school photo.

95

THE USUAL SUSPECTS

"I'm Keyser Soze..." "No, I'm Keyser Soze!" "Hang on, I thought I was Keyser..." etc.

During the mid '90s, revealing the key turning point of Bryan Singer's twisty, playful thriller was tantamount to standing next to a queue heading into *The Empire Strikes Back* in the early '80s and screaming, "Darth is Luke's father!" Or parading up and down outside *The Crying Game* with a big banner reading, "She's a man!" Even as late as the turn of the millennium, *Total Film* regularly got e-mails of complaint every time we casually mentioned that Keyser Soze was... well, we'll come to that in a minute.

Singer's movie is an unsettling masterclass in expertly choreographed confusion

Singer's movie is an unsettling masterclass in expertly choreographed confusion. Nothing is what it seems to be and nothing you see can actually be trusted. Every time the film throws you a standard thriller bone, or a basic movie set-up or scenario, it's only purpose is to distract you from something else. *The Usual Suspects* is misdirection moviemaking at its very finest. And the whole thing starts so simply too. An opening teaser that hints at the end of the story, followed by a flashback to the events that lead up to it, with a handy let's-make-everything-easy-for-you narration courtesy of Kevin Spacey's debilitated con-man, Verbal Kint.

Five crooks pulled together for a line-up, decide on a little payback, pull a revenge robbery and set in motion a chain of events that puts them at odds with a mysterious crime lord, Keyser Soze, who has a worryingly fierce reputation. One thing leads to another and to clear their debt they have to pull off a killing on a cargo ship crammed with heavily-armed foreigners. Which puts us roughly back where we began.

Running parallel to all this is Verbal's interrogation by Custom's agent Dave Kujan (Chazz Palminteri). It's Verbal who lays out the events of the tale, Verbal who spins out the core yarn for the hugely sceptical Kujan: "I'm smarter than you and I'm gonna find out what I wanna know, and I'm going to get it from you whether you like it or not".

As a director, Singer's got the vocabulary of the hard-boiled thriller down pat. Shadowy close-ups, Hitchcockesque music, jagged pacing flipping from the slowburn to the breakneck in a heartbeat... he can do the lot. He even throws in some cold-blooded action sequences for good measure, with the SWAT-team-style hit on the boat as good as anything seen before.

All of this is a blind, though. The film's real thrills come in the last 15 minutes. What Singer and writer Christopher McQuarrie are playing on is cinema's greatest illusion: that what you see is the truth. But

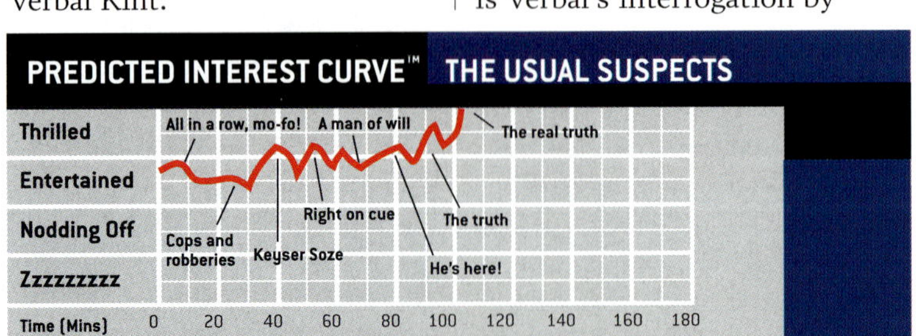

all that we see is what Verbal describes. What if it's all been a lie? What if every bit of the flashback sequence is an elaborate fiction?

As the movies end draws near, Singer's first trick is to convince us, despite all we've seen, that Soze is Gabriel Byrne's character, Keaton. Kujan pulls together elements from the story to persuade Verbal, and then us, that the crooked former cop set it all up; that Keaton was playing on the Soze myth to fake his own death for a second time. Cue that first jolt of reality-twisting shock.

But it's not enough. Just as that's settled in, Singer hits you again, reinterpreting events for the second time in a few minutes. Now Verbal walks out of jail and his limp slowly disappears as he straightens up and sparks up a fag with the gold lighter we see in the first flashback. Of course! Verbal is Keyser Soze! And he's spun the entire tale out of things he's seen in the office in which Kujan interrogates him – facts on bits of paper, logos on notice boards, names on random police reports and the like. And bingo... "The greatest trick the devil ever pulled was convincing the world he didn't exist. And poof! Just like that, he's gone." Screen goes black.

But the beauty of *The Usual Suspects* is that it's never really over. Like any good puzzle, you just keep turning it over in your head. Is Verbal actually Keyser Soze? Maybe not. What if it's all been made up? What if there is no Soze? Suppose he's just an absurdly long con dreamt up by this self-confessed trickster? What if it's all just a complex plot drawn up between Verbal and the man in the car that picks him up at the end – who's not named Kobayashi, that's just the name on the coffee mug, and may not even be a lawyer at all. Like all good thrillers it leaves the audience on a knife edge.

For Singer, the answers are less important than the host of unsettling questions. "This isn't an Agatha Christie mystery," he quips when you press him on it. "It's up to the audience." And audiences are still playing the game, returning to *The Usual Suspects* time and again to enjoy one of cinema's most enduring mind-messing movies.

Ceri Thomas

NEED TO KNOW

Year 1995
Running time 106 mins
Director Bryan Singer
Stars Kevin Spacey, Gabriel Byrne, Chazz Palminteri, Stephen Baldwin, Benicio Del Toro, Kevin Pollak
Buy it on Region 2 SE
Tagline "Five criminals. One line-up. No coincidence."
Best line "The greatest trick the Devil ever pulled was convincing the world he didn't exist." – Verbal Kint
Critic's view "Vivid, audacious, relentless intelligence." – *The Sunday Times*
Best watched when... You've finished the crossword and Sudoku doesn't do it for you.

94

MAGNOLIA

Gain from pain in Paul Thomas Anderson's long, dark, amphibious night of the soul...

Three hours for one smile. But *what* a smile. A twinkle of heart, of hope. After all the pain, the fear, the loathing. After all the "piss and shit". Maybe they'll all live happily ever after, after all...

In *Magnolia*, everybody hurts. Everybody has given up, fucked up, beaten themselves up. They've paced and they've paced and they've dug a comfortably dumb little furrow. We join them all on the edge of their darkest hour. They're dry and choked, in need of rain. Living on practised smiles; gradually losing the strength to keep the floodgates closed. They need to wake up, wise up. They need a miracle...

After his low-key 1996 debut, *Hard Eight*, Paul Thomas Anderson went head-rush hi-fi with *Boogie Nights*. But, although his sexed-up, San Fernando valley hedonists embraced their proxy porno community like a fresh-start family, there was sadness behind their eyes. The ageing Julianne Moore matriarch, with her cocaine hunger and custody quarrels, is Anderson's blueprint for the fragile flower at the core of his *Magnolia* melodrama: Claudia (Melora Walters), the little girl oh-so lost.

"I found that I couldn't write in the chaos of *Boogie Nights* coming out," says Anderson. "But, because of all the expectations, I thought if I just made another one right away, I'd cut 'em all off at the pass..."

Anderson spent eight months of 1998 writing *Magnolia*, but admits that "the majority of the work really only happened in the last two weeks." Retreating to William H Macy's cabin in Vermont, he was visited by an unlikely muse. "There was a snake outside the door and I was too scared to leave. It kept me in there, writing."

In *Magnolia*, everybody hurts. They're either abusive/negligent parents, gnawed down by guilt and remorse, or estranged and loveless kids. Mostly, it's a tale of two fathers. Quiz-show host Jimmy Gator (Philip Baker Hall) is a terminally ill sadsack who just wants to make peace with abused daughter Claudia. Anderson devises a significant concept for Gator's show – children vs adults – and sneaks him the film's defining line ("We may be through with the past, but the past ain't through with us.")

In *Magnolia*, everybody hurts – they're gnawed down by guilt

Before the shoot, Anderson screened Sidney Lumet's *Network* for cast and crew. Gator is the spiritual descendant of *Network*'s wronged TV anchor Howard Beale, whose on-air collapse echoes *Magnolia*'s watershed wake-up call ("You've got to say, 'I'm a HUMAN BEING! My life has VALUE!'").

The other sad dad, Earl Partridge (Jason Robards) – also being savaged by cancer – is alienated from cold-fish daughter Linda (Moore) and son Frank (Tom Cruise), who has channelled his inexpressible rage into a feral alter ego: 'TJ' Mackey. A motivational guru who smothers his own emotional impotence by urging

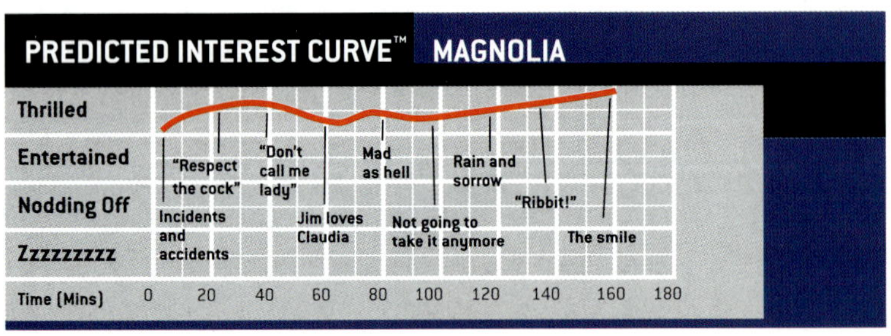

other men to posturing dominance ("Seduce and destroy!"). Despite the role's ugliness, Anderson sold it to Cruise as "the showcase, a real smorgasbord for an actor. You get to say 'cunt' and you get to cry at your daddy's bedside and get redeemed at the end."

Earl and Frank's reunion is far from a syrupy, air-clearing, Hollywood-style slosh of sentiment. Rasping out his final breaths, Frank shaking with sorrow by his side, Earl slurs out his repentance in a shattering rage against the dying of the light ("The regret, the regret!").

Soon after the tears, the clouds burst and Anderson pulls his critic-baiting twists of magic realism. Time freezes and disbelief suspends while we prowl around this drowned world of damaged souls, all lip-syncing to Aimee Mann's sweet and wistful 'Wise Up'. And then, down comes the miracle: a blessing disguised as a plague of frogs. A freakshow for the freaks. As though God himself has had enough of the weeping.

Anderson makes *Magnolia* flailing and flashy (neck-ache camera sweeps, busy-busy tracking shots) but also simmering and intimate. He swoops right on down and in tight but isn't afraid to make the emotion widescreen, operatic.

After so much success with the bleak stylings in *Boogie Nights*, the 29-year-old helmer could so easily have rambled on down the QT-apeing road of guns and gangsters. Instead, he had the balls to go deeper, to try to make audiences care about characters rather than chortle at their comic demise.

In *Magnolia*, everybody hurts. If only they could get a break, communicate... most of them just need change and catharsis. For life to finally find a way, all those muffled demons have to be confronted and tackled. For Claudia and bumbling cop Jim (John C Reilly), it's the connection that counts. There's no romance in their first kiss, just pure *need*.

And so, just shy of the three-hour mark, Anderson catches Claudia and slowly closes in on those sweat-lashed features. And... yep. She definitely smiles – *into camera*.

Blackout.

Everything – including you – is gonna be alright, after all.

Andy Lowe

NEED TO KNOW

Year 1999
Running time 188 mins
Director Paul Thomas Anderson
Stars Tom Cruise, Julianne Moore, William H Macy, Philip Seymour Hoffman, Melora Walters
Buy it on Region 3 Korean SE
Tagline "Things fall down. People look up. And when it rains, it pours."
Best line "Now that I've met you, would you object to never seeing me again?" – Claudia
Critic's view "Dry wit, bravura staging, intricate design, wondrous performances." – *Chicago Tribune*
Best watched when... You're getting guilt pangs about not having called your folks for a while.

93

SALVADOR

Oliver Stone's first furious assault on America abroad retains its power to shock and awe.

Perhaps it's the dangerously romantic supposition of a film journalist who's never seen any real hardship which suggests Oliver Stone's early, best work is so touched because he had been so close to death. The further the Vietnam War veteran travels from being the college drop-out who volunteered to fight for his country, so his films become less accomplished – still interesting, stylish and aggressive, sure, but the aggression has come to feel a little like a pose. *Salvador* has the taste of death. It is a film with a thousand-yard stare.

Stone had written *Platoon* long before, but no one in Hollywood was quite ready to pick the scab of the Vietnam war with such first-hand ferocity. He was making a living as a screenwriter and had won an Oscar for Alan Parker's *Midnight Express* (1978) – a grubby, heavy-handed, arguably racist and certainly dull true-life tale of how daft it is to try and smuggle drugs in Turkey. But his work on *Scarface* (1983) was far more accomplished. Brian De Palma's cellophane-shiny story of a Cuban illegal immigrant who lives and dies the American Dream was the gangster picture as written by Karl Marx. Well, that goes much too far, but it was at least written by someone who'd *heard* of Karl Marx.

Oddly, Tony Montana, the coke-snorting, sister-fancying, anti-communist psycho of *Scarface*, would indirectly help *Salvador*, at least for a time, when Stone opted to shoot in the titular El. *Salvador* is often referred to as Stone's debut and he'd certainly like you to forget his earlier films – the 1974 horror *Seizure* and the enjoyably rubbish Michael Caine shocker *The Hand* (1981).

Prepping production on a tight budget, Stone talked his way into a meeting with El Salvador's military leaders and gave them a doctored version of the script, which presented the government army as the good guys. They agreed to provide the film with weapons, troops and vehicles for free and the Salvadoran soldiers, in particular, adored the director.

"These guys were carrying weapons on their hips and slapping us on the back, drinking toasts to Tony Montana," he would later recall. "They kept talking about their favourite scenes and acting out the killings. They'd be going, 'Tony Montana, muchos cojones! Ratta-tat-tat! Kill the fucking communists!'"

The plan to film there fell through, though, when Stone's government contact was killed by rebel troops. It was probably just as well, given that if the authorities had realised the true nature of Stone's film, they might have killed him. He wanted to bring the world's attention to the suffering of the country under these thugs,

Had the authorities realised Stone's true intentions, they might have killed him

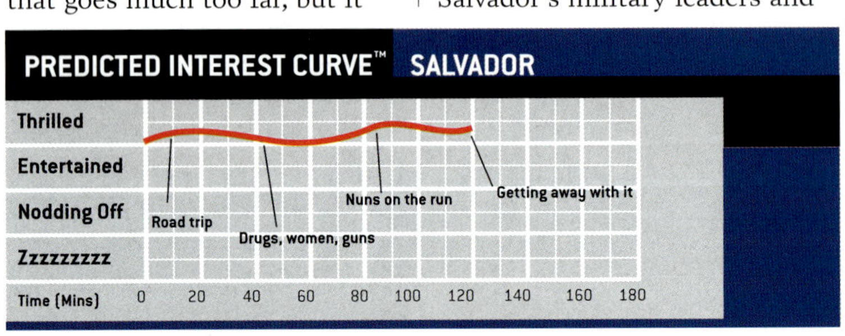

who – with funding from the Reagan government – would kill 70,000 of their own people during the 1980s.

"I was trying to say, 'Look, this is what's really happening in El Salvador right now and nobody here in the US is paying attention,'" the director reflects. "I wanted the movie to strike home 'in your face' like the agitprop films of the Soviets during the revolution. No wonder it bombed."

All of which is a roundabout way of saying *Salvador* has passion; it has guts, fire, scuffed edges and is alive with the possibilities of cinema. It's both personal and political, micro and macro – and gripping.

The story is 'Gonzo goes guerrilla', based loosely on the real-life exploits of journalist Richard Boyle. James Woods plays the Hunter S Thompson-style hack at 110 mph, ditching his life Stateside to investigate what's going on down south, dragging his disc jockey friend Dr Rock (James Belushi) to a place which promises "good beer, beautiful women and cheap rent". He neglects to mention the occasional summary execution, rape and murder of nuns and the assassination of an archbishop.

Woods is both punchable and pitiable, the character always ready with a wisecrack but the actor showing, through stuttering eyes, a man whose cynicism shields a strong heart. He tries to isolate himself from the horror of the world in which he finds himself – the more he shouts and pouts, the less he has to care, but beneath the sarcasm, it's getting to him.

There's always an 'anti-' to this 'hero', but as rage and incredulity grind him down, what's left is a human face to a distant tragedy. The film doesn't just boil the situation down to one man's heartache, but through him it allows us a window to that world and shows a country under the heel.

The picture ended up nominated for Oscars at the same ceremony *Platoon* won Best Picture. That remarkable film was more polished and portentous and – like so many 'Nam films – painted America as a sort of victimised aggressor. In contrast, it's *Salvador's* greatness that you never forget who it's really about.

Nev Pierce

NEED TO KNOW

Year 1986

Running time 123 mins

Director Oliver Stone

Stars James Woods, James Belushi, Elpidia Carrillo, John Savage, Michael Murphy

Buy it on Region 1 SE

Tagline "Based on a true story..."

Best line "I hope you all get anal herpes!" – Richard Boyle

Critic's view "*Salvador* is as raw, difficult, compelling, unreasonable, reckless and vivid as its protagonist." – *Variety*

Best watched when... You're thinking about jacking everything in and doing something real.

92

BACK TO THE FUTURE

A tale of two decades as Michael J Fox goes back in time to meet the parents...

After ecstatic preview screenings saw it shunted forward to a Fourth of July weekend release, *Back To The Future* raced to the top of the US Box Office. No surprises there. The, ahem, comedy adventure science fiction time-travel love story was a born crowd pleaser even at script stage. More eyebrow-raising is that the number two slot was held, for a week at least, by the somewhat less spectacular *Teen Wolf*. And, rounding off a ratings hattrick, the pleasant but hardly earth-shattering sitcom *Family Ties* was making a serious bid to be crowned America's favourite TV show.

It manages two rare feats for an '80s blockbuster – charm and timelessness

Providing the Midas touch for all three was Michael J Fox. Like an '80s Cary Grant (albeit shorter, Canadian and a little less dapper), Fox was one of those leads with such easy charm and naturalistic style that, at the time, people often didn't realise how good he was. Not so *Back To The Future*'s director Robert Zemeckis. Four weeks into production, he became aware he didn't have a movie without Fox. Problem was, he didn't have Fox. The role of Marty McFly had been given to Eric Stoltz because Fox was tied to, um, *Ties*. But some 28 days into the shoot, it was clear Stoltz was struggling. "Eric was terrifically dramatic," observed executive producer Steven Spielberg (it was the Beard's third collaboration with Zemeckis), "but not mining the humour Bob was trying to get out of him."

Filming ground to a halt. Stoltz was released, desperate negotiations finally got Fox on board (working on a sleep-rarely-an-option schedule of TV show during the day and film at night) and *Back To The Future* as we know it began to take shape. (Albeit $3 million over the original budget...)

"I didn't know where I was a lot of the time," admitted Fox later. "Every waking moment was about work. It was my dream to be in the film and TV business, I just didn't know I'd be in them at the same time."

Nonetheless, it was only when the lead was in place that everything else began to click on set. "Once Michael came onto the picture, everybody gelled together, everybody got the tone of the humour," acknowledged Zemeckis.

And what humour. Warm, knowing, exuberant and with just enough satirical edge to stave away tweeness, the film manages two rare feats for an '80s blockbuster – charm and timelessness.

"Capra meets the Twilight Zone" is how Spielberg described the tale of the '80s youth who travels back to the '50s and meets his parents as teenagers only to discover – hey – they were once just like him. Albeit nerdier, hornier and possibly with a higher alcohol intake. Spielberg has a point. It's one of the film's key

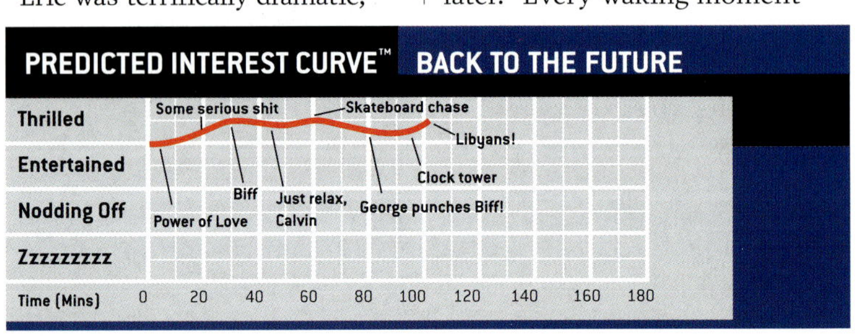

strengths that the Capra-esque heart is kept in check by just such observations. If Dad wasn't such a hopeless nerd, and Mum a lush with nympho tendencies, the mix could quickly have become syrupy. Instead it never stops having fun with the predicaments of its protagonist and the clash of cultures from different decades of American life.

Marty has to contend with match-making a mother who wants to seduce him (even if she does think he's wearing some boy called Calvin Klein's pants) and a father who couldn't get a woman to talk to him, never mind mother his children. Zemeckis admits the plot, while delicious, was a nightmare to get right. He and writer-producer Bob Gale spent months just resolving how Marty would escape the clutches of his own mother.

"We knew we had a great story that got us to this place, but then we didn't know what to do. The breakthrough only came when we came up with the line, 'It's like I'm kissing my brother'. From that we were able to make the whole thing work."

Not only is the plot a doozy, the performances are uniformly excellent. Christopher Lloyd is spot-on as the almost-crackpot Doc Brown. Best known as the slouching, mumbling Reverend Jim from hit sitcom *Taxi*, he bristles with the nervous energy of an electric shock therapy patient. Stand-up comic Thomas F Wilson makes Biff a baddie to boo and ridicule, being simultaneously both bully and buffoon. But perhaps most impressive are Crispin Glover and Lea Thompson who manage to thrice convince – as teenagers, failed parents and, ultimately, affluent yuppies in the film's near-perfect tying up of loose ends.

Inevitably, success led to sequels. The almost Godard-like experimentation of *II* and the slightly more straightforward western themes of *III* both have their merits. But it's the original that remains the gem. In the decades since, few blockbusters have provided such a warm marriage of script and spectacle. Or, to paraphrase the wise words of Huey Lewis, offered such compelling evidence that the power of love really is a curious thing.

Aubrey Ganguly

NEED TO KNOW

Year 1985
Running Time 111 minutes
Director Robert Zemeckis
Stars Michael J Fox, Christopher Lloyd, Lea Thompson, Crispin Glover, Thomas F Wilson
Buy it on Region 2
Tagline "17 year old Marty McFly got home early last night. 30 years early."
Best line "If you guys ever have kids and one of them, when he's eight years old, accidently sets fire to the living room rug... go easy on him, will ya?" – Marty
Critic's view "It puts nostalgia gently in perspective." – *The New York Times*
Best watched when... You can't relate to your parents.

91

DEKALOG

Polish legend Krzysztof Kieslowski lists 10 things God hates about you...

A thriller about a serial killer bumping off people in accordance with the seven deadly sins sounds hellishly exciting. But a 550-minute, ten-part, ten Commandments-inspired Polish drama set in Warsaw sounds excruciatingly hellish.

"Real knowledge is knowing how to live, why we live" KRZYSZTOF KIESLOWSKI

Of course, anyone with even a passing interest in World Cinema knows that *Dekalog* is the work of the late, great Polish director Krzysztof Kieslowski; something to luxuriate in rather than avoid. But if your knowledge of Polish film is restricted to cartoons featuring a plasticine man being pursued by a pack of buildings, then chances are that you've a) never seen a single episode of *Dekalog* and b) have no intention to.

Obtuse ideas never intimidated Kieslowski. Indeed, in the final years of his life, the former documentary filmmaker dedicated himself to making three pictures based upon the principles of liberte, egalite and fraternite – the sublime *Three Colours* trilogy. Next to *Dekalog*, though, the this series seemed about as intellectually imposing as the Indiana Jones saga. Okay, so it's not too hard to see how a filmmaker might make a movie about the wrongs of killing. But there hasn't been much call for a drama about coveting thy neighbour's ox since Moses descended Mount Sinai with God's prescription for mortal peril. No matter – Kiewslowski imbues each of the ten episodes with enormous intelligence and compassion, fashioning a tapestry that manages to be both metaphysical and accessible, examining the BIG questions even as it roots around in every day life.

After 20 years in film, Kieslowski understood how to make such a project work. Considering himself more artisan than artist, the director possessed a combination of immense skill and unquenchable curiosity that made him the perfect person to bring *Dekalog* to life. "Real artists find answers," he once remarked during an interview. "The knowledge of the artisan is within the confines of his skills. For example, I know a lot about lenses, about the editing room. I know what the buttons on the camera are for. I know all that, but that's not real knowledge. Real knowledge is knowing how to live, why we live. My films are trying to capture a truth which I myself haven't found."

Made for television but distributed theatrically, *Dekalog* is best known for its adultery and murder installments – both were remixed to feature length (just) and released as *A Short Film About Love* and *A Short Film About Killing*. The latter, arguably Kieslowski's finest achievement, juxtaposes the brutal killing of a taxi driver with the state execution of the murderer. In confronting both homicides with the eye of the non-fiction filmmaker, he

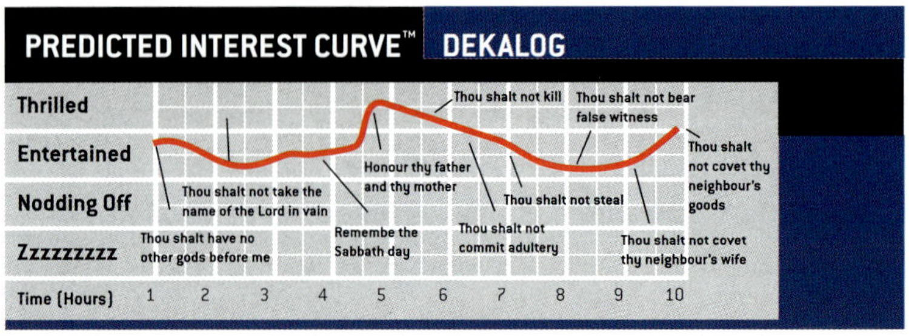

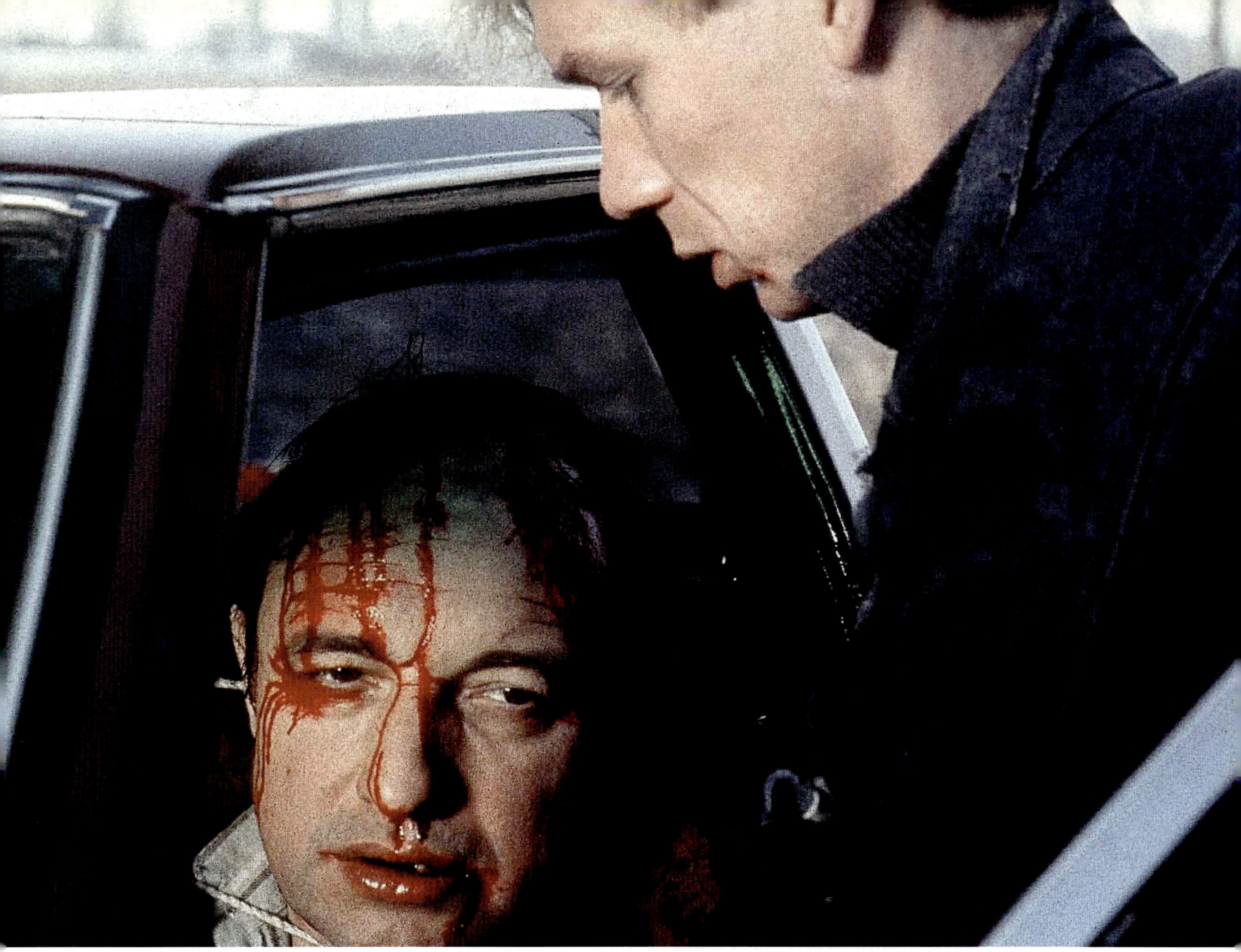

created a picture with the power to rattle even the keenest proponent of the death penalty. "I like chance meetings... Every day, without realising it, I pass people whom I should know. In *A Short Film About Killing*, the fact that the future killer and the lawyer fail to meet each other is the key. Had they met, had they acknowledged one another, how different their lives would have been."

Despite its title, *A Short Film About Love* made for equally confronting drama. The story of a postman who spies on his neighbour, the seemingly straightforward tale rapidly dissolves into an account of infatuation, obsession and suicide. It's what *Sliver* might have been had it a brain big enough to match its libido.

Of course, sex and death have long been cinematic staples. But if the other aspects of the Lord's design for life seemed short on intrigue and impact, this couldn't prevent Kieslowski from carving them into always gripping and often ennobling dramas. *In Honor Thy Father And Thy Mother*, a long-lost letter threatens a girl's relationship with her father. *Thou Shalt Not Steal* is the tale of a woman tormented by her inability to raise her son. And *Thou Shalt Not Take The Name Of Thy Lord God In Vain* sees a doctor faced with a dilemma involving a patient who may be dying of cancer and said patient's pregnant (by another man) wife.

Although co-written by regular collaborator Krzysztof Piesiewicz, *Dekalog* is very much Kieslowski's baby. Certainly, the series would have been less potent had his words been brought to life by a different director, as was the case when his premature death in 1996 led to German helmer Tom Tykwer bringing his screenplay for *Heaven* – first part of a trilogy to be completed by *Hell* and *Purgatory* – to the screen. Sitting through the episodes, it becomes clear that this odyssey through God's laws is less about mankind in general than one man in particular. A director who claimed he made movies "because I don't know how to do anything else." *Dekalog* has much to say about Kieslowski's life, and it's humbling that he invites us on this highly personal journey.

Richard Luck

NEED TO KNOW

Year 1989
Running time 550 minutes
Director Krzysztof Kieslowski
Stars Henryk Baranowski, Miroslaw Baka, Krystyna Janda
Buy it on Region 0 Polish Edition
Best line "What kind of a life is this?"
Tagline N/A
Critic's view "Kieslowski movingly demonstrates the unexpected connections that strangers make, and ponders the metaphysical forces that not only bind us, but also redeem us."
– San Francisco Chronicle
Best watched when... You've got a few mates over. If you want to dump said friends and have a night on your own.

90

PSYCHO

Wet-behind-the-ears mommy's boy makes for cinema's prototype slasher.

Faced with interviewers asking philosophical questions about the 'meaning' of his films, Hitch liked to respond, deadpan, that his sole aim was "to put the audience though it". By this criterion, *Psycho* must rank as his supreme cinematic achievement. Plenty of Hitchcock films have had the audience on the edge of their seats, but *Psycho* was surely the first one to have people hiding under them, screaming.

It was also the biggest box-office hit of his career. Shot quickly and cheaply in black-and-white, using Hitch's pared-down television team rather than his usual film crew, *Psycho* was finished for around $800,000 and grossed $15m on its initial US release alone.

So lasting was its impact that over 20 years later, three inferior sequels could be made, all starring Anthony Perkins and confidently relying on audiences' recall of the original – especially of the masterly shower-scene. Think about it: how many subsequent thrillers/slasher movies have settled for the camera-tracking-slowly-towards-a-drawn-shower-curtain trick, knowing that just this simple image will spook the hell out of viewers? And how many lazy critics have since described a movie as, "Does for [insert noun] what *Psycho* did for showers"?

Yet, even though we've all seen the movie at least once, if not dozens of times, so that we know just what's about to happen and can recite the dialogue off by heart, *Psycho* is still one of the scariest movies ever made, and for so many reasons, too: Bernard Hermann's trenchant strings-only score, jabbing and tearing like a flock of ruthless beaks; Josef Stefano's laconic boiling-down of Robert Bloch's pulp novel; John L Russell's encroaching shadows in every corner, waiting to pounce; Janet Leigh's terrified and touchingly vulnerable Marion Crane; Tony Perkins, in the role that made and forever ruined his career.

Even though we know what's about to happen, *Psycho* is still one of the scariest films ever

But above all, of course, there was Hitch at the very top of his form, using pure cinematic technique to manipulate our reactions and tear at our tautened, wailing nerves, all the while insisting that it was just "a fun picture". He may have lived an orderly life, but when it came to his movies, he loved to break the rules. Flashbacks can't lie? They do in *Stage Fright*. Can't shoot a whole film without editing? *Rope* does just that. Don't give away the twist half-way through the movie? See *Vertigo*. And most shockingly of all, you can't kill off your heroine 40 minutes into the film. Can you?

That shower scene must be the most famous bit of editing in all Hitchcock's films, indeed

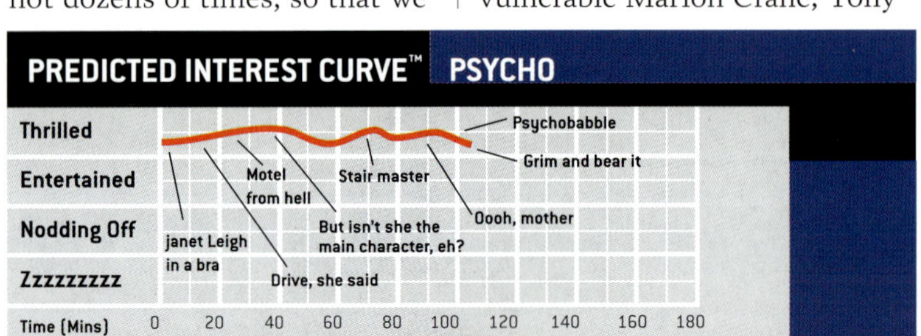

in all cinema – over 70 shots in just 45 seconds. Rumours that it was directed by Saul Bass are apparently untrue. We never see the knife enter the woman's flesh, but we're convinced we do through sleight of hand, sound effects, Hermann's shrieking violins and the assault on our emotions.

And now Hitch pulls his cruellest trick. Having been brutally deprived of Marion Crane, our identification figure, we're forced to identify with Norman – only to gradually realise that we've switched our allegiance to a psychotic killer.

Another ingenious, though less widely-noted, piece of camera trickery comes with the stabbing of the detective Arbogast (Martin Balsam). As Balsam climbs the stairs to the first floor, Hitch's camera lurks just in front of him, tracking backwards as he makes his ascent. Then he reaches the landing but instead of levelling off, the camera keeps going at the same angle. Result? By the time 'Mrs Bates' erupts out of her room, knife poised, we're positioned above her head. If Hitch had cut to a shot of the back of her head, we'd have wondered what he was hiding from us. As it is, there's been no cut, just a continuous, camera movement. Nothing to alert our suspicions.

Always the master-publicist, Hitch decreed that no-one would be allowed in after the picture started. Maybe because this applied to the critics too, several panned the film with the same hostility that had greeted Michael Powell's *Peeping Tom* the year before. But unlike Powell's movie, which was largely shunned by audiences, the public flocked to *Psycho*.

Hitch was delighted. "It's tremendously satisfying," he told François Truffaut, "to be able to use the cinematic art to achieve something of a mass emotion. It wasn't a message that stirred the audience, they were aroused by pure film."

Some members of the public weren't quite so satisfied. Hitch had a letter from a woman complaining that her daughter, who had refused to take baths since seeing *Les Diaboliques*, was now too traumatised to take a shower. What should she do? "Have her dry-cleaned," came Hitchcock's response.

Philip Kemp

NEED TO KNOW

Year 1960
Running time 108 mins
Director Alfred Hitchcock
Stars Anthony Perkins, Janet Leigh, Vera Miles, John Gavin, Martin Balsam
Buy it on Region 2 Collector's Box Set
Tagline "Don't give away the ending – it's the only one we have!"
Best line "Mother isn't quite herself today."
– Norman Bates
Critic's view "A reflection of a most unpleasant mind, a mean, sly, sadistic little mind." – *Esquire*
Best watched when... You're having to spend the night at a strange motel.

89

RIO BRAVO

"Sorry don't get it done, Dude..." Howard Hawks' witty tribute to friendship and heroism.

The inimitable Quentin Tarantino, on one of his favourite films: "When I'm getting serious about a girl, I show her *Rio Bravo* and she better fucking like it." Some viewers may wonder that the master of quick, aggressive verbiage and stomach-scrunching violence should cherish a Western starring John Wayne, the perceived conservative icon, who chastised Clint Eastwood for the brutality of his pictures. But the imprint of Howard Hawks' joyous actioner is on every Tarantino film: from the coffee shop 'Like A Virgin' exchange of *Reservoir Dogs* to the bong-hitting hilarity of Bridget Fonda and De Niro in *Jackie Brown*. "I watch it every couple of years," says Tarantino. "It's just like, 'I know these people now.' I watched it once, got the storyline out of the way and now I just hang out with them."

Rio Bravo is a superb 'hang-out' film: put it on when you're on your own and suddenly you've got your best friends round. There's an ease and a camaraderie to it that few films possess, with characters content to stroll together and give you time to get to know them. The unhurried nature should not be confused for laziness (as several critics at the time did, claiming Hawks stretched the story thin and indulged himself too much); this is its charm. The dialogue is a delight: never a word wasted, it gives fresh laughs and insight with each viewing. The action scenes, when they come, are elegantly edited and brilliant in their apparent simplicity (watch the 'Muddy boots' saloon showdown which Dean Martin's reforming drunk deputy Dude orchestrates and the 'Ezekiel 25:17' sequence in *Pulp Fiction* for an idea of Hawks' influence over Tarantino).

"When I'm getting serious about a girl I show her Rio Bravo" QUENTIN TARANTINO

The characters drive the story, each finding or trying to maintain self-respect: whether it's Martin's heart-broken Barachon (slang Spanish for drunk), Walter Brennan's crippled ex-rancher, Angie Dickinson's widow-with-a-past or Wayne – endearingly bashful when faced with her love for him. These scenes with Dickinson are particularly rich, as the director toys with Wayne's tough, no-nonsense persona and relishes Dude tying his tongue in knots trying to deal with his emotions. There's a lightness to Wayne here that belies his reputation and yet an authority and charisma elsewhere that ensures any of the alternate casting considered (Burt Lancaster, Gregory Peck) is unthinkable. Wayne in *Rio Bravo* is a picture of grace under pressure. There was never any real possibility of the character of John T Chance (named after the French model, Chance de Widstedt, who Hawks held a candle for) being played by anyone else. In an early script treatment the character was even called John Wayne.

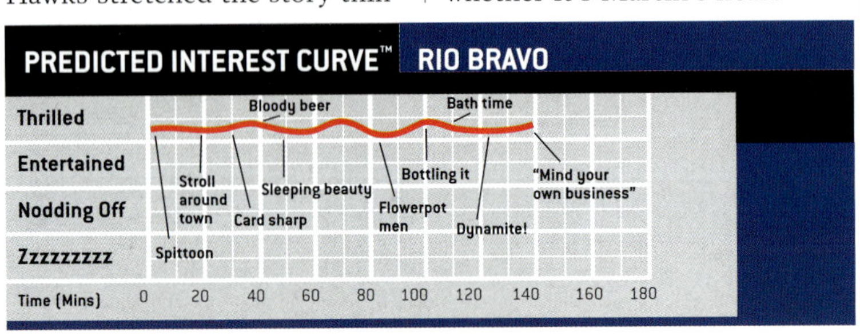

In contrast, Dean Martin wasn't even on the 19-name long-list for the casting of Dude, which was topped by Montgomery Clift (who turned it down) and included Frank Sinatra (which would have been a disaster) and Cary Grant (probably an interesting mistake). But Martin – who earned the role by chartering a private jet and flying to meet Hawks after a night working in Las Vegas – is perfect as the crumpled alcoholic. Watch the scene where Dude, struggling with the DTs, punches his leg to stop it from shaking; or any scene which closes up on his sweaty, screwed-up ball of a face. Martin was much more than stunt casting: this is a truly great performance. Ricky Nelson, in contrast, was cast the box office potential of a young rock'n'roll star, although he's fine as the smart gunslinger Colorado. The character was originally intended to be older and Robert Mitchum, Lee Marvin and James Garner were considered.

Hawks welcomed the input of the actors (the cigarette scene, for example – where Dude is shaking so bad he can't manage a roll-up – came out of rehearsal). He was an auteur unafraid of genuine collaboration, and the vitality and good humour of the production is evident in every frame. The film was conceived as an antidote to the neediness of *High Noon*, which both Wayne and Hawks hated. "I didn't think a good sheriff was going to go running around town like a chicken with his head cut off asking for help and finally his Quaker wife has to save him," said the director, and it is a stronger, more satisfying picture: self-reliant yet not devoid of compassion and never weighed down by a sense of its own importance.

It's precisely this lack of portentousness that still leads grave critics to dismiss it. Never mind that it subtly examines friendship and love and decency; it doesn't furrow brows or gaze at navels. It's just damn entertaining. Take Ward Bond's sceptical wagonmaster when he says, "A game-legged old man and a drunk. That's all you got?" To which Wayne replies: "That's *what* I got." It's simply perfection.

Nev Pierce

NEED TO KNOW

Year 1959
Running time 141 mins
Director Howard Hawks
Stars John Wayne, Dean Martin, Ricky Nelson, Angie Dickinson, Walter Brennan, Ward Bond
Buy it on Region 2
Tagline "You've seen nothing like 'em together... and in the heat and hate of Rio Bravo nothing can tear 'em apart!"
Best line "Sorry don't get it done, Dude. That's the second time you've hit me. Don't ever do it again." – Sheriff John T Chance
Critic's view "One of the year's better class oaters." – *Variety*
Best watched when... You want the company of friends.

88

GET CARTER

Brutal, bleak and bold, Caine swaps cockney charm for killer calm...

Before the making of *Get Carter*, Michael Caine had a bee in his bonnet. "I had a bee in my bonnet," he said (that was the clue), "because several British gangster films had come out in which the gangsters were universally either funny or stupid. But I knew from personal experience that they were neither. So I wanted to make a film about a gangster who was very, very clever and very, very mean."

It's Get Carter's spiteful savagery that makes it such a brutal masterpiece

Caine's wish was granted with *Get Carter*, the stark tale of a London gangster who comes up north to find his brother's killer. It was certainly a departure from Caine's previous incarnations. The chirpy Alfie, the roguish Charlie of *The Italian Job* or even the laconic Harry Palmer hardly prepared viewers for the cold-blooded killer on display here. But Caine's impatience with cartoonish characters was timely. After all, this was the decade that saw public terrorism come to London. Letter-bombs and embassy attacks would shape headlines; violence and ugly attitudes would simmer around the country. There was corruption exposed in industry and local government. The colourful but naïve optimism of the '60s simply didn't suit the landscape.

Carter's director, Mike Hodges, was equally aware of the shift in the nation's mood, having worked on Granada TV's investigative reporting show, *World In Action*, where he'd witnessed some ugly realities: "Working on that show affected me," he admitted. "I had seen a certain element of truth which Britain was trying to keep hidden. It was as corrupt as every other country – and it was worse, in a sense, because it pretended it was something else."

Get Carter reflected all of this and marked a shift in tone for British film. Gone were the Pop Art stylings of the previous decade. In their place came a sourer, greyer viewpoint – more cynical or more realistic, depending on your politics. Meanwhile, Hollywood, going through America's own period of dissatisfaction and loss of naiveté, would provide *Get Carter* with peers, in films like *Point Blank* and *Dirty Harry* – all three detailing tough men travelling treacherous paths on their own. Similarly bleak is Sean Connery's turn a year after *Carter* as the policeman who kills a suspected child-molester in Sidney Lumet's *The Offence*. Unfortunately, without the benefit of such hindsight-led perspective, critics were not initially taken with Hodges' debut feature. "Cheap", "Sleazy and second rate", "Inept... almost pornographic" were among the barbs delivered on release.

But time has been kind to this brutal gangland thriller. Caine's cold, controlled performance now chills and perhaps marks the point at which the film star also became a credible actor. Wolfgang Suschitzky's bleak

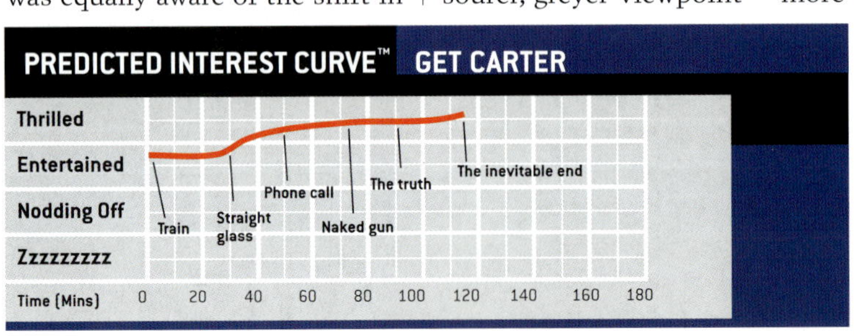

photography captures the sense of waste and regret emerging in Britain's industrial towns, where the '60s boom led to high wages, a macho workforce and rampant consumption, rather than earnings to climb the social ladder. Roy Budd's melancholic score seems entwined with the films own world weariness and nihilism. (The assassin who comes for Carter at the film's end is actually visible on the train at the beginning. Carter's fate is already sealed.)

Equally impressive is Hodges' own unsentimental but eminently quotable screenplay which feels more contemporary with each passing year ("You know, I'd almost forgotten what your eyes looked like. They're still the same, piss holes in the snow"). Little wonder that Tarantino cites it as his favourite British film. Behind the camera, too, Hodges doesn't put a foot wrong. Every composition is carefully constructed, every character contrasted or isolated by their surroundings. The overall effect is bleak and remorseful.

And rampaging through it all is Carter. As the search for his brother boils over into a bloody mess of abuse and betrayal, the gangster, Samurai-like in his focus, mows down any man, woman or child that stands in his way but somehow still elicits our support – surely a reflection of the power of Caine's performance and screen persona.

In the '90s, 'lad mag' culture saw Caine deified as the ultimate lad and his body of work hailed as ideal viewing. But while some of his other roles may have made him the perfect poster-boy for such campaigns, Carter's bleak, hard misery seems a little out of place in the celebrations. Carter is a nasty piece of work and *Get Carter* is a deliberately nasty film. But its spiteful savagery is what makes it such a brutal masterpiece.

Meanwhile, Hodges is just grateful that people have rediscovered an interest in his once-maligned debut. As he observed philisophically, "I've come to regard making films as putting a message in a bottle. If you manage to get whatever you are talking about into the bottle, at least it's out there on the ocean somewhere and it may float in and hit the shore at some point or another."

Aubrey Ganguly

NEED TO KNOW

Year 1971
Running time 111 mins
Director Mike Hodges
Stars Michael Caine, Ian Hendry, Britt Ekland, John Osbourne, Bryan Mosley
Buy it on Region 2
Tagline "What happens when a professional killer violates the code? Get Carter!"
Best line "You're a big man but you're out of shape. With me it's a full time job. Now behave yourself." – Jack Carter
Critic's view "No amount of picturesque violence can redeem *Get Carter*'s perfunctory plot."
– *Monthly Film Bulletin*
Best watched when... You're out for revenge.

87

DONNIE DARKO

Experience the best bunny flick since Watership Down...

There's this boy, Donnie, who's friends with a giant rabbit called Frank. But the rabbit's not really there. Anyway, a jet engine falls on Donnie's house, but, well, Frank's taken him to a golf course. So he survives. But then he floods the school. Donnie, that is. Or Frank. And then he discovers time travel. Donnie, that is. Or Frank. And Patrick Swayze plays a pervert."

As if selling *that* pitch to the good folks of middle-America wasn't going to be hard enough, *Donnie Darko* was saddled with the most unfortunate release schedule in cinema history: it came out weeks after 9/11, when having bits of plane crashing into buildings didn't really equate to entertainment.

Richard Kelly's astonishing debut could very well have sunk without trace. Fortunately, however, its UK release date was held back to late 2002, by which time its plane engine McGuffin had exited the no-fly zone and critical buzz had morphed into anticipatory word-of-mouth. America may have blinked and missed it, but Britain wasn't about to do the same: we were ready for a subversive, anthropomorphised bunny tale of the twisted conservatism of '80s Republican America.

There's no denying it's a head-scratcher. Studio suits didn't get it

There's no denying it's a head-scratcher, though. "I don't know how to explain this movie," said Noah Wyle, who plays lefty science teacher Prof Kenneth Monnitoff. "My part is the only part I could understand." Not surprising, really, given his 25-year-old director was fond of describing his elaborate calling card as, "a black comedy-ensemble suburban drama-science fiction thriller-character study-'80s period piece". Form an orderly queue please...

Studio suits, of course, didn't get it at all. "We got no after no after no, for a year and a half," Kelly said, until Drew Barrymore and her Flower Films Production company responded to the film's "intelligence without arrogance" and "its spiritual, thoughtful questions."

Barrymore herself would play Donnie's free-thinking English Lit teacher, sacked for studying Graham Greene's *The Destructors*. Vince Vaughn almost came on board as Donnie before Jake Gyllenhaal signed up as the angsty anti-hero. It was a perfect fit, and the cute casting of real-life sister Maggie as on-screen equivalent Elizabeth just added to the symmetry.

Donnie seizes you from the off: a scruffy boy awakening on a mountain pass to the chiming chords of Echo & The Bunnymen's 'The Killing Moon' before cycling home to call his sister a "fuckarse". From there it blends every genre imaginable, plus one or two more besides, as Donnie embarks on a mindfucking magical mystery tour to save the lives of those around him, maybe even the

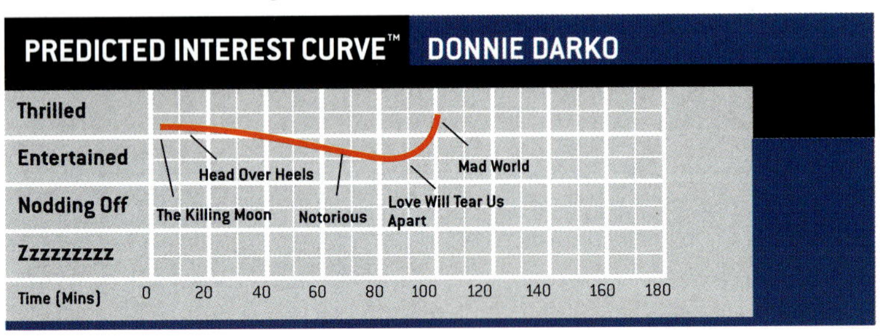

world. And through it all glides through Kelly's fluid camera (who can forget the long, twisting slow-mo/fast-mo steadicam shot as we enter Middlesex High School to Tears For Fears' 'Head Over Heels'?), its slippery journey coming to rest – to graceful peace – as 'Mad World' plays over the closing montage. It's a moment of beauty, the perfect-fit lyrics (*"I find it kind of funny, I find it kind of sad/But the dreams in which I'm dying are the best I've ever had"*) slipping into your ears to lodge in your brain.

If 'Mad World' is the pay-off though, it's at the very least equalled by other words, glances and actions throughout – pitched by Kelly squarely at the weepy adolescent within us all. Donnie's Mum Rose (*Independence Day*'s First Lady Mary McDonnell) answering her son's "How does it feel to have a wacko for a son?" question with "It feels wonderful". Gretchen (Jena Malone) and Donnie ridding each other of their cherries to 'Love Will Tear Us Apart'. Also, depending on your interpretation, the last word Donnie utters to his Mum is "Bitch". Rose's pain is clear when, in the dénouement, she's left an empty shell, pushed beyond tears.

Kelly's treatise on the unbearable pain of teenhood is extraordinary, funny ("Sometimes I doubt your commitment to Sparkle Motion!") and touching.

On this evidence, he could, just could, blossom into one of the filmmakers of his generation, though the unsatisfactory, handholding director's cut released in 2004 suggests otherwise. Unwisely building concrete bypasses over gossamer plot strands, it steers us through a spaghetti junction of possible meanings when all we really want to do is get lost.

Whether Kelly can deliver on his gargantuan promise will be answered by the forthcoming *Southland Tales*. "You can't fuck up your first movie, because you won't get a second," he said on the penultimate day of shooting *Donnie Darko*. As the only director in this list with just one film to his name, it would be a horrendous waste if his career was snuffed out before it really ever got going. It would, indeed, suck a fuck.

Jonathan Dean

NEED TO KNOW

Year 2001
Running time 102 mins
Director Richard Kelly
Stars Jake Gyllenhaal, Noah Wyle, Maggie Gyllenhaal
Buy it on Region 2 SE (which has both cuts)
Tagline "You can never go too far."
Best line "What if you could go back in time, and take all those hours of pain and darkness and replace them with something better?" – Gretchen
Critic's view "Richard Kelly displays an imagination almost as unbridled as that of the unstable protagonist." – *Variety*
Best watched when... You start seeing large, imaginary furry friends.

86

KIND HEARTS AND CORONETS

Ealing's blackest comedy: a triumph of satire... and Alec Guinness in eight roles.

These days, Ealing comedy conjures up images of cosy middle England, with chirpy cockney commoners and crumpets for tea. Fair enough – there's certainly plenty of that going on in the likes of *Passport To Pimlico, Whisky Galore!* and *The Titfield Thunderbolt*. But there was also a darker, more subversive strand stitched through the London studio's output. *The Man In The White Suit, The Ladykillers, The Lavender Hill Mob*... all mixed chewy lumps of satire in amongst the usual slapstick. And *Kind Hearts And Coronets* is the darkest, riskiest and strangest of them all. Not to mention the funniest.

It's all about Alec Guinness, right? Well, he's a huge part of what makes *Kind Hearts* crackle with wit and vigour. Playing all eight members of the D'Ascoyne clan (from strapping young posh lad to suffragette auntie and gun-happy duke), the then 34-year-old Guinness delivers a tour de force of make-up, mannerisms and mortality as they're killed off in turn by a murderous social climber from the family's bastard line. The scene where Guinness appears as six of the D'Ascoyne's at once took two days to shoot. These days it would be patched together with CGI trickery in no time; back in the late '40s, it had to be shot on a specially built platform with only a small part of the film being exposed for each character and then wound back manually to shoot the next one.

Guinness delivers a tour de force of make-up, mannerisms and mortality

It was the part/parts that – hot on the heels of Fagin in *Oliver Twist* and Herbert in *Great Expectations* – turned the man who would be Obi Wan into a movie star. Not bad for Guinness' fourth film. But brilliant though he undoubtedly is, Guinness isn't even the best thing in *Kind Hearts...*

The sleight-of-hand trick with a comedy this black – it is about a sociopathic serial-killer, after all – is pitching the tone perfectly. Beginning at the end, not the beginning, with the murderous Duke Louis Mazzini (Dennis Price) penning his memoirs in his prison cell the night before his hanging, director Robert Hamer slings us straight into the world as the deliriously amoral Louis sees it. Harnessing a fearsomely witty, stiletto-stab script (where else could a character hope to get away with describing a stained glass window as possessing, "all the exuberance of Chaucer, without, happily, any of the concomitant crudities of the period"?) to a structure that leads audiences towards the most lethal and deceptive of narrative man-traps, it's an energetic stroll towards a hugely ambiguous, double surprise ending of which Hitchcock would have been proud.

By overlaying black-and-white cinematography straight out of an Edwardian photo album on top of some gloriously

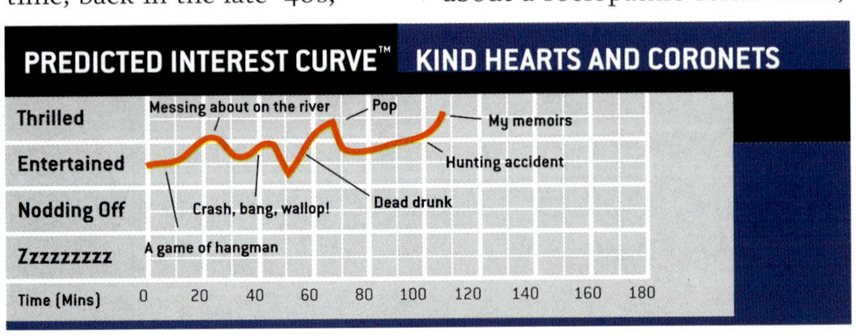

slapsticky deaths (a sinking ship, a plummetting hot-air balloon, exploding caviar, poisonous port...), Hamer keeps things teetering brilliantly between guffaws and grimaces. If it tipped too far one way, *Kind Hearts* would have easily become little more than a *Wacky Races* farce. Too far the other and it would have drowned in desolation.

The key to it all is Dennis Price. "I am a second-rate feature actor," Price once claimed. "I am not a star and never was – I lack the essential spark." Any viewing of Price's performance as Louis Mazzini, the man killing his way up the family tree with his eye on a title, shows that statement for the overly modest bollocks it so clearly is. Carrying out Louis' lethal exercise in self-serving class warfare, Price giftwraps a performance of impeccably restrained glee by folding his clipped, educated vowels around a script which is packed with the juiciest of dialogue: "It is so difficult to make a neat job of killing people with whom one is not on friendly terms"; "He exhibits the most extraordinary capacity for middle age that I've ever encountered in a young man of 24"; "I shot an arrow in the air, she fell to earth in Berkeley Square..."

With Louis as both narrator and lead character, his performance shapes *Kind Hearts*, while Guinness supplies the ornamental trimmings. He's a bastard – in almost all senses of the word – but a lovably debonair one. Nudging viewers with a raised eyebrow here, or a sardonic glance there, Price masterfully butchers his way through the extensive D'Ascoyne family tree, romances two very different women ("I never admired Edith as much as when I was with Sibella, I never longed for Sibella as much as when I was with Edith...") and charms his way past the usual audience defences with the grace of, yes, a real star.

Literary, slyly erotic, amoral, clever, hilarious... Any filmmaker who even thinks of shooting a black comedy should be forced to watch this before the cameras start rolling. Young Louis only made it as far as Duke; *Kind Hearts* is the uncontested king of the genre.

Ceri Thomas

NEED TO KNOW

Year 1949
Running time 106 mins
Director Rupert Hamer
Stars Dennis Price, Alec Guinness, Joan Greenwood
Buy it on Region 2
Tagline "A hilarious study in the gentle art of murder."
Best line "As the Italian proverb says, 'Revenge is the dish which people of taste prefer to eat cold.'" – Duke Louis Mazzini
Critic's view "Enlivened with cynicism, loaded with dramatic irony and shot through with a suspicion of social satire." –*The Daily Telegraph*
Best watched when... You've been insulted by a posh bloke and you're itching for payback.

85

THE KING OF COMEDY

Big Botherer: Jerry Lewis is stalked by Robert De Niro in Scorsese's jet-black comedy.

Martin Scorsese has helped to bring to life some of the most fascinating monsters in modern movies – think Travis Bickle in *Taxi Driver*, Jimmy Doyle in *New York, New York* or Jake La Motta in *Raging Bull*. What all these men have in common – apart from being played by Robert De Niro at his most disconcerting – is that they use violence or bullying to express what they can't articulate. But Scorsese and De Niro's most disturbing character by a long chalk is Rupert Pupkin, the celebrity-obsessed would-be stand-up who lives with his mum and performs an imaginary chat-show in the basement alongside a cardboard cut-out of Liza Minnelli. Next to Rupert, Travis looks like an upstanding member of society, Jimmy a hot date and Jake a happy little bunny.

De Niro first brought Paul Zimmerman's screenplay for *The King of Comedy* to Scorsese's attention shortly after they'd finished their first collaboration, *Mean Streets*, but the actor was always more enthusiastic about it than the director. Then, in 1980, after the 'kamikaze' experience of making *Raging Bull*, Scorsese was itching to plunge into another project, and De Niro finally persuaded him that the time was right for *The King of Comedy*. It's true that the script, about Rupert's obsession with the chat-show king Jerry Langford – which leads him eventually to kidnap Langford and demand a slot on his show by way of ransom – had ripened with the growth of celebrity culture in the US. But in retrospect, Scorsese wondered if he had been right to direct the picture. "I didn't feel comfortable with it. *King Of Comedy* was something that De Niro liked and I had to be convinced to do. If I have to be convinced to do something, I shouldn't do it. I realised that I only want to do pictures that come from me."

'I lost my energy. I only wanted to do pictures that come from me' MARTIN SCORSESE

It was conceived as a quick, guerilla-style shoot after the lengthy production of *Raging Bull*, as well as a pick-me-up for Scorsese after a bout of pneumonia. But it didn't turn out that way. "I didn't make the film fast enough," he said. "I lost my energy. Every day I had to get myself back into why I wanted to make the picture."

Odd to think that the movie was considered plum material for a breezy shoot: its defining characteristics include a painstakingly slow pace and an over-deliberate fixation on images that convey the emptiness of celebrities and those who stalk them. You can see that from the off, when Scorsese freeze-frames the image of a fan's hands slammed against the window of Langford's limousine. This tableaux is made all the more bizarre by being caught in the lightning glare of paparazzi

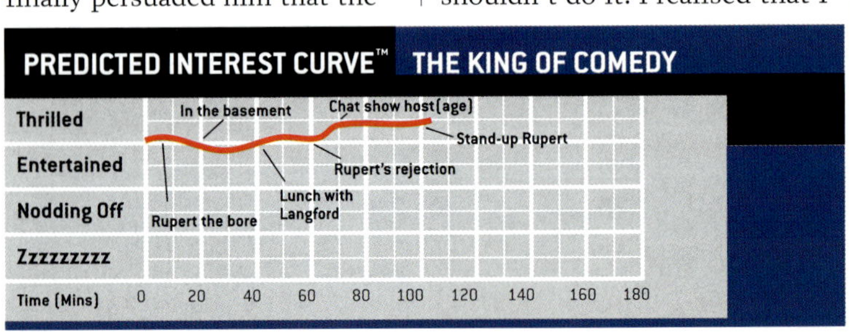

flashbulbs. We have to look at that image for so long as the credits play over it that we want to scream.

That's the reaction Scorsese was going for. So many of the scenes here are protracted for maximum audience discomfort. Even devotees of Alan Partridge or *The Office* will be squirming when Rupert takes his friend Rita to Langford's country house for a lunch date that exists only in his own warped mind. The social embarrassment when Langford confronts his uninvited guests is agonising; the massacre at the end of *Taxi Driver* is like musical comedy in comparison.

With his slicked hair, ingratiating manner and Huey Lewis dress sense, De Niro gives a grotesque performance devoid of vanity, but there's sound work too from Jerry Lewis, impressively implacable as Langford. The celebrity resonance invoked in the casting of this giant of US showbusiness works to the film's advantage. Scorsese had been turned down by Johnny Carson, and had even considered Frank Sinatra for the part, but it's unlikely that either of them would have been so game, or so glum, as Lewis. His performance is like one long Mexican stand-off with his co-stars, whether it's De Niro weaseling his way into his limo, or real-life comic and former friend of Madonna Sandra Bernhard stripping for him after first mummifying him with parcel tape.

With its despairing worldview, dislikeable characters and callous humour, *The King Of Comedy* is not easy to warm to, though it has provoked widespread admiration. The 1980s were difficult for Scorsese: after the glory of *Raging Bull,* he slipped into a series of unambitious projects not originated by him (*After Hours, The Colour Of Money*) before expending enormous energy on his troubled pet project *The Last Temptation Of Christ*. But while *The King Of Comedy,* like most of his 1980s output, was a box-office flop, respect for it continues to grow among those who see its view of a culture that prizes celebrity above all else as alarming and pertinent in this age of *Big Brother*.

Ryan Gilbey

NEED TO KNOW

Year 1983
Running time 109 Minutes
Director Martin Scorsese
Stars Robert De Niro, Jerry Lewis, Sandra Bernhard, Diahnne Abbott, Shelley Hack.
Buy it on Region 2
Tagline "No one knows Rupert Pupkin, but after 11.30 tonight no one will ever forget him."
Critic's view "With *The King Of Comedy*, Mr. Scorsese again confirms his reputation as one of the most authentic, most original voices of his film generation."
– *The New York Times*
Best Watched When...
You've just returned from the Comedy Store.

84

METROPOLIS

The sci-fi classic that you've already seen, even if you haven't...

I have recently seen the silliest film," mused HG Wells in 1927. "I do not believe it would be possible to make one sillier." Death would spare Wells all eight *Police Academy* movies, but even for us less-fortunate souls, it's still hard to clock the fact that the suddenly-myopic sci-fi prophet was talking about *Metropolis*.

A sci-fi epic packed with sex, violence, titanic effects and thunderous acting

HG was the exception. Because when it came to influencing people, Fritz Lang was damn near untouchable. His *Dr Mabuse* trilogy cut the template for criminal geniuses everywhere. *M* invented the serial-killer movie. *You Only Live Once* is definitive text for American crime noir. But in *Metropolis*, the director created not only the most influential sci-fier ever made, but quite probably the most influential movie. Ever.

And it was no more than Lang had planned. In 1925, the Austrian helmer set out to beat Hollywood at its own game. He would simply produce the biggest movie of all time: a sci-fi epic packed with sex, violence, titanic effects and thunderous acting. Two years and one million dollars later, he'd done it – and practically bankrupted German cinema.

Despite later claiming that *Metropolis* was inspired by his first look at the New York skyline, Lang and his wife, co-scripter Thea Von Harbou, had already begun a novel that formed the film's core. Their vision was of a futuristic upstairs-downstairs, an awesome techno-city where the wealthy elite frolic as the workers toil in subterranean depths. With effects whiz Eugene Schufftan combining actors, mirrors, full sets, miniatures and stop-motion, it remains an amazing spectacle – Lang's German Expressionism and Bauhaus architecture colliding with Von Harbou's kitsch futurism. Soaring towers glitter with light, traffic cruises along high-wire skyways, while planes buzz through the air and the streets stream with cars. But then, you already know this: you've been there many, many times... In *Blade Runner*'s LA, *The Fifth Element*'s New York, *Dark City*'s spaceship, *Batman*'s Gotham and *Star Wars'* Coruscant.

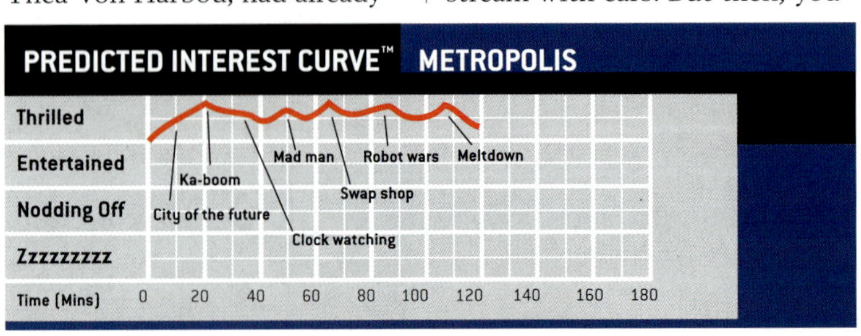

Back in *Metropolis*, we find Freder (Gustav Frohlich), son of the city's ruthless dictator, venturing into the lower depths to help the workers and, more specifically, cop an eyeful of their beautiful revolutionary leader Maria (Brigitte Helm). Incensed, his father hires mad genius Rotwang (Rudolf Klein-Rogge) to capture Maria and transfer her face to a robot in order to fool and control the workers.

Now we'll be straight with you. Story-wise, *Metropolis* isn't exactly copper-bottomed. Lang here is at his most excessive, packing clunking morals, swiss-cheese logic and one of the crappest endings to any great film. But this is a meisterwerk of stunning images: a robot burning at the stake; a machine-god devouring workers in its jaws;

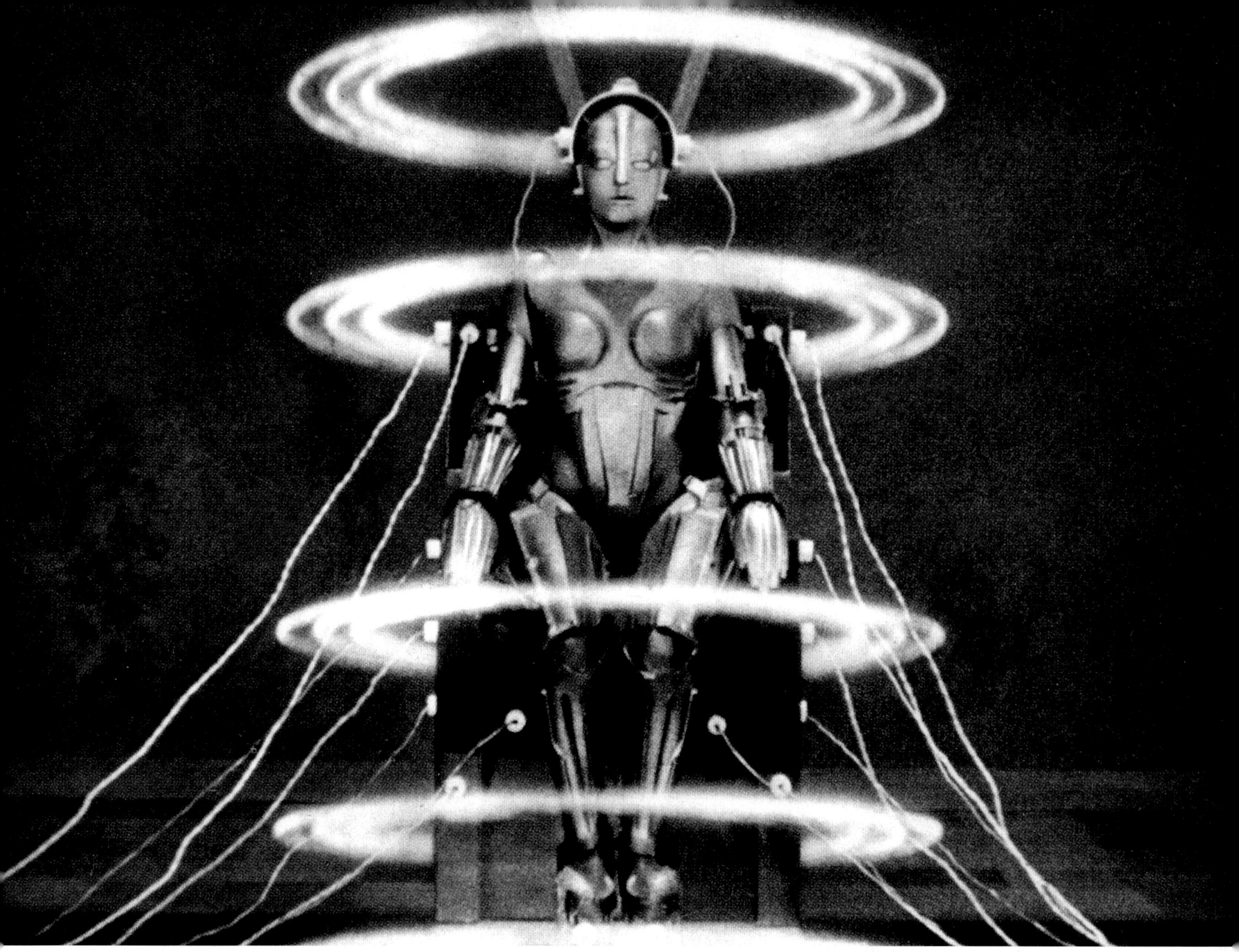

men heaving the heavy hands of a giant clock... Our pick, though, is the birth of the False Maria: an eye-popping array of electrical arcs, bubbling beakers and glowing halos.

According to press releases, Lang employed eight leads, 750 supporting cast, 26,000 male extras, 11,000 females, 750 children, "100 negroes and 25 Chinese". He gave every one of them merry hell. Pushing his actors to exhaustion, the mad perfectionist nearly drowned half the extras during the flood scenes and torched Helm for real during the robot-burning finale. At the end of it all, Lang blew up his giant sets and, by all accounts, enjoyed it mightily.

That, of course, was anything but the end. Even outside its visionary supercity, *Metropolis'* shadow falls across every decade and every genre: from horror (*Bride Of Frankenstein*'s lab) to comedy (*Dr Strangelove*'s hand) to music vids (Queen's 'Radio Gaga'). *Metropolis'* metallic femme fatale teaches the emotional confusion of machines in human form (*Blade Runner, Westworld, Terminator, AI, The Matrix...*), while C-3PO is obviously Maria's fruity cousin.

The film's grunting thematic payload – Madonnas and whores, medieval occult versus modern science, politics, design, industry, blah, blah, blah – is a whopping muddle. But, through its sheer overspill, Lang's mythic melting-pot continues to channel fresh relevance for every era. Hitler, for example, loved the dictatorialism so much that he offered Lang (who loved the anti-authoritarianism) the Nazi film industry. Lang duly jumped the next plane to America, leaving Thea ("that Nazi bitch") behind. Eighty years later, the dystopian nightmare of wage-slave drones filing through the catacombs as clock-faces count down a lifetime of work should ring familiar to commuters the world over. Sliced'n'diced through the second half of the last century, *Metropolis'* newly restored DVD is something to cherish. Because what Lang's film adds up to, far more than an art director's cheat-sheet, is a living museum of 20-century culture. Set in 2000 – a new millennium of fear, desire, science and despair – it's become a self-fulfilling prophecy that even Lang could never have dreamed.

Jonathan Crocker

NEED TO KNOW

Year 1927
Running time 118 mins
Director Fritz Lang
Stars Gustav Frohlich, Brigette Helm, Rudolph Klein-Rogge, Alfred Abel, Fritz Rasp
Buy it on Region 2
Tagline "There can be no understanding between the hands and the brain unless the heart acts as mediator."
Best line N/A
Critic's view "A work so audacious in its vision and angry in its message that it is, if anything, more powerful today than when it was made." – *Chicago Sun-Times*
Best watched when... You're feeling like an underworld wage slave.

83

THE WIZARD OF OZ

No childhood would be complete without MGM's Technicolor fantasy...

It doesn't matter how many times you've seen *The Wizard Of Oz*, it still feels fresh with every new viewing. That's an enviable cinematic achievement that's as rare as a surviving pair of Dorothy's ruby slippers. As a Technicolor beacon in a time of dark, angry politics, *Oz* was drenched in homespun heartland values ("Next time I go looking for my heart's desire, I won't go further than my own backyard," blubs Dorothy after she's returned from Oz). As a gleaming escapist fantasy created by a studio at the peak of its powers, it's brimming with talent, including Judy Garland in a performance of simmering openness, and Margaret Hamilton as that wiry, green-skinned harridan, the Wicked Witch Of The West, a cackling icon who's plagued a few children's dreams in the past 66 years. *Oz*'s screenplay was decked with easy insight and snappy catchphrases, while the musical score is peerless, strewn with unforgettable tunage that almost everyone can chant along to ("Ding dong, the witch is dead..."; "We're off to see the Wizard/ The Wonderful Wizard Of Oz!").

For what's at heart a pretty simple adventure story, *Oz* sprang from chaotic origins, with 14 writers and five directors having a hand in its formation.

Casts a magical shadow over every kids' film that stakes its claim to greatness

Victor Fleming got the final director's credit, but not before footage was scrapped, sets rebuilt, the script revamped and Garland's look refined (goodbye blonde wig). A tough-talking man's man, you can credit Fleming for the honest simplicity of the central performances – some of them having to blare through thick coatings of make-up. But he still went through hell getting *Oz* in the can (leaving King Vidor to finish the job, as he moved over to MGM's other big production, *Gone With The Wind*). Apart from crash-landing flying monkeys, fornicating Munchkins and Margaret Hamilton getting second-degree burns during her witchy vanishing act, original Tin Man Buddy Ebsen was felled by his character's toxic aluminium face paint and replaced by Jack Haley. "People say, 'It must have been fun making that picture,'" recalls Haley. "Like hell. There was nothing fun at all about it."

Adapted from L Frank Baum's 1900 children's novel, the film audaciously mixed its top-and-tail, sepia-toned Kansas sequences with the candy-coloured fantasia of Oz (in an industry that stayed defiantly black-and-white until the late '60s). But generating an entire dreamworld using real sets and actors was *Oz*'s true triumph, even if the movie's special-effects – viewed through our CGI prism – are glorious only in a tacky, old-fashioned Hollywood way. You can spot every seam, wire and matte backdrop, but the marvellous imagination at the film's heart

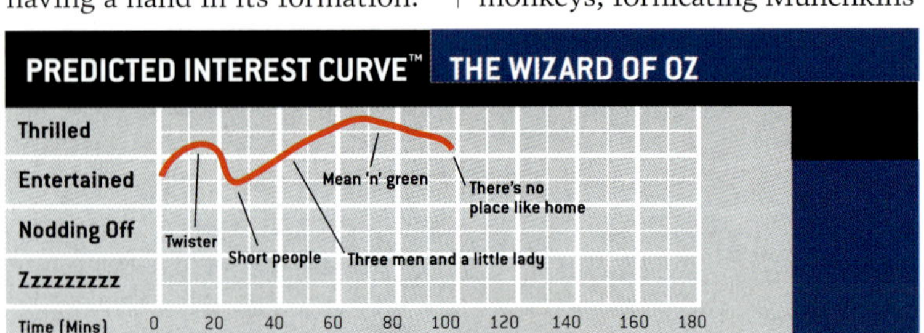

transcends the limitations of its patchwork techniques.

Rumours persist that Ray Bolger, Jack Haley and Bert Lahr – a grizzled trio of Broadway veterans – refused to give an inch to their adolescent co-star, but whatever... Their chemistry with Garland is a joy to behold, while their misfit antics are a riot, from the Cowardly Lion's (Lahr) goofy malapropisms to the Scarecrow's (Bolger) floppy physicality. And amidst all the burlesque clowning lies real pathos. When the Cowardly Lion tearfully bares his soul, it's a heartfelt cry of inadequacy, an aching yearning to fit into a world that's often terrifying. And, in the dominion of Oz, terror comes in fearsome form, as the Wicked Witch deploys balls of flame, drug-laced poppy fields and her simian Luftwaffe to snatch those red heels off Dorothy's feet.

But the emotional glue holding this fanciful tale together is a little girl who no one believes. *Oz* would be nothing without the right Alice in its wonderland, and 16-year-old Garland won the role of farmgirl Dorothy over MGM honcho Louis B Mayer's first choice, dimpled sprite Shirley Temple. Thank the gods, because it's unthinkable to imagine the picture without Garland's wide-eyed, girl-next-door ordinariness and tremulous, emotion-choked singing (although her signature song, 'Over The Rainbow', barely survived the final cut). Dorothy's desire to get back to Kansas is painfully palpable – and Garland's turn achieves extra resonance in our awareness of the actress' drug-overdose death at 47.

Enshrined in the cultural pantheon thanks to television repeats, *The Wizard Of Oz* casts a long, magical shadow over every children's film that stakes its claim to greatness, from *ET* to any of Disney's animated classics. Handed down from generation to generation like a precious keepsake, *Oz* retains its power to transport you in an evocative and unexplainable way. "We don't get any residuals, but we have immortality," Bolger said about the film's ageless appeal. Next time you want to find your heart's own true desire, slip in a DVD of the adventures of Dorothy, Toto and friends. There really is no place like Oz.

Matt Mueller

NEED TO KNOW

Year 1939
Running time 98 mins
Director Victor Fleming
Stars Judy Garland, Ray Bolger, Jack Haley, Margaret Hamilton
Buy it on Region 2
Tagline "It's Metro-Goldwyn-Mayer's Technicolor Triumph!"
Best line "Pay no attention to that man behind the curtain!" – The Wizard of Oz
Critic's view "A work of almost staggering iconographic and emotional meaning, this is one vintage film that fully lives up to its classic status." – *Variety*
Best watched when... Your nasty neighbour has just threatened to call the council because your pet crapped on the pavement in front of her house.

82

ETERNAL SUNSHINE OF THE SPOTLESS MIND

Just when you thought Charlie Kaufman couldn't get any weirder

Gondry and Kaufmann have their work cut out balancing fantasy and reality

There are certain names which, when they appear on a movie's credits, you can think to yoursel, 'Phew. Everything's going to be fine. We're in for something special.' With screenwriter Charlie Kaufman, you know you're in safe hands. Or rather, thrillingly unpredictable hands that will mess with your head and reshape the world in the space of two hours.

His collaborations with director Spike Jonze – *Being John Malkovich* and *Adaptation* – were mindbending slaloms through uncharted territory. Kaufman had a tough time, however, watching his script for *Confessions Of A Dangerous Mind* get mangled, coming out spitting bile at director George Clooney and producer Steven Soderbergh. It looked like a Kaufman screenplay without Jonze's guiding hand was doomed. And then came the miracle of *Eternal Sunshine Of The Spotless Mind* (the title comes from Alexander Pope's epistle 'Eloisa To Abelard'.)

Teaming up again with Michel Gondry, Kaufman launched one of his characteristic high-concepts into another universe altogether. The script owes something to Philip K Dick, but there's the beguiling whiff of pure Kaufman all over it. The whole picture is built around a labyrinthine structure that it would be unfair to discuss here, since one of the chief pleasures is the moment when everything clicks into place. But suffice it to say that it charts the process by which Joel (Jim Carrey) has all memories of his former girlfriend Clementine (Kate Winslet) erased from his mind after he discovers that she has done the same to him – courtesy of an organisation called Lacuna, Inc. Everything is played arrow-straight, the better to give the most bizarre touches a realistic underpinning.

The brain-wiping process itself is visualised with great eloquence. Joel wanders in his pyjamas through the memories as they fade from view; he drifts into the office where the procedure is taking place and sees himself unconscious; as he hurries through a bookshop, the lights switch off behind him, representing the memory he is losing. It was brave, and even a little theatrical, of Gondry to rely so much on shifts in lighting, but the further the film veers away from conventional effects, the more powerful its impact.

Of course, sometimes things go a little crazy: cars fall from the heavens; people's faces are physically erased, leaving a deformed expanse of flesh where their features should be. But generally Gondry achieves his most poetic effects simply: Joel and Clementine waking up in bed on a beach, Clementine's wild red hair clashing with the lush white sand.

This is a film that is not afraid to shock, but in fact it

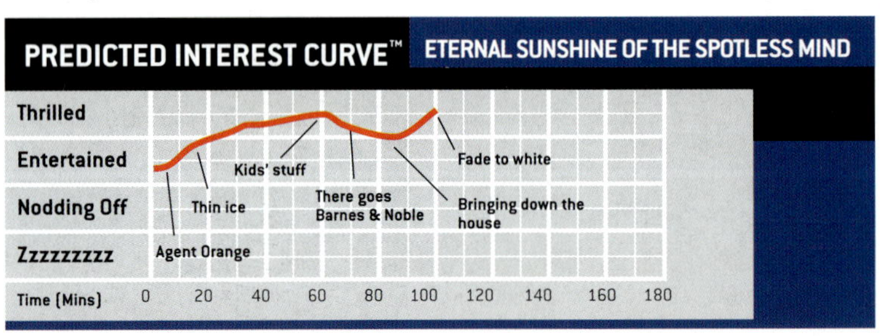

was poised to become even darker: Kaufman had a subplot in his original draft about a woman who was raped and wanted that traumatic memory erased. Such provocative material might have been too hard to confine to the margins, though; and as it stands, Gondry and Kaufman have their work cut out balancing fantasy and reality, present tense and past tense. In this respect, Jon Brion's delicate score, and the use of 'Everybody's Got To Learn Sometime' as a haunting refrain, help to bind together the disparate moments in the film's challenging timescale.

Sunshine's weird mix'n'match cast also work beautifully: Carrey, more touching here than in a self-consciously 'straight' piece such as *Man On The Moon*, comes off as shy and reserved beside the gloriously manic Winslet, who told director Gondry, "I'll be Jim Carrey instead of Jim being Jim Carrey." Let loose to be as anarchic as possible in the movie's freaky landscape, Winslet is nothing short of a revelation. Many of her most inspired moments – her little sidewalk dance, the mighty punch she lands on Carrey's shoulder – were entirely improvised, and you can feel how liberated she feels in the film. There is also impressive work from Tom Wilkinson as Dr Mierzwiak, who performs the procedure on Joel, and Elijah Wood, Kirsten Dunst and Mark Ruffalo as Lacuna staff.

The runaway imagination at play is astounding, but it wouldn't amount to much without the film's painful emotional core. There's almost too much agony and anxiety in images such as Joel standing in the middle of a vast frozen lake at night shouting, "I don't want this any more! I wanna call it off," as his memories are being stripped away from inside him. Or in the flashbacks to traumatic childhood episodes, which provide Gondry and Kaufman with their most thrillingly wacko detour, as Joel drags Clementine into his youth; one scene has the two of them miniaturised and bathing in Joel's mother's kitchen sink. Words cannot convey the potency of Gondry's images; *Eternal Sunshine* is a movie that must be seen to be disbelieved.

Ryan Gilbey

NEED TO KNOW

Year 2004
Running time 108 mins
Director Michel Gondry
Stars Jim Carrey, Kate Winslet, Tom Wilkinson, Mark Ruffalo, Kirsten Dunst
Buy it on Region 1 SE
Tagline "A comedy for anyone with a past they'd rather forget"
Best line "Drink up, young man. It'll make the whole seduction part less repugnant." – Clementine Kruczynski
Critic's view "This deft, witty, and vastly enjoyable movie is a head trip." – *Village Voice*
Best watched when... You've just come round from having a lobotomy.

81

THE SHINING

All work and no play makes Jack a cray-zeee boy in Kubrick's haunted hotel.

Let's face it, Stanley Kubrick films make for demanding viewing, his tantalisingly elusive, stubbornly austere style making his movies as hard to pin down as the man himself. And while *2001: A Space Odyssey* remains his most ambiguous work, this haunting adaptation of Stephen King's novel is equally unafraid to pose teasing questions.

Searching for his next project after 1975's *Barry Lyndon*, Kubrick was ploughing through a stack of paperbacks. Most hit the wall after he'd sampled the opening few pages; *The Shining* stayed glued to his sweaty mitts, Kubrick's long-standing interest in the paranormal tickled by King's tale of a writer holed up in a haunted hotel.

"I thought it was one of the most ingenious and exciting stories of the genre I had read," he would later say. He was right – King's book is a belter, the best spook story since Shirley Jackson's *The Haunting Of Hill House*. But while Kubrick had discovered something that tweaked his interest in King's novel, he wasn't about to stay faithful to the prose. "The plot is for the most part extremely well worked out and for a film that is often all that really matters," he said, in something of a back-handed compliment. His own interpretation would ditch the book's literally explosive ending and speed up Jack Torrance's descent into madness by casting Jack Nicholson's leer. What for King had been a tale about the tragic breakdown of one flawed man and the subsequent break-up of his family became, in Kubrick's icy hands, a film about screaming insanity. (After seeing the movie, King would describe Kubrick's take "as a great big beautiful Cadillac with no motor inside. I would do everything different". He did, too – by churning out a rubbish TV mini-series in 1997.)

'It was one of the most ingenious stories of the genre that I had read' STANLEY KUBRICK

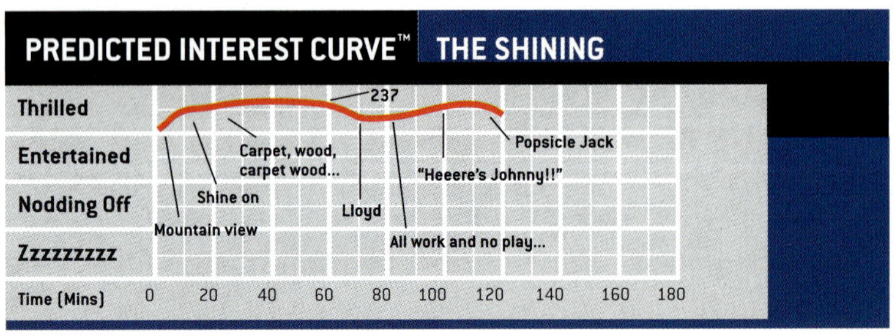

Despite King's misgivings ("The real problem is that Kubrick set out to make a horror picture with no apparent understanding of the genre"), *The Shining* is a disconcerting picture. Terrifying, even. It starts as it means to go on, setting the ominous mood with a helicopter shot of an ant-sized car creeping along a mountain road. Jack is on his way to take up a winter caretaking post in the isolated Overlook Hotel; he'll wind up trying to bury an axe in his wife (Shelley Duvall) and son (Danny Lloyd).

Everything in *The Shining* is designed to agitate, Kubrick chipping away at our composure like the genial spooks that sculpt Jack into a drooling madman. And just as the director infamously tortured Duvall until the harangued actress and her character were hardly discernable – both weeping, screaming wrecks – he does everything in his considerable powers to unsettle

the audience, losing us in the Overlook's maze of identical corridors, doors, patterned wallpaper and garish carpets. Mirrors, too, provide a symmetrical view, but the outlook at the Outlook is rarely a true reflection: Jack talking to himself at the bar where Lloyd suddenly appears; his encounter with the sexy woman/rotting hag in room 237; and the revealing of the true-meaning of Danny's repeated "Redrum. Redrum" mutterings. We're also unnerved by the director's pioneering use of technology, particularly his employment of the newly-invented Steadicam which tracks Danny on his tricycle. The title-cards ('SATURDAY, 'A MONTH LATER', 'WEDNESDAY') further confuse, offering a mock timeframe that's of zero value. (As *New Yorker* critic Janet Maslin would comment in her 1980 review, "*The Shining* may be the first movie that ever made its audience jump with a title that simply says 'Tuesday.'") We're not even really sure if we should believe what we're being shown: whether Danny's anxious visions and Jack's genial conversation with Lloyd are real (well, 'real' in terms of being spectres unleashed by the hotel) or the fantasies of warped minds.

"As the supernatural elements occur you search for an explanation and the most likely one seems to be that the strange things that are happening will finally be explained as the product of Jack's imagination," Kubrick explains. "It's not until Grady, the ghost of the former caretaker, slides open the bolt of the larder door, allowing Jack to escape, that you're left with no other explanation but the supernatural."

King was at least pleased with the sustained ambiguity – he chastised himself for letting on too early in the novel that it was the hotel, definitely the hotel, that was behind the carnage, and openly praised Kubrick's introduction of the hedge-maze as an extension of the hotel-as-metaphor-for-Jack's-twisted-mind metaphor. It's to Kubrick's credit, however, that viewers won't really care where the scares are coming from. The tidal wave of blood out the lift doors, the axe in the chest, the chase through the maze... trust us, you're too *scared* to care where the scares are coming from.

Scott Russon

NEED TO KNOW

Year 1980
Running time 115 mins
Director Stanley Kubrick
Stars Jack Nicholson, Shelly Duvall, Danny Lloyd, Scatman Crothers, Dick Hallorann Barry Nelson
Buy it on Region 1
Best line "HERE'S JOHNNNY!" – Jack Torrance
Critic's view "Stanley Kubrick's spellbinding foray into the realm of the horror film." – *The New York Times*
Best watched when... You've just cancelled that expensive weekend for two at the picturesque old hotel in the Rocky Mountains.

80

DAY FOR NIGHT

French New Wave master François Truffaut charms Hollywood...

"I don't give a shit what you think of La Nuit Américaine" FRANÇOIS TRUFFAUT

François Truffaut was no greenhorn when he made one of his most fondly regarded pictures, *Day For Night*, a film about filmmaking that takes its title from the practice of shooting nocturnal scenes in daylight using filters. (The French title – *La Nuit Américaine* – arguably embodies the film's affectionately prickly spirit even better.) Like his countrymen and contemporaries Eric Rohmer, Claude Chabrol and Jean-Luc Godard, Truffaut had graduated from film critic on the incomparably brilliant *Cahiers Du Cinema* to world-class auteur. His reputation was founded on his early features, like his 1959 debut, *The 400 Blows*, an autobiographical tale of childhood rebellion that epitomised the freewheeling spirit of the French New Wave.

Of all the New Wave directors, Truffaut always seemed the one most destined to hit paydirt in Hollywood. Sure, Godard was interviewed by Warren Beatty as a possible director for *Bonnie & Clyde* – but only at Truffaut's recommendation, and because Truffaut himself had already passed on the project. And by making *Day For Night*, partly in English, Truffaut confirmed what his fans (as well as some dissenters) always knew about him: his cinema was too universal, too passionate, to be restricted to arthouse audiences. The film's box-office success confirmed this, as did the approbation of the Academy: the movie was nominated for four Oscars, including Best Director, and walked off with one for Best Foreign Language Film. Soon he became Official New Best Chum to Spielberg, who cast him in *Close Encounters Of The Third Kind*, suggested the US title for Truffaut's *L'Argent de Poche* (*Small Change*) and made *E.T. The Extra-Terrestrial* with Truffaut's encouragement.

Every frame of *Day For Night* brims with joy and enthusiasm for the filmmaking process. It's almost immaterial that the picture focuses on the shooting of a film (*May I Introduce Pamela*) that would command rather less admiration than Truffaut's own work. Truffaut himself plays Ferrand, the filmmaker who is presiding over the unedifying material as well as talking us through the pitfalls of life on set. "Shooting a movie is like a stagecoach trip," he intones in the picture's most famous line. "At first you hope for a nice ride. Then you just hope to reach your destination."

Day For Night belongs to that intriguing sub-genre of movies that dish the dirt on behind-the-scenes goings-on, but it has none of the overriding cynicism of *Beware Of A Holy Whore* or *The Stunt Man*, nor the muted despair of *Sweet Liberty*, the cutesiness of *State And Main*, or the suspenseful comedy of *Living In Oblivion*. *Day For Night* is more wistful and more levelheaded than any of them (the only modern movie to have

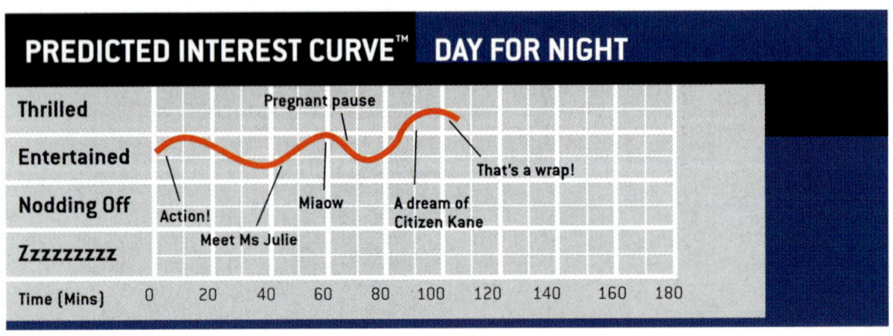

approached its tone is probably Tim Burton's *Ed Wood*).

The key to its magic lies in the loose, anecdotal structure, which builds at a leisurely pace, Pierre-William Glenn's camera glancing around the participants with the curiosity of someone who has simply wandered on set one day and decided to stay. In place of the glamorous lie that is sold to us about moviemaking, we get the boredom of killing time between takes, the petty rivalries, the stresses suffered by the lowly crew, the agony of trying to work with animals, the intricacies of being a stunt driver. There is sympathy and wryness in equal measures for this band of itinerant misfits: a former star (Valentina Cortese, Oscar-nominated for Best Supporting Actress), who consoles herself with booze; a seasoned actor (Jean-Pierre Aumont) ambling belatedly out of the closet; and a classy American actress (Jacqueline Bisset) coping with the attention of the lead actor (Truffaut regular Jean-Pierre Leaud, who had the lead in *The 400 Blows*, and played Antoine Doinel in four subsequent movies).

There's nothing judgmental, just the scrappy business of making movies shaped into a vague narrative by Truffaut. But what some of us prize about the film – its gentle nature, ebbing rhythms and understated humour – others see as a betrayal of the once-daring Truffaut. Indeed, *Day For Night* was the reason for Truffaut's rift with Godard, who wrote to him to complain of what he saw as the film's dishonesty about the realities of filmmaking: "Yesterday I saw *La Nuit Américaine*. Probably no one else will call you a liar, so I will."

Truffaut responded: "I don't give a shit what you think of *La Nuit Américaine*, what I find deplorable on your part is the fact that, even now, you continue to go and see such films, films whose subject matter you know in advance will not correspond to either your conception of cinema or your conception of life... Why? In the hope of finding something that will fuel your contempt for the rest of us, that will reinforce all your new prejudices?"

It's rare that Godard was wrong. But this is one occasion when he was.

Ryan Gilbey

NEED TO KNOW

Year 1973
Running time 115 mins
Director François Truffaut
Stars Jacqueline Bisset, Valentina Cortese, Alexandra Stewart, Dani, Jean-Pierre Aumont
Buy it on Region 1
Tagline "A movie for people who love movies."
Critic's view "A movie for the movie-struck, the essentially naïve – those who would rather see a movie, any movie... than do anything else." – Pauline Kael, *The New Yorker*
Best watched when... You're considering a career change to become a director.

79

THE WICKER MAN

Lust, murder, human sacrifice, Britt Ekland starkers and Christopher Lee in drag...

The Wicker Man snuck into British cinemas like a hand-grenade rolled quietly down the aisle – unpublicised, unpreviewed, slotted in as the unassuming support feature to Nic Roeg's *Don't Look Now*. Many cinema managers, assuming it was a travelogue fronted by blazered TV personality Alan Whicker, billed it as *The Whicker Man*. Audiences got the surprise of their lives.

For a start, they were confronted by a movie that takes religion seriously – in all conscience, a rare enough event in British cinema. *Wicker Man* pits dour, Scots-Presbyterian Christianity against exuberant paganism – and exposes the flaws in both of them. Witty, irreverent and revelling in the cut-and-thrust of doctrinal combat, Anthony Shaffer's script hits its peak in the clash between Edward Woodward's uptight mainland cop Sergeant Howie and Christopher Lee's urbane Lord Summerisle. "And what of the true God? What of Him?" protests Howie, appalled at the realisation that pagan eroticism is the island's official creed. "He's dead," responds Summerisle cheerfully. "He can't complain. He had his chance and – in modern parlance – blew it."

Made right at the weary fag-end of the British horror cycle, *Wicker Man* shrugs off all the gothic fangs-and-capery of the Hammer stable in favour of the limpid sunlight and blossom of a Hebridean spring. (Still more of an achievement, given that it was shot, for logistical reasons, in a dank October with a shivering cast and plastic flowers taped to the boughs.) Which was essential since, as Summerisle explains in the film's jaw-dropping climax, Howie must come "of his own free will", eyes open (but seeing nothing) in broad daylight to the place of sacrifice. Right through the film, pious police sergeant Howie, the fool-king-virgin, is led by the nose – literally so, when he's in his Punch costume – by everyone on the island: the hunted leading the hunters, believing he's tracking down his quarry when the quarry is actually Howie himself.

What's more, the pagans play fair. Neil Howie, chastely saving himself for his marriage bed, has temptation offered him – thrust at him, even – in the comely shape of Britt Ekland, the landlord's lascivious daughter, gyrating stark buttock naked outside his bedroom as he writhes to contain his lust. Had he succumbed and popped his cherry, he'd presumably have been saved. (Dissent here, incidentally, over why Ekland needed a booty-double for the full-length shots. Some accounts say she demanded it, but Britt herself insists she knew nothing about it – and furthermore complains that her substitute's bum was too big.)

The film's greatest asset –

Witty, irreverent and revelling in cut'n'thrust doctrinal combat

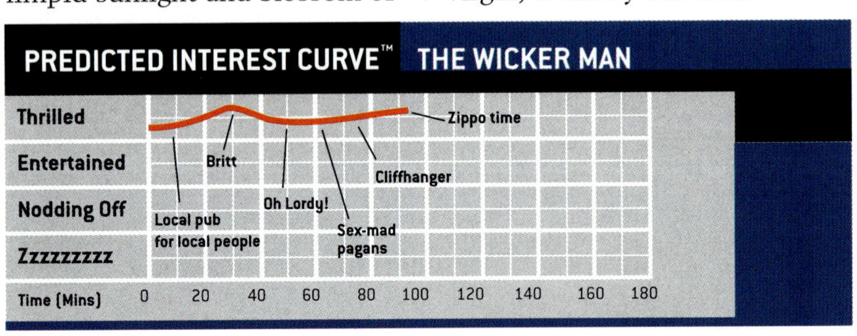

besides Lee's performance – is Shaffer's amused, coolly intelligent script. The island's religion, founded (we're told) by the present laird's granddad, offers just the kind of loopy mishmash you'd expect from a solemn Victorian free-thinker – a hotchpotch of ancient lore, druidical mumbo and chunks ripped shrieking out of Frazer's Golden Bough. Even better, here's a movie that has the courage of its convictions – not just to state them proudly, but to follow them right through to their logical, ruthless conclusion. As the flames crackle higher and the copper's desperate howls of "The Lord Is My Shepherd" are counterpointed by the islanders' joyous chant of "Summer Is Icumen In", you wait for the filmmakers to chicken out, for the Highland Calvary to come thundering over the hill. But no. Listen to the echo of those first audiences' jaws hitting the floor.

Even though what they saw on the screen was actually a mutilated torso. British Lion, recently taken over by new management, loathed what they'd financed, chopped the movie down with a blunt axe and shoved out the remains with zilch support as a B-picture. The negative was accidentally (or, as Christopher Lee claims, deliberately) chucked out and buried under the M3 motorway. Luckily, a full print had been sent to Roger Corman in the USA. As *The Wicker Man*'s reputation blossomed from minority cult rave to full-on masterpiece, the missing bits spliced back in to restore the film almost to the original director's cut. (The Region 2 release carries both versions.)

What few have noticed, though, is that *The Wicker Man* is a cunning reworking of another Scots-set classic, *Whisky Galore!* Far-fetched? Okay, consider. The people of a remote Hebridean island, faced with a life-threatening dearth, conspire to resolve it by illegal means. To do so, they hatch a plot against an outsider, the representative of authority and the only man of conventional morality on the island – and sacrifice him in the pursuit of the greater good. With not a shred of remorse. Now if only *Whiskey Galore!* had featured naked teens fornicating in the open air...

Philip Kemp

NEED TO KNOW

Year 1973

Running time 102 mins

Director Robin Hardy

Stars Christopher Lee, Edward Woodward, Britt Ekland

Buy it on Region 2 Classic Collection Box Set

Tagline "Flesh to touch... Flesh to burn! Don't keep the Wicker Man waiting!"

Best line "They do love their divinity lessons" – Summerisle, watching naked girls dancing

Critic's view "It's the kind of film that needs the transforming hand of a good director. The raw material is there, but in Robin Hardy's hands it remains raw material." – *Financial Times*

Best watched when... You're saving yourself for marriage.

78

THE GRADUATE

Scuba gear, sex and Simon and Garfunkel... the growing pains of Benjamin Braddock.

Let's begin at the end. Benjamin and Elaine sitting on the bus. No climactic kiss. No knowing look at each other. Just the slow draining of adrenaline from their vacant, youthful faces.

Years later, when asked what happened next, director Mike Nichols replied: "They probably ended up like their parents."

More than simply a slice of '60s counter culture, it's the saddest comedy ever

More than simply another late '60s slice of counter culture, *The Graduate* remains perhaps the saddest comedy ever.

Like 1967's other big hit, *Bonnie And Clyde*, it quickly found favour with America's college population. As the Vietnam War escalated and dissatisfaction grew, young Americans tapped into the idea of Hoffman's Benjamin Braddock, an innocent who's seduced and betrayed by an older generation unwilling to admit their own mistakes.

But, as Nichols recognised, the vast majority of those disenfranchised young teenagers packing the nation's cinemas would not be holding rallies and protests forever. Eventually the placards would be lowered, the light of indignation dimmed and new concerns would permeate their days – jobs and cars and houses and families. In effect, they too would become their parents. This is the heart of *The Graduate* – not a youthful yell of rebellion but a depressing, world-weary sigh.

To this end, Dustin Hoffman's lugubrious features perfectly suit Benjamin Braddock, the titular character 'worried about his future'. It proved to be Hoffman's breakthrough role and although it seems hard now to imagine anyone else playing Ben, initial plans had focused on more traditional leading men. Warren Beatty was first lined up for the part before Robert Redford screen tested, while even Jack Nicholson was considered. The producers started to move away from the obvious when they cast Charles Grodin as Ben but disagreements over his salary saw him walk.

Even the role of Mrs Robinson went through revision. Famously, Doris Day turned it down (without having seen the script – her husband was too 'disgusted' by it to pass it on). Judy Garland was also considered while Nichols wanted her to be French and had Jeanne Moreau in mind.

The producers were aghast. They insisted on an American actress and also tried to veto Nichols' other demand – a Simon and Garfunkel soundtrack. Eventually a compromise was reached. Moreau was out, the songs could stay.

Strangely, for years after, the one element of the film not embraced by the critics was the iconic soundtrack. Paul Simon's haunting tunes were seen as 'dating' the movie, and locking it to the times. But as the decades have passed and pop

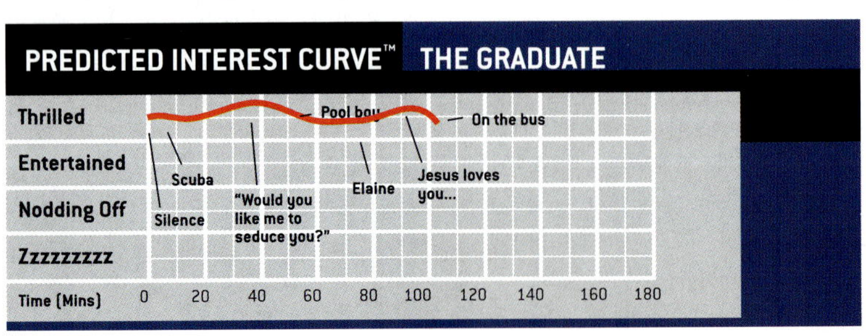

music has cannibalised itself, the year of a song seems irrelevant. Contemporary films happily employ music from previous decades without fear. If the song suits the mood of the visuals, where's the problem? And rarely have songs so suited a mood as they do in *The Graduate*. From the opening credits' use of 'The Sound Of Silence' to the stuttering 'Mrs Robinson' as Benjamin races to Elaine's wedding, the marriage of music and images has rarely been bettered.

Visually too, the film is a treat. Nichols, who won a Best Director Oscar for his efforts, never misses an opportunity to let what's in the frame emphasise the underlying themes. The film opens with Benjamin isolated on a crowded plane, then static on an airport walkway and finally staring through the glass of his aquarium tank. In all three shots he is alone and floundering. When he comes downstairs for the party, he passes a framed picture of an unhappy clown. The role he is about to take at the party.

Throughout, he is seen behind glass or under water, and bleak composition follows bleak composition (Mrs Robinson's nudity reflected in her daughter's portrait, Elaine's face coming into focus as it dawns on her that her mother and Ben have had a relationship).

But despite the melancholia, the film still manages to draw laughs. Hoffman excels as the nervous Benjamin, while all the adult characters (who – unlike Benjamin and Elaine – are never referred to by their first name, to emphasise the generation gap) are absurd and comic. Apart from the towering Mrs Robinson, who is, in her own words, neurotic, alcoholic and available. Naturally, Anne Bancroft's portrayal of callous sexuality instigated a million teenage fantasies.

By the movie's ending though, we are back where we started. Benjamin is still alone. Only now, Elaine is alone next to him. Both are about to encounter the coming of age that all of us face, the move from teenager to adult, the realisation that we all have to grow up. Nichols' bitter coda is that we may not have as much choice as we think in who we will ultimately become.

Aubrey Ganguly

NEED TO KNOW

Year 1967
Running time 105 minutes
Director Mike Nichols
Stars Dustin Hoffman, Anne Bancroft, Katherine Ross, William Daniels, Murray Hamilton
Buy it on Region 2
Tagline "This is Benjamin. He's a little worried about his future."
Best line "Just one word... plastics." – Mr McGuire
Critic's view "*The Graduate* is funny, not because of sight gags and punchlines and other tired rubbish, but because it has a point of view." – *Chicago Sun-Times*
Best watched when... You're pursued by an older woman.

77

LAWRENCE OF ARABIA

TE Lawrence gets his just 'deserts' in David Lean's landmark epic...

They used a psychological recipe. Take an ounce of narcissism, a pound of exhibitionism, a pint of sadism, a gallon of bloodlust and a sprinkle of other aberrations and stir well." By all accounts, AW Lawrence was less than impressed by how his brother, legendary British adventurer TE Lawrence, was portrayed in David Lean's film. But what would he know, eh? An incredible life deserves an extraordinary movie, and they don't come much better than Lean's magnificent desert saga. It might play fast and loose with historical fact, omit some characters and amalgamate others, and ultimately become as seduced by the feral beauty of Arabia as its subject was. But if any picture deserves the title "epic", it's this one: a tale of heroism, friendship, ambition and hubris, played out on the grandest stage imaginable yet rooted in the psychology of one flawed, fascinating individual. To quote Steven Spielberg, it truly is "a miracle of a film".

A story played out in the grandest scale yet rooted in the psychology of one man

Of course, it could all have been very different. Having seen *The Bridge On The River Kwai* scoop seven Oscars, Lean's first notion was a Gandhi biopic with Alec Guinness as the Mohatma and Laurence Olivier as Lord Mountbatten. (How ironic that when Richard Attenborough did bring his Gandhi biopic to the big screen it should mirror *Lawrence* so closely, right down to the gambit of commencing with its protagonist's death.) Producer Sam Spiegel was unconvinced, however, and steered him towards Lawrence, mainly because he was sure it would be the perfect role for Marlon Brando. "Lawrence and Brando are very much alike," said the producer. "Both have that mystic, tortured quality of doubting their own destiny."

But Brando turned the part down, as did Albert Finney. So the role went to Peter O'Toole, a virtual unknown who Lean remembered from 1960 crime caper *The Day They Robbed The Bank Of England*. It would prove to be an inspired choice. With his piercing blue eyes and glistening blond hair, the Irish actor had a magnetic presence on camera. (As Noel Coward quipped, "If he'd been any prettier they'd have had to call it *Florence Of Arabia*.") He also really wanted the role and was prepared to do anything his director demanded – even spending three months in the desert to acclimatise himself to the searing heat. Bit by a badly behaved camel, roasted by the blazing sun and nearly blinded by a misfiring squib, O'Toole would end up completing the 23-month shoot a good two stone lighter than when he started. But he also came out of it a star.

He wasn't the only one. Few actors have been gifted a more memorable entrance than Omar Sharif, emerging slowly out of

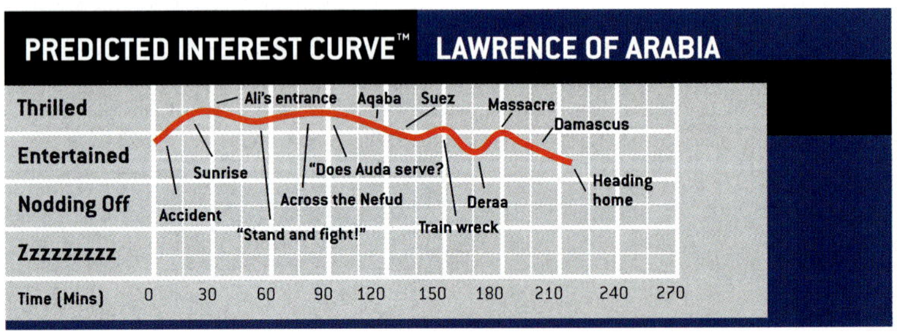

the haze like a mirage come to life. "David wanted it to last a lot longer," reveals the Egyptian. "But the studio thought it was boring. They thought he was mad making an entrance that long, where you see nothing and the silence." Sharif himself was initially sceptical about the film: "It was about Arabs on camels crossing the desert from left to right and from right to left. There were no women, no love story and no action. It was an incredible gamble." Still, he believed in Lean's ability to pull it off. "There was so much care given to every shot. We used to wait a whole day for a cloud that was *here* to go *there*. You couldn't imagine that all this was not going to make a good film."

The Academy certainly thought so, nominating *Lawrence* for 10 Oscars. (In the end, like *Kwai*, it won seven.) The studio, however, had cold feet, forcing Lean to snip 20 minutes off his masterpiece – an act of savagery only corrected in 1989 when the movie was restored, under Lean's supervision, to its full, three-and-three-quarter hour glory. Cynics at the time sneered it was little more than a *Boy's Own* adventure writ large that skirted the issue of Lawrence's latent homosexuality and ignored his postwar flirtations with fascism. The majority, however, gladly surrendered to its eye-popping spectacle and sweeping grandeur, captured for all eternity by Freddie Young's 70mm photography and to the unforgettable strains of Maurice Jarre's beautiful score.

Best moment? Too many to mention. For sheer jaw-dropping brilliance you can't beat the train wreck, shot in Almeria, Spain, on more than two miles of specially constructed track. But if we have a favourite scene, it has to be the one where a Suez Canal ship sails across the crest of a sand dune – an image of such breathtaking, absurd beauty you can only watch agape. We hope O'Toole liked it too when he finally got round to seeing the picture in 1980. Probably not, though. "Who is that pudding, that poor, coy twit with the twinkling blue eyes?" he gasped at the time. "My God, it's me!"

Neil Smith

NEED TO KNOW

Year 1962
Running time 228 mins (restored version)
Director David Lean
Stars Peter O'Toole, Omar Sharif, Alec Guinness, Anthony Quinn, Jack Hawkins
Buy it on Region 2 SE
Tagline "A mighty spectacle of action and adventure!"
Best line "Do you think I'm just anyone? Do you?" – TE Lawrence
Critic's view "Here is a wonderful film that makes all other epics look like peanuts." – *The People*
Best watched when... You want to take a holiday without leaving your sofa.

76

CLOSE ENCOUNTERS OF THE THIRD KIND

Steven Spielberg urges us to watch the skies. And makes mountains out of mash-hills...

Exploding swamp gas reflecting off the light of Venus. Mind control by sinister government bodies. Top-secret air force craft being tested in civilian areas. None of these theories about alien visitations are mooted – or even mentioned – by Steven Spielberg in *Close Encounters Of The Third Kind.*

Neary's obsession is so identifiably human, we're swept along with him

After exploring primal terror in *Duel* and *Jaws*, Spielberg abandoned himself with his fourth film to the expression of that childlike sense of wonder that's come to define his career. In a sense, he'd already made the film, having borrowed $400 from his father while still in high school to make *Firelight*, a two-hour epic about UFOs. So this, along with *ET*, is the director's most primal example of channelling his inner child, and the sort of otherworldly experience he'd want to have. The clue's in the title: the aliens in *Close Encounters* are exactly what you'd hope beings from another planet would be – affable, intelligent, noble, and, perhaps, bringing a message of love and peace to a bellicose planet. Indeed, Spielberg's only nod towards conspiracy theory is the military's attempt to keep the public away from the immense mothership's landing site. And the only debate about these extraterrestrial interlopers is what sort of junk food one of their ships resembles: an ice cream cone or a cookie?

While *Close Encounters* does drift off into the realms of fantasy, and gloriously so, Spielberg deftly keeps us anchored to awed reality by revealing the extraordinary events through the eyes of a very ordinary, working man. Roy Neary (Richard Dreyfuss) becomes ensnared in the earth-shattering events surrounding the aliens' arrival by accident rather than intention. His first experience of the space-dwellers' presence rocks him to his core, propelling him on an urgent mission to find out what's happening, risking alienation (no pun intended) from his family to fulfil his quest. Neary's obsession is so identifiably human, we're swept along with him.

He's not a hero, nor a man in control of his destiny who understands what he's getting himself into. The best hope humanity has for understanding is a quirky man of science (François Truffaut), whose passion for the subject matter matches Neary's. But even he falters in the face of this unfathomable event, his logical brain struggling to come up with an answer or explanation. Kind of what you imagine would really happen if alien ships suddenly landed in desert sands. And that gives *Close Encounters* its power: in the absence of black-and-white heroes and villains, what Spielberg leaves us with is a wide-eyed voyage of discovery, of having everything we believe

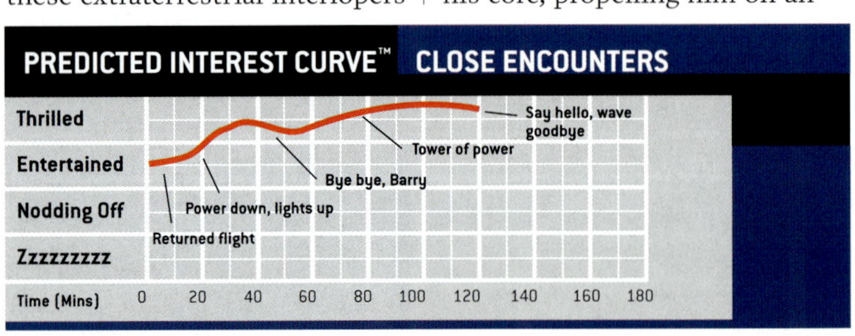

in and trust torn from our eyes, and how we cope with that.

Then at the peak of his Hollywood powers, and in many ways a quintessentially '70s movie star, Dreyfuss is perfect casting for the role of Neary, portraying a flawed man's struggle to determine the truth and his quiet breakdown with subtle grace – even as he had to rely on his own imagination for a lot of the effects work. "Steven did not know what the UFOs looked like when we were shooting. So he would say to me, all the time, 'So you're looking up in awe – more awe!'" laughs the actor. Spielberg guides him through the story with some magnificent and – yes – iconic imagery: from the mashed potato replica of the Devil's Tower monument that Roy fashions with clinical purpose at the dinner table, to the alien mothership itself, a colossal construct that employs the power of music to confirm that this particular group of grey-skinned galactics come in peace. This final effect is a glorious, triumphant, uplifting finale – even if it gave the young director technical nightmares: "A nightmare in lighting," Spielberg recalled. "At least 40 electricians had to be flown in to handle it."

Close Encounters is a sci-fi epic for grown-ups, easily holding its own against brasher, flashier youth-oriented contenders like *Star Wars*. At its best, its sublime meditation on alien interaction compares favourably with the writings of the best sci-fi authors. With brains to go with its blockbuster heft, Spielberg refuses to allow spectacle to override emotion.

Some critics argue that Spielberg never should have shown the aliens, that by doing so, he tipped the scales in favour of schmaltz. But they're the ideal cap for the film, the tantalising reward for all the chaos and disruption they've thrust into these characters' lives. As Roy is led away by his new alien friends, it's the thrilling climax of an extraordinary film that sends you out humming the five-bar communication shared between the two species and watching the skies. Whether or not aliens really exist, *Close Encounters Of The Third Kind* makes you wish that they did.

James White

NEED TO KNOW

Year 1977
Running time 135 mins
Director Steven Spielberg
Stars Richard Dreyfuss, François Truffaut, Teri Garr
Buy it on Region 2 Collector's Edition
Tagline *We are not alone.*
Best line "We didn't choose this place. We didn't choose these people. They were invited!" – David Laughlin
Critic's view "Whether or not you believe it, this climax involves the imagination in surprising ways. This is a day in which the earth might have stood still." – *The New York Times*
Best watched when... Those strange lights in the sky turn out to be more than just the local nightclub's laser display.

75

THE WILD BUNCH

Sam Peckinpah locks'n'loads to fill the Old West with ragged, bloody holes...

The passing of the Old West – that was where Sam Peckinpah's heart always lay. Other great directors visited there, of course: John Ford (*The Man Who Shot Liberty Valance*), Anthony Mann (*Man Of The West*), John Huston (*The Life And Times Of Judge Roy Bean*), Don Siegel (*The Shootist*) and plenty more – but that elegiac moment of transition was what always captured Peckinpah's imagination the most powerfully, right from *Ride The High Country* through *The Ballad Of Cable Hogue* to *Junior Bonner* and *Pat Garrett And Billy The Kid*. And, of course, in his definitive statement of that cherished theme, *The Wild Bunch*.

Just a glance down the cast list tells us where we're at. William Holden, Robert Ryan, Edmond O'Brien, Warren Oates, Ben Johnson, Ernest Borgnine – a terrific line-up of craggy, well-loved actors, all heading into the twilight of their careers. (Although, remarkably enough, Borgnine's still with us and still working.) It's 1914, the whole world's about to fly apart and down on the Tex-Mex border, Pike Bishop (Holden) and his gang of old-time outlaws are dreaming of that last "one good score". Obviously they won't make it – we know that. But that's not what matters. What matters is whether Pike, along with those who ride with him, can (to borrow a line from Joel McCrea in *Ride The High Country*) "enter his house justified".

Despite all the violence, this is a movie about honour, chivalry and comradeship

For, despite the violence, this is a movie about honour, chivalry and comradeship.

"When you side with a man you stay with him," says Pike, "and if you can't do that, you're like some animal." So the film's most tragic figure isn't Pike or any of his gang, but Deke Thornton (Ryan), a former associate who's been coerced into helping hunt down the gang by the threat of being returned to jail and tortured. Leading a motley bunch of scuzzy bounty-hunters, his whole body weighed down with a sense of betrayal, Deke mutters, "We're hunting men – and I wish to God I was with them." Only right at the end, when he's sent the bounty-hunters off to their deaths, can he regain his self-respect and link up with Sykes (O'Brien), the last surviving member of Pike's gang, who tells him, "Ain't like it used to be – but it'll do."

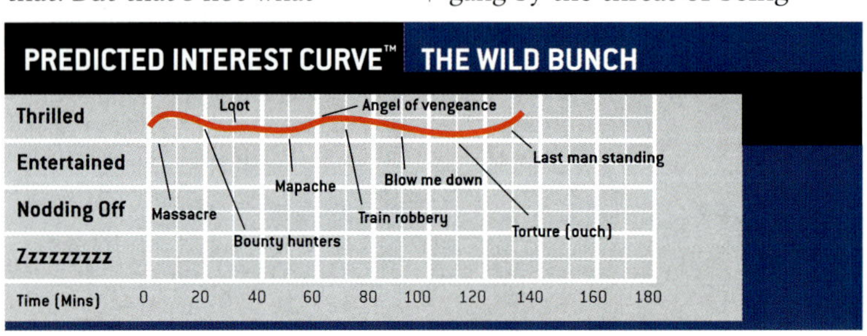

Violent? Well, yes, of course. Though those reviewers who complained the movie was one long sequence of gore-spurting were wide of the mark. *The Wild Bunch* begins and ends with two of Peckinpah's trademark slow-motion blood-letting sequences. But in between, the greater part of the movie is lyrical and gentle – especially the sequence set in a Mexican village, whose people seem to know that these gringos

are riding to their last fight. There's gentleness, too, in the relationship between Pike and his second-in-command Dutch Engstrom (Borgnine) – these are men who've known each for years and can trust and respect each other.

Maybe more shocking than the violence – which in the age of Tarantino doesn't look so excessive – is Peckinpah's use of children to present the worst aspects of human nature. The first image we see, in the build-up to the shoot-out at the bank, is a group of kids happily tormenting scorpions by putting them into an ants' nest. By the time the shooting's over, the kids have progressed to setting light to ants and scorpions alike. When Angel, the youngest member of the gang, is being dragged behind a car, a bunch of sweet-faced Mexican youngsters take turns sitting on his tormented body. And it's another angelic young boy who gives Dutch his final coup de grâce.

As so often with Peckinpah (*Ride The High Country*, *Ballad Of Cable Hogue*), it's a motor-car that spells the beginning of the end. In this case the car owned by General Mapache. Mapache – brutal, venal, treacherous – is the polar opposite of Pike and his gang. Dutch isn't slow to point it out: "We ain't nothing like him," he drawls. "We don't hang nobody." And just to underline Mapache's ill-faith, Peckinpah furnishes him with a couple of advisers from the German Imperial Army – which is maybe slightly over-egging the pudding.

NEED TO KNOW

Year 1969
Running time 138 mins
Director Sam Peckinpah
Stars William Holden, Robert Ryan, Ernest Borgnine, Warren Oates, Edmond O'Brien
Buy it on Region 2
Tagline "Nine men who came too late and stayed too long."
Best line "We gotta start thinking beyond our guns. Those days are closing fast." – Pike
Critic's view "It represents a conscious exercise in the glorification of the kill." – *The Morning Star*
Best watched when... You're convinced that chivalry is dead.

Lucien Ballard's cinematography casts a rich autumnal glow over the whole film. For once, it's a Peckinpah movie that wasn't mutilated before its release; there was none of the trauma and frustration he experienced over *Major Dundee* and *Garrett*. Only a few brief scenes were cut, most showing flashbacks to Deke Thornton's torture in jail, and these were restored a few years later. Rumours still circulate of a 175-minute version, but it seems this was merely an initial rough cut that Peckinpah played around with before making his final cut.

Oh, and John Wayne loathed the movie. But then, what else would you expect?

Philip Kemp

74

RAIDERS OF THE LOST ARK

Spielberg and Lucas combine brains to build the ultimate cinematic thrill-ride.

It all came together on a Hawaiian beach the weekend *Star Wars* opened. George Lucas and his good buddy Steven Spielberg were building sandcastles and talking movies when Spielberg confessed that he'd always wanted to direct a Bond movie. And so Lucas told him about an idea he'd come up with around the same time as *Star Wars*, again recycling the Saturday morning serials of his youth, about an archaeologist adventurer racing to beat the Nazis to the Ark Of The Covenant. For Spielberg, he was better than Bond. He was a new hero for a new generation. "I committed there and then on the beach," he recalls.

Lucas initially saw Indiana Jones, named after his dog, as a 007-type character, a suave playboy in a tux surrounded by fast girls and faster cars. But Spielberg pressed his buddy to recast him as a dishevelled, world-weary hero – as American critic Roger Ebert later described, "a taciturn, understated, stubborn character who might be the Bogie of *The Treasure Of The Sierra Madre* with his tongue in his cheek."

Raiders is so full of choice moments, it's like its own greatest hits compilation

Movie history also remembers that Tom Selleck was first choice to play the globetrotting artefact-hunter, although whether that was with or without the moustache is uncertain. But with Selleck unable to extricate himself from his contract for TV detective series *Magnum PI*, the role went to Harrison Ford who, despite having played Han Solo in *Star Wars*, had gone back to carpentry. After *Raiders*, Ford would never again have to put up anybody else's shelves.

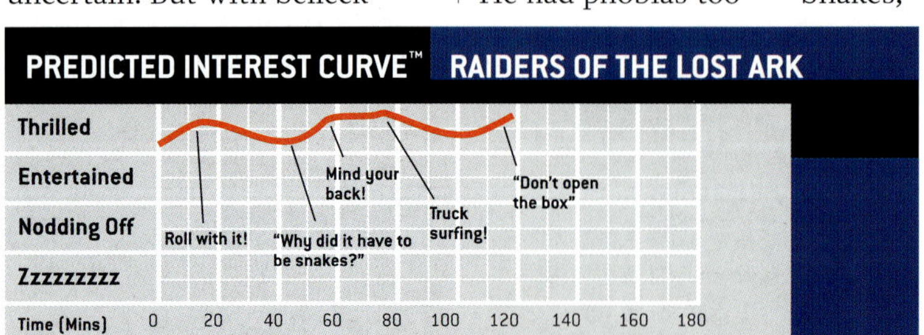

A bespectacled college professor with adoring female students and an intrepid sideline in raiding tombs, Ford's Indiana Jones made archaeology look cool, proving himself to be a dab hand at finding old stuff, although, to be fair, not so good at holding on to it for very long. He had phobias too — "Snakes, why'd it have to be snakes?" — and took as much punishment as he dished out.

On that Hawaiian beach back in 1977, Spielberg was the blockbuster wünderkind of *Jaws* and soon to be *Close Encounters Of The Third Kind*. But heading into *Raiders*, he was coming off his first flop, the bloated, critically savaged World War Two comedy *1941*, and felt he had a point to prove, particularly about his ability to stick to a schedule and budget. Spielberg shot *Raiders* in a torrid 73 days, 12 ahead of schedule — *1941* had taken more than twice that — ploughing that speed and energy directly into the film. Apart from *Duel*, it's his leanest film.

As scripted by Lawrence Kasdan, from a story by Lucas and Philip Kaufman, who was originally going to direct, there was no waste and little time spent on extended set-ups. The viewers find themselves thrust, Bond-like, directly into

the action, joining Jones mid-adventure as he's about to enter a Peruvian temple to plunder the precious artefact inside. He barely escapes with his life, double-crossed by his own helper and narrowly avoiding countless booby traps and a runaway giant boulder. But his death-defying deeds amount to nothing, as the little golden idol is snatched from his grasp by his insipid French rival, Belloq (Paul Freeman), who proves to be a much bigger thorn in his side as the film progresses. As openings go, it was a doozy.

The rest of *Raiders* concerns itself with non-stop, breathless entertainment – Kasdan's narrative a convenient framework for Jones' race to secure the legendary Ark Of The Covenant, the Hebrew casket containing the remnants of the Ten Commandments – said to be a telephone to God – before it falls into Hitler's hands. Of course he succeeds, though in the end it's taken away by shady US Government suits who lock it away in a crate-filled warehouse – a nod to *Citizen Kane* – for who knows what purpose. Before then, the plot expertly hops from the jungles of South America to the mountains of Tibet to the deserts of Africa, via a short detour into academia, before culminating in a special effects extravaganza on a deserted island. Along the way, Jones must team with feisty, spunky Marion Ravenwood (Karen Allen), daughter of his former mentor and once the love of his life, who gives as good as she gets as the heroine and makes a great foil; Indy doesn't know whether to punch her or kiss her, so does both.

Spielberg pays due homage to those Saturday morning cliff-hangers that so inspired Lucas, with one astounding stunt and/or chase sequence after another, throwing motorbikes, submarines, trucks, planes, even horses into the mix, and Jones, armed with only his whip, pistol, hat and wits, facing-off against a rogue's gallery of broad villains, including the most comically sadistic Nazis you've ever seen. (This was, after all, 12 years before Spielberg made *Schindler's List*.) Raiders is so full of choice moments, it's like its own greatest hits compilation: the Nepalese bar shootout; the

NEED TO KNOW

Year 1981
Running time 115 mins
Director Steven Spielberg
Stars Harrison Ford, Karen Allen, Paul Freeman
Buy it on Region 2
Tagline "The creators of *Jaws* and *Star Wars* now bring you the ultimate hero in the ultimate adventure."
Best line "It's not the years honey, it's the mileage." – Indiana Jones
Critic's view "A movie that will leave you breathless, dizzy, wrung-out, and with a silly grin on your face." – Chicago Sun-Times
Best watched when... You've just witnessed the horror that is *The Mummy Returns*.

flaming plane; the raising of the Ark; Indy beneath a truck, a tribute to Yakima Canutt's stunt in John Ford's *Stagecoach*.

One of the best was the result of a dodgy tummy. During the Tunisian leg of the shoot, many of the *Raiders* cast and crew fell ill — all except for Spielberg, who had brought his own tinned food from England. Ford himself had had dysentery for five weeks and come the day he was due to film an elaborate fight scene with an Arab swordsman, he simply wasn't up for it. "Let's just shoot the fucker," said Ford, and so Indy unholsters his pistol and shoots his adversary instead. It's the film's biggest laugh, though given Lucas' and Spielberg's retrofitting of their films on DVD, it can only be a matter of time before we have a version in which the Arab fires first.

Ironically, even with the combined might of Lucas and Spielberg, *Raiders* initially proved a tough sell. When they first took the idea around Hollywood, nobody bit. Part of the reason was their terms. As Tom Shone recounts in his excellent book *Blockbuster*, Lucas and Spielberg wanted a piece of the distributor gross plus sequel rights and eventual ownership of the movie. They wanted to be treated as equals by the studio, and nobody was interested until Michael Eisner, then CEO of Paramount, caved in, much to the distress of the other studio heads. Hollywood deal making would never be the same again.

Neither would Ford's career, nor that of his director — they would go on to make two more *Indiana Jones* films, although plans for a fourth film remain mired in development hell. *Raiders* wasn't even an immediate hit, proving to be a box-office slow-burner that just wouldn't go away, steadily raking in enough money week in, week out, to wind up as the biggest hit of the year. It was also, perhaps, the last time Spielberg would make a film as unfussy, uncluttered and exhilarating — the sequels, for sure, were far more mannered and a lot less fun. *ET* made more money, *Schindler's List* made him 'respectable' (and won him an Oscar), but *Raiders*, even more so than *Jaws* or *Jurassic Park*, remains his most rip-roaringly perfect popcorn movie, the adrenaline-rush purity of its adventure showing no signs of diminishing almost a quarter of a century later. TF

Mark Salisbury

STATE AND NAME

In honour of Indiana Jones – hey, at least they didn't call him Arkansas – here are a few other movie names that flirt with daftness...

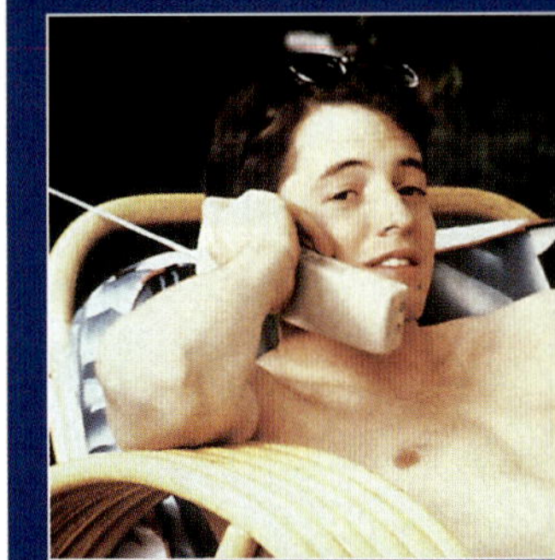

FERRIS BUELLER
(Matthew Broderick, *Ferris Bueller's Day Off*)
The real reason Ferris Bueller pulled a sickie from school? Someone found out his middle-name was Wheel...

DR CHRISTMAS JONES
(Denise Richards, *The World Is Not Enough*)
In a franchise populated by women called Pussy Galore, Holly Goodhead and Kissy Suzuki, this still goes down as the stoopidest lady-name in Bond's history.

NATURELLE RIVIERA
(Rosario Dawson, *25th Hour*)
A name even the most desperate drag queen would reject outright...

SNAKE PLISSKEN
(Kurt Russell, *Escape From New York*)
John Carpenter claims he got the name from a real hombre. Still, it's a damn sight better than Hyena Plissken, his name for the Italian release.

DAKOTA FANNING
(Dakota Fanning, many films)
Take a precocious starlet named after a Native American tribe, with a surname sounding like a US term for bottom and what do you get? Giggles at the *Total Film* office.

73

NEED TO KNOW

Year 1994
Running time 170 mins
Director Steve James
Stars William Gates, Arthur Agee, Emma Gates, Curtis Gates
Buy it on Region 1
Tagline N/A
Best line "People always say to me, 'When you get to the NBA, don't forget about me'. Well, I should've said back, 'If I don't make it to the NBA, don't you forget about me.'" – William
Critic's view "One of the great moviegoing experiences of my lifetime" – *Chicago Sun-Times*
Best watched when... Demon-chimp Bush is starting to make you a little too nostalgic for Clinton's America.

HOOP DREAMS

Director spends years following NBA wannabes... and invents the crossover doc.

With its widescreen emotional scope and sweeping cultural critique, *Hoop Dreams* slaps down any idea of the documentary as TV drama. In showing that fact *can* be rangier than fiction, it laid all the groundwork for the multiplexification to come.

It's an intoxicating cocktail: a film about sport with a novel's richness of humanity and narrative texture. Over three hours it shapeshifts, weaving in layer after layer. It's like one of those time-lapse, zoom-out nature films that starts with a pore on a finger and ends up at the backside of the universe. First, it's about basketball, then poverty, then family, then inner-city culture, then racism, until it eventually reveals itself to be a comment on America – and the modern, fitful version of the American Dream.

Back in 1986, Steve James and producer Peter Gilbert's plan was to track two inner-city kids, William Gates and Arthur Agee, as they put themselves through the US college basketball system, fantasising about an eventual step-up to the cash and kudos of the NBA. "When we started, we knew that the subject matter had a great wealth of experiences that we could put on screen," says Gilbert. "But we had no idea how compelling the kids and their families were gonna be. It just kept growing exponentially as the years went on, bringing in more complex issues at every twist and turn."

Six years later, it took them another two-and-a-half years to edit 250 hours of material. Further crafting coaxed out an epic taking in poverty, drugs, ambition, success, failure, teenage pregnancy... There's a delicious dramatic imbalance from the start, with William's background the more stable, but Arthur (dirt-poor, estranged from his fuck-up dad) the mercurial talent.

Not only do James and Gilbert capture the kind of jaw-flooring events that would be scoffed at in a fictional sports movie, they also isolate moments that lesser directors might have dismissed as incidental. When Arthur's beaten-down mother overcomes self-doubt to graduate from nursing school, they linger for just as long as they do when William is charged with a crucial free throw to beat a much stronger upstate team.

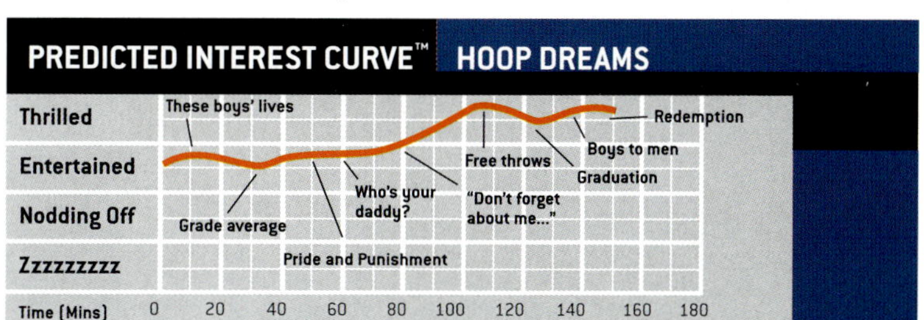

At the core of the film's complexity is an unschmaltzy story of hope and humanity. The theme of the downtrodden reaching for the stars provides the magic, but, due to the sheer length of time the filmmakers spent with their subjects, *Hoop Dreams* is even more satisfying as an intimate portrait of coming of age, striving to move on up, while continuing to nurture the instinctive ties of family love and conflict.

But here's the fun bit... no Oscars. Not one. Not even Best Documentary. Not even a *nomination* for Best Documentary. William Goldman was almost right. In Hollywood, nobody knows anything – but the Academy knows even less.

Andy Lowe

72

THE TERMINATOR

James Cameron's tech-thriller blasts a ragged hole in '80s action cinema...

Every pulp movie should begin in the fevered dreams of its writer/director – at least that's if *The Terminator* is anything to go by. And we're not talking metaphorically. Relentless robo-assassin T800 literally stalked James Cameron's nightmares as he battled to pump out his debut feature *Piranha II: The Spawning*, the aspiring writer/director awakening with the image of a cyborg killer masquerading as a human burned to the back of his eyeballs. Scribbling the story notes down in a clammy hurry (guerilla fighter travels back from machine-ruled 2029 to save his in-utero rebel resistance leader from the bullet of a similarly time-travelling robo-hitman), Cameron then bashed out a script and started slinging it around Hollywood with the singleminded purpose of his titular assassin.

Who knew that Linda Hamilton would prove to be the perfect action heroine?

Banged out on the cheap? Sure, but that's part of *The Terminator*'s success: it arrives sweaty and nightmarish and full of restless energy, with the grinding electronica-style soundtrack found on so many '80s movies – a perfect accompaniment to the impending doom. Cameron's background in schlock and short filmmaking also proved to be the ultimate boon – his was a sleek, pared-down style, which was perfectly suited to fashioning science-fiction with a limited budget (pretty hard to believe when you're three hours into *Titanic*...).

Not that Cameron was the only hungry pup intent on sinking its teeth into *The Terminator* and shaking it to within an inch of its life. Let's start with the effects team, a rag-tag group of professionals whose insatiable appetite allowed them to conjure alarming, unforgettable images by rubbing pennies. Okay, so some of the stop-motion techniques now look dated but their power remains, the sight of the merciless, unstoppable, flesh-stripped killer dragging its way through the final reel is still guaranteed to clog your dreams. And as today's technology continues apace and machines continue to get smarter, is there anyone who doesn't find themselves picturing the blackened, blasted future-war scenes that haunt the movie?

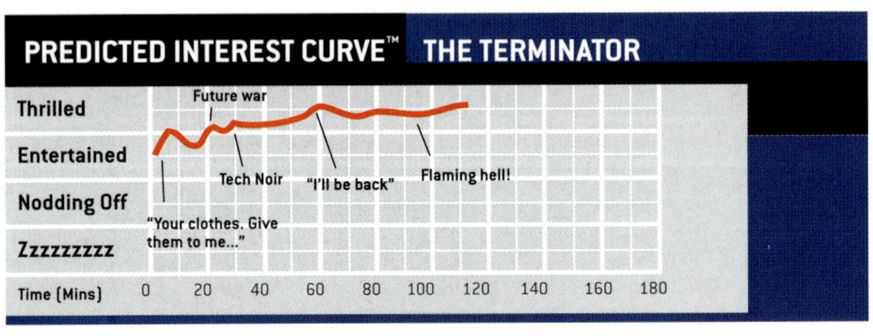

Next up is the cast, Cameron milking miracles from unexpected sources. Who knew that mouse-like Linda Hamilton (*Children Of The Corn*) would prove to be the perfect action heroine, or that lock-jawed Michael Biehn (TV dross and a handful of feature films you've never heard of) had such range? Again, it's down to the hunger: Cameron giving his leads the chance to chomp into roles of substance. Hamilton turns from big-haired Barbie to tenacious survivor, determinedly pointing her Sarah Connor towards the pumped-up

action heroine she'd become in *T2*. Biehn, meanwhile, makes a surprisingly credible stab at portraying a layered Tortured Hero – a man with an emotional burden so great and yet so precious he has little ability to express it. No wonder the love scene between the two leads doesn't amount to much: their minds seem to be fixed on the small matter of an indestructible soldier of death pursuing them with a stubborn single-mindedness that would put Michael Myers to shame.

But the biggest surprise was a certain Mr Universe with an Austrian accent thicker than his thighs. Unbelievably, Cameron's first choice for the title role was OJ Simpson. Thankfully the director had a change of heart, casting the Teutonic oak and turning his limitations into whopping great assets. No doubt about it: Arnold Schwarzenegger as the mechanical, monosyllabic terminator proved to be an inspired match (who else could blurt, "Fuck you, asshole" with so much menace and so little life?). He also proved to be a poster boy for Reagan's '80s; hair-brained and hair-triggered. And don't even get us started on him being the right man to govern California...

Part technological nightmare, part sci-fi time-traveller, part actioner and part slasher film, *The Terminator* mashes genres to create an exhilarating, volatile atmosphere. Biehn's Kyle Reese sums it up perfectly: "You still don't get it, do you? He'll find her. That's what he does. That's all he does! You can't stop him. He'll wade through you, reach down her throat and pull her fucking heart out."

As with the killer cyborg, so the film. *The Terminator* is relentless; a mean-machine that pounds along at 100mph, all muscle and metal. Cameron's *Terminator 2: Judgment Day* would put on a little flab yet remain a phenomenal achievement, especially as a sequel; Jonathan Mostow's *Terminator 3: Rise Of The Machines* went the other way, emerging malnourished and weak. But it's *The Terminator*, the original and still the best, that rewards repeated viewings, year after year. "I'll be back?" It's never been away.

James White

NEED TO KNOW

Year 1984
Running time 108 mins
Director James Cameron
Stars Linda Hamilton, Arnold Schwarzenegger
Buy it on Region 2 Ultimate Edition
Tagline "The thing that won't die, in the nightmare that won't end."
Best line: "It doesn't feel pity, or remorse, or fear. And it absolutely will not stop, ever, until you are dead." – Kyle
Critic's view "A blazing, cinematic comic book, full of virtuoso moviemaking, solid performances and a compelling story." – *Variety*
Best watched when... A killer cyborg is attempting to slaughter your unborn child.

71

NORTH BY NORTHWEST

Hitchcock's most entertaining film... but is it his best?

Alfred Hitchcock claimed *North By Northwest* contained the essence of all his American films. And even those sniffiest of critics, who yearn for the haunting layers of *Vertigo*, the voyeuristic complicity of *Rear Window* or the stark violations of *Psycho*, will acknowledge its one of his most enjoyable romps. But could it be that *North By Northwest* is actually Hitch's finest hour (okay, two and a bit hours)?

Well, it's certainly his most fully-realised film. As it should be, with over a year spent on the script (credited solely to Ernest Lehman, but as usual covered in Hitch's pawprints) and a budget of $4 million that's pretty much all visible on screen. Even MGM's attempts to cut the film's running time were comfortably deflected – Hitchcock's iron-clad contract giving him complete and final artistic control.

The result is a film that's still a bestseller five decades later – pick it up on Amazon and they'll claim it's "a strong candidate for the most sheerly entertaining and enjoyable movie ever made by a Hollywood studio." So, fair to say it's got timeless appeal.

The fantastic (in every sense of the word), labyrinthine and blatantly Kafka-esque plot still grips today: Roger O Thornhill (Cary Grant) is a successful, some would say shallow, ad exec, with two failed marriages and a domineering, wise-cracking mother (the excellent Jessie Royce Landis). While at The Plaza Hotel's Oak Bar (a regular Grant haunt in real life) he gets mistaken by foreign spies for 'George Kaplan' – a US agent who doesn't actually exist... which makes it somewhat difficult for Thornhill to prove he isn't said agent as he can't produce the real Kaplan. Confused? Stick with it...

Thrilling, smart and stuffed with some of the best set-pieces in movie history

After being kidnapped and taken to the Long Island country estate of his captors, Thornhill narrowly averts death in a thrilling car chase (forcibly inebriated, he careers his vehicle precipitously close to disaster). Our hero is locked up in a police cell (one of Hitch's pet fears) before returning to the scene of his abduction only to find no evidence at all of foul play.

Determinedly continuing his quest, Thornhill visits the United Nations, where the actual owner of the country estate, a UN diplomat, is promptly killed by agents trying to assassinate 'Kaplan'. Thornhill is photographed holding the murder weapon, a knife, and promptly flees for his life. With both assassins and the authorities now after him, he has to find the 'real' Kaplan (whom the audience already knows doesn't exist). Oh yeah, then it gets worse...

Thornhill meets the beautiful Eve (Eva Marie Saint) who, in the space of a few erotic, dramatic and ultimately romantic scenes, hides him from police, tries to have him killed (via a crop

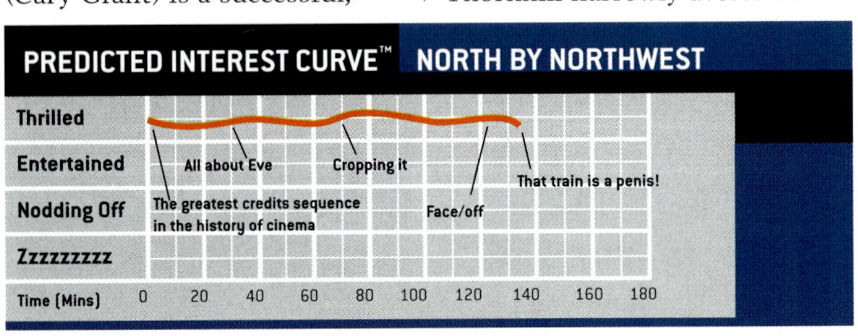

duster) and falls in love with him (well, he is Cary Grant...).

Thornhill then discovers she's a double agent, and his constant badgering has now put her life in danger. The only way to restore her credibility with the bad guys is for them to see her 'kill' him, or rather Kaplan. (Keep calm, we're almost there...)

Unfortunately, the fake death doesn't quite convince the evil, and possibly homosexual, Leonard (Martin Landau), henchman to the even more evil Phillip Vandamm (James Mason). Which means Thornhill will have to try and rescue Kendall before they kill her.

Which still leaves time for one more epic set piece atop Mount Rushmore before things wrap up with the most blatantly phallic shot in film history.

Now, sidestepping any miseries who claim the tangled plot is ludicrous and full of holes (Why does he pick up the knife? Why would you use a crop duster to kill someone? You couldn't build a house on Mount Rushmore), there's little doubt this is one of the most thrilling movies ever made.

Why? Because it's stuffed with some of the best set pieces in movie history, including the drunken car chase, the UN stabbing, the crop duster attack, the auction scene, and the Mount Rushmore finale (to name just a few). Not enough for you? Then consider the arch dialogue ("Maybe you're planning to murder me?"; "Shall I?"; "Please do..."), a career best performance from Grant (plus a thoroughly underrated turn from Saint) and enough existentialism to please the sternest intellectual. (The O in Thornhill's name stands for nothing; he's dwarfed by his surroundings; the crowds are reflected in the skyscraper's windows like ghosts; fleeing provides Thornhill with a pilgrimage, a journey of growth; his emergence as hero is a signifier of the self-realisation he lacked at the start; the phallic ending is the ultimate sign of creating life... etc.)

But enough brain fodder, is this Hitchcock's finest?

Well, a flick through these pages is evidence that the debate will go on (and on). But here's a test. Watch a Hitchcock a night for a week. And at the weekend, see which you one you fancy watching again...

Aubrey Ganguly

NEED TO KNOW

Year 1959
Running time 136 mins
Director Alfred Hitchcock
Stars Cary Grant, Eva Marie Saint, James Mason, Martin Landau, Leo G. Carroll
Buy it on Region 2
Tagline "Only Cary Grant and Alfred Hitchcock give you so much suspense in so many directions."
Best line "I'm an advertising man, not a red herring. I've got a job, a secretary, a mother, two ex-wives and several bartenders dependent on me."
Roger O Thornhill
Critic's view "The year's most scenic, intriguing and merriest chase." – *New York Times*
Best watched when...
Nobody believes a damn word you say.

70

DAWN OF THE DEAD

Romero's zombie saga hits its finest, bloodiest peak...

The Godfather Part II of horror. The *Empire Strikes Back* of gore. George Romero's zombie masterclass may not just be the greatest undead movie of all time, but the greatest sequel of all time, too.

Certainly never before has a film had so many different versions, all lapped up by its fans. Romero's 156-minute Ultimate Cut, the Cannes Cut, the Dario Argento Cut, the German Theatrical Cut, the Screwdriver In The Ear Cut, the Shotgunned Head Cut... Some were merely simple updates, Lucas-like tinkerings if you will. Mostly, though, the varying running times are down to Tom Savini's breathtaking effects work, pruned to different extents by the gasping censors in each territory. "It's a weird thing being a special-effects guy and having the MPAA cut your work," Savini remarked in 1984. "One part of you hates the fuckers, the other part feels proud – if they've thought that it looks too real and gruesome then you've basically done your job the best you can."

A never-bettered cascade of bloody, increasingly disturbing, violent imagery

Recently back from Vietnam, where he had spent his tour of duty photographing the horrors he encountered on a daily basis – heads, he noted, exploded "like watermelons", limbs could be shorn clean off with horrific ease – his effects were personal therapy at the time and remain a genre landmark, a never-bettered cascade of bloody, increasingly disturbing, violent imagery that no amount of CG trickery will ever improve upon. (See Zack Snyder's slick but soulless 2004 remake.)

Nevertheless, when he later complained that the fake blood he was made to use looked like "melted red crayon" Savini was for once missing the point. Romero's desire to shoot with a cartoon aesthetic is what makes the movie so powerful, a fantasy horror-comic imbued with a dreamlike quality that is impossible to shake. While its predecessor, *Night Of The Living Dead*, was a claustrophobic, monochrome allegory of a troubled America and civil rights, *Dawn Of The Dead* is a colourful yet stark, haunting, apocalyptic premonition for the future of all mankind.

After setting *Night* in the desolate countryside, Romero locates *Dawn* firmly in an urban arena, opening with a SWAT team attack on a tower block ravaged by the reanimated. With no more room in Hell, the dead are indeed now walking the Earth, and as the city descends into chaos a small band escapes in a helicopter, finding refuge in that all-American of institutions, the mall. "What are they doing? Why do they come here?" Francine asks Stephen as they look down upon the zombie hordes. "Some kind of instinct. Memory, of what they're used to do. This was an important place in their lives," he replies. While Peter

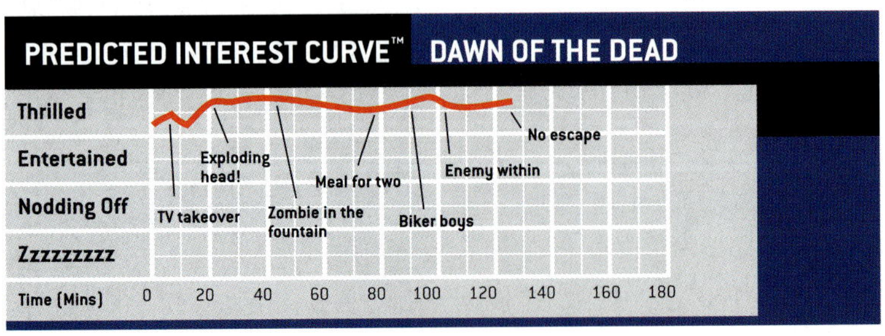

later adds: "They're after the place. They don't know why, they just remember. Remember that they want to be in here... They're us, that's all."

Romero plays out his anti-consumerist message in an arch Western structure. After they've cleared the building of the shuffling natives, our heroes (the cowboy frontiersmen) run riot in their materialist playground, going on joyous 'shopping' sprees (note the Wild West-themed gun store) before having to defend it against a gang of bikers (the Injuns), hellbent on looting. All the while the zombies simply follow their own natural instincts, unaffected by greed or Machiavellian motivations. Amid the madness – at one point the humans even shoot at them for sport – they remain blameless; innocent even. Is this, as the critics at the time had it, a depraved movie? Or, rather, a movie about depravity. According to Romero, America is literally eating itself.

But as much as it is pessimistic and bleak, Romero's satire is often pin-sharp funny – zombies falling into fountains as music plays in the background, special offer announcements tinkling over the tannoy as they travel up and down escalators on a grim loop – and never paints its protagonists in black and white. Funny, noble and alone, trapped in their strip-lit prison, when their words sometimes fail them (even adamant fans will concede the screenplay is rather one-note) their characters shine through with a genuine, touching spirit.

Dawn was followed by the talky *Day Of The Dead* and this year's interesting but malnourished *Land Of The Dead*, but it remains a bonafide classic. Rooted in the flipsides of humanity, it refuses to bend to genre cliché, keeping it stark all the way. Reports still disagree as to whether an alternate ending was shot (in which Peter shoots himself and Fran kills herself by sticking her head up into the helicopter's blades), but regardless, *Dawn*'s climax still resonates starkly. "How much fuel do we have?" Peter asks Fran as they fly over the zombie masses, desperately looking for somewhere safe. Her answer? "Not much..."

Mark Dinning

NEED TO KNOW

Year 1978
Running time 126 mins
Director George A Romero
Stars David Emge, Ken Foree, Scott H Reiniger, Gaylen Ross
Buy it on Region 1 Ultimate Edition
Tagline "When there's no more room in Hell the dead will walk the Earth."
Best line "You'll take care of me when I go, won't you, Peter? I don't want to be walking around like THAT!" – Roger
Critic's view "A dreadful picture by a director who should know better." – *Guide For The Film Fanatic*
Best watched when... You're not suffering from a hangover.

69

SIDEWAYS

Seventies-style smarts in Alexander Payne's witty, warm road trip.

Neurotic, divorced, possibly alcoholic Paul and horny, hedonistic, soon-to-be-hitched Jack take a road trip. For Paul, it's a break from an unfulfilling life. For Jack, it's a pause before the plunge into something approaching responsibility.

Exhibits an unfussy style and no recourse to narrative gimmicks

Consequently, Paul wants to drink and dull the pain while Jack wants to fuck around. Wine and girls follow. Paul falls in love. Jack falls in lust. There may be consequences.

Sideways starts simple and lets the characters dictate the pace. The plot unfolds leisurely, personalities and flaws are slowly revealed, the laid-back setting seduces and, before you know it, you're beguiled.

Unsurprisingly, critics went crazy for it. After the overlooked *Citizen Ruth*, the toothsome *Election* and the gentle *About Schmidt*, Alexander Payne's already-impressive résumé took a leap forward with a fourth film that wouldn't sit uncomfortably among the likes of *Five Easy Pieces*, *Harry And Tonto*, or *California Split*. No doubt about it: *Sideways* exhibits a freewheeling charm rarely seen in recent decades, an unfussy style that lets the warmth and intelligence of the material shine through with no recourse to narrative gimmicks or tommygun edits. Repeat viewings only emphasise the film's languid charms.

Of course, there's an inherent risk in labelling any new film an instant classic. Primarily, that you'll end up looking stupid. Modern movies have mastered the habit of a quick seduction only to reveal hidden shallows on second look.

But *Sideways* has been around longer than you think, quietly maturing before it earned all that acclaim last year. "I actually wrote it back in 1999," acknowledged Payne, "and I'd been looking forward to making it ever since. But then, the wheels of fate were set in motion for *About Schmidt* to happen first. It just worked out that way."

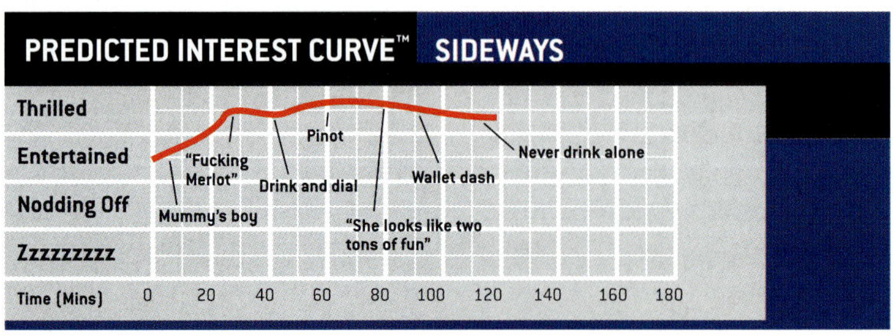

After *Schmidt*'s success, and Jack Nicholson's Oscar-nominated turn, Payne's ripening *Sideways* script began to garner attention from Hollywood A-listers thirsty for a decent role. Jim Carrey and George Clooney were two of those pushing for the part of Jack, the hedonistic, washed-up actor, while 'bootleg' versions of the script had even started swapping hands between agents.

"It's true. My agent sent me the script," confessed Thomas Haden Church. "He said, 'Don't tell anybody you have it. It's a bootleg script. When you meet the director, don't say you've read it.' But as soon as I walked through the door, Alexander said, 'So, did you read one of the black market copies of my script?' I couldn't lie to him!"

Perhaps the honesty helped. More likely, Payne just knew that Church was right for the role. The actor had shown

sparks in the little-regarded (but Charlie Kaufman-penned) TV show *Ned And Stacey* and had previously auditioned for Payne for his earlier films ("He assured me we'd work together eventually," says Church).

The years between script and filming may have hardened Payne's resolve or strengthened his vision of what *Sideways* should be. After all, it's hard to imagine there wasn't pressure to alter the casting (who could honestly say the film would have made less money if Clooney or Carrey had played Jack...?) but, for the director, it was non-negotiable. He pitched the film as a package, with his cast already attached.

"His attitude was, 'I don't want movie stars, I want it to be about mood,'" said Paul Giamatti. "He didn't want people thinking, 'Oh look, it's Julia Roberts playing a waitress'. He wanted the movie to really come through."

Hence the unlikely foursome of Church, Giamatti, Virginia Madsen and Payne's own wife Sandra Oh – a decision vindicated when the reviews came out. "A quartet of actors who qualify as a cinematic dream team," gushed *Rolling Stone* in a summation echoed by most commentators.

They have a point. View *Sideways* and rarely a minute goes by without a moment of perfection from one of the four. Be it the way Jack slugs from the bottle or how Stephanie flirts, the kindness in Maya's eyes or the frustration in Miles'. These are four real people and we feel like we're watching real struggles. Which has always been Payne's preferred area to focus on. Never is this more apparent than in the film's outstanding sequence, where Miles and Maya discuss the qualities of the Pinot Noir grape and, in the process, open up to each other. Not only does it contain some of the prettiest dialogue in recent memory, it also glows with measured acting and a fragile metaphor. Not for the first time, the Academy's lack of taste (Masden nominated but scandalously not a winner, Giamatti absurdly not even nominated) proved depressing. More encouragingly though, Payne's success may mean the return of that particularly '70s habit: films for grown ups.

Aubrey Ganguly

NEED TO KNOW

Year 2004
Running time 123 mins
Director Alexander Payne
Stars Paul Giamatti, Thomas Haden Church, Virginia Madsen, Sandra Oh
Buy it on Region1
Tagline "In search of wine. In search of women. In search of themselves."
Best line "Did you drink and dial?" – Jack
Critic's view "The emergence of Mr Payne into the front ranks of American filmmakers isn't just cause for celebration; it's a reason for hope." – *New York Times*
Best watched when... You're just back from Oddbins.

68

THIS IS SPINAL TAP

Two visionaries, a temporary drummer and a preserved moose. Must be the Tap...

Eric 'Stumpy Joe' Childs (1945-1974). Choked on (someone else's) vomit...

Before *The Office* made mock-doc modish, there was once a very metal Brit-band modelled as an unholy hybrid of Black Sabbath and Iron Maiden, with bits of Uriah Heep and Led Zeppelin chucked in. Oh, and definitely a dash of Whitesnake.

They were birthed from a flimsy, malfunctioning, oversized egg

They were birthed (from a flimsy, malfunctioning, oversized plastic egg) in 1978, when then-TV producer Rob Reiner compiled a one-off comedy special, *The TV Show*. It featured a sketch, written by Reiner, Michael McKean, Christopher Guest and Harry Shearer, where a limp-brained rock band performed a schlocky little signature tune called 'Rock 'n' Roll Nightmare'. In early 1980, Reiner pitched the idea of a feature-length version...

Reiner, McKean, Guest and Shearer researched rock concert footage and documentaries, absorbing all the format conventions – as well as the sights, sounds and smells. The idea was to build up the band's characters and history by improvising all the dialogue. That way, they'd nail the naturalistic air that would stop it tipping over into an overplayed, extended sketch.

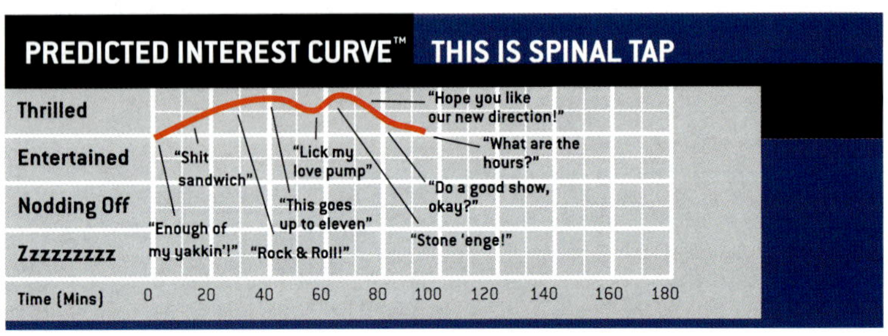

They shot a demo, wrote the band's abysmal, sub-adolescent numbers 'Sex Farm', 'Big Bottom', and 'Stonehenge', and just got on with it. "The actors got the joke and flew with it," says McKean. "Every day's shooting was at least as much fun as the day before."

Joe 'Mama' Besser (1944-). Missing, presumed dead...

After a limited cinema release, the culty mock-doc eventually found a natural, repeat-play home on the tour buses of genuine bands. Fuelled by their own day-to-day dealings with hapless handlers, toxic internal politics and petty creative tantrums, jobbing musicians really connected with the tale of *Spinal Tap*'s disastrous US comeback tour.

Um, apart from Liam Gallagher, who still thinks it's real. "We saw them play at Carnegie Hall," Noel recently told the *Observer Music Monthly*. "'You know they're not even English', we told Liam. 'They're all American actors. One of them [Guest] is married to Jamie Lee Curtis!' 'I'm not fuckin' 'avin' that,' he says, and storms off."

Peter 'James' Bond (1949-1977). Spontaneously combusted on-stage...

This Is Spinal Tap is more than just an acutely observed parody of an overblown heavy metal band. 'Tapspeak' has crossed over into the everyday language of people who probably haven't even seen it, for example, 'rockumentary', and something

'going up to eleven'. It's prescient: witness cricket bat-wielding manager Ian Faith with his pre-spin doctor explanation of *Tap's* dwindling ticket sales, "It's not that they're becoming less popular. Their appeal is becoming more selective".

Mick Shrimpton (1948-1982). Exploded on-stage (left green globule on drum seat)...

It's a credit to the writers' fastidious backstory design that a largely improvised film should come out with everything feeling so right: the passionate pseudo-profundity: "Every movie in every cinema is about death. Death sells!"; the laughable moral tangle of artistic self-justification: "With a song like 'Sex Farm', we're taking a sophisticated view of the idea of sex and... putting it on a farm". Nothing is overplayed. All the character names are also note-perfect: Nigel Tufnel, Derek Smalls, David St Hubbins, PR gadabout Bobbi Fleckman, starchy record company owner Sir Denis Eton-Hogg, and of course, put-upon promoter Artie Fufkin.

Richard 'Ric' Shrimpton (1948-). Sold dialysis machine for drugs, assumed dead...

With subtlety lavishly invested in the foreground, all the out-and-out comedy is reserved for the songs: 'Sex Farm': *"Scratching in your henhouse/ Sniffing at your feedbag"*; 'Big Bottom': *"My baby fits me like a flesh tuxedo/I like to sink her with my pink torpedo"*.

Like all great comedy, *Spinal Tap* is idea-packed and funny enough to bear endless repeats. "We've achieved that magical thing: shelf-life," says McKean.

John 'Stumpy' Pepys (1943-1969). Bizarre gardening accident...

The *Tap's* legendarily high drummer turnover has its own queasy punchline. Jeff Porcaro, drummer with Toto, may have actually died in a bizarre gardening accident in 1992. He supposedly inhaled too much insecticide he was spraying on his garden.

Andy Lowe

NEED TO KNOW

Year 1984
Running time 82 mins
Director Rob Reiner
Stars Rob Reiner, Michael McKean, Christopher Guest, Harry Shearer, Tony Hendra
Buy it on Region 0 Criterion Edition
Tagline "Does for rock'n'roll what *The Sound Of Music* did for hills."
Best line "It's a fine line between stupid and clever." – David St Hubbins
Critic's view "It hardly ever gets more spot-on than this." – *The Austin Chronicle*
Best watched when... You've noticed your dreaming is becoming a little part-time.

67

L'ATALANTE

Argy-bargy in the soul-tickling swansong of a tragically short-lived filmmaker...

Jean Vigo's entire cinematic output – one full-length feature, one short feature and a couple of documentary shorts – runs to less time than *Titanic*. Despite which, this indisputable genius, who died aged 29, is a hugely influential figure in the history of cinema. Everybody who's anybody in French cinema drew inspiration from Vigo, from Cocteau and Renoir through Malle and Truffaut to Jean-Pierre Jeunet and André Téchiné. He was a god to the Nouvelle Vague. You can see his influence on just about every indie filmmaker – Cassavetes, Jarmusch, Todd Solondz. And Lindsay Anderson's *If...*, a movie that so nearly made this list, would never have happened without Vigo's *Zéro De Conduite*.

Son of a Spanish-French anarchist who died (most likely murdered) in a French jail when his son was 12, Vigo blended his father's politics with the expressionist surrealism of the '20s. He was especially taken with the work of the great Soviet avant-garde director Dziga-Vertov (*The Man With A Movie Camera*), and Vertov's brother, Boris Kaufman, acted as cinematographer on all Vigo's movies.

This indisputable genius is a hugely influential figure in the history of cinema

His first feature, the satirical 44-minute *Zéro De Conduite*, took a fusty suburban boys' boarding school as an allegory for constipated French society. The boys are lively, imaginative, mischievous. Their teachers, with one exception, are pompous, mentally stunted and hopelessly inadequate in their jobs, lacking in any sense of imagination and with no idea how to stimulate it in their pupils. The film is grotesque and dreamlike, culminating in a rebellion when the boys climb up on the school roof and hurl missiles at the assembled staff and governors. Not surprisingly, the French authorities loathed the movie and banned it for being "anti-France". It wasn't seen at all until after the end of the war.

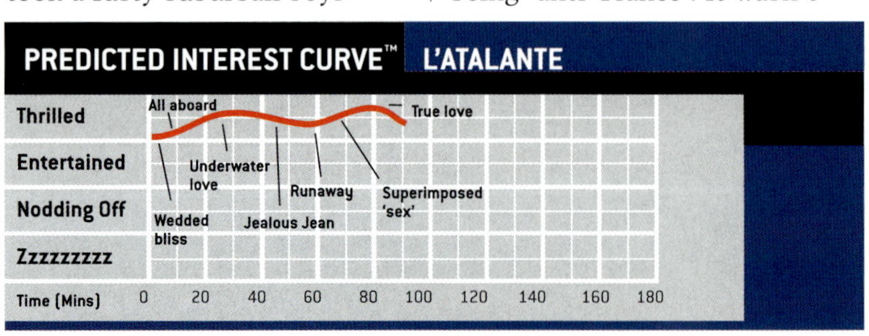

Desperately ill and in dire need of funds, Vigo accepted a commission from his producer, Jacques-Louis Nounez. The assignment was a script by one Jean Guinée, *L'Atalante*, about a young country girl, Juliette (Dita Parlo), who marries Jean (Jean Dasté), the captain of a Seine canal barge. As written, it was conventional, clumsy and sententious. Vigo took it on reluctantly, but found that Guinée was quite amenable to changes and started to rework it completely. By the time he started shooting, all that was left of the original script were the names of the characters and the bare bones of the plot. Vigo transformed his banal subject into a lyrical, intensely personal vision.

There's much less satire here than in *Zéro De Conduite*, though the villagers in the opening wedding procession to the barge, recall the

respectable speech-day bourgeoisie of the earlier film. But Vigo's far more interested in the relationships on board the hermetic society of the barge. The arrival of the bride upsets the all-male camaraderie of the captain, a young boy who remains nameless and the glorious, eccentric mate, Père Jules, played by the great Michel Simon in one of his finest performances. Surrounded by dozens of cats, showing off his collection of junk and telling stories about his adventurous life, Père Jules is the spirit of benign anarchy, blithely indifferent to social convention. Jean, conscious of his dignity as the captain and newlywed husband, mistrusts the easy intimacy that develops between his bride and the old man.

Perfection was never Vigo's aim, and continuity in *L'Atalante* is often hard to locate. Hardly matters, though, as this just adds to the overall atmosphere of sensuous surrealism that pervades the movie. Objects, like Père Jules' collection of exotica, or the dress that he makes and then grotesquely models for Juliette, take on dreamlike significance. As the tensions increase between Jean and Juliette – she wants to see Paris, he jealously forbids her – so does the mood of rhapsodic eroticism. In the film's most intense sequence, Vigo intercuts between Jean, on the barge and believing Juliette has left him, and Juliette in a hotel. Both are in bed, each dreaming of the other, until Vigo's superimposition makes it look as if they're in bed together – a powerful expression of overwhelming erotic yearning.

L'Atalante was way ahead of its time in its freshness and poetic imagination. Too much so, even. By the time the movie was completed, Vigo was near to death and in no state to defend his work. Gaumont, who were distributing, decided it needed "popularising". They recut it and retitled it *Le Chaland Qui Passe* (*The Passing Barge*), after a hit song of the period. Vigo died just three weeks after the release of this mutilated version. Not until some 20 years later was the movie restored the way he'd wanted it and at long last hailed as the classic it's now become.

Philip Kemp

NEED TO KNOW

Year 1934
Running time 89 mins
Director Jean Vigo
Stars Michel Simon, Jean Dasté, Dita Parlo
Buy it on Region 1
Tagline N/A
Best line "Oh, these hands! What haven't these hands done? Once even, in a Shanghai back street one evening... like this... tighter... tighter..." – Père Jules
Critic's view "The story is awkwardly told and the visual quality one expects of a director is not well presented. One can trace many good intentions, but deprived of craftsmanship and skill, it remains of little interest." – *Le Journal*
Best watched when You're heading off on a canal-boat holiday.

66

SE7EN

The serial killer movie reborn, redefined and reinvigorated...

Hard now to think of a world before David Fincher, and, most of all, before *Se7en*. This powerhouse director and his breakthrough movie have been so influential that the style and pace of modern thrillers have since changed irrevocably in its wake.

The same thing happened after *The French Connection* in the early '70s: suddenly, the verité approach, with barely audible dialogue, juddery camerawork and an abiding appetite for all things seedy, began to seep into mainstream cinema.

Se7en introduced a downbeat grunginess into a genre that had always previously been prized for its cheap thrills. The modern thriller was low-rent and dog-eared. *Se7en*, with its big ideas and sophisticated twists, injected some much needed intelligence into the genre. And it certainly didn't make things easy for you. Several cinemas were forced to display large notices in their auditoriums along the lines of, "Don't complain that the opening scene is inaudible – it's meant to be", after cinemagoers griped that they couldn't hear the dialogue properly.

Andrew Kevin Walker had been bashing out the film's screenplay at about the same time that Fincher was nearing implosion point on *Alien 3*. That troubled blockbuster could have killed off his directing career, but *Se7en* offered him a spectacular second chance, as well as introducing the world to an abrasive but playful Fincher aesthetic that continued in *Fight Club* and *Panic Room*. Top marks in this respect to *Se7en*'s quite brilliant cinematographer, Darius Khondji, who crisply rendered the director's visual sensibility, best described as Goya-by-flashlight; a grisly and grotesque tableaux depicted with such teasing, taunting haste that they almost qualify as subliminal (plenty of viewers still maintain they actually saw that severed head in the box, whereas in truth Fincher and Khondji are perfectly discreet).

Grisly and grotesque, visually *Se7en* is Goya-by- flashlight

Nonetheless, the terror is real. From the moment the scratch-video opening kicks in, which ranks as one of the most inventive credits sequences in cinema, accompanied by the bristling angst of the *Nine Inch Nails*, the movie is horribly unsettling. It's set in an unnamed, rainswept American city where a serial killer is notching up victims according to the seven deadly sins; crucially, though, we only ever see the stomach-churning scenes of his crimes, rather than the murders themselves. The only on-screen execution is in fact carried out by a detective, which may be a sick joke on the part of Fincher and Walker.

Everything about the film ticks along with awe-inspiring precision: the interplay between Morgan Freeman's world-weary Detective Somerset and his

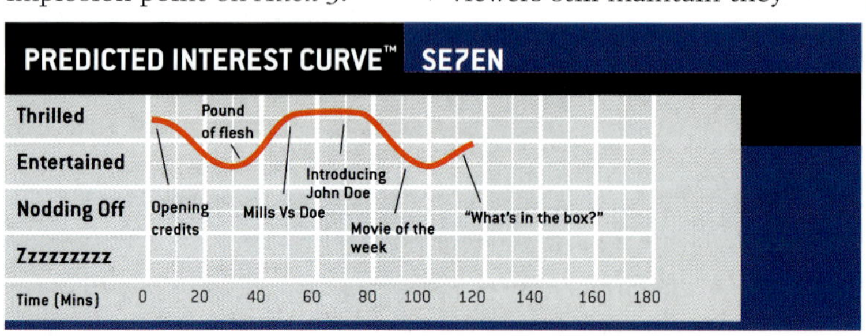

impetuous new partner Mills (Brad Pitt) never capitulates to buddy-movie conventions, or settles into wisecracking familiarity. The heroes, like the audience, are always on edge.

The supporting actors are perfectly cast, from Richard Roundtree (*Shaft*) as a dubious District Attorney, to the gruff R Lee Ermey (*Full Metal Jacket*) as Mills' and Somerset's boss, while Freeman gives one of the defining performances of his career as the sage counterpoint to the film's violence. The 'detective solving his last case before retirement' is one of the hoariest clichés in cinema, but Freeman dispels any staleness with a performance of measured calm and concentration.

A decade on from the film's release and the ace up its sleeve is still genius. As Fincher commented at the time, the end-of-second-act twist was one of the main reasons he got involved. "We've seen all this terrible stuff up until now," he said, "and then, out of the blue, the killer just shows up and hands himself in? I was reading the script and I checked the page number: it was something like 100, out of 135. And I thought, 'Well, something *really* bad's gonna happen now.'" He's right – killers do not simply surrender. But then John Doe is no ordinary killer. Sensibly, Kevin Spacey rejected the offer of top billing, reasoning that the shock of his appearance would be much greater if audiences weren't primed for it. Along with *The Usual Suspects*, *Se7en* was the making of him, and the perfect distillation of his oily, untrustworthy charisma.

NEED TO KNOW

Year 1995
Running time 127 mins
Director David Fincher
Stars Brad Pitt, Morgan Freeman, Kevin Spacey, Gwyneth Paltrow, R Lee Ermey
Buy it on Region 1
Tagline "Seven deadly sins. Seven ways to die."
Best line "Just because the fucker's got a library card doesn't make him Yoda." – David Mills
Critic's view "One can already tell that this film is on to something special during the opening credits..." – *Chicago Reader*
Best watched when... You think someone was following you home.

Which is not to say that the film is perfect. Gwyneth Paltrow deserved much better than the pathetic role of sacrificial lamb. And it's hard not to feel disappointment when John Doe turns out to be one of those murderers whose catalogues, scrapbooks and interior decorating choices articulate those things about him that the writer couldn't express in any other way.

But these are minor flaws that wilt in the shadow of the film's greatest achievement – casting a spell that refuses to evaporate when the lights go up. Fincher's forthcoming *Zodiac* – another serial killer movie – has a lot to live up to.

Ryan Gilbey

65

8 1/2

Fellini turns the backstage melodrama on its head. Because he can.

You're Federico Fellini. You're 42-years-old, and so far you've made seven movies and three collaborations. You've recently won a Palme d'Or, you've got three Oscar nominations under your belt, and everybody you know is bugging you about your latest film. What's it about? Who's got the starring role? When will it start shooting? You don't let them know the truth, but you're actually going through a rather alarming patch of writer's block. You're thinking about making another autobiographical film, like your 1954 breakout movie, *La Strada*, but you're not sure. You want to do a more fantastical picture too, like your Cannes victor, 1960's *La Dolce Vita*, but you don't want to repeat yourself either. You're even contemplating making a sci-fi flick, because you love comics and used to write *Flash Gordon* serials during World War Two. In the end, still stifled by writer's block, you decide to do something even more audacious: you will make a film about all three subjects, *plus* a film about the writers block, *plus* a film about the making of this film. You will call it *8 1/2* (after the number of movies you've made: seven, plus three halves, arithmetic fans).

To the viewer unaccustomed to the style of high-period Fellini (think Emir Kusturica with a couple of dashes of Fincher, Scorsese, Bergman and some clowns – Fellini ran away to the circus when he was a kid), *8 1/2* can be a bewildering experience. Sweeping camera moves, multiple characters engaged in near overlapping dialogue, scenes bleeding into scenes into dream sequences into flights of fancy and back into scenes, and we've only just begun. Here especially, with such an ambitious remit (four films for the price of one), Fellini offers no comforting CliffsNotes as he darts between biography, fantasy and production story, pinning an increasingly bamboozled and angst-ridden director protagonist (and Fellini surrogate) Guido (Marcello Mastroianni) centre stage as his world whirls uncontrollably around him. As screenwriter Carini (Jean Rougeul) says to Guido, surveying the creative chaos that is constantly surrounding him, "You need to add clear-cut features to this hazy crowd of characters!"

And yet, the well-worn idea that *8 1/2* is a chaotic, circus-like movie is the single greatest deception that the film plays on its audience. For although Nino Rota's propulsive score, plus added ear-splitting bursts of high-octane Rossini, suggest something approaching a nervous breakdown, the movie is coolly calculated in everything it does. For instance its opening traffic jam dream sequence (later reverentially replicated by Joel Schumacher for the opening scene of *Falling*

Dizzying? Yes. Head-wrecking? Certainly. Out of control? Never!

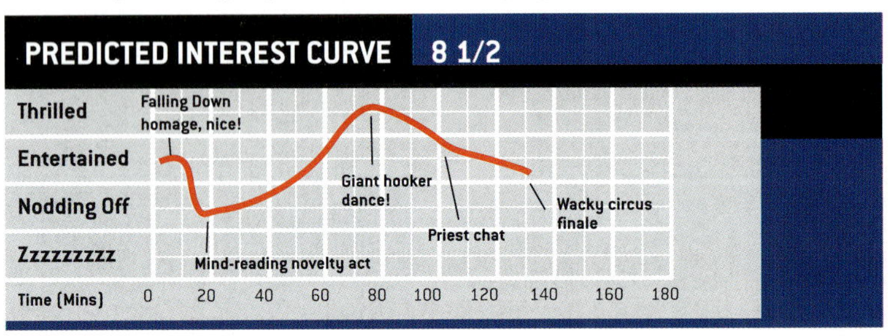

Down) sets the thematic tone for the entire film, depicting Guido floating heavenwards into the ethereal and spiritual realms, yet ending with his producers lassoing his floating body by the ankle and yanking him unceremoniously back down to earth. The sequence soon segues into a hotel scene in a spa town outside Rome, where fading French actress Madeleine (Madeleine LeBeau) harangues Guido about her upcoming role.

This is then followed by another in the production offices (of *8 1/2*) where a costume designer asks Mastroianni's opinion on the costume that's just been worn by Madeleine LeBeau in the last 'scene' that wasn't supposed to be a scene! Dizzying? Yes. Head-wrecking? Certainly. Out of control? Never!

Consequently, within all this controlled chaos, when Fellini decides to slip in a few emotional depth charges, the effect is far greater because they feel so unexpected. The justly famous sequence where the young schoolboy Guido dances the rumba with a hulking prostitute (American actress Eddra Gale) on the beach has an inexpressible tenderness to it, especially as it comes right in the middle of the older Guido's slightly ponderous dialogue with a Roman cardinal on the nature of salvation. "There is no salvation outside the church!" says the cardinal, and then, bang, there we see it, beauty incarnate, boy and big-breasted behemoth, dancing a rumba in the noonday sun. Similarly, when Guido announces, "I want to make an honest film, with no lies of any kind," you just know that it's coming directly from Fellini's own mouth. If you're still not convinced, take this casual exchange between Guido and a priest. "Married?" says the Priest. "Yes," replies Guido. "Any children?" comes the next question. "Yes," says Guido, before correcting himself... "No". In 1945, Fellini and wife Giulietta Masina had a son, who survived for only two weeks. Guido's stuttered response is more telling than ever. The level of agonising biographical detail that Fellini puts into *8 1/2* isn't just an attempt at self-reflexive artistry. It's filmmaking honesty of the highest order.

Patrick Donovan

NEED TO KNOW

Year 1963
Running time 138 mins
Director Federico Fellini
Stars Marcello Mastroianni, Claudia Cardinale, Anouk Aimee, Sandra Milo, Rossella Falk
Buy it on Region 1 Criterion
Tagline N/A
Best line "I have absolutely nothing to say. But I want to say it anyway."
– Guido Anselmi
Critic's view "Fellini is a magician who discusses, reveals, explains and deconstructs his tricks, while still fooling us with them."
– *Chicago Sun-Times*
Best watched when... You've just trashed your 20th attempt at a debut screenplay.

64

THE CONVERSATION

Hearing is disbelieving in Francis Ford Coppola's minimalist thriller...

It was the *Godfather* films that established Francis Ford Coppola as the most ambitious of the '70s Movie Brats: grand, wide-reaching and lovingly detailed, they showed a filmmaker skilled enough to retain a personal touch while working on the largest possible canvas. But the question of whether Coppola could do 'intimate' as well as 'epic' was answered with the movie that was sandwiched between those two Mafia masterpieces.

Coppola had written the first draft of *The Conversation* between 1967 and 1969, inspired not, as is commonly thought, by Michelangelo Antonioni's thriller *Blow Up* (with which Coppola's picture shares the same basic premise of a voyeur who chances upon sinister dealings) but by a comment from the director Irvin Kershner. "We were talking about surveillance," Coppola recalled. "He mentioned that the safest place for two people who wanted to have a conversation in private would be outside in a crowd. Then he added that he had heard of microphones that had gun sights on them that were so powerful and selective that they could, if aimed at the mouths of these people in the crowd, pick up their conversation. I thought both what an odd device and what a great motif for a film."

Gene Hackman's performance sucks us into the film's stark, spare sense of dread

Indeed, the picture begins with the surveillance wizard Harry Caul (Gene Hackman) – known, in a line which always gets a snigger from UK audiences, as "the best bugger on the West Coast" – deploying sophisticated technology to eavesdrop on a couple (Frederic Forrest and Cindy Williams) meeting illicitly in a busy park. This is where we first get an earful of what quickly emerges as the movie's most striking feature – Walter Murch's innovative multi-layered sound design, which interweaves overlapping conversation, on-location sound and abstract noise to create an aural jigsaw in which a few pieces are always, tantalisingly, missing.

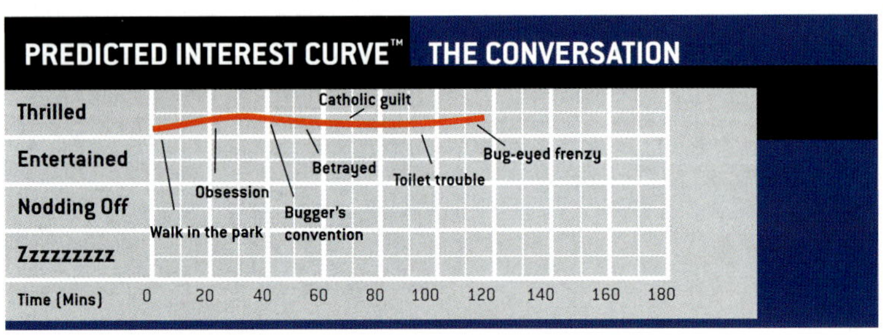

Murch had worked with Coppola on *The Godfather*, as well as with George Lucas on *THX 1138* and *American Graffiti*, but nothing had hinted at the revolutionary sound design that he would attempt here. Together with Richard Chew's precise editing, there is a fascinating interplay of sound and image... not to mention an exploration of the meanings and misunderstandings that arise from this relationship, as Harry's investigations spiral out of control. Coppola is a fine filmmaker, but arguably in this instance, Walter Murch is the movie: he turns *The Conversation* into a mystery that you can feast your ears on.

Also crucial to the picture's stark, spare sense of dread is Gene Hackman's downbeat, economical performance. Hackman actually does very little that is demonstrative – he's all interior. But he sucks

us in. And his flashes of panic or vulnerability, as this control freak realises that he's losing the control he has exercised over his life, are more revealing than the rather redundant backstory that Coppola supplies. Also excellent is the strong supporting cast – the cadaverous John Cazale, whom Coppola had cast as Fredo in *The Godfather*, is Harry's sidekick Stan, who defects to join Harry's chief rival (a brilliantly overbearing Allen Garfield); a rumpled Robert Duvall is the fat cat paying Harry to spy on his adulterous wife, and there's a small but sinister role for Harrison Ford as Duvall's corporate stooge. Teri Garr brings an important flash of brightness to the glum milieu as Harry's lover, neglected and undervalued by him in his quest for privacy.

The spectre of Catholic guilt haunts the movie, but even that was overshadowed by unforeseen external events. Halfway through shooting, the Watergate scandal broke, and suddenly Coppola found himself making a film that commented, albeit inadvertently, on modern America. "Watergate is a funny accident," he later said. "I never meant it to be so relevant. I almost think the picture would have been better received had Watergate not happened."

That *The Conversation* did not receive the universal acclaim afforded to the *Godfather* movies was a source of consternation to Coppola. Which is not to say that the film didn't have its ardent supporters – after all, it walked off with the Palme d'Or at the 1974 Cannes Film Festival. It may be a little earnest in its imitation of the '60s European arthouse aesthetic, which had influenced strongly most of the Movie Brats, but it fused that brilliantly with the paranoid sensibility of the political thriller, which was at its height in the '70s thanks to films like *Klute*, *The Parallax View* and *Three Days Of The Condor*. *The Conversation* may seem insular in focus, with its withdrawn, shuffling hero and its domestic murder plot. But its implications, as Harry realises that he cannot divorce his actions from their consequences, are massive. It's a morality tale that just happens to be a gut-wrenching, nail-gnawing thriller.

Ryan Gilbey

NEED TO KNOW

Year 1974
Running time 113 mins
Director Francis Ford Coppola
Stars Gene Hackman, John Cazale, Teri Garr, Robert Duvall, Frederic Forrest
Buy it on Region 2
Tagline "Harry Caul is an invader of privacy. The best in the business. He can record any conversation between two people anywhere. So far, three people are dead because of him."
Best line "He'd kill us if he got the chance."
Critic's view "A taut, intelligent thriller" – Chicago Sun-Times
Best watched when... Some bugger's bugging you.

BE THE ONE
Experience The Matrix through the eyes of The One and decide your own path.
Assume the role of Neo and relive your favorite scenes and battles from the blockbuster movie trilogy.
• 1000's of martial-arts-style fighting moves • Battle hundreds of Agent Smiths • Over 15 major characters from all 3 movies as well as brand new ones • Never-before-seen training levels prepare you for the most memorable battles • Director's Cut of movie footage from all three Matrix™ films • Epic new ending to the Matrix™ Trilogy written and directed by the Wachowskis.
16+
www.pegi.info
PC DVD ROM
ONLY DVD COMPATIBLE
XBOX
The Matrix: Path of Neo Software © 2005 Atari, Inc. All Rights Reserved. All trademarks are the property of their respective owners. Manufactured and marketed by Atari, New York. © 2005 Shiny Entertainment. All rights reserved. Shiny Entertainment is a wholly-owned division of Atari, Inc. "PlayStation" and the "PS" Family logo are registered trademarks of Sony Computer Entertainment Inc. Microsoft, Xbox, and the Xbox logos are either registered trademarks of Microsoft Corporation in the U.S. and/or in other countries and are used under license from Microsoft. The ratings icon is a trademark of the Interactive Digital Software Association.

THE
MATRIX
PATH OF NEO™
www.thematrixpathofneo.com
PlayStation®2
Shiny Entertainment
Interactive Entertainment WB™
ATARI
TM & © Warner Bros. Entertainment, Inc.
WBIE LOGO, WBIE SHIELD, TM & © Warner Bros. Entertainment, Inc.
(s05)

63

THE MATRIX

The Wachowskis dream up a brave new world and high-kick Jar-Jar in the face...

Simply always destined to be more than popcorn entertainment

Appearing through a vortex of green digits, a woman clad in sexy, black bondage gear sits facing the wall. A cop squad, shining bug-eyed torches, closes in. Outside, a carload of FBI-like stooges pull up – one of them passionlessly muttering that the men inside are "already dead". Back in the building, the woman rises... spins mantis-like, near-freezes in mid-air and picks them off, cop by cop. Moments later, she's danced across the rooftops, squatted back on the ground, taken a phone call and almost been crushed by a thundering truck. Welcome to *The Matrix*. Welcome to something you had simply never seen before...

Back in 1999, there was just one sci-fi epic on everyone's minds – a certain *Star Wars: Episode I – The Phantom Menace*. However, crashing the kids' party like a high-kicking S&M freak came a teasingly-tagged curiosity. "Unfortunately, no one can be told what *The Matrix* is... You have to see it for yourself" gave nothing away. "What Is The Matrix?" was even less helpful. What indeed? Hordes trekked to the cinema to find out. It wasn't just the lure of Keanu Reeves either. Rather, a nagging feeling that a cult was being born and it would be good to say you were there at the start.

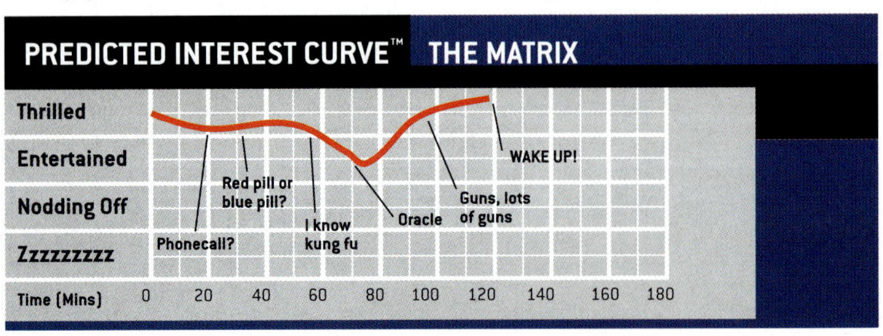

At the time, Warner Bros big cheese Lorenzo Di Bonaventura said the film "could really impact on how we view a genre... I think people will mimic it." Flow-mo? Bullet-time? Cod-philosophical bullshit? He was spot-on.

Given he was previously renowned for *Bill & Ted* slacker hits and pout'n'posture actioner *Speed*, Reeves' presence hardly suggested a metaphysical masterwork, but, remarkably, his hilarious mumblings – "The icon representing God loses its connection to God... then you have a simulation of an icon until it's on your car's dashboard. A decay of meaning" – were almost apposite, dude. "I had to read Baudrillard and *Out Of Control* which is about systems, evolution and robots and Evolutionary Psychology," Reeves said, as philosophy profs everywhere cringed, knowing their lectures on Descartes' 'Demon Hypothesis' (look it up) would never be the same again. Passable philosophical/biblical metaphors aside, however, there's a murkier monkey on this cyberpunk parable's back. Yep, drugs. "Ever had that feeling that you're not sure if you're awake or still dreaming," asks Neo (Reeves) before meeting Morpheus (Laurence Fishburne) for the first time. Head-to-toe in dealer black, he offers Neo a "truth" drug. Scampering down the rabbit hole, Neo takes the red pill and is reborn in another reality far more terrifying and dangerous than his safe 1997, but certainly more alive. Huge needles jack people in and out of The

Matrix; Neo rejects his first hit and, when bio-technically wired into The Matrix, can fly; and eventually, he becomes unbeatable. Sure, it cheapens the fanboys' quasi-religion, but, frankly, it makes more sense.

The Wachowskis prefer to let the audience work it out for themselves. A synthesis of everything that had ever interested the brothers, their vision perplexed studio execs, who doubted whether a pair with just the *Assassins* screenplay to their name had the know-how to handle a multi-million dollar blockbuster. So, Warners challenged them to prove their mettle by directing a $5 million test-film and, one Sapphic fantasy fulfillment flick later (*Bound*), the brothers were granted an initial budget of $65 million for *The Matrix*. With the readies to take conceptual designer Geof Darrow's eye-ballooning pencil drawings to the screen, the gorgeously glossy Wachowski world was realised – enhanced by state-of-the-art CG, intense kung-fu training and actor-pushing acrobatics (Carrie-Anne Moss broke an ankle, Keanu was restricted due to the fusing of the two top vertebrae on his back). Visual effects supervisor John Gaeta said the brothers "wanted to go completely over the top and demonstrate that previous models of action scenes are old and stale". Subsequent imitation suggests they succeeded.

Released Stateside a fortnight before the Columbine High School massacre, *The Matrix* also attracted unwanted homages. Attempts to blame the film for the shooting largely failed, but, in the next few years the loony-sounding "Matrix Defence" cropped up in US courtrooms as an 'excuse' for various murders. Shrinks said the film was used by people with fractured lives to excuse their differences without admitting they had a problem, while parent-killer Josh Cooke said, "Wouldn't it be cool if that was real? What if we were in *The Matrix*? When I would watch Keanu Reeves shooting people, I remember thinking, 'That's me.' I kind of put myself in that position." There's no denying that *The Matrix* made guns even 'cooler' than they already were – "Guns. Lots of »

NEED TO KNOW

Year 1999
Running time 130 mins
Directors Andy Wachowski, Larry Wachowski
Stars Keanu Reeves, Laurence Fishburne, Carrie-Anne Moss, Hugo Weaving, Joe Pantoliano
Buy it on Region 4 has the best picture quality.
Tagline "What is The Matrix?"
Best line "I imagine that right now, you're feeling a bit like Alice. Hmm? Tumbling down the rabbit hole?" – Morpheus
Critic's view "A wonderfully enjoyable pulp classic... An unalloyed pleasure crammed with hi-tech, high-camp action sequences and spiffy effects." – *The Guardian*
Best watched when...
You wake up unsure if you're a butterfly who dreamed of being a man or a man who dreamed of being a butterfly.

guns" is a sexy line, while the trenchcoat-wearing entrance hall demolition is a slo-mo orgy of orgasmic violence – but its descent into legal excuses for murderers is depressing.

More intriguingly, *The Matrix* was always destined to be more than just popcorn entertainment. Aside from the hypothetical mumbo-jumbo, the Wachowskis and their team imbued their fixation with motifs only noticeable once you know they're there. For starters, everything in the actual Matrix is tinged in the green glow of an old computer screen, whereas nothing in the world of the Nebuchadnezzar ship, except of course the on-screen Matrix code, is hued as such.

Cinematographer Bill Pope said The Matrix was designed to be "slightly decayed, slightly monolithic and grid-like, like a machine would make it", whereas the 'real' world is more human, more lifelike. Sure, the overall design is flawed – why don't the Agents just smash all the phones in The Matrix to keep out interlopers? Does Morpheus really have to spout quite so much exposition? – but these are piffling gripes for a film that grabs you by the throat and rabbit punches you to the gut 'til you're choking on your knees. *The Matrix* is a movie that changed cinema.

The Wachowski Brothers' foresight, though, has also been their burden – their exemplary benchmark was *so* innovative it left itself open to imitation, ridicule and merciless lampooning. Still, if you can just ignore the piss-takes, rip-offs and consequential interest in the balletic/chin-stroking martial arts of *Crouching Tiger, Hidden Dragon* and co, you're still faced with a sci-fi mindbender.

Of course, the sequels did their best to muddy the shine. Our advice? Ignore everything that happened after SuperNeo flew skyward to the chug chug of Rage Against The Machine's 'Wake Up' and put yourself back on the edge of your cinema seat, circa June 1999... Yes, it was exhilarating wasn't it? TF

Jonathan Dean

GHOSTS OF THE MACHINE

A handful of choice cuts from the unstoppable slew of Wachowski-inspired 'homages' that followed...

SPACED (1999-2001)
Tim and arch-enemy Duane Benzie face-off in the paintball arena and, like Neo and Mr Smith, are both out of bullets.

CROUCHING TIGER, HIDDEN DRAGON (2000)
Would this have been as popular without *The Matrix*? Check out the bar scene for obvious debt.

SCARY MOVIE (2000)
Ah ha ha – devoid of original ideas? Crib others and grab a cheap laugh from them instead. How to kill Ghostface? Use kung-fu!

SHREK (2001)
Cameron Diaz is treading softly as Princess Fiona until she meets a Robin Hood gang and needs Neo-kicks to sort them out.

THE SIMPSONS (1989-)
Sure, *The Simpsons* mock any phenomenon going, but Bart's slow-mo ascent in black ninja outfit is a sure nod to the Wachowskis.

62

NEED TO KNOW

Year 1955
Running time 88 mins
Director Charles Laughton
Stars Robert Mitchum
Buy it on Region 2
Tagline "The wedding night, the anticipation, the kiss, the knife, but above all – the suspense!"
Best line "A man with $10,000 hid somewhere, and a widder in the makin'." – Harry Powell
Critic's view "It makes us fall in love again with an experimental cinema that truly experiments." – *Cahiers Du Cinema*
Best watched when... You need reminding how scary movies could be when you were a kid.

THE NIGHT OF THE HUNTER

Robert Mitchum's scary as hell in Charles Laughton's tale of right hand, left hand...

Charles Laughton didn't mince his words when he pitched the role of Harry Powell to Robert Mitchum. "He's a terrible, evil shit of a man," he said of the bogus preacher who stalks *The Night Of The Hunter*'s child heroes across the Depression-battered South. "Present!" replied the actor who, having recovered from a potentially career-threatening prison term for marijuana possession, was keen to test himself by working with a giant of the English stage.

Together they created one of cinema's true originals: a twisted Gothic parable, part film noir, part expressionist fairy tale, that ranks alongside *Citizen Kane* as one of the greatest pictures ever made by a first-time director.

It's certainly one of the most influential. Spike Lee used Mitchum's "left-hand, right-hand" soliloquy almost verbatim in *Do The Right Thing*, while the reveal showing Shelley Winters dead at the bottom of the river was copied by the Coen brothers in *The Man Who Wasn't There*.

Imitation might be the sincerest form of flattery, but at its best, *The Night Of The Hunter* is inimitable. And in Robert Mitchum – dressed in inky black with knife in pocket and the words 'Love' and 'Hate' etched on his knuckles – the film gave us one of cinema's all-time scariest psychopaths: a murderous misogynist on a mission to rid the world of "perfume smellin' things, lacy things, things with curly hair", who shacks up with the widow of a hanged cellmate who's stashed the proceeds of a robbery in his daughter's doll.

On the flip side, Laughton presented a symbol of unblemished good in the form of Lillian Gish's Miss Cooper, the kindly spinster who takes runaway children John and Pearl Harper in, and safeguards them from Mitchum's evil predations.

"I have to go back to DW Griffith to find a set so infused with purpose and harmony," said the actress, although it wasn't always as harmonious as she claims. Ordered by the producer to go home after turning up to work drunk, Mitchum responded by unzipping his fly and pissing in his car. On another occasion, Laughton silenced a complaining Winters by slapping her around the face. Mitchum loathed his co-star with a passion, joking that he'd wanted them to use the real Shelley for the underwater scene instead of a wax dummy.

Still, none of this stopped *The Night Of The Hunter* being an artistic triumph – making its failure at the box office all the more crushing. Laughton was so heartbroken he vowed never to direct another film; he kept his word, dying in 1962 without stepping behind a camera again. Had he lived, he would have seen his film championed by a generation of critics, filmmakers and cineastes. He would also have seen his movie given the ultimate accolade: a character in *The Simpsons* with 'Luv' and 'Hat' tattooed across his three-fingered hands.

Neil Smith

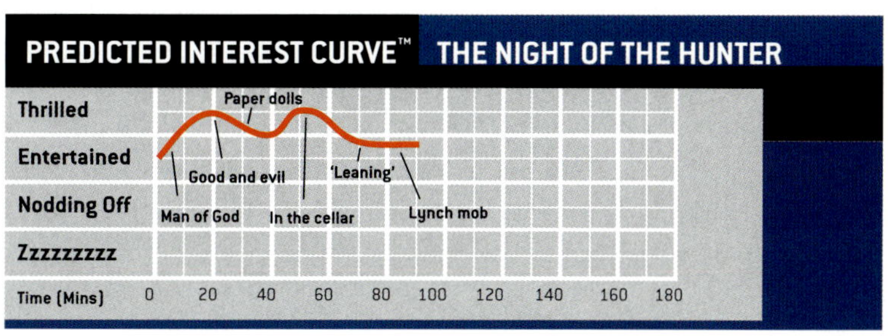

61

HALLOWEEN

Seminal '70s horror sharpens the knives for screen psychos...

You know, I look at *Scream* and *Scary Movie* and they're fun," John Carpenter told *Total Film* back in 2003. "But for me horror shouldn't be fun. Horror should be unflinching. Scary as fuck."

Carpenter has never come closer to achieving his remit than with *Halloween*. Credited as having honed the modern-day slasher conventions, only to see them carbon-copied and parodied ever since (most notably in *Scream*'s clever-clever piss-take), its power to shock should by all rights have been diluted by now – watered down by the years of sorority house rip-offs, Zucker-esque ribbings and its own lame sequels. All seven of the damn things. That it hasn't and that – unlike the Freddys and Jasons of this world – its main man hasn't turned into a panto ponce, is testament to its flawless design, machine-like momentum and singular purpose. Were it not for those pesky *Blair Witch* kids, it would still be the most successful independent movie of all time. And quite rightly so. Through the fog of Carpenter's recent output it seems unlikely, but make no mistake: 27 years on, *Halloween* is still perfect, tapping into fears so raw and primal that it will forever defy the process of ageing.

Halloween taps into fears so raw and primal that it defies ageing

Working from a shoestring structure – murderer escapes from a mental institution and returns to his hometown with mayhem on his (fractured) mind – and shot in 21 days on a threadbare $325,000, the early signs for *The Babysitter Murders* (its working title) weren't rosy. Famously, of course, budget constraints meant that Carpenter's killer, Michael Myers – so named in a twisted thank-you to the European distributor of his previous movie, *Assault On Precinct 13* – was forced to wear a spray-painted, re-jigged William Shatner mask, as opposed to the "fucked-up clown face" originally envisioned. The weather conditions meanwhile were far from ideal (a hazy spring having to pose as a chilly October) and the tight schedule meant that repeat takes were at a premium. And then there was Jamie Lee Curtis...

Today she's as synonymous with the series as Michael himself. Back in 1978, though, she was a 20-year-old TV actress of, well, TV ability. Carpenter wasn't keen – preferring instead Anne Lockhart, daughter of *Lassie*'s June, for his lead – but was talked round by his producer/then-girlfriend Debra Hill. "I knew that casting Jamie Lee would be great publicity for the film because her mother was in *Psycho*," Hill says. "And John eventually agreed."

With the movie shot out of sequence, Carpenter came up with the idea of a "fear metre" to help the actress, giving each scene a rating out of 10 so she knew beforehand the level of intensity required. And boy, did it work, Curtis turning

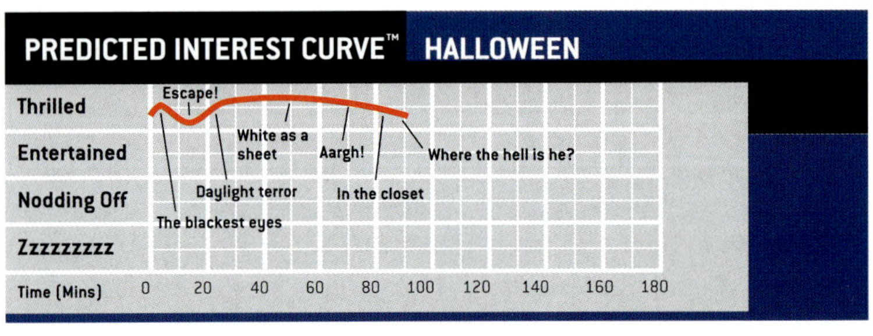

in a performance of which Mum would've been proud.

But it's not just Curtis' screams, Carpenter's forever-iconic score and a surprising lack of gore that meant *Halloween* became the *Psycho* for a new generation. Riffing on both Hitch and Michael Powell's *Peeping Tom*, as well as employing an autumnal colour scheme reminiscent of the Halloween sequence in *Meet Me In St Louis*, Carpenter showcased his technical smarts, using an array of POV shots to create a voyeurism that permeates every frame. From the rightly revered opening sequence, in which we watch through young Michael's eyes as he spies on, then slaughters his sis – all captured in a Steadicam tracking shot that looks seamless, but in fact contains two ingenious cuts – the audience is complicit in the carnage. When Curtis' Laurie is attacked in the closet, the camera sticks us in there with her. As she runs down the road screaming for help, Carpenter's dolly shot gives us the same panicked perspective. And when Myers escapes the loony bin and drives back to Haddonfield, we're crouched in the back seat – helpless passengers on his nightmare ride.

The use of widescreen too gives Carpenter the scope to skew shot compositions, allowing his monster an ocean of shadow in which to lurk. Never does the director properly reveal his nemesis. Michael (aka The Shape) is born of the darkness; an inhuman menace. He may have been based on *Westworld*'s robot, but he's in fact more akin to Jim Cameron's Terminator. He can't be bargained with. He doesn't feel pity or remorse or fear. And he absolutely will not stop, ever, until you are dead. Especially if you've just got laid.

"What, if you fuck you get fucked? People have always said that about *Halloween*, that the key to survival is to remain a virgin, that if you have sex then you're next... but that was never the intention," Carpenter maintains. "But I'll tell you: there isn't anyone who watches the movie and then thinks about going home to make out. It's movie birth control."

Ladies and gentlemen, *Halloween*: the sleekest, purest, rawest horror movie ever made. And a contraceptive to boot.

Mark Dinning

NEED TO KNOW

Year 1978
Running time 91 mins
Director John Carpenter
Stars Jamie Lee Curtis, Donald Pleasence, PJ Soles
Buy it on Region 2 20th Anniversary Edition
Tagline "The night HE came home!"
Best line "I met this six-year-old child with this blind, pale, emotionless face... I spent eight years trying to reach him and then another seven trying to keep him locked up." – Loomis
Critic's view "The cold sweat in the palm of my hands never had time to warm up" – *The Sunday Telegraph*
Best watched when... You're not babysitting on 31 October.

60

THE OUTLAW JOSEY WALES

Clint Eastwood comes of age as a director of Westerns, tapping into a great tradition...

With *The Outlaw Josey Wales*, Clint Eastwood comes into his own as a director of Westerns. His first foray into the genre, *High Plains Drifter*, a brutal revenge saga tainted with misogyny, was patterned very much after the spaghetti Westerns that had made his name. *Josey Wales* starts off rather the same way, with Clint as a peaceful farmer whose wife and son are killed by Unionist militia. Joining the Confederate guerillas, he sets out to fight terror with terror. Looks like we're in for more of the same: massive slaughter, with our hero riding off into the sunset, avenged but alone.

But with the ending of the war, and Josey as sole survivor of his band hunted down by Captain Terrill (Bill McKinney), the leader of the militia who killed his family, the movie starts to take an unexpected turn. As he rides southwest towards Texas, Josey the embittered loner begins to accumulate companions. Not that he wants to, but they just keep tagging along: a starchy old lady and her fey granddaughter, a taciturn Indian woman, an old Mexican vaquero, a broken-down cowboy – and, first and anything but least, an elderly Cherokee, Lone Watie, superbly played by Chief Dan George, who wryly explains his inability to "sneak up on" people by his tribe's close contact with the white man: "We're called the civilised tribe because white men have been doing it to us for years."

With The Outlaw Josey Wales, Eastwood really comes into his own as a director

What's happening, quite unpredictably, is that a tough, formulaic revenge Western is turning into a dark-edged comedy of redemption. As Josey resignedly accepts yet another recruit to his ill-assorted band ("He might as well ride along with us. Hell, everybody else is"), he gradually becomes humanised again, taking on a surrogate family to replace the one that was brutally wrenched from him. This fertile mixing of genres, it's only fair to say, can be partly ascribed to the film's screenwriter and original director, Philip Kaufman, who Eastwood replaced a week into shooting. It was a controversial step, and one which prompted the Directors Guild of America to institute a ban on any current cast or crew member replacing the director on a film – a statute which, ever since, has been known as the 'Eastwood rule'.

Both Kaufman and Eastwood know their classic Westerns backwards, of course, so the film's nods to some of the great directors of the past are absolutely intentional. The dance as an image of society coming together and healing itself harks back to John Ford; the journey as a process of redemption and reintegration into the community recalls Anthony Mann; the forging of a motley crew of individuals into an efficient fighting unit was a favourite theme of

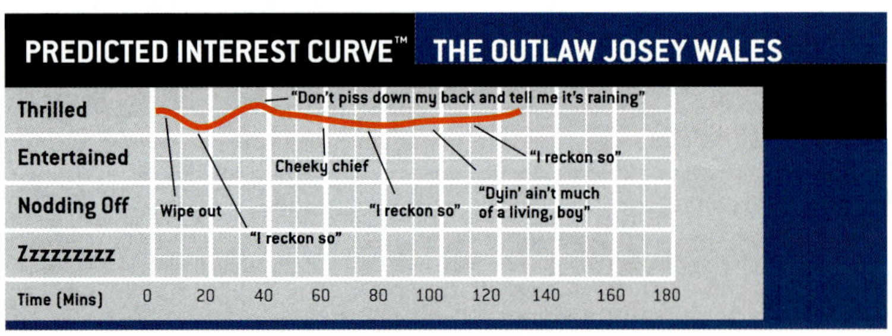

Howard Hawks; and the detail of Josey's former comrade, Fletcher, being forced into joining in his pursuit is an explicit reference to Sam Peckinpah's *The Wild Bunch*. For all its nods and winks, though, *Josey Wales* never feels derivative: the sweep and colour of the narrative, the touches of offbeat humour and the crisp, delineated characters (Lone Watie in particular) give the film a flavour all its own.

The more outcasts and stray dogs that Josey manages to gather around himself, the more his character softens. To start with, he's a mythical killer, pretty much The Man With No Name he played in the spaghettis – monosyllabic, chewing on a cheroot, shooting first and not bothering to ask questions afterwards. But because his uninvited companions refuse to treat him as a myth, or as anything but a man, and regard the purpose of his journey as no more important than theirs, he's obliged to start seeing himself on those terms – and seeing even the least deserving others as human too. He's even prepared to give bounty hunters a fair chance: "This isn't necessary. You can just ride on," he tells them, though of course they don't have the good sense to do so. And when a showdown with the Comanche seems inevitable, rather than mount a pre-emptive strike, he simply rides alone and unarmed into their camp and barters on equal terms with their chief to make peace. (Worth noting, incidentally, that in none of his Westerns has Eastwood ever killed an Indian.)

Josey's final attempt to return to his old, solitary life is a complete, triumphant failure. Riding out early in the morning from the farmhouse where his surrogate family have settled, he gets no further than a hundred yards out before his pursuers ambush him. But at once a rifle appears at every window and the Unionist militia are routed and killed. Josey chases Terrill back into town and kills him with his own sword, and Fletcher, along with two Texas Rangers, accepts the blatant fiction that Josey Wales is dead. As, in a way, he finally is.

Philip Kemp

NEED TO KNOW

Year 1976
Running time 135 mins
Director Clint Eastwood
Stars Clint Eastwood, Chief Dan George, Sondra Locke, Bill McKinney, John Vernon
Buy it on Region 2
Tagline "...An army of one."
Best line "I didn't surrender neither. They took my horse and made him surrender." – Lone Watie
Critic's view "Although the film is as violent as some of them come nowadays... it has an extraordinary undertow of sweetness and redemption to its tale of pursuit and revenge." – *Evening Standard*
Best watched when... Your family are *really* bugging you.

59

BLUE VELVET

Now it's dark: David Lynch brings small-town sadomasochism out of the closet.

Pauline Kael called it "an anomaly". JG Ballard declared it "the best film of the 1980s". Yes, you can pin many labels to *Blue Velvet*: postmodern noir, pop-surrealist nightmare, Freudian mind-fuck. But perhaps the best way of defining this indefinable film is to say that it's a coming-of-age classic. In more ways than one.

Because with *Blue Velvet*, the David Lynch we know today truly arrived. The Montana-born auteur had already helmed three movies – two of them stunners (1977's *Eraserhead*; 1980's *The Elephant Man*) – but this was the one that ordained him as cinema's czar of the subconscious, the most influential avant-gardist since Luis Buñuel. Yoking his inky thematic obsessions to fresh storytelling rigour, it stuck a bomb under the boundaries of mainstream culture, the effects of which we're still feeling.

This wild flower grew from seeds of failure. Emerging from the box-office desert of *Dune* (1984), Lynch plunged into his most personal project since his cult debut. *Blue Velvet* was bankrolled by *Dune* producer Dino De Laurentis, who limited Lynch's budget but gave him the freedom of final cut.

Imagination unfettered, the director set about moulding a masterpiece whose roots lay in a fantasy he'd had of spotting a clue to a mystery while spying in a girl's room. This obnoxious brain-burp spawned the movie's primal scene: hidden in the closet, the preppy Jeffrey (Kyle MacLachlan) watches as nightclub chanteuse Dorothy (Isabella Rossellini) is horrifically abused by the bestial Frank (Dennis Hopper), a blue-velvet-fetishising, gas-mask-toting gangster. This is the point where the film's id erupts and Lynch doesn't flinch. There have been forewarnings: take the brilliant opening sequence, where the Norman Rockwell images of flowers and waving firemen give way to battling insects in giant close-up. But nothing quite prepares you for one of the most disturbing moments in '80s cinema – or any cinema. And once we've crossed the line, there's no going back. "I'm seeing something that was always hidden," muses Jeffrey, whose Oedipally complex arc puts him in touch with his inner Frank when he embarks on a sadomasochistic affair with Dorothy. As Jeffrey makes his passage from innocence to experience, we see a warped reflection of our own darkest, dirtiest impulses. "Certain aspects of sex are troubling," Lynch has said. "The way it's used as power, or the way it takes the form of perversions that exploit people. These things are not good, but I think a lot of people find them a real kick and it's fairly common."

Yet the kink that's key to unlocking *Blue Velvet* isn't S&M or fetishism. It's something

"Certain aspects of sex are troubling, the way it's used as power" DAVID LYNCH

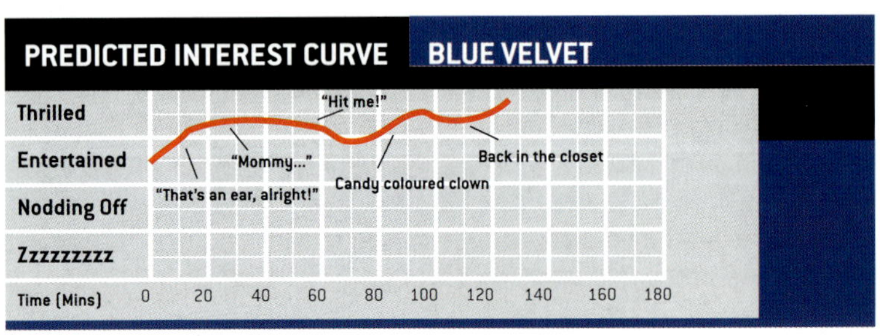

anyone who's ever sat in a gloomy auditorium can relate to: voyeurism. "David found that spot in people's subconscious where there's a little bit of voyeur," says DoP Frederick Elmes. "He was very curious about what could be seen that shouldn't be seen. I think everybody has a bit of that [in them] and that's why people got into the film."

Of course, the lushness of Elmes' lensing didn't hurt either, his painterly palette mixing the brooding shadows of Edward Hopper with Francis Bacon's livid flesh tones. Aurally too, it's a triumph, from sound design (the flickering candle; Frank's distorted roar) to soundtrack (Angelo Badalamenti's first gig for Lynch, a collaboration that's endured to this day).

But while no one can dispute the beauty of *Blue Velvet*'s style, some have questioned its content. "It's not a film for everybody," Lynch once said. "Some people really dug it. Others thought it was disgusting and sick. And, of course, it is, but it has two sides. You have to have the contrasts." While über-critic Pauline Kael embraced it ("its vision isn't alienating – this is American darkness, darkness with a happy ending"), Roger Ebert thought that the cornball depictions of small-town life undercut the raw sexual realism. "This is the way America is to me," argues Lynch. "There's a very innocent, naive quality to life and there's a horror and a sickness as well."

A modest box office performer, *Blue Velvet* earned Lynch his second Best Director nod from Oscar. And its influence? Seismic. It sired Lynch's soap noir *Twin Peaks*, which in turn begat shows like *The X Files*, *Wild Palms*, *The Kingdom*, *Six Feet Under*, *Desperate Housewives*... And on the big screen, you can see the *Velvet* touch in films as diverse as *Heathers*, *Lantana*, *Secretary*, *American Beauty*, *Happiness* and countless others. Trouble is, of course, that exposing the dark underbelly of white-picketed suburbia has become a cliché. But here's the thing: what's most shocking about *Blue Velvet* is that it's still shocking. Age and imitation haven't muted its pain, its terror, its mysteries. Take another look at *Blue Velvet*: it's still a strange world, isn't it?

Matthew Leyland

NEED TO KNOW

Year 1986
Running time 120 mins
Director David Lynch
Stars Kyle MacLachlan, Isabella Rossellini, Dennis Hopper, Laura Dern, Hope Lange
Buy it on Region 0 SE
Tagline "It's a strange world."
Best line "I looked for you in my closet tonight" – Dorothy Vallens
Critic's view "When you come out of the theatre after seeing *Blue Velvet*, you certainly know you've seen something" – Pauline Kael, *The New Yorker*
Best watched when... You feel like being a peeping tom without leaving the comfort of your own living room.

58

DIE HARD

Willis' wisecracking redefines the action genre for a new generation...

"One hundred million terrorists in the world," gripes Bruce Willis' John McClane. "And I gotta kill one with feet smaller than my sister..."

Fuck the yippee-ki-yays. What still elevates *Die Hard* above Hollywood's traditional action output isn't its iconic one-liners but its consistently knowing, movie-savvy script. "This time John Wayne does not walk off into the sunset with Grace Kelly," sneers Alan Rickman's uber-villain, Hans Gruber, near the climax. McClane's response? "That was Gary Cooper, asshole."

With Hollywood starting to greenlight a number of projects based on the tragic events of 9/11, *Die Hard*'s high-rise histrionics now feel even more good-natured than they did 17 years ago. A pinnacle of action-movie engineering, *Die Hard* exploded on the unsuspecting world, raking in more than $150 million from a budget of $28 million and setting a template for the genre that didn't shift significantly until the arrival of *The Matrix*, 11 years later.

Beyond all the wanton destruction, it's the relationships that make it tick

Director John McTiernan and cinematographer Jan De Bont have each turned in some prize turkeys since, but here their sleek, slick visuals deliver a thrill-a-minute momentum that forever altered the landscape, sparking a raft of *Under Seiges*, two sequels and rumours to this day of a *Die Hard 4.0*.

It turned Willis – who was reputedly fifth choice after Arnold Schwarzenegger, Sylvester Stallone and, believe it or not, Burt Reynolds and Richard Gere – from 'That Smart Alec in *Moonlighting*' to international A-lister overnight and earnt him a cool $5 million (astounding for a TV actor whose face wasn't even considered commercial enough to put on the original poster). Ironically, the book behind *Die Hard*'s inspiration was hardly explosive. Written by real-life detective Roderick Thorp, *Nothing Lasts Forever* was the follow-up to his previous effort, *The Detective*, which had been picked up by Twentieth Century Fox and turned into a movie starring Frank Sinatra in the late '60s. Sinatra, however, turned down the sequel, leaving it languishing in the Fox archives for Joel Silver to stumble upon 15 years later...

At the time, Silver was flush from the success of *Lethal Weapon* and on the lookout for another cost-effective cash cow. *Die Hard* proved ideal. Shortly before writing, Thorp had read *The Glass Tower* – filmed later as *The Towering Inferno* – and had chosen to offer a humble 'homage' by locating his story in a skyscraper. Factor in the fact that Fox had just built the brand new, 34-storey Fox Plaza in Century City (a character in its own right in the movie) and the touchpaper was lit. Let the machine-gunning begin.

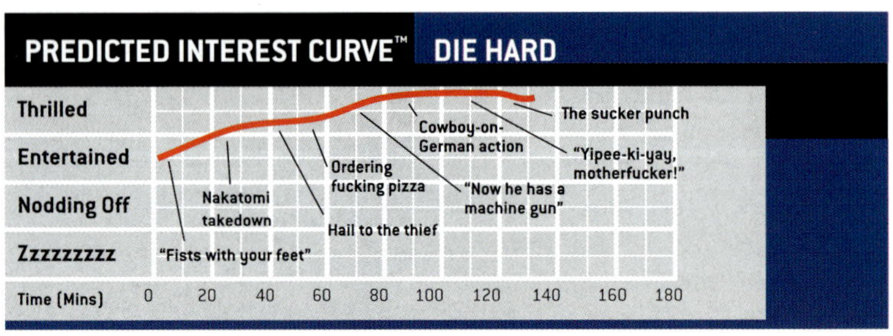

Beyond the wisecracks and wanton destruction, though, what makes *Die Hard* really tick is its relationships: McClane and his absent wife (Bonnie Bedelia); McClane and his cuddly cop buddy, Sgt Al Powell (Reginald Veljohnson); and, most important, McClane and his terrorist adversaries. From CB backchat to cheeky notes – "Now I have a machine gun. Ho ho ho" – the bond between them is wonderfully played. In an arena of typically faceless baddies, not only are the goons properly drawn characters, but our hero at one point even writes their names on his arm. How's that for wearing your heart on your sleeve?

Rickman is terrific as McClane's sauve, pseudy nemesis, Hans Gruber. Cast after Silver and McTiernan caught him in a Broadway adaptation of *Les Liaisons Dangereuses*, his snooty intellectualism is the perfect foil for McClane's blue-collar rozzer. An aversion to guns aside – despite numerous takes, you can still see him wince in the scene where he shoots the cocky dealbroker in the head – Rickman has a ball in his Hollywood breakthrough, turning in a performance that saw him instantly added to a thousand casting agents' rolodexes. His death, meanwhile – a 30-storey swandive reminiscent of Hitchcock's *Saboteur* – is a corker, largely due to the look on his face as on set he found himself dropped 20-feet onto a crash-mat on the count of two, not three.

NEED TO KNOW

Year 1988
Running time 131 mins
Director John McTiernan
Stars Bruce Willis, Alan Rickman, Bonnie Bedelia, Reginald Veljohnson
Buy it on Region 1, two-disc SE.
Tagline "40 Stories Of Sheer Adventure!"
Best line "Oh my God, the quarterback is toast."– Theo
Critic's view "*Rambo* for snobs" – *NME*
Best watched when... You're wearing comfortable shoes.

Ultimately, however, this is Willis' movie. Barefoot and vest-chested, he's an everyman action icon. When he's shot, he bleeds. When he's hurt, you feel his pain. (And having performed most of his own stunts, he certainly felt the pain.)

Is there a message behind the mayhem? The death of the '80s 'Greed is good' mantra, where yuppies trying to do million-dollar deals get their brains blown out and people are only saved by letting go of their gold Rolexes? Or is it about McClane's workaholic wife and their subsequent marriage troubles; a sexist morality tale about working women and a loss of family values? Not really. But you'll be having too much fun to care.

Mark Dinning

57

SWEET SMELL OF SUCCESS

Brit helmer dissects the Big Apple to find a core of pure cyanide...

I love this dirty town," announces Burt Lancaster, eyes glinting behind killer hornrims, as he surveys his kingdom – the violent, nocturnal streets of Manhattan. Even now, 50 years on, no movie has captured more acutely the neurotic energy of New York, the pungent mix of visual and emotional aggression. Startling, then, that it was made by a director fresh from that most reassuringly British of studios, Ealing. But then, even at Ealing, Alexander Mackendrick had shown signs of a disposition too dark and too cynical to chime with the studio's mild ethos. No wonder he pounced on the opportunity to helm Ernest Lehman's adaptation of his own snarling, downbeat short story set in the murky twilight of Manhattan showbiz journalism.

"A director often does his best work under intense pressure" ALEXANDER MACKENDRICK

It was, as Mackendrick put it, a huge chance "to get out of a reputation for cute British comedies".

Originally, Lehman planned to script, produce and direct *Sweet Smell Of Success* himself. But his production company was Hecht-Hill-Lancaster, the first of the independent actor-agent combines that broke the hold of the Hollywood studios. A notoriously devious and ruthless trio, HHL (agent Harold Hecht, screenwriter James Hill and actor Burt Lancaster) soon eased Lehman out of the director's seat. Not long after, he succumbed to a spastic colon – brought on, he believed, by the strain of dealing with HHL – and bowed out, leaving 'minor rewrites' still needed on the script.

Offered a new screenwriter, Mackendrick picked Clifford Odets – golden-boy hero of '30s leftist theatre, now down on his luck and politically tarnished after caving in to the McCarthyite witch-hunters. Odets tore into Lehman's work with gusto – too much gusto, if anything. The "two-week rewrite" took four months. Mackendrick was forced to start shooting "with no script at all, while Clifford reconstructed the thing from stem to stern". Holed up in the Essex House Hotel on Central Park, Odets dispatched the pages straight to Mackendrick and crew on the streets below.

But what pages. Nothing else that Odets wrote for the screen can match *Sweet* for caustic stylisation, gutter-baroque poetry or sheer intensity. "Listen," sneers a crooked cop, "rectify me a certain thing..." "I'd hate to take a bite of out of you," megalomaniac columnist JJ Hunsecker tells his press-agent sidekick Sidney Falco (Tony Curtis). "You're a cookie full of arsenic." "Maybe I left my sense of humour in my other suit," responds Sidney. Okay, so no one really talks like this, but why let realism get in the way of dialogue as dangerous as a razor-wire chastity belt?

The tensions of the production – Mackendrick shooting his first ever US movie on location

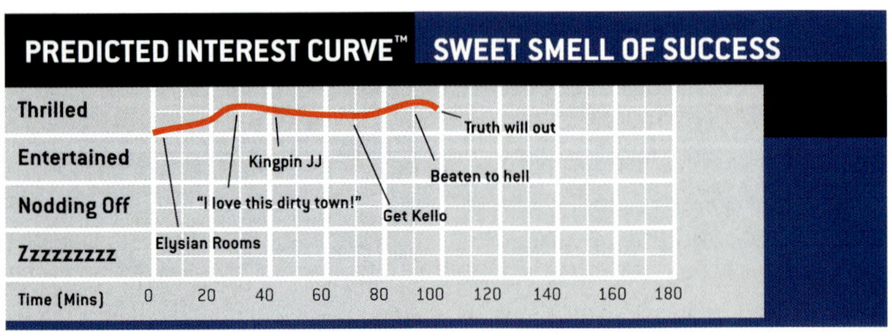

in Times Square, beset by hordes of teenage Curtis fans, as script pages trickled in with minutes to spare and producer/star Lancaster glowering over his shoulder – might have scuppered the film. Instead, they force-fed adrenaline into it, quickening the unrelenting pace and sharpening the hysterical edge. "At those moments," the helmer recalled, "the desperation you work from becomes a kind of strength... A director often does his best work under pressure, because decisions have to be made from the subconscious."

It's this sense of sheer, sanity-shredding terror that fuels *Sweet,* where the Manhattan streets seem not so much rain-wet as slick with the sweat of fear, and nightclubs are hazed with the smoke of burning reputations. This is a world of competitive degradation: the fouler your motives and the worse you treat people, the more power you accumulate. As Hunsecker, who can degrade more people more lethally than anyone else, Lancaster gives a riveting performance, reining in his habitual athleticism as he locks his arms to demonstrate a powerful man channelling all of his force into psychological warfare. But the revelation here is Tony Curtis. As determined as Mackendrick to escape from typecasting, the former pretty-boy star hurls himself headlong into the part of of Sidney Falco, the "boy with the ice-cream face", who uses his helpless grin and sex appeal to cheat, seduce, betray and sink to ever slimier depths of self-loathing.

NEED TO KNOW

Year 1957
Running time 96 mins
Director Alexander Mackendrick
Stars Burt Lancaster, Tony Curtis, Susan Harrison, Marty Milner, Sam Levene
Buy it on Region 2
Tagline "This is the story of JJ – but not the way he wants it told."
Best line "Match me, Sidney." – JJ Hunsecker
Critic's view "A brilliantly executed slice of evil and perversion, with a fascinating surface that far nobler films lack." – *Film Culture*
Best watched when... You're starting to believe what you read in the papers.

Inevitably, it all backfired. Audiences in the '50s were nowhere near ready for such a dark view of America – and Curtis fans certainly weren't ready for this new take on their idol, as Mackendrick realised at the preview. "You could see them curling up, crossing their arms, recoiling from the screen." HHL tried to salvage matters by taking the film and recutting it – only to realise that it would only work the way he'd planned it. Despite some respectful reviews, *Sweet* flopped. Lancaster, for some reason, blamed Lehman for the debacle. At a party he told the writer, "You could have made this a better picture. I ought to beat you up." "Go ahead," retorted the scribbler. "I could use the money."
Philip Kemp

56

THE SHAWSHANK REDEMPTION

Frank Darabont transforms a meat-and-veg prison flick into a religious experience...

"It landed," says Frank Darabont, "with a hollow thud at the box office." But then so did *Citizen Kane* and *It's A Wonderful Life*... *The Shawshank Redemption* clawed back only $18 million of its $25 million budget. It seemed that, in 1994, audiences just didn't have the stomach – or the buttock resilience – to head down to the multiplex and spend two-and-a-half hours in the company of some hangdog prison flick with the second-most-unappealing title in movie history (the first being *The Hudsucker Proxy*, also starring Tim Robbins).

Sneered at by critics, it quietly snagged the hearts and minds of real people

But after seven Academy award nominations (it won none), the film seeped into the culture via a slowburn word-of-mouth based on TV repeats and video rental (it was the most-rented tape of 1995). *Shawshank* is always high up in the IMDB Top 250 list, regularly jostling for the number one slot with the likes of *The Godfather* and *Star Wars*. It's a film overlooked and sneered at by reviewers; handed only a grudging acknowledgement on the showbiz back-slap circuit; misunderstood, mispronounced, underestimated... A doe-eyed underdog that quietly padded in from the critical cold to snag the hearts and minds of a broad sweep of real people (suicidal urban teens, buttoned-down Bible-belters, battered ex-cons). It's a rich and rewarding feel-good movie with such an effortless take on universal themes (despair, hope, injustice, friendship, overcoming adversity, seizing the moment) that it's become a sort of industry standard for intelligent crowd-pleasers.

Back in 1993, Darabont picked up the rights to his friend Stephen King's novella, *Rita Hayworth And The Shawshank Redemption* for a quick buck. He scribbled a spec screenplay and sent it to the writer (King: "I thought it was amazing. Just a mind-blowing piece of work.") Darabont had faithfully adapted King's story about a wrongly imprisoned man who spends two decades chipping away at a tunnel in his cell – the escape route hidden behind a poster of Rita Hayworth.

His script drew interest from Tom Cruise, Charlie Sheen, Nicolas Cage and Brad Pitt (who had his eye on young firebrand/sacrificial lamb Tommy Williams). But Darabont preferred the cool authority of Morgan Freeman for the role of prison smuggler Red and Tim Robbins for the lead of Andy Dufresne. "He has an enigmatic quality," says Darabont. "It was perfect, because Andy has to look like he's hiding this little secret."

While Robbins prepared by spending some time in solitary confinement, Darabont scouted a creepy, disused reformatory in Ohio to double as austere '40s state penitentiary Shawshank. The mood was set with an early

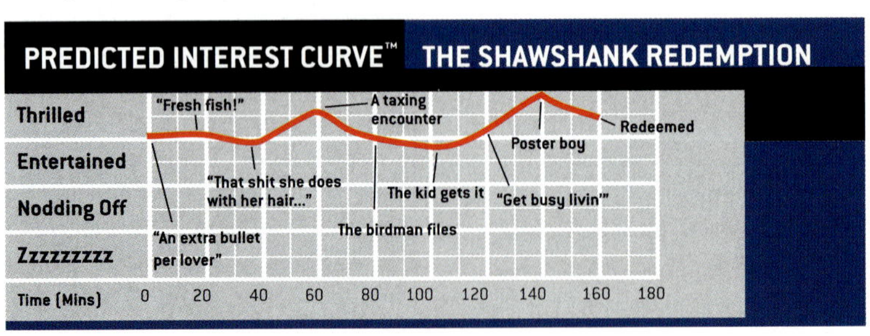

helicopter shot that soared up and over the mixed Gothic/cathedral stylings of the prison as hundreds of identically overalled inmates crowd towards a van-load of new arrivals ("fresh fish"). With Andy yet to emerge, there's a hint of unwitting worship, of pilgrims flocking to their future redeemer.

Robbins plays Andy with heart *and* heft, hitting the perfect note of stoicism and righteous grace ("Everyone's innocent in here," says Red, of all the alleged non-sinners) but he's also firmly one of the people. The turning point, when Andy earns his co-workers a "bottle of suds" with some timely tax advice to a warder, was filmed on an exposed rooftop in 100-degree heat. "In those conditions," says William Sadler, who played cynical con Heywood, "when someone hands you a cold beer, acting relieved ain't hard." As with *Million Dollar Baby*, *Shawshank* is a memory tale and Morgan Freeman patents his soulful voiceover with cast-iron integrity, carrying the narration even when it teeters on the edge of cheese.

Darabont used extended rehearsals to sensitively draw out solid, unmannered performances from a rack of supporting character actors. Bob Gunton is monstrous and Nixon-like as boo-hissable Warden Norton, simmering with easy sleaze, casual corruption and Old Testament hypocrisy ("Put your trust in the Lord. But your ass belongs to me"). Even better is Clancy Brown as Shawshank's bestial chief enforcer Hadley, a pitbull-tough echo of *Full Metal Jacket*'s Gunnery Sergeant Hartman, with a similar line in ugly/beautiful outbursts ("What is your problem, you fat barrel of monkey spunk?").

When he first read Darabont's script, King thought it would never be made because the novella-sized characters and conventions would seem too corny on a broader, prison-movie canvas (guy who can get things, shower rape, evil warden, birdman...). But with a calm, clear-sighted alchemy, Darabont renders the whole much more than the sum of its hackneyed parts. With just a touch of vaseline on the lens, he transforms what could have been a grim, gloomy and claustrophobic eye-roller into a fertile melodrama — without »

NEED TO KNOW

Year 1994

Running time 142 mins

Director Frank Darabont

Stars Tim Robbins, Morgan Freeman, Bob Gunton, William Sadler, James Whitmore

Buy it on Region 2 SE

Tagline "Fear can hold you prisoner. Hope can set you free."

Best line "Hope is a good thing, maybe the best of things. And no good thing ever dies." – Red

Critic's view "A simple story, elegantly told." – *Boston Globe*

Best watched when... You've been dumped, bereaved, rejected or could otherwise use a damned good cine-hug.

skimping on the raw, primary qualities (the violence is surprisingly nasty).

Mostly, it works because he keeps it simple. The storytelling is clipped into progressive, digestible chapters: none of yer auteur-style narrative juggling here. It's shot-for-shot, by-the-book structure all the way. Darabont and King – both down-the-line, red-meat-and-Bud types – were made for each other. *The Shawshank Redemption* is as mainstream as bread and water, but there are moments of transcendence that elevate it to a much higher frequency. Take James Whitmore as birdman Brooks, who enriches his character's off-the-peg prison-movie cliché into something more than the standard skeletal stereotype. His sad, dignified, beautifully written and acted suicide speech is the film's shining moment of classical tragedy ("I'm tired of being afraid all the time. I've decided not to stay").

Elsewhere, Darabont aims even higher – to the heavens. Andy's mission is to bring humanity to an inhumane place, and *Shawshank*'s most iconic moment comes when he locks himself in the prison tannoy room and illegally broadcasts a burst of Mozart, giving his defeated colleagues a fleeting taste of the sublime. It's a lyrical act of defiance that further emphasises Andy's divinity and spiritual stamina ("There are places in the world that aren't made out of stone. There's something inside that they can't get to"). It's easy to read Andy as a Christ figure, particularly from his speech about wanting to live by the ocean which, he says, has "no memory". He craves to be born again; for a forgiving, non-judgemental, divine force to wipe away his messy history.

The rebirth/resurrection notion extends to Andy's escape from the entombment of the prison – out through the sewage pipe and back into the world. (Just in case you miss the significance, Darabont has him adopt a cross-shaped gesture up towards the pelting, purifying rain.) It's a film about stoicism, perseverance and sacrifice, but it's also full of joy and life and – yep – hope. It's all about how Earthly friendship and human connection are crucial for the heart, but faith – in whatever form – is good for the soul. *That's* why *Shawshank* has found such a universal audience connection: because it expertly uses a straightforward moral-bound story to carry such weighty baggage. That is, pure fairytale. TF

Andy Lowe

MAINE MAN

Adapting Stephen King is a treacherous business. *Shawshank* is a classic. Here's the pick of the clag...

CUJO (1983)
Cuddly Saint Bernard bitten by a rabid bat. Broken-down car. Keep away from the foamy-mouth dog. The end.
Quote: "Fuck you, dog!"

SILVER BULLET (1985)
Werewolves terrorise smalltown America. Nothing else really happens to speak of.
Quote: "I hate you, you booger!"

MAXIMUM OVERDRIVE (1986)
Based on King's 'Night Shift' short story, 'Trucks'. Lorries and machines come to life. King directed it himself – very badly.
Quote: "This machine just called me an asshole!"

GRAVEYARD SHIFT (1990)
Clammy mutant doings in the basement of a textile mill. Incredibly, it has pretensions to be a sort of inland *Jaws* – with rats.
Quote: "I don't mind telling you, this place is infested."

THE MANGLER (1995)
Laundry machine gets taste for blood. Death by folding! Other appliances go bad. This film contains a scene of two men having a fight with a fridge.
Quote: "Have you considered the possibility that the machine may be haunted?"

55

NEED TO KNOW

Year 1955
Running time 98 mins
Director Robert Aldrich
Stars Ralph Meeker, Albert Dekker, Paul Stewart, Gaby Rodgers
Buy it on Region 2
Tagline "Blood red kisses! White hot thrills! Mickey Spillane's latest H-bomb!"
Best line "First, you find a little thread, the little thread leads you to a string, and the string leads you to a rope, and from the rope you hang by the neck." – Velda
Critic's view "Here it is, the crime film of tomorrow." – Claude Chabrol
Best watched when... You're about to pick up a hitchhiker...

KISS ME DEADLY

Robert Aldrich's brutal masterpiece punches hard, fast and below the belt...

Night, dark as death. Out of the blackness a girl – terrified, barefoot, naked under a raincoat – running hell for leather down the centre strip of a two-lane blacktop, waving desperately at the oncoming headlights. She hurls herself in front of an open-top Jaguar that screeches to a halt, picks her up. As she gasps for breath, the credits come scrolling down the screen in reverse, top to bottom, like a sentence of doom, and on the car radio, Nat King Cole pours warm dark syrup into the night. Minutes later, the girl's been stripped and tortured to death with pliers while the fellow who gave her the ride – tough-guy PI Mike Hammer – is tipped over a cliff with her body to burn to death in his car.

From here on the punches just keep on coming. Aldrich wanted his movie "to depict my utter contempt and loathing... for the cynical, fascistic private eye, Mike Hammer". Freely adapted by Al Bezzerides from Mickey Spillane's sub-Chandleresque pulp novel, and centred round a sneering, charmless performance from Ralph Meeker, *Kiss Me Deadly* anchors itself in the deep-noir, paranoid world of the Cold War mid-'50s where the sex is loveless, corruption all-pervasive and no holds are barred in the pursuit of the Great Whatsit – a mysterious metal box that's hot to the touch and, when opened, emits a burning dazzle of light and hisses like 10,000 devils.

En route to the dénouement – a nuclear explosion in a Malibu beach-house, no less – Mike Hammer, the cultured sadist, reads Christina Rossetti sonnets, snaps treasured Caruso discs, fends off passes from pretty girls and casually brutalises damn near everyone he meets. Those he doesn't, the heavies dispose of. You start to wonder why everybody's so pleased to see this guy.

The whole film is permeated with anger and violence. Aldrich uses his camera like a weapon, assaulting us with bizarrely tilted shots, jagged cuts, overlapping staccato dialogue, hysteria boiling around the edges of the screen. Unexpected objects – a newsstand, a fence-rail – suddenly glare, unnaturally bright, out of the encroaching darkness. This is film noir by flashes of lightning. And in Gaby Rodgers' Lily Carver – short blonde gamine-crop, twitchy, helium-voice – it has just about the most improbable femme fatale in movie history.

Kiss Me Deadly was shot in less than three weeks. For years, poorly edited prints cut the movie short: as the wounded Mike struggles to get his secretary/lover Velda out of the beach house, we cut to outside as it goes up in a cataclysmic explosion. But more recently, prints have restored Aldrich's own ending: Mike and Velda watching from a distance as the Great Whatsit ignites the end of the world. When the film was released, the Kefauver Commission named it as the year's No. 1 menace to the morals of American youth. Aldrich took it as a compliment.
Philip Kemp

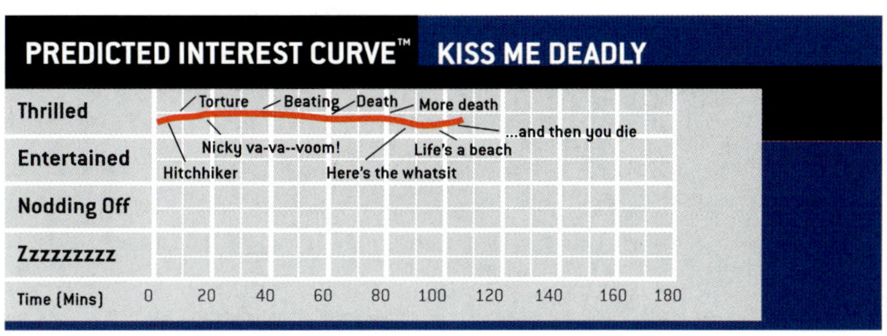

54

MILLER'S CROSSING

Gangland America as it never was – but maybe should have been...

"I'm talkin' about friendship. I'm talkin' about character. I'm talkin' about... Hell, Leo, I ain't embarrassed to use the word: ethics." So says Johnny Caspar (Jon Polito), rising Italian-American gang boss, to Leo O'Bannion (Albert Finney), ageing Irish-American crime-king of the city whose power is on the wane. It's a great line in a movie packed-to-bursting with great lines – well, this is the Coen brothers, after all – and what makes it even funnier and more telling is that we know that Johnny, as amoral and treacherous as anyone in his line of work, actually means what he's saying. Or imagines he does.

When and where are we? The brothers aren't saying, but think Prohibition-era Chicago or New Orleans and you won't be far out. But then this isn't a straight gangster movie (how many Coen movies are straight anything?) so much as a lovingly executed, ironic pastiche of all those classic gangster movies of the '30s, a rich, complex, dark, comic exploration into the heart of one of the most cherished of all American myths. The characters converse in a dazzlingly stylised, slang-ridden prose that's part invented, part resurrected from the novels and films of the period, making not the least pretence at realism. "I get you smart guy, I know what you are. Straight as a corkscrew. Mr Inside-Outsky. Like a goddamn bolshevik, picking up your orders from Yegg Central," says one gangster to his opposite number. For the poetry of sheer improbable gutter-baroque, *Miller's Crossing*'s only rival is Clifford Odets' dialogue for *Sweet Smell Of Success*.

A rich, complex, dark, comic exploration of the most cherished of American myths

But then, plausibility was never an issue here. In the film's funniest, most violent and most brilliantly choreographed scene, Leo is relaxing on his bed in his dressing-gown, listening to a record of 'Danny Boy', when a bunch of Caspar's goons arrive to rub him out. In one single practised movement, Leo dons his monogrammed slippers, slides under the bed, empties his revolver into the ankles of one of the hitmen, grabs his Thompson gun, exits via the bedroom window, guns down the second hitman as he appears at the window, then strides into the road and continues firing at the car in which the remaining goons are fleeing. The car swerves, crashes and bursts into flame. During all this, Leo's still in his dressing-gown and the glutinous old Irish ballad has played uninterrupted on the soundtrack.

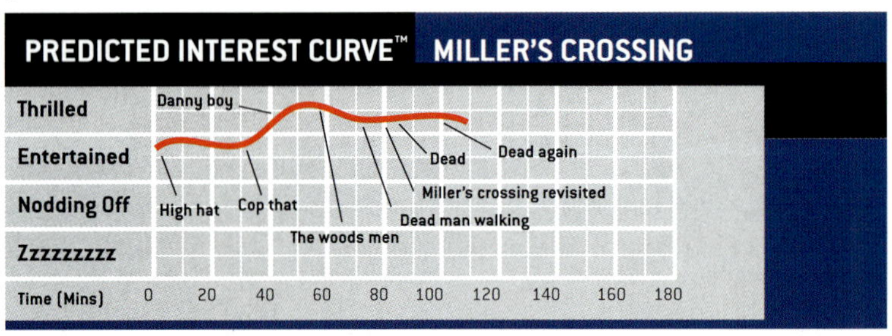

As Leo, Albert Finney throws himself into the role with unmistakable gusto, even though he wasn't the Coens' original choice for the role. (That was Trey Wilson, the tycoon from *Raising Arizona*, who died aged 43 two days before production started.) But Finney makes the role utterly his own. He's surrounded by

some of the finest of the Coens' personal stock company: John Turturro, Jon Polito, Steve Buscemi and, chilling as Caspar's henchman Eddie the Dane, the always-underrated JE Freeman. In a stunningly assured screen debut, Marcia Gay Harden plays Verna, the icy broad who comes between Leo and his adviser Tom Reagan (Gabriel Byrne). It's Tom who's the centre of the tangled plotline, where everybody's out to get an angle on everybody else and loyalty is just another chip on the poker table. "You double-cross once," muses the ill-fated Caspar, "where's it all end? An innaresting ethical question."

But then, as Tom notes, "Nobody knows anybody. Not that well." Certainly nobody knows Tom – and that includes us. Bitterly conscious of not only having some genuine residual code of ethics but of being one of the rare intelligent men in a society ruled by violence and short-term greed, he despises everybody around him (including Leo, for whom he feels a perverse protective loyalty) and despises himself for having sunk to their level. Byrne, with his lugubrious face and hooded, seen-it-all eyes, makes perfect casting – though he's one of the few actors who didn't love working with the Coens. Maybe because the plot has him getting beaten up about every five minutes. Even Verna takes a sock at him.

The picture looks beyond gorgeous – this is a fully-functioning fictional world, lovingly designed and lit with the gloss and rich depth of an old master. Every hand-crafted detail, both physical and verbal, glows – from the delirious slang ("What's the rumpus?" is the universal greeting, occasionally varied to "What's the disposish?") to the deftly over-stylised costumes. The much-loved Coen trademark – fat people screaming – makes its appearance. Oh, and then there's the hats. Fedora-style hats figure prominently in every scene – dropped, chased, stolen, retrieved, pulled low for menace, often awarded their own close-up. "What did the hat mean?" demanded the frustrated critics, but met with the brothers' usual teasing deadpan. "We wanted to make a movie about men in long coats wearing hats."

Philip Kemp

NEED TO KNOW

Year 1990
Running time 110 mins
Director Joel Coen
Stars Gabriel Byrne, Marcia Gay Harden, Albert Finney
Buy it on Region 2 SE
Tagline "Up is down, black is white, and nothing is what it seems."
Best line "I figure a thousand bucks is reasonable. So I want two." – Tom Reagan
Critic's view "It is likely to be most appreciated by movie lovers who will enjoy its resonance with films of the past. What it doesn't have is a narrative magnet to pull us through." – *Chicago Sun-Times*
Best watched when... You're wondering what's the rumpus.

53

THE DEER HUNTER

Cimino snubs 'Nam heroics to zoom in on the before-and-after effects…

Opening credits. A heartstopping little something plucked out by acoustic ace John Williams – 'Cavatina'. Its syrupy grace suggests a kind of softness – maybe schmaltz – to come. Title. *The Deer Hunter*. A story of star-crossed Southern folk? Trouble in Appalachian paradise? Not quite…

"This is this! This ain't something else. From now on, you're on your own" ROBERT DE NIRO

Before this, Michael Cimino's sole director credit had been a feisty Clint Eastwood/Jeff Bridges buddy pic, *Thunderbolt And Lightfoot*. For a more jarring shift of tone, you'd need a *Weekend At Bernie's/Schindler's List* double-bill.

Three years after the Vietnam war, *The Deer Hunter* went head to head with Hal Ashby's Jane Fonda-starring, anti-war *Coming Home*. 'Hanoi Jane' loathed *The Deer Hunter*'s arty, equivocal approach to an issue she saw as black and white and, according to Cimino, she called him a "fascist right-winger". With the opulent opera of Coppola's *Apocalypse Now* almost two years away, Cimino's film was the first to ignore the politics and focus on the personal.

There's no condemnation, or justification; it's a layered, lingering lament for a group of close friends forever fractured and dehumanised by their experiences of combat. Cimino milks his big idea of minimising scripted dialogue in favour of intimate, naturalistic exchanges (locker-room banter, beery horseplay, cultural quirks).

He pitched it over a one-hour meet with United Artists mogul Dino De Laurentis. "I had to do it verbally", says Cimino. "Because Dino didn't like to read." After firing his co-writers, Cimino took on the script himself. He seduced Method-man box-office-banker De Niro by touring him around Pennsylvania's steel towns, setting him up with lodgings in a real steel worker's house.

The film opens amid the steel mill's deafening, pyrotechnic fury: shimmering, spark-spewing rivers of molten lava illuminating the otherworldly visors of our hazard-suited heroes. It's a kind of hell; a teasing foreshadow of the battlefield's formalised chaos. Cimino then takes his time – around an hour – insinuating the audience into his characters' lives and loves, hopes and suspicions. During a lavish wedding party, we learn of their do-or-die companionship; the importance they invest in extended family; the swirling resentments and twitchy infidelities so easily reared up by barrel-loads of booze.

On a post-wedding hunting trip, we learn the pecking-order of the men's tight, blue-collar world: all hard work and rough play. Nick (Walken) is the thrusting, risk-addicted young buck who "never eats"; Steve (John Savage) is the sensitive guy, the mediator between the extreme personalities. Mike (De Niro) is the stag; the eldest and

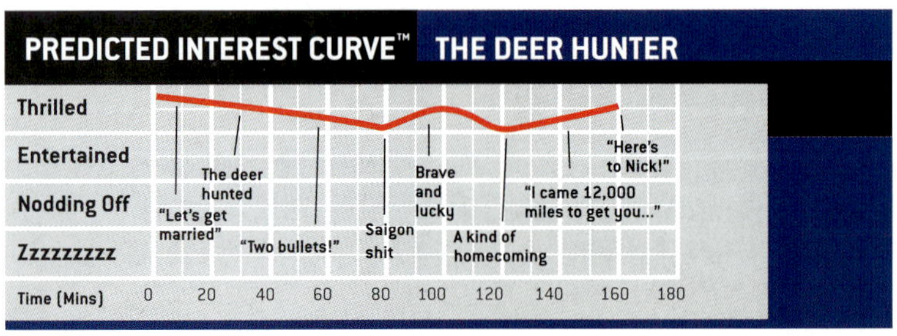

smartest who, with all three due to leave for their tour of duty, lectures about taking their last trip seriously: "This is this! This ain't something else. From now on, you're on your own."

After the trip, where Mike bags an elk with his focused and exacting "one shot" philosophy, Cimino cuts to a twilight bar scene and there, in the grip of a comedown, the group lapse into sozzled reverie as Steve plays a mournful Chopin piano lament. This is both their point of exit and entry, as they prepare to shed one brand of uneasy camaraderie for another.

The notorious Russian Roulette sequence has been criticised for its sensationalist edge. (Nick and Mike pop the empty chambers while a traumatised Steve languishes in a rat-riddled, semi-submerged bamboo cage). But Cimino was aiming more for metaphor than conscientious historical precision. "How *do* you evoke the experience of combat?" he insists. "That is, the pure terror of waiting for random death? Russian Roulette has all the elements of battle boiled down."

After the highs of the opening sequences, Cimino lashes on a horrendous barrage of cruelty and carnage: women and children senselessly machine-gunned; pigs fighting over charred human remains; immolation by flamethrower. He insisted that, for the jungle sequences (shot in Bangkok), the actors should suffer a little, "I told them not to take a shower, not to change their uniforms, not to take a shave."

NEED TO KNOW

Year 1978
Running time 182 mins
Director Michael Cimino
Stars Robert De Niro, Christopher Walken, Meryl Streep, John Cazale, John Savage
Buy it on Region 2 SE
Tagline N/A
Best line "I feel a lot of distance. I feel far away." (Michael)
Critic's view "A heartbreakingly effective fictional machine that evokes the agony of the Vietnam time." – *Chicago Sun-Times*
Best watched when You're feeling angry and disjointed and you have three hours to kill.

Cimino presented a four-hour cut to EMI execs who insisted on test-screening a short (two hours) and long cut (just over three). He sabotaged the short version screening by having the projectionist burn the film and delay its replacement. The unsettled audience gave it a low score, and the long version prevailed.

The Deer Hunter is about as flawed as masterpieces get, but it has much to say about loyalty to companion and country, and how war – for whatever reason it was fought, whoever 'wins' – is bad for the soul. We came in with a wedding and we close on a funeral, soundtracked by the most irony-drenched, buried-resentment-loaded rendition of 'God Bless America'.

Andy Lowe

52

SULLIVAN'S TRAVELS

The Player? Bowfinger? Nah, Preston Sturges' Hollywood satire remains the one to beat...

Read all the film treatises about *Sullivan's Travels* and you'll likely come away with the wrong impression. According to the experts, you'll need to pay close attention to the European influences that Preston Sturges draws upon from his youth spent travelling abroad, and be sure to take in all those subtle messages about the human condition. Hokum. What makes this comedy a solid-gold, copper-bottomed classic – Sturges' best out of a crowded field that includes *The Lady Eve*, *The Palm Beach Story* and *Hail The Conquering Hero* – is that it's so damn witty. "I wrote *Sullivan's Travels* to satisfy an urge to tell [*my fellow directors*] that they were getting a little too deep-dish," said Sturges. "Leave the preaching to the preachers."

We get pratfalls, one-liners, Hollywood hedonism, murders... and a little sex.

Sturges' masterpiece opens with golden boy helmer John L Sullivan (Joel McCrea) – creator of *Ants In Your Pants Of 1939* – deciding to ditch the escapist piffle and make something worthy. He will make a difference. He will adapt breadline novel *O Brother, Where Art Thou?* ("I want this picture to be a... document," he says. "I want to hold up a mirror to life. I want this to be a picture of dignity... a true canvas of the suffering of humanity." "But with a little sex in it?" replies a fretting exec.)

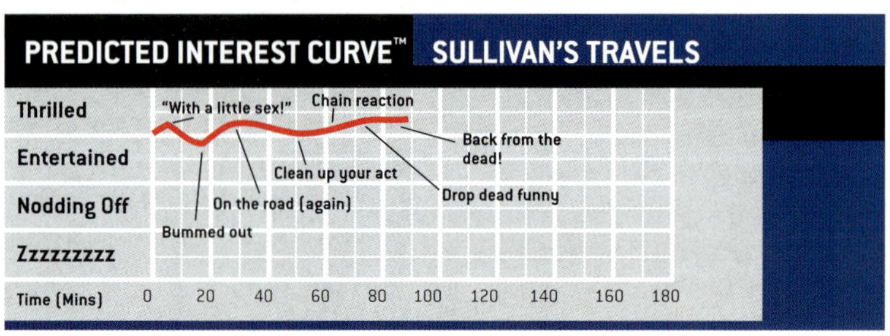

The studio heads would naturally prefer a sequel to *Ants...*, and cunningly point out that Sully knows nothing about poverty. Bad mistake, the pampered director setting off on the road as a penniless tramp to experience true hardship – with unforeseen events conspiring to put Sully, minus his memory, on skid row... and then in jail. How's that for research?

It's this embracing of real pain that makes *Travels* all the more funny. Unlike so many ho-hum comedies that hang on the most slender thread of conflict, afraid to nudge the audience out of the fuzzy comfort zone (think Charles Grodin wrangling an unruly, oversized St Bernard or Macaulay Culkin braining an unruly, undersized Joe Pesci), *Travels* understands that the deeper the torment, the more satisfying the laugh. Hence we get pratfalls, chain gangs, flophouses, one-liners, murder, Hollywood hedonism... and a little sex. All in the same movie.

The sex, of course, is courtesy of an iridescent Veronica Lake, here playing a wannabe actress who teams up with Sully on his travels. Credited simply as The Girl, her inclusion is one of the movies' many in-jokes: "There's always a girl in the story. What's the matter, don't you go to the movies?" says Sully when the suits beg him to work a little flesh into his social drama. Cue our nomadic hero picking up Lake at a roadside diner... and Sturges getting her to sportingly strip for a communal shower.

But if Lake provides the sex, it's McCrea who brings the heart. His is one of those

performances that critics often overlook because it's carried off with such lightness of touch – there's no grandstanding here for the Academy to cling onto. Look again, and you'll see just how much he brings to what could have been a thanklessly straight arrow role, part social conscience, part do-gooding rich boy. You'll also see that his comic timing is near-flawless: it's McCrea who often acts as Sturges' biting mouthpiece, giving vociferous voice to the director's growing frustration with the moviemaking system.

It's these performances bolted to a fiendishly intelligent, big-hearted script and Sturges' assured direction that allow *Travels* to walk its dangerous tightrope with such insouciance. Why dangerous? Because *Travels'* message ("There's a lot to be said for making people laugh") could have easily been as lightweight as *Ants...*, and the wordless sequences of the downtrodden poor could have smacked of ivory towered, bleeding-heart condescension. Luckily, Sturges is ahead of us: "I have never been sympathetic to the caricaturing of the poor and needy, sir," says Sully's butler as the helmer sets out. "Who's caricaturing? I'm going out on the road to find out what it's like to be poor and needy and then I'm going to make a picture about it," responds Sully. "If you'll permit me to say so, sir, the subject is not an interesting one. The poor know all about poverty and only the morbid rich would find that topic glamorous."

NEED TO KNOW

Year 1941
Running time 90 mins
Director Preston Sturges
Stars Joel McCrea, Veronica Lake, Robert Warwick
Buy it on Region 1 Criterion
Tagline "Veronica Lake's on the take."
Best line "There's a lot to be said for making people laugh. Did you know that's all some people have? It isn't much, but it's better than nothing in this cockeyed caravan" – John L Sullivan
Critic's view "A deftly sardonic apologia for Hollywood make-believe." – *The New York Times*
Best watched when... *Are We There Yet?* has numbed your funny bone and faith in humanity.

Sturges was reputed to be an all-round nice guy, popular with just about everyone in Hollywood. But he was also dedicated to his vision, willing to buck the system and stand his ground. It was this iron will that enabled him to strike out and pen his own scripts at a time when it was practically a commandment that you work in teams... and that meant he then had the guts to insist that he direct them. The first writer/director of the sound era, Sturges died in 1959 having won only one Oscar for screenwriting (*The Great McGinty*). Insanity. But that's the problem when you write comedies too innovative and too smart for the room: too few know exactly how to honour them.

Dennis Brabham

51

ALIENS

James Cameron sends Ripley on a bug hunt of the worst kind.

We're almost as surprised as they are at the extreme carnage inflicted on them...

Back in 1983, the later self-proclaimed king of the world was still an unknown, with *Piranha II: The Spawning* the only somewhat fishy directing credit on James Cameron's CV. His breakthrough feature, *The Terminator*, was only just entering the latter stages of pre-production, and it would be another year before Cameron and his cyborg-portraying star Arnold Schwarzenegger would stomp all over the big screen on their way to becoming two of the most significant movie players of the last quarter of a century. Yet *The Terminator*'s apocalyptic premise was enticing enough to bring Cameron to the attention of Walter Hill and David Giler, with the producing duo inviting him to pitch them future projects.

Once he was there, though, Cameron's pitches sank faster than the Titanic. But as he got up to leave the room, empty-handed and depressed, Giler interjected, "We do have something else." Dramatic pause. "It's a sequel to *Alien*." "Hmmm," replied Cameron, doing everything he could to stop his jaw from smacking into the office's plush carpet, "that sounds kind of interesting."

It was a once-in-a-lifetime offer which, following in the wake of *The Terminator*'s box-office rampage, would cement Cameron's reputation as the undisputed king of adrenaline-fuelled action cinema. He went straight to work, turning around a 40-page treatment for a ballistic sequel to Ridley Scott's 1979 sci-fi horror. Fortuitously, Cameron had his building blocks, adapting a script he'd already written called *Mother*, about an alien sneaking onboard a space station and wreaking merry havoc; all he had to do was drop in *Alien*'s sole survivor, Ellen Ripley (Sigourney Weaver), do a bit of nipping and tucking, and he was set. Suffice to say, his second encounter with Hill and Giler proved a lot more satisfactory. And so the 29-year-old Canadian, without a proven pedigree or any real box-office credentials, was hired as writer/director for the sequel to one of the most acclaimed sci-fi films of all time.

In what's now established Cameron style, the director fearlessly grabbed hold of the project and made it his own – made it, in fact, brasher, ballsier, and, yes, better than Scott's deliberately-paced psychological horror. Yet Cameron was also respectful and, more importantly, shrewd enough to bridge the two films by riffing on Scott's cool, smoke-whisping style during the film's opening scene, in which a deep-space salvage team discover the hibernating Ripley in the Nostromo's escape pod. With the transition deftly dealt with, Cameron propels the audience into a full-on, xenomorph smackdown.

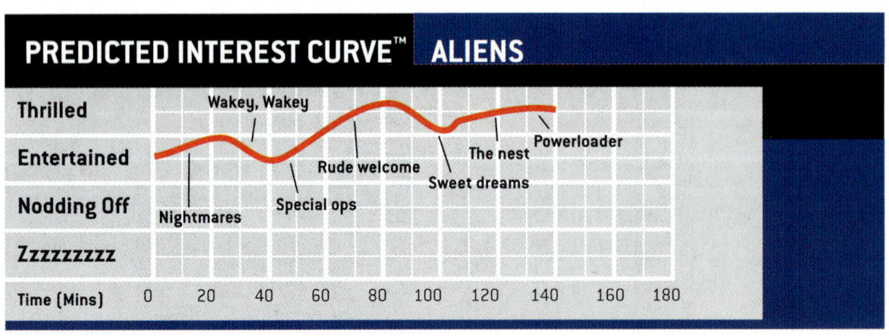

Cameron, a child of the '60s, drew on his own TV memories of Vietnam War broadcasts to create a comparative story about a technologically-advanced army getting their arses whipped by a determined and underestimated enemy.

Sensitively setting up Ripley's motivation for returning to the now-colonised LV-426 (the planet where John Hurt got up close'n'personal with the first face-hugger) – it's a chance for her to banish her nightmares and save the colonists, cleverly appealing to Weaver's own liberal sentiments – Cameron then surrounded her with a rabble of military grunts who the audience couldn't help rooting for.

Cocksure and gung-ho, but also immensely likeable, the Colonial Marines were a wise-cracking, swaggering, tooled-up bunch who were too cool for school – and Ripley. The fact that you knew they were about to go into gruesome battle with some extraterrestrial scum made them all the more appealing. But despite the ominous foreboding that these poor suckers (including *The Terminator*'s Michael Biehn and Bill Paxton) are in for one helluva scrap, we're almost as surprised as they are at the extreme carnage inflicted on them in the movie's first major set-piece, which results in half the platoon's computer-monitored vital signs suddenly flatlining.

Despite a mostly blistering 148-minute running time, Cameron still had 20th Century Fox execs griping about the first act's relative lack of action and apparent 'goofing around'. As is too often the case, the suits missed the point: the pacing was pitch perfect, Cameron lulling the audience into a false sense of security before the homicidal xenomorphs pounce. From that moment on, you're left in no doubt where the film is going: the tables have turned and the acid-blooded beasts are a far greater adversary than anyone, even Ripley, imagined.

It's easy to forget now, in an age where CGI offers filmmakers whatever they want, whenever they want and wherever they want it, that *Aliens'* special effects were not conjured by digital means. Genius (and Oscar-winning) monster maker Stan Winston was on hand to craft alien body suits with »

NEED TO KNOW

Year 1986
Running time 148 mins
Director James Cameron
Stars Sigourney Weaver, Michael Biehn, Bill Paxton, Lance Henriksen, Carrie Henn
Buy it on The Alien Quadrilogy Region 2 box set
Tagline *This time it's war*
Best line "That's it man, game over man, game over! What the fuck are we gonna do now?" – Private Hudson
Critic's view "I have never seen a movie that maintains such a pitch of intensity for so long" – *Chicago Sun-Times*
Best watched when... You want an action-flick that's more intelligent than *Predator* but no bullet-count compromise.

velcro attachments for the film's stuntmen, as well as provide animatronic puppets, models and miniatures, achieving a convincing level of realism that's one of the film's primary strengths. The power-loader that Ripley uses in her climactic clash with the Alien queen was constructed out of lightweight plastic, and housed a hefty stuntman supporting Weaver, while the drop ship was constructed out of a couple of model kits that Cameron 'Frankensteined' together.

It wasn't the only example of Cameron's passion driving the film – the scene in which the drop ship plummets from the Soluco and is buffeted violently by turbulence was achieved when the director literally wrestled with the camera as an operator tried to film. Cameron also had to ride out his own turbulence at Pinewood, where the majority of his inherited British crew were continually on the verge of mutiny. And lest he take all the credit, Weaver was justifiably nominated for a Best Actress Oscar, no small achievement considering the Academy is notoriously dismissive of the sci-fi genre.

After an intense 65-day shoot and a budget that passes for indie these days ($18 million), Cameron's *Aliens* script had made a triumphant transition from page to screen. As well as laying the foundations for Cameron's reputation, the film also bestowed 20th Century Fox with a solid box-office hit and gave birth to a highly lucrative franchise. The most impressive element, however, is that almost 20 years on, *Aliens* still stands the test of time, remaining one of the most exhilarating adventure rides in cinema history. If you haven't already, climb aboard Cameron's express elevator to hell... going down. TF

Scott Russon

REPEAT BUSINESS

Give your all to Cameron and he'll use you again and again and again...

LANCE HENRIKSEN
Worked on *Piranha II: The Spawning* (1981). The director had him in mind to play the Terminator; he was recast as a detective. Popped up as Bishop in *Aliens*.

BILL PAXTON
Met on *Battle Beyond The Stars*, where Bill was a carpenter. A bit part in *The Terminator* was followed by his career-making role as Private Hudson in *Aliens*, the deep-sea investigator role in *Titanic* and parts in *True Lies* and *Ghosts Of The Abyss*.

MICHAEL BIEHN
The hero in *The Terminator*, Biehn became Corporal Hicks in *Aliens* when James Remar was replaced due to "creative differences". Other Cameron films include *The Abyss* and *Terminator 2: Judgment Day*, with Biehn bitten on the hand in three of his four Cameron movies.

JENETTE GOLDSTEIN
Blue-eyed Goldstein played gun-toting Private Vasquez in *Aliens* (with brown contacts to help the Latino look). A role as John Connor's doomed foster mom in *T2* was followed by the gentile "Irish mommy" in *Titanic*.

50

NEED TO KNOW

Year 1934
Running time 105 mins
Director Frank Capra
Stars Clark Gable, Claudette Colbert, Roscoe Karns, Alan Hale, Jameson Thomas
Buy it on Region 1
Tagline "Together... for the first time!"
Best line "Excuse me lady, but that upon which you sit is mine!" – Peter Warne
Critic's view "Both leads play as if they really like their characters and therein lies much of the charm." – *Variety*
Best watched when... You're in love with someone who's out of your league.

IT HAPPENED ONE NIGHT

Get on the bus for the Frank Capra classic that redefined romantic comedy...

Stop us if you think you've seen this one before: a guy and a gal, emotional opposites, are thrown together on a wacky journey, during which their initial antagonism defrosts into sweet lurve. Oh, and one of 'em is engaged to a deadbeat the audience doesn't care about. It's the formula for a million movies, from *Bringing Up Baby* to *Forces Of Nature* to *The Honeymooners*. And it was minted right here, with the original – and still one of the very best – screwball comedies.

Spawning a sub-genre isn't the film's only contribution to the history books. *It Happened One Night* was the first flick to bag the top five Oscars (Picture, Director, Actor, Actress, Screenplay). Its success broke 'Poverty Row' studio Columbia into the Hollywood big leagues. Heck, thanks to Clark Gable's carrot-munching (and other character quirks), it even inspired Bugs Bunny. Not bad for a four-week, $325,000 production that suffered multiple casting headaches.

But ignore the legacy for a moment. Consider instead how this classic sleeper struck a chord with Depression-pummelled punters. They lapped up the idea of a spoiled runaway heiress (Claudette Colbert's Ellie) roughing it with a journo (Gable's razor-witted Peter) who teaches her to respect the coarser things in life, like dunking doughnuts and night-bus singalongs. Adapting from a *Cosmopolitan* article, helmer Frank Capra and scripter Robert Riskin crafted a touching, sincere fanfare for the common man that showed the soulful poor redeeming the spiritually impoverished rich.

Of course, all the class politics would have been for nowt if the leads' chemistry hadn't combusted as powerfully as it did. Legend may have it that Colbert sulked her way through the shoot, but on screen she has a blast, fighting, flirting and falling in love with Gable, whose rugged romantic persona hadn't shone like this before. The settings may be seedy and the supporting cast cartoonish, but this is a sexy picture, the horny highlight being Colbert's literally traffic-stopping show of leg in the hitchhiking scene. A firm believer in the power of suggestiveness, Capra mused, "There is more sex in a flash of pretty ankles than there is in a scene of a thousand bare legs; more allurement in what is not shown than in that which is crudely smeared on the screen to the point of nausea."

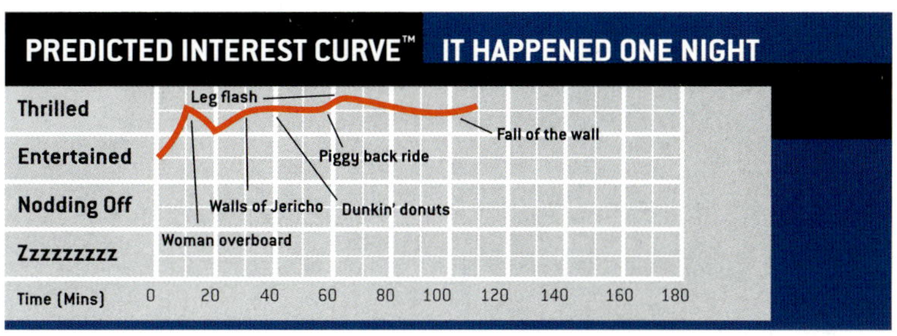

Mind you, blatantness and crudity were out of favour in 1934, the year Hollywood began rigorously kow-towing to the Production Code. It was a turning point for Capra too, the popularity of *It Happened One Night* knocking him sideways. "I didn't want to make any more pictures," he later confessed. "How could I top this?" But he did make more pictures, albeit darker, bleaker ones like *Meet John Doe* and *It's A Wonderful Life*. Sure, he was still able to warm cockles, but the films were more about screwed-up lives than screwball laughs. Sharp and sparkling, *It Happened One Night* was Frank Capra's lightest, brightest hour.
Matthew Leyland

49

PULP FICTION

Fatale femmes, killer lines, murderous motives. Let's twist again...

The plaster on the back of Marsellus Wallace's (Ving Rhames) neck is covering the scar where his soul was removed – the very soul sitting glowing in the briefcase that Jules (Samuel L Jackson) and Vincent (John Travolta) are sent to retrieve with deadly force...

Flips a cool middle-finger at the arthouse Euro-purists

Well, that's one of the many myths that has lingered ever since Tarantino's cinematic colonic of cool hit the screens in 1994. And it's a testament to the movie's immediate, enduring power that it inspires such fevered chatter to this day.

After his genre-redefining debut (*Reservoir Dogs*), the pressure was on QT to follow up with force. But there's nothing in *Pulp Fiction* to show that he felt any of the pressure, as he delivered a sizzling sophomore effort that easily matches, and at times surpasses, *Dogs'* impact. Never happier than when he's messing with our heads, QT takes us on a wild, chronology-fucking ride through several interlinked storylines: Jules and Vincent's quest for the suitcase and the various lowlifes they encounter along the way; Mob-ruled boxer Butch (Bruce Willis) choosing conscience over conspiracy in a fight-rigging scam – much to his boss Marsellus' dismay; opportunistic stick-up artists Pumpkin and Honey Bunny (Tim Roth and Amanda Plummer) who end up at the wrong end of Jules and Vincent's furious vegeance... And Mia, of course. Mia – wife of Marsellus, who spends an eventful evening with Vincent.

Caught your breath yet? On paper it seems utterly brain-blending, but Tarantino skilfully links the stories into a solid whole with a consistent grimy tone – something most old-handers would struggle with, let alone a young director under a mass of pressure to deliver his 'difficult' second.

As the post-*Reservoir Dogs* hype-storm died down, Tarantino took a six-month break in Amsterdam. Drugs? Sleaze? Countercultural milieu? "There was a Howard Hawks festival on," he says. Alternating between phoneless hotel room and favourite hash-bar (the 'Betty Boop'), he wrote the first draft of the *Pulp Fiction* script off an increasingly complex aim ("I wanted to write a crime anthology. But when I sat down, I saw there was much more gold there and it would be neat to have three separate stories, but have the same characters floating in and out.")

He sent the finished script to producer Danny DeVito ("I thought either it was brilliant or I was sick"). He'd written many of the characters with specific actors in mind (Jules for Jackson, The Wolf for Keitel, Pumpkin and Honey Bunny for Roth and Plummer). *Reservoir Dogs* fan Bruce Willis was brought in by Keitel and Tarantino personally selected Uma Thurman for the part of

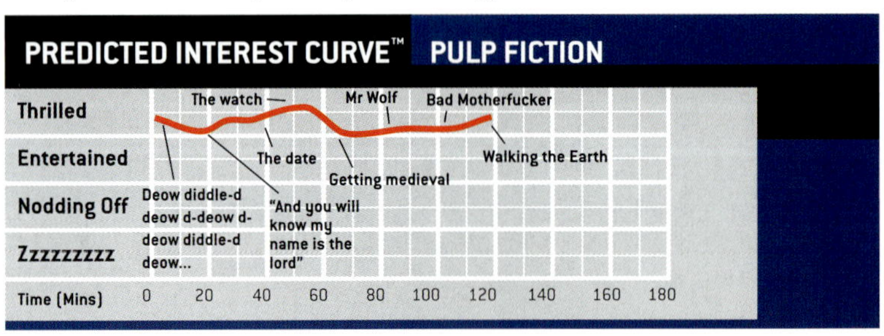

slinky moll Mia because she had really nice feet. He'd written smackhead hood Vincent for Michael Madsen, who dropped out to do, erm, *Wyatt Earp*. So he turned to one of his favourite actors, John Travolta, then in career freefall. Producer Lawrence Bender thought he was crazy. ("You can get anyone in the world. Why do you want John Travolta?")

But Tarantino wasn't just stunt casting. He was simply putting together a group of people he really wanted to work with and felt he knew well enough, through their movies, to get the best out of. And it worked. Jackson has never been better as the soulful hitman who finds religion. Travolta more than repays Tarantino's faith as the petulant, dope-smoking foot-massager who finds his ordered life suddenly falling apart around him when he's thrown off-balance by Mia (Thurman, funny and seductive). Willis is surprisingly layered, torn between career and life-limiting moves. And there's a truckload of superb supporting parts, from Roth and Plummer's soppy robbers to Harvey Keitel, all unspoken knife-edge and predatory politeness as "fixer" Mr Wolf.

Sure, it's sweary and violent, but it's also shot through with a keen humour that somehow blends perfectly with the blood and guts. So confident is the material that the tone shifts naturally from horror to laughter, often in the same scene. (Take Mia's half terrifying/half farcical adrenaline awakening). And how many modern films have aged so well that their language lives on, ten years later ("Bring out the gimp", "I'm gonna get medieval on your ass")? Well done, American Film Institute, for overlooking *Pulp Fiction* in its list of '100 Greatest Movie Quotes'.

NEED TO KNOW

Year 1994
Running time 154 mins
Director Quentin Tarantino
Stars John Travolta, Uma Thurman, Samuel L Jackson
Buy it on Region 1 LE (Limited Edition)
Tagline "Girls like me don't make invitations like this to just anyone!"
Best line "Pretty please. With sugar on top. Clean the fucking car!" – The Wolf (Harvey Keitel)
Critic's view "It's the movie equivalent of the novel where you check how many pages are left and hope there are more." – *San Francisco Chronicle*
Best watched when... You need to learn how to look good while being bad.

At Cannes 1994, the Euro-purists sneered at Tarantino and his vulgar entourage. He strode onstage to pick up the Palme d'Or to a chorus of hisses and catcalls. *Pulp Fiction* was an all-American film inspired by the arthouse – and the arthouse crowd didn't like it. Trophy in hand, he focused on the general direction of the jeers, held out an upturned fist and flipped up his middle finger.
James White

48

SINGIN' IN THE RAIN

Gene Kelly and Stanley Donen's effervescent, heart-soaring Hollywood hoofer...

Even if you've never seen this vibrant, postmodern musical, you'll intrinsically know the famous scene in which Gene Kelly twirls, splashes and grins his way down a sodden street, ebulliently crowing the title song, thanks to Morecambe and Wise, that VW advert or *A Clockwork Orange*'s dark subversion. Described by critic Peter Wollen in his BFI book as "the single most memorable dance number on film", it's a joyous piece of cinematic originality and verve that captures Kelly at his most twinkle-toed and charming. Not bad for a film that started out as a cynical studio ploy to bolt some of its old songs together and cash in on the public's hunger for glitzy Technicolor sensations.

MGM-contracted songwriter Arthur Freed originally put together a load of his '20s showtunes and hired writers to fit a story around them. The song 'Singin' In The Rain' had already cropped up in a number of previous flicks and was not initially conceived as a set-piece, but when Kelly (hot after his success with *On The Town* and *An American In Paris*) came on board, a routine sing-song picture became an innovative and glorious event movie loaded with breathtaking hoofing. It was so perfect a combination of song, dance and drama that it won the accolade of most popular movie musical of all time in a recent AFI poll.

In a case of art imitating life, *Singin' In The Rain*'s premise of a silent-movie idol desperately trying to keep a foothold on fame by adapting his latest film to sound mirrors Kelly's own determination to mould the project to his own advantage. No whippersnapper when he became a star and aware of his limited shelf-life, Kelly was a demanding perfectionist who reduced teenage co-star Debbie Reynolds to tears (she couldn't keep up with the dancing and ended up getting lessons from Fred Astaire). He also antagonised MGM honcho Louis B Mayer and bullishly imposed his creative ideas on the production – eventually taking a co-directing, choreographer and acting credit. But take a look at the film now and his vision is validated.

Kelly brought in physically dexterous dancer Donald O'Connor as his on-screen sidekick Cosmo and had clowning song 'Make 'Em Laugh' written for him to perform. In a world of *Matrix*-style CGI, it's still hard not to view his no-wires pratfalling, running up walls and somersaulting backwards as anything other than sheer, breathtaking magic (especially when you consider he twice hospitalised himself filming it). O'Connor also provides most of the film's funniest moments, his subtle timing balancing out

In a world of *Matrix*-style CG, the dance numbers still amaze

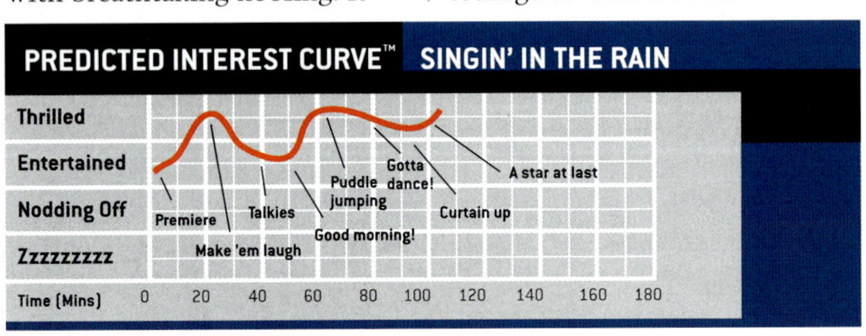

Kelly's propensity to mug. Kelly also had 'Broadway Melody' written and he choreographed everything in the stunning 15-minute dream sequence, from his own energetic whirling to the casting of Cyd Charisse as a long-legged moll. Big, bright and beautiful, this film-within-the-film shows off Kelly's inimitable dance style to perfection, his effortless-looking, manly, athletic moves the antithesis of Astaire's come-dancing pizzazz. It's that same elegant-but-butch quality that makes his rain-soaked title ditty so mesmerising. Despite struggling with a sky-high fever and a constantly shrinking suit under a milk-laced sprinkler system (it made the drops stand out on Technicolor), Kelly tangibly conveys the euphoria of romance with a balletic twirl around a lamppost, a sluice under a drainpipe and, most endearingly, his stamping about in a puddle. Only the hardest heart could fail to feel the love.

In a further postmodern blurring of fact and fiction, this sweet musical also demonstrates a dark wit in its view of Hollywood – a sort of precursor to *The Player*. "Almost everything in *Singin' In The Rain* springs from the truth. It is a conglomeration of bits of movie lore," Kelly said of lampooning contemporary stars, the power of gossip columns and the magic/deception of movies. Kelly's own films have the piss ripped out of them (the film his character, Don Lockwood, works on satirises his own flick *The Three Musketeers*), celebrity soundbites are revealed as a pack of lies and, in a film about a star's voice being dubbed to preserve the public view of her, Reynolds' own singing was dubbed by Betty Noyes.

Sharper than your average '50s musical, boasting dance numbers that would be hard to replicate today (even for you, Baz Luhrmann) and an ending so predictable but uplifting that it transcends corn, *Singin' In The Rain* is a triumph of creative perseverance over the studio factory system. And although he was awarded a special Oscar for choreography in *An American In Paris*, Kelly's awe-inspiring work here is testament to a one-off star at the very top of his game.

Jane Crowther

NEED TO KNOW

Year 1952
Running time 99 mins
Directors Gene Kelly, Stanley Donen
Stars Gene Kelly, Debbie Reynolds, Donald O'Connor
Buy it on Region 2 SE
Tagline "What a glorious feeling!"
Best line "I'm singin' in the rain..." – Don Lockwood
Critic's view "All the elements in this rainbow programme are carefully contrived and guaranteed to lift the dolors of winter and put you in a buttercup mood." – *The New York Times*
Best watched when... You're unappreciated at work and want a spring in your step.

47

BLADE RUNNER

Ridley Scott's future shock still looks like the most prescient sci-fi film ever made.

B*lade Runner* redefined people's idea of science fiction. Turning away from bright, glossy *Star Wars* utopias towards something grubbier, something evolutionary, something real, Ridley Scott's story of a weary "blade runner" hunting down escaped replicants (artificial humans used as slave labour) across a rainy futurescape now casts a huge shadow across books, comics and cinema.

But it wasn't always that way. After a torrid and expensive shoot, *Blade Runner* tanked on its first cinema release in 1982, taking, at the US box office, barely half what it cost to make. Critics were confounded. Even those, like *The New Yorker's* Pauline Kael, who admired the look of the film described it as cold and devoid of emotion. Warner Bros took the hint and yanked it from cinemas.

But from the jaws of defeat, *Blade Runner* snatched a strange victory – becoming one of the first films truly rescued from permanent obscurity thanks to the rise of video. Diehard fans watched it over and over again, picking out background details they might have overlooked. People who missed it (or just missed the point) could now discover it for themselves.

But the 1982 version wasn't the film Scott wanted to make. When the shoot went over budget, completion guarantee company Tandem stepped in and started meddling with the director's vision. Tandem orchestrated the hard-bitten noir voiceover, reluctantly spoken by Harrison Ford, and denied Scott the chance to shoot a sequence showing Roy Batty and the other replicants' original escape. Scott finished shooting the movie, but it was Tandem, responding to poor test screenings, that assembled the final cut. They removed sequences and even changed the ending, inserting an uplifting closing scene that showed Ford's Deckard and Sean Young's Rachael flying off into a pristine countryside (offcuts from Stanley Kubrick's *The Shining*) to live happily ever after. Scott despised it.

Fortunately, he got the last laugh. In 1992, Scott was able to release a new cut that was much closer to his original vision. The Director's Cut (then a new phenomenon) was based on workprints that Scott had prepared before the various test screenings and Tandem's recutting. It wasn't entirely how he'd envisaged the film – no reshooting was done, so none of the scenes axed for budgetary reasons appear – but it's close to his original plan.

Is it really the best version, though? Despite Scott's tinkering, lots of people still champion the original cut. We think his redux edges it. *Blade Runner DC* has all the best bits of the film we already know – the obsessive detail, the soaring imagination, the sheer poetry of

"All those moments will be lost in time, like tears in rain. Time to die" ROY BATTY

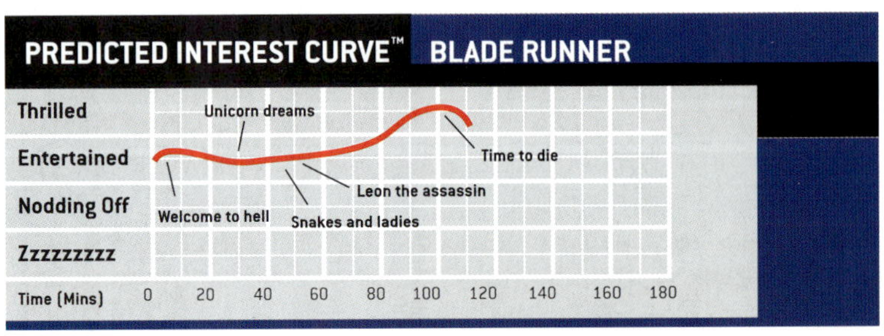

Roy Batty's demise – but adds something new: ambiguity. The result is a film that's darker, nastier and ultimately much more worrying.

There are three significant changes. Firstly, Ford's voiceover is largely dropped – he's now just part of the story, not the storyteller, and is less obviously sympathetic (you suddenly don't feel so inclined to forgive this trained killer). Second, the happy ending has been scrapped and replaced with the original, less conclusive finish. Third, there's the unicorn reverie...

The latter is certainly Scott's most contentious modification. Ford's character dreams of a unicorn and then finds an origami model of one left outside his apartment by fellow blade runner Gaff (Edward James Olmos). Coincidence or design? If design, how did Gaff know what Deckard dreamt? Is Deckard himself a replicant?

Scott's admitted that he fully intended audiences to realise Deckard was also an imitation human. It's obviously a key plot point that he never bothered to share with his cast, though. "We had agreed that he definitely was *not* a replicant," Harrison Ford has harrumphed since. Somehow, though, it only fits more neatly with *Blade Runner*'s themes of identity and what makes someone human that Ford was kept in the dark...

The first cut was a search for answers. The second just throws up more questions. Those backgrounds are as involving as ever, but now the story matches them in complexity. Once you've watched the Director's Cut, the 'original' 1982 version never quite seems grown-up enough any more.

With every year that passes, *Blade Runner*'s prescient vision creeps closer. Video phones and retina scanning are here already. Global warming? Ecological breakdown? That's why it always rains in *Blade Runner*'s 2019 Los Angeles. Huge corporations dominating the Earth? Think about that the next time you boot up your computer. And replicants? Well, one minute it's cloned sheep, the next it's Roy Batty watching C-beams glitter off the Tannhauser Gate.

Good sci-fi always tries to predict the future. Only the very best actually gets it right.

Ceri Thomas

NEED TO KNOW

Year 1982
Running time 116 mins
Director Ridley Scott
Stars Harrison Ford, Rutger Hauer, Sean Young, Edward James Olmos, Daryl Hannah
Buy it on Region 2SE.
Tagline "Man has made his match. Now it's his problem."
Best line "I've seen things you people wouldn't believe. Attack ships on fire off the shoulder of Orion. I watched C-beams glitter in the dark near the Tannhauser Gate. All those moments will be lost in time, like tears in rain. Time to die." – Roy Batty
Critic's view "Great in any version." – *Washington Post*
Best watched when... It's dark and rainy outside.

46

NASHVILLE

The master of multiple storylines delivers three sublime hours of music and menace...

It's often said that we're still awaiting the arrival of the Great American Novel. Perhaps so. But the closest thing we have to it, with all the scope, breadth, insight and formalist invention implied in that phrase, is a movie called *Nashville*. Nudging three hours, and with interweaving storylines distributed among 24 characters, the picture has an astonishing power and a deeply affecting compassion. It's the film that Paul Thomas Anderson – whose *Boogie Nights* and *Magnolia* would not have existed without *Nashville* – would kill to have made. It's the film that exposes the likes of *Love Actually*, *Playing By Heart* and *This Year's Love* for the bogus hack jobs they really are. And it's a testament to the blazing vision of Robert Altman, which shows little signs of dimming nearly 40 years on from his debut.

By the time *Nashville* was released in 1975, Altman, who began on TV shows like *Bonanza* and *Alfred Hitchcock Presents* but scored his first movie hit with *M*A*S*H* in 1970, was firmly established as one of the brightest lights in new American cinema. He may not have been part of the Movie Brats club that comprised the likes of Scorsese, Spielberg, Coppola and Lucas, nor did he display any of those directors' Hollywood aspirations. But the gems that he produced at a prolific rate in the early '70s assured his critical reputation (even if, after *M*A*S*H*, he didn't have another hit for two decades). He'd already made one masterpiece – the strung-out, opium-tinged 1971 Western *McCabe & Mrs Miller* – and the iconoclastic thriller *The Long Goodbye* among others when he began trying to raise the budget for the period crime drama *Thieves Like Us*. United Artists tried to interest him in making a movie in Nashville with Tom Jones; Altman passed on the Tom Jones part, but agreed to develop a Nashville-based project in exchange for the money for *Thieves Like Us*. He got his regular crew on board, including assistant director Alan Rudolph (later to become a fine auteur in his own right) and dispatched the screenwriter Joan Tewkesbury to Nashville to drum up script ideas. Her diary of the weeks she spent there formed the backbone for the picture. "I was sitting in the Exit Inn listening to a woman croon out a hopeless tune," she said. "There was a girl sitting next to me who had overdosed on something and another man telling me he just got out of jail. In the midst of these simultaneous events, it came to me that these elements were the making of a great movie."

Her instincts were right. On their own, any of the plotlines might have been diverting: the on-stage breakdown of country superstar Barbara Jean (Ronee Blakley), hired by election campaigners to play at a rally

It exposes other films for the hack jobs they really are

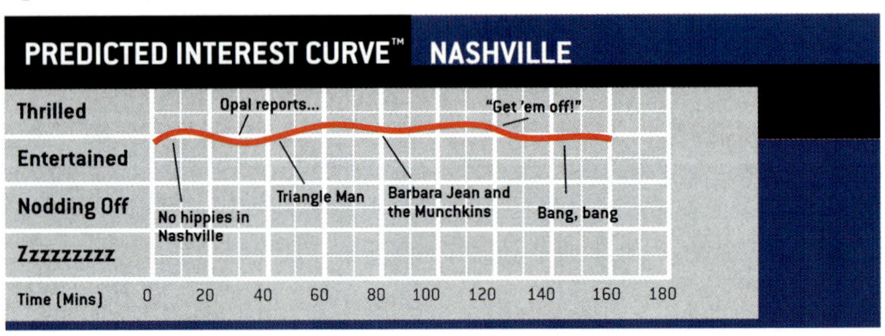

for an unseen Presidential candidate; the various attempts of dubious singer Sueleen Gay (Gwen Welles) to hit the big time; the tensions between folk trio members Bill, Mary & Tom (Allan Nicholls, Cristina Raines and Keith Carradine); the unwillingness of a lawyer (Ned Beatty) to relate to his deaf children; not to mention any of the misfits and hangers-on, played by the likes of Jeff Goldblum, Shelley Duvall and Scott Glenn. Woven together, peppered with songs written by the cast (including the Oscar-winning, Carradine-penned 'I'm Easy'), this stuff was dynamite. "They're little soap operas that aren't particularly extraordinary on their own," Altman observed. "They're common stories of ordinary people, but I show you such a mass of them that they comment on themselves."

The magic was in Altman's balancing of action and tone, his instinct for improvisation and his stunning use of sound: as is customary on an Altman film, every actor in every scene was miked, but no one was certain where the camera would place its emphasis. The director uses long lenses, slow zooms and tiny microphones to capture the details of every scene – details with which lesser filmmakers litter the cutting-room floor. He has no time for stars; even those actors who appear fleetingly as themselves – Julie Christie, Elliott Gould – arrive and depart without fanfare. And while the movie builds to a cataclysmic event, the real drama is in things half-glimpsed, minor tragedies that take place off the beaten track: Sueleen's striptease to a crowd of drunks, or Tom's string of empty conquests. "They're gonna kill you in this town," Sueleen is warned and, all at once, we realise that an atmosphere of menace has been whipped up amidst the sinister political wrangling.

Who knows what else would have been revealed had Altman got his way and reshaped the original movie as a six-hour marathon using material cut out first time round. Fact is, it's perfect the way it stands. Well, almost. Only BBC reporter Opal (Geraldine Chaplin) oversteps the line, becoming as irksome to us as she is to the characters. If only the assassin's bullet had been aimed at her...

Ryan Gilbey

NEED TO KNOW

Year 1975
Running time 160 mins
Director Robert Altman
Stars Karen Black, Henry Gibson, Lily Tomlin, Keith Carradine, Ronee Blakley
Buy it on Region 1
Tagline "The home of country music"
Best line "Y'all take it easy now. This isn't Dallas, it's Nashville! They can't do this to us here in Nashville!" – Haven
Critic's view "It's his masterpiece. He went beyond what others were doing. He had his finger on the pulse at that time." – *Entertainment Weekly*
Best watched when... You're considering a dramatic career change.

45

MEAN STREETS

How Scorsese, De Niro and Keitel became movie legends almost overnight...

Asked what he learned from mentor Roger Corman, Martin Scorsese fondly remembered his first meeting with the B-movie behemoth. "Roger took me to one side and said, 'Marty, you've got to get a good first reel because people want to know what's going on. Then you need a good last reel because people want to hear how it turns out. Everything else doesn't really matter.'"

Although he was fond of saying Corman's comment represented "the best sense I've heard", kicking around with him didn't do a great deal for Scorsese's career. Summoned to LA to bang out crime drama *Boxcar Bertha* for the mogul's company, AIP, Scorsese was so disappointed with the final result he became obsessed with the idea that he'd have to draw on his own life if his work was going to have any integrity. Keen to make a movie about Italian-American toughs growing up in New York, Corman promised to bankroll the picture provided Scorsese make one small alteration – turn the white boys into Afro-Americans.

Baulking at the chance to make an early Blaxploitation picture, Martin Scorsese took his first step on the journey that led to *Mean Streets*, the first of his great pictures.

A story of decent men trying to do good and bad men having to accept their fate

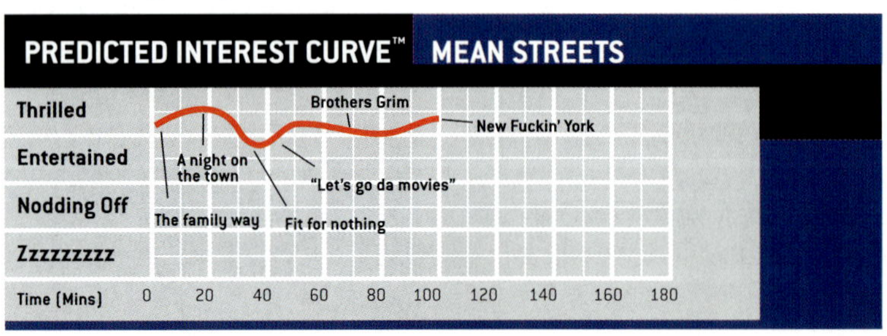

Indeed, even with *Taxi Driver*, *Raging Bull*, and *GoodFellas* to his name, there are many who still rewind to 1973 for their favourite Scorsese film. Far and away his most personal movie ("I knew these guys and many of them are still very good friends," he once said), *Mean Streets* is the film that reveals the forces that shaped the New Yorker both as a man and a filmmaker. And, by way of a bonus, it captures the moment when two actors became stars.

Now movie titans, it's easy to forget how inconsequential Robert De Niro and Harvey Keitel were when they made *Mean Streets*. But like three volatile elements, Marty, Bobby and Harvey proved an extraordinarily combustible combination when thrown together. "Working with Bobby and Harvey has been amongst the best experiences of my career," Scorsese would later remark. "And working on *Mean Streets*, when we were young and wanting to make our mark, well... it doesn't get better than that."

To look back at De Niro's Johnny Boy, a thug-cum-psycho who can't stay out of trouble, is to see the great actor create the first of those brutal, broken souls who somehow snag on the jagged part of our subconscious. Meanwhile, Keitel's Charlie Cappa – a Catholic boy whose life is blighted by his explosive best friend – is but the first of countless complex characters this performer viscerally brought to life. And with these two hugely talented actors at his disposal, Scorsese weaves

an amazing story of decent men fighting to do good and bad men reluctantly having to accept their fate.

Which all sounds pretty grim, but with a visionary director at the helm, *Mean Streets* whips along at a pace where, not only does it cease to be bleak, it becomes sublime. "I wanted to make my movie my way," explains Scorsese. "People kept saying, 'You can't do that', like in the drunk scene where we strapped the camera to Harvey. But I stuck to my guns." The upshot of his self-confidence are moments, such as when The Ronettes strike up as Keitel's head hits the pillow, where you go beyond watching a movie into experiencing cinema at its purest.

Shot largely in LA because of its miniscule budget, *Mean Streets* is an epic drama in miniature, its minor scraps elevated to major confrontations. It's also the film where Scorsese first got to grips with the politics of masculinity, a predominant theme throughout his career. Indeed, as his success and influence have grown, so the director has been given a more expansive canvas on which to pursue his favourite subject. However, while *Mean Streets* could've been bankrolled with *Gangs Of New York*'s catering budget, a boost in resources hasn't led to an increase in insight. "I wish I'd had the money to shoot for another 10 days on *Mean Streets*," he whinged while promoting *The Aviator*, unaware that what you don't have is sometimes more important than what you've got.

With hunger in general and a longing for recognition in particular key aspects of any young man's existence, it's no wonder that Scorsese was at the peak of his powers when he made *Mean Streets*. "There was a real burst of energy in making it," he says. "We had 26 days shooting mostly in LA, faking interiors for New York. A lot of stuff I couldn't get on screen but I like the music, I like the actors and it's a story that's very close to me."

That he never had more in common with his characters goes a long way to explaining why *Mean Streets* remains among Scorsese's finest contributions to da movies.

Richard Luck

NEED TO KNOW

Year 1973

Running time 107 mins

Director Martin Scorsese

Stars Robert De Niro, Harvey Keitel, David Proval

Buy it on Region 2 SE

Tagline "You don't make up for your sins in church. You do it in the streets..."

Best line "Twenty dollars! Let's go da movies!" – Johnny Boy

Critic's view "*Mean Streets* isn't so much a gangster movie as a perceptive, sympathetic, tragic story about how it is to grow up in a gangster environment."
– *Chicago Sun-Times*

Best watched when... You're wondering why you stick by that mate who's always landing you in trouble.

44

ANNIE HALL

Laugh, cry, then laugh some more at Woody Allen's breakthrough hit.

Comedy didn't begin with Woody Allen, but it wouldn't be what it is today without him. His influence has been everywhere for over two decades – it screams out at you from the work of Wes Anderson, Zach Braff, Edward Burns, Albert Brooks, Richard Curtis, the Farrelly Brothers, Neil LaBute, Whit Stillman, and on television, in everything from *Seinfeld* to *The Simpsons*, *Arrested Development* to *Sex And The City*. But let's get specific for a second. While Woody Allen has inspired countless writers, directors, actors and comedians, there is one of his movies in particular that can leave no viewer unaltered, untouched, unsmiling. That movie won four Oscars (for Picture, Actress, Director and Screenplay), introduced its own fashion sense and catchphrases, taught a generation of men to be charmingly self-deprecating and a generation of women to be adorably kooky, twisted cinematic conventions until they were gloriously misshapen, and ended up as the romantic comedy par excellence. *Annie Hall*, take a bow.

A lean, pithy comedy that can leave no viewer unaltered, untouched, unsmiling...

Ah, but here's a question: would Allen's sweet-and-sour 1977 masterpiece have figured on this list in its original form under its original title? *Annie Hall* started life as *Anhedonia*, after a condition that prevents the sufferer from experiencing happiness. Allen had planned the movie as a departure from his early, blissfully silly confections (including the goofball satire of *Bananas* and the sci-fi slapstick of *Sleeper*).

"I really feel it was a major turning point for me," he said later. "I had the courage to abandon clowning around and the safety of broad comedy." The first draft, co-written with Marshall Brickman, was a light-hearted thriller in which Alvy Singer and his girlfriend Annie Hall uncover a murder plot. But as Allen and Brickman wrote, Alvy and Annie's relationship proved fertile enough to be foregrounded, and the thriller idea was jettisoned (later to return in the 1993 cracker *Manhattan Murder Mystery*).

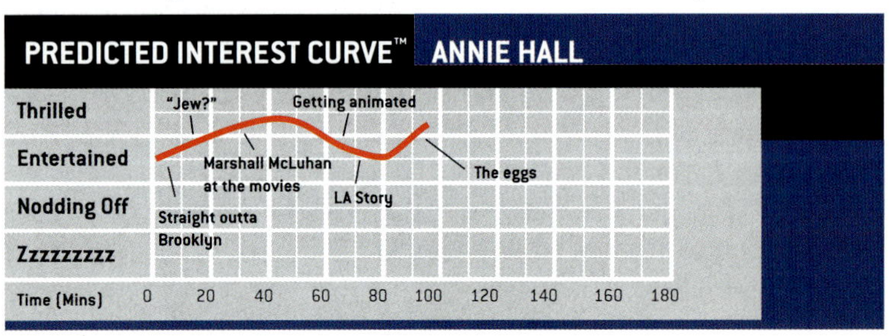

But this still wasn't the *Annie Hall* we adore today. The three-hour cut that Allen and his editor Ralph Rosenblum were faced with pruning was peppered with elaborate fantasy sequences taking in the Garden of Eden, Nazi headquarters, and an *Invasion Of The Body Snatchers*-style skit in which Alvy and Annie are almost replaced by pods during a visit to Los Angeles. But it soon became apparent that these digressions were impeding the central love story. Once Rosenblum had finished snipping, what was left was a lean, pithy comedy with a punch in every punchline.

The key to *Annie Hall*'s success is its authenticity. No matter how triumphant the

gags, or how daring the flights of fantasy, they would be nothing without the sparky double-act of Allen and his then-girlfriend Keaton (neé Hall; the movie is named after her). If you want a distillation of romantic chemistry, check out the scene when Annie calls Alvy out in the middle of the night to kill a spider; their scenes together exude a good-humoured warmth that shows just how manufactured most movie partnerships are.

Then there's the sheer breadth of the picture's imagination. The eclectic styles and techniques on display include voiceover, straight-to-camera monologues, stand-up and animation. There are flashbacks in which the modern characters mingle with their younger selves, split-screen sequences and subtitles that divulge Alvy and Annie's true thoughts. Most dramatically, there is no score. You either get it on its own terms, without a string section telling you when to shed a tear, or you don't get it at all. Despite the gentle nature of Allen's comedy, there is something confrontational about that refusal to toe the line; you can see it too in the unfussy white-on-black titles, and the melancholy that overwhelms the final scenes.

Woody Allen has arguably made even better movies – *The Purple Rose Of Cairo* and *Husbands And Wives* – but nothing he's done since has been as influential, or as ambitious, as *Annie Hall*. There are so many peerless scenes and much to cheer: the magnetism of Keaton, la-di-dahing all over the place in her waistcoats; Allen being gloriously self-righteous in a cinema queue and shaming the opinionated boor pontificating behind him; a cast including Shelley Duvall, Paul Simon, Carol Kane and glimpses of Jeff Goldblum, Christopher Walken and Sigourney Weaver; handsome photography by Gordon *Godfather* Willis.

Allen seemed embarrassed by the success, and chose to play his regular jazz gig rather than collect his Oscars. In recent years, he has even slighted the film, calling it a "reinforcement of middle-class values". Don't listen to him. If you've ever loved, lost or longed for anyone, you need *Annie Hall* in your life.
Ryan Gilbey

NEED TO KNOW

Year 1977
Running time 93 mins
Director Woody Allen
Stars Woody Allen, Diane Keaton, Tony Roberts, Carol Kane, Shelley Duvall
Buy it on Region 2
Tagline "A nervous romance"
Best line "My grammy never gave gifts. She was too busy getting raped by Cossacks." – Alvy
Critic's view "More superb gags in one minute than most movies manage in 90. It's like drinking champagne." – *The Guardian*
Best watched when You've fallen in love with a nerdy stand-up comic, or a woman who wears men's clothes.

43

HEAT

Michael Mann's concrete classic traps De Niro and Pacino in a city on fire...

A man walks through a hospital unnoticed and steals an ambulance. Another buys explosives from a builders' merchant. A third picks up a co-worker in a truck on the way to a job. Five minutes later, three other men lie dead in the wreckage of an armoured-car robbery. Three hours, two more robberies and at least half-a-dozen deaths later, two men from different sides of the law find themselves hunting each other down on the fringes of a Los Angeles landing strip... Welcome to *Heat*.

Michael Mann's über-crime thriller is an exercise in stripped down, frill-free, armour-piercing drama. A script he'd been sitting on for decades – he'd already used "40 percent of it" to make TV movie, *LA Takedown* – every sentence, every word, heck, every comma in *Heat* feels like it's been means tested to within an inch of its life. Despite being a movie whose most famous scene is a coffee-shop chat between a crook and a cop, this is a film where the silence – well, the ambient noise really, whether that's plates clattering or machine guns rattling – matters just as much as the words.

An armour-piercing drama where the silence matters as much as the words

That scene between Al Pacino's hyper-tight cop Vincent and Robert De Niro's disciplined robber Neil. It earns its place in Holly-history for having the two great men share the screen for the first time. It earns its place in the movie, though, for what you see, as much as what you hear. The dialogue is so good it's worth repeating – Vincent: "You do what you do and I do what I gotta do... if I'm there and I gotta put you away, I won't like it. But I tell you, if it's between you and some poor bastard whose wife you're gonna turn into a widow, brother, you are going down." Neil: "There is a flip side to that coin. What if you do got me boxed in and I gotta put you down? We've been face to face, yeah. But I will not hesitate. Not for a second."

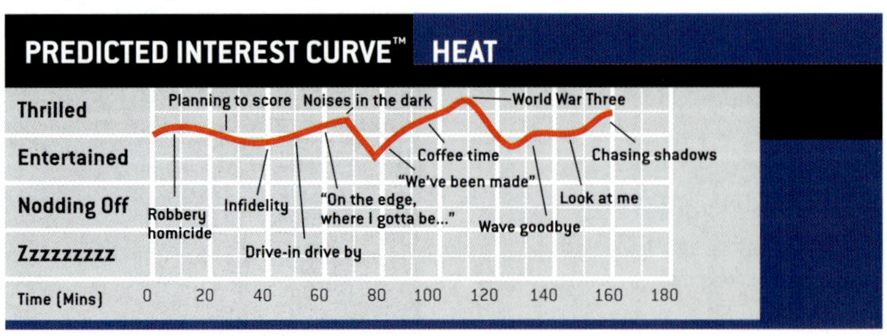

No doubt about it, this is a dynamite crystallisation of the mirror-imaging theme that sits at the chronological, emotional and narrative centre of the film. But the dialogue isn't what's really important. Watch the scene again. Look at their faces. Look at the way Mann holds on their features in the quiet moments between spiel. That's where the real conversation is happening – in the eyes, in the flickers of the face, in the tiniest of gestures. It's the best example, but just watch any moment and you'll get so much more out of *Heat* than just the words – the film is crammed with almost subliminal detail.

The crisp, deadly way Val Kilmer's Chris handles an automatic weapon, Hanna's instant understanding of a crime scene, the fact that Tom Sizemore's Michael makes time to smooth his hair down after leaving a robbery, Neil finishing checking a room is clear before he returns to the fatally injured

body of a buddy... these are the little, precisely observed things that allow Mann, a ceaseless perfectionist to rival Kubrick, to give *Heat* its absolute authority.

How many other films have well-staged robberies, impeccable surveillance scenes and huge, sprawling gunbattles? More than we have room to mention here. Mann knew that for *Heat* to be different, to be better, it had to feel real, almost documentarian – there could be no room for anyone to question the reality of what they were seeing. The cast visited Folsom prison to get a feel for convicts; famed US crook and author Eddie Bunker was hired as techinical consultant; and Mann went out with a policeman friend answering real-life crime calls. SAS veteran Andy McNab, meanwhile, was brought in to train everyone up in weapons and tactics. "He had us out on the range to learn to shoot guns," remembers Pacino. "I've done it before. But never with real bullets!" It paid off – few actors have ever looked as comfortable tooled up as *Heat*'s. Legend has it that footage of Kilmer changing a rifle clip in the middle of the bank robbery is now shown to marine recruits as part of basic training. It's that good.

All too often when people talk about Mann's Los Angeles films – *To Live And Die In LA*, most recently *Collateral* – the image that comes up is sleazy neon. *Heat*'s theme is concrete, though – the streets and freeways, the buildings being robbed, the houses the protagonists live and work in, the huge blocks Vincent and Neil shoot it out between... all hard, unforgiving, brutal, everyday concrete. Take it as a metaphor for the ties that bind the main players together and hold them apart or just accept that it's Mann rubbing audience noses in the reality of the film. Both work.

It's a movie with no breaks in concentration, no moments in its close-to-three-hour runtime that let you disengage. When the excitement comes, whether it's the tingling thrill of a sudden realisation or the ballsy adreno-rush of a shoot-out, you're there, on the street, on the rooftop, in the bank, holding the hand of a man you've just shot as his life ebbs away. Mann's never made a better film. The '90s produced no better thriller.

Ceri Thomas

NEED TO KNOW

Year 1995
Running time 164 mins
Director Michael Mann
Stars Al Pacino, Robert De Niro, Val Kilmer, Tom Sizemore, Diane Venora
Buy it on Region 2 SE
Tagline "An epic tale of crime and obsession and two men on opposite sides of the law."
Best line "Don't let yourself get attached to anything you are not willing to walk out on in 30 seconds flat if you feel the heat around the corner." – McCauley
Critic's view "Mann binds sound, music and pictures into one hypnotic triaxial cable and plugs it right into your brain. He makes this almost-three-hour experience practically glide by." – *Washington Post*
Best watched when... You've just got out of prison.

42

ONE FLEW OVER THE CUCKOO'S NEST

One flew East and one flew West... Jack Nicholson rages against the machine.

If you can experience the zither-themed finale of *One Flew Over The Cuckoo's Nest* without tears freshening your eyes you should consider whether cinema isn't a little wasted on you. There are few scenes, few films, as bittersweet and elevating; so inspiring, but without the self-conscious affectation that word often implies. It's an extraordinary end and a beautiful beginning: a stinging injustice and a hope for the future. In the death of one comes the birth of another. "Let's go," says Chief Bromden (Will Sampson) to the blank-eyed McMurphy (Jack Nicholson) and in this heart-breaking moment – emotionally draining the first time you see it – is redemption and a kind of resurrection. There is sorrow and rage and a sense of love.

It's hard to see past Jack Nicholson, so perfect is his performance...

The book, based in part on author Ken Kesey's experiences working in a mental institution, was published in 1962 and adapted for the stage a year later, with Kirk Douglas playing the rabble-rousing criminal committed to an insane asylum, Randle Patrick McMurphy (Gene Wilder played stuttering youngster Billy Bibbit, the role Brad Dourif would make his own on screen). Douglas was desperate to make it into a movie but couldn't get a studio interested in the transgressive material, with its foul-mouthed hero and anti-establishment tone. He did send a copy to a young Czech filmmaker he'd met, Milos Forman, and was frustrated not to hear back. Forman, in turn, was disappointed when nothing arrived from this American movie star. It turned out Czech customs had confiscated the book. Forman flew West after the Soviet crackdown of 1968 and received the book again, 10 years later, from Michael Douglas, who had taken over his father's quest and teamed with Saul Zaentz to try and get the movie made. They clicked. Douglas recalls he and Zaentz crying when they realised they had a director who shared their passion for the source. From a first draft by Lawrence Hauben, Bo Goldman and Forman reworked the material, always according to the director's mantra: "It must be real." The book was told from the perspective of Bromden, the apparently deaf/mute Indian, but the script discarded his internal monologue and the more hallucinatory passages (which featured a harvesting 'Combine' forcing everyone into conformity) in favour of a more conventionally unconventional narrative (Kesey, who had used the book royalties to become a counter-cultural icon with his acid-fuelled Merry Pranksters, as documented in Tom Wolf's extraordinary *The Electric Kool Aid Acid Test*, was furious at the change and refused to watch the film.) Casting was key for McMurphy. James Caan was offered, and turned down, the

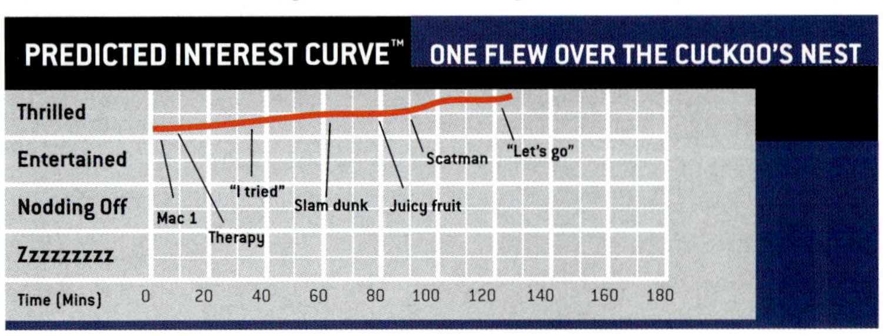

role. Marlon Brando and Gene Hackman were considered and Forman was keen on Burt Reynolds for his "cheap charisma". Then Douglas saw Nicholson in *The Last Detail* – Hal Ashby's brilliant road trip about two hard-assed sailors delivering an innocent youngster (Randy Quaid) to the stockade. "That was the first picture where you really felt the size of Jack," he later said, and it's true that after the Stoner lawyer of *Easy Rider* and the elegant wastrel of *Five Easy Pieces* here, finally, was a Man. Billy "Bad Ass" Buddusky is a proto McMurphy – except he shrugs and strolls on in the face of injustice, whereas Randle just can't give up.

It's hard to see past Nicholson in Cuckoo's Nest – so perfect is his performance. He's ferociously charismatic, but charisma has its pitfalls and the film would feel hollow if beneath the arched eyebrows and devilish/wolfish/shit-eating/pick your cliché grin there wasn't a deep sense of restlessness and longing and a man whose moral bearing will out. He is a catalyst and changes the inmates, for sure, but they ignite a change in him, or bring out his long-buried centre. He arrives a convict for statutory rape ("she told me she was 18") looking for an easy escape from hard time, a man driven by kicks and self-interest. Yet he can't ignore the struggles of those around him – the impotent Harding (William Redfield), needy Cheswick (Sydney Lassick), timid Billy – and will turn away from, at least, three chances to escape in favour of trying to help the inmates. There's much more to McMurphy than twisting the noggin of Nurse Ratched (Louise Fletcher), even though it's their clash of wills which propels the story. Fletcher, like Nicholson, landed the role only after others (including Anne Bancroft and Angela Lansbury) turned it down. And, like Nicholson, she is frighteningly good. It's a performance of incredible control. Where it would be easy to boil over, she simmers. And where a lesser actress might have made Ratched consciously evil – darting eyes and scheming beats – Fletcher is terrifying because of her sincerity. Ratched believes she is fighting the good fight »

NEED TO KNOW

Year 1975
Running time 128 mins
Director Milos Forman
Stars Jack Nicholson, Louise Fletcher, William Redfield, Sydney Lassick, Brad Dourif, Danny DeVito
Buy it on Region 2
Tagline N/A
Best line "Well, I tried, didn't I? Goddamnit, at least I did that." – Randle Patrick McMurphy
Critic's view "A film so good in so many of its parts that there's a temptation to forgive it when it goes wrong." – Roger Ebert, *Chicago Sun-Times*
Best watched when... You feel the world closing in and just want to get out.

(see Tony Blair for the most recent high-profile example of such well-intentioned psychosis).

For the inmates under her control Forman collated a group of deliberately contrasting kooks, from future-names such as Danny DeVito to rising character actor Redfield, who was dying from leukemia. The camera kept rolling and the actors were always "on", never sure where Haskell Wexler's lens was pointed. Despite being a 90 per cent interior film, it was shot on location at the Oregon State Hospital. By the end of production, some actors were sleeping in their characters' beds on location. Douglas became concerned that Lassick might actually be going cuckoo. Christopher Lloyd later recalled that anyone visiting "might have had difficulty deciding who were the inmates and who were the actors". Buildings can have a sadness and weight to them – Tim Robbins said as much about the real-life prison used in *The Shawshank Redemption* – and *Cuckoo's Nest* has the atmosphere of a place where sanity has worn thin. But if there's one thing the movie makes clear it's that this line is often rather blurred. Is 'Mac' mad for kicking and screaming against conformity? He's certainly living on the edge. But in our age of button-down politics and sound-bite morality, living there looks more appealing than ever. TF

Nev Pierce

CRAZY TALK

Cuckoo's Nest scribe Bo Goldman on his acclaimed adaptation...

"The nurse was never a problem for me because my mother-in-law was a nurse. You have to get a doctorate in the institution of Passive Aggression and then you create this frigid female who has tremendous sexual potency at the same time."

"How do you describe the Nicholsonian exuberance? That mad cackle which is giving the finger to the world? From the moment we're born we're enjoined to become part of a system and what are we on this Earth for except to invent ourselves? And McMurphy, in his criminality, in his madness and in his obsession, knows that better than anybody."

"The last scene between the Chief and McMurphy, I remember Saul saying, 'I think he's got to hug McMurphy.' I was concerned about the sentimentality of it and yet I remember putting down the stage direction – 'And then he embraces McMurphy' – and thinking, 'This is right, this is right.' But what was the Chief's last line? I couldn't find it and Milos said, 'What is it?' and I said, 'I think he wants to say, "Let's go!"' Milos said, 'That's it!' It's the best line I've ever written. It told the whole story. They were going to take a trip together; that one of them was going to be dead made no difference."

THE UK'S BEST-SELLING DVD MAGAZINE...

More reviews than any other monthly DVD magazine!

41

THE LAST PICTURE SHOW

Love, loss and longing. The end of an era in smalltown America...

"If that cocksucker isn't out of Texas by tonight, I'm going to borrow a hunting knife from one of these good ol' boys and kill him..."

Safe to say, Peter Bogdanovich was not enamoured of producer Stephen Friedman's visit to the set of *The Last Picture Show* – especially after Friedman had made comments to Cybill Shepherd about her performance.

But then, the director didn't seem too keen on anyone talking to Shepherd. As the actress noted in her ribald autobiography, "The joke on set was, if you want to get fired from the picture, talk to Cybill Shepherd." Whether this was the director protecting his star or just jealously coveting his soon-to-be-lover is difficult to know. Bogdanovich's wife Polly Platt was the film's set designer but an affair between Shepherd and the director began anyway. Bogdanovich and Platt would subsequently divorce and the director and his actress became, at least for a while, Hollywood's golden couple (until 1974's *Daisy Miller* and 1975's *At Long Last Love* proved critical and box-office disasters).

Technically excellent, beautifully paced and warmly informed by cinema's past

But none of this should distract from his achievement with *The Last Picture Show*, one of the finest films from Hollywood's most consistent decade. A former stage-director and film historian and writer, Bogdanovich got his directorial break working for king of the B-movie Roger Corman, where as well as cobbling together the forgettable *Voyage To The Planet Of The Prehistoric Women*, he made the rather better *Targets*. But *Picture Show* was his baby. Based on the elegiac novel of the same name by Larry McMurtry, the film follows the lives, loves and other frustrations of the small town folk of Anarene, Texas in the early '50s.

From the younger generation, there's high-school athlete Duane (Jeff Bridges), his quiet, serious friend Sonny (Timothy Bottoms) and the girl they will both love (or at least lust after), the wilful, trouble-seeking temptress Jacy (Shepherd). Older and wiser are ex-cowboy Sam 'The Lion' (Ben Johnson), neglected coach's wife Ruth (Cloris Leachman) and Jacy's mother Lois (Ellen Burstyn) a once-beautiful now lonely alcoholic.

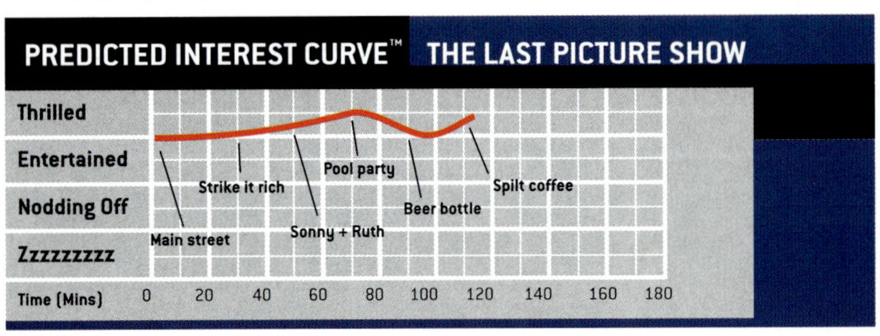

Over the course of a year, friendships break and are re-built, love rears its head and two deaths occur. Underpinning everything is the unrelenting march of time and the changes that come with 'progress'. It's a theme that's been touched on before, notably in Orson Welles' *The Magnificent Ambersons*, which tapped into how the arrival of the automobile marked the passing of an earlier way of life. But with *Picture Show*, television is the catalyst, the town's only picture house about to fall victim to the small screen's growing popularity. Bogdanovich had already struck up a friendship

with Welles (he would go on to author the excellent *This Is Orson Welles*) and, like *Ambersons*, *Picture Show* uses forthcoming change merely as a torch to shine light on a whole host of things that happened to America in the early '50s.

Anarene could be any small town in 1951, between two wars (World War Two and the Korean war); bemused by the world at large; the older generation out of touch with the cynicism of their offspring; a dying economy offering an apparently bleak tomorrow. The evocation of period is perfect. Clothes, styling, decor, music, all feel spot on. Bogdanovich chose to shoot in black and white because he felt it would be "less distracting" although Robert Surtees' crisp lensing is so beautifully evocative, it can easily turn the eye.

US critic Roger Ebert claimed the film was so accurate in its depiction of the era it was like watching "the best picture of 1951", although no film made then would have had the frank tone of Bogdanovich's work. The sexuality is raw. There's a '70s frankness to its depiction and a lack of sentimentality that simply didn't exist in the fifties.

Critics at the time also responded, hailing the director as a Wellsian wonder, while the film received eight Academy nominations (and two wins, for Cloris Leachman and Ben Johnson).

Some of the reaction is understandable. *Picture Show* is technically excellent, beautifully paced and warmly informed by cinema's past. There are blatant, affectionate nods to Howard Hawks' *Red River* and John Ford's *The Grapes Of Wrath* as well as Welles' *Citizen Kane*. Plus, for many critics, the film was evoking the very era they grew up in, when a visit to the local picture house was still a magical thing.

But to the modern audience, perhaps none of this matters. Take away the evocation of era and the film references and what are you left with? Well, actually, something still very special. A rich character study of youthful aspirations, middle-aged decline and pre-death wisdom, tenderly acted and totally engrossing. *The Last Picture Show* remains a beautiful and compelling study of the human condition.

Aubrey Ganguly

NEED TO KNOW

Year 1971
Running time 118 mins
Director Peter Bogdanovich
Stars Timothy Bottoms, Cybill Shepherd, Jeff Bridges, Cloris Leachman, Ellen Burstyn
Buy it on Region 2
Tagline "Anarene, Texas, 1951. Nothing much has changed."
Best line Sonny: "Coulda been worse" Sam: "You can say that about nearly everything, I guess."
Critic's view "*The Last Picture Show* is a great deal more complex than it might at first seem." – Roger Ebert
Best watched when... You feel the times they are a-changin'.

PERONI
ITALY

PERONI

PERONI
ITALY

peroniitaly.com

40

E.T. THE EXTRA-TERRESTRIAL

No phoned-in performances during this miraculous tale of intergalactic friendship.

There aren't many films that can make grown men cry every single time, but this magical exploration of lost innocence, love found and faith restored reliably reduces audiences to bawling tots during the final reel. Even hard-hearted critical maven Pauline Kael had to admit to being "enchanted" by Spielberg's life-affirming story of the friendship between an intergalactic turd and a small earth boy.

A director at the very pinnacle of his game, Spielberg managed to perfectly capture the freedom, discovery, imagination and trust of childhood. Who among us would not have risked everything for a friend like ET? How keenly can we remember being able to love so open-heartedly without worry of ridicule and hurt clouding the equation? And can't we all recall pedalling our BMXs as furiously as Elliot when he makes his escape from authority figures?

The story of a being from the heavens with otherworldly powers who unites people, inspires a group of loyal followers and goes through a resurrection thanks to love and faith, *ET* has been likened to a Christ allegory, a theory strongly denied by both Spielberg and screenwriter Melissa Matheson. To Spielberg, it was simply the story of an isolated, fatherless boy who finds friendship and understanding. "Perhaps *ET* was a subconscious fantasy of mine since childhood, to make myself feel less lonely in my life," he said, referring to his own father's departure from the Spielberg homestead. "It was a childhood dream of a special friend who rescues a boy from the sadness of divorce."

It's a snapshot of a sweeter age when children could run off for hours at a time

Thought up on the set of *Raiders Of The Lost Ark* and given life by Matheson, this kiddie movie rises above teeth-rotting sweetness thanks to the 'simpatico' team of talent involved. Spielberg, of course, demonstrated a canny ability to channel his inner ankle-biter, shooting most scenes from waist-level, a child's eye view. Industry pioneers ILM delivered the kind of special effects not seen since, well, *Close Encounters Of The Third Kind.* And John Barry's soaring score ensures viewers' hearts take off to accompany Elliot and ET on their iconic bike flight.

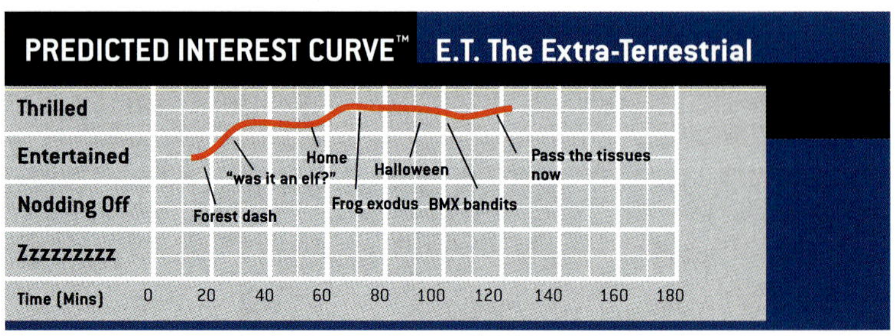

But the soul of the film is Thomas, who almost didn't make the cut after cocking up his initial audition with Spielberg. Thankfully he got another chance to convince The Beard, winning him over by making him weep as he recalled his dead dog.

Watch *ET* again and you'll notice that it's the wide-eyed nipper, even more than Drew Barrymore's terrifically cute younger sister Gertie or the eponymous lump of putty, who makes the film utterly convincing. It's his veracity

that suspends disbelief as Elliot facilitates ET's journey home via infantile cunning, good will and dogmatic optimism. It's his wobbling bottom lip and agonizing yelping as ET's life is threatened that has us accepting a rubbery puppet as worthy of our emotions. And it's the single tear rolling down his stricken face in the climactic farewell that shatters our hearts, now as then.

Thomas' performance, like those of the rest of the spot-on kiddie cast, is aided tremendously by Spielberg's astute decision to shoot most of the film in sequence. This allowed the kids to grow into their roles and to respond to events as they unfolded with real conviction, culminating in an outpouring of genuine sorrow, as they shot the tearful goodbye on their last day.

Spielberg also allowed his cast to improvise and filmed rehearsals to retain the freshness of their performances. The heartwarming result made *ET* the biggest film of all time (until that infernal ship sank) and spawned a rash of boy-befriends-alien/robot copycats.

Although ET continues to be a touchstone to new and old fans, it's also a capsule movie that perhaps wouldn't be made with the same naivety today. Viewed now, it looks like an artefact from an era of national wealth and post-'70s optimism; it's a snapshot of a sweeter age when children could run off for hours at a time, safe in the knowledge that the scariest thing they could find watching them in the garden shed was a grey alien with Albert Einstein eyes. To wit Spielberg's PC, tinker for the 25th anniversary re-release. Guns and the word 'terrorist' have been excised because bad things CAN happen. Now Spielberg's aliens are the community-destroying, unforgiving and horrifying creatures that stride through *War Of The Worlds*.

To watch *ET* is not only to celebrate and miss our own innocent past but also to lament the loss of our collective innocence and reaffirm our belief that goodness does exist. As Spielberg himself admits: "I think that *ET* is for the people we are, the people we have been, and the people we want to be again."

Jane Crowther

NEED TO KNOW

Year 1982
Running time 115mins (original) 120mins (re-release)
Director Steven Spielberg
Stars Henry Thomas, Drew Barrymore, Dee Wallace, Robert MacNaughton, Peter Coyote
Buy it on Region 2 SE
Tagline "He is afraid. He is alone. He is three million light years from home."
Best line: "I'll believe in you all my life" – Elliot
Critic's view "The most moving science-fiction movie ever made on earth." – Pauline Kael, *The New Yorker*
Best watched when... You've missed your last plane home and don't speak the lingo.

39

MONTY PYTHON AND THE HOLY GRAIL

History goes hysterical as the Python lads launch their first feature...

Why exactly does *The Holy Grail* work so well? Money. As in, the Pythons didn't have a lot of it. Which meant they applied a fearsome collective intelligence and talent for comedy that spanned many levels at full power to overcome the budgetary obstacles. The grimy, low-rent look of the costumes and props even helped, as it established the film's world as a vital, real, dirty, bloody medieval place, where peasants are covered in mud and armour is rusty, dented or both. Plus, while we're always hearing that directors don't have the cash to realise the true glory of their "vision", sometimes a good kick up the wallet is necessary to spark the fires of genius. So it is with *Holy Grail*, an achievement in comedy that still sparkles today. Ask yourself: how many of today's comedies will be remembered with such vigour? Or can claim so many utterly quoteworthy and instantly recognisable lines? And the final, true test: how many movies made in the '70s have locations that fans still flock to?

Songs, satire and lobbed scimitars – it's an embarrassment of comedy riches

Star Wars, you say? You'll never find a *Star Wars* location where the owners hand out coconuts so the faithful can recreate their own "horse"-riding madness. Yet *Grail* has Doune Castle, where you can find exactly that.

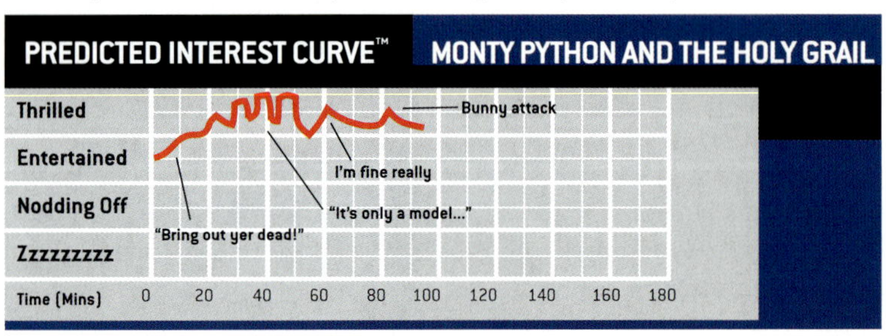

Ah yes, the coconuts... Yet another symbol of how the film's chronically British low budget (estimated at around £229,000) pushed the team to the hilt in their writing. With coconuts for horses (though one real nag does show up as the mount ridden by the knight who beheads the historian early on), and knitted wool sprayed silver for chainmail, the look of *Holy Grail* is strictly DIY, while the comedy is an embarrassment of riches. The film's laughs derive from the sort of humour that history students dream of perpetrating upon dry, dull myths and legends, with the added bonus that it's being written and performed by the Python team. Using Graham Chapman as the straight man plays brilliantly on the typical "hero" type, the stiff upper-lipped sort who rides obliviously though such fantasy lands. Today, putting Chapman in that role seems like a no-brainer, his dry expression and deadpan delivery perfect for King Arthur. But don't forget that back then it fell more on the brain-pain side, as Chapman battled alcoholism, forgot swathes of dialogue and continually panicked that he was screwing it up for everyone else.

He didn't. And what remains is still considered – alongside *Life Of Brian* – to be the Pythons' strongest excursion on to celluloid. Breaking free of their sketch-show roots, *Grail* is a much more mature (if such a word can be applied to the film) beast: one of the greatest comedies ever put on screen. And while the two

Terrys — Gilliam and Jones — would spark so much tension that they refused to ever share directing duties again, the final result bears no obvious scars from their fragmenting on-set relationship. Gilliam's insane animations perfectly complement the live action, adding million-dollar sparkle to the film while costing a fraction of that. Thanks to the American Python, the team were bringing comedy visions of God to the screen long before the likes of *The Simpsons*. And with the face of classic cricketer WG Grace, no less, whose beardy countenance is a weirdly perfect fit for the role.

Cartoon deities fit easily into a plot that manages to kitchen-sink-in just about every form of gag. Broad farce is heavily and happily represented (the Black Knight's mocking, soon-to-be-limbless taunting) but this is not just a showcase for the wacky. Subtle satire can be seen in the moments where "reality" (or at least some semblance of it) interrupts the flow of the film — or, in the case of the abrupt finale, brings it screeching to a halt. And who can forget Eric Idle's long, memorable diatribe that deconstructs several layers of government even as you're chuckling over such phrases as "moistened bint" and "lobbed a scimitar" as Arthur tries to assert his Excalibur-given right to rule over the "Britons"? Witty word-play and some stellar song-writing ("Brave Sir Robin!") also contribute.

NEED TO KNOW

Year 1975
Running time 91 mins
Directors Terry Gilliam, Terry Jones
Stars Graham Chapman, John Cleese, Eric Idle, Michael Palin, Terry Gilliam, Terry Jones
Buy it on Region 2 boxset
Tagline "Makes *Ben-Hur* look like an epic!"
Best line "I blow my nose at you, so-called 'Arthur King,' you and all your silly English K-nig-hts!"
Critic's view "Performed in whimsical fashion with Graham Chapman an effective straight man as King Arthur." – *Variety*
Best watched when...
You need to accurately quote Arthurian legend, but couldn't give a monkey's about research.

Arthur and his "ke-nikkets" search for the mystical Grail, the team manages to send up the legend, courtly love, fidelity, bravery, costume movies, movie violence and ornithology. You might have watched the likes of *The Naked Gun* and been impressed by the comedy credits, but this is where they were perfected, years ahead of their time. For all the craziness up on screen, you're always aware that there's a blazing brain-trust behind it, the team honing and crafting the jokes until they shine. Or in the case of the peasants, pouring on the mud until they, er, don't shine.

Grail's legacy lives on today, if only because the team behind it occasionally find themselves a bit short of cash. The story has been turned into more >>

than one computer game and those well-loved lines have filtered down through our culture, popping up in the most unlikely places. *Grail* devotees can drink Holy Ail (with the "Gr" handily crossed out on the bottle) and there is even a huge Broadway musical based on the story – *Spamalot* – as written by Eric Idle, which attracted no lesser name than Mike Nichols to direct it on the stage. You don't see anyone planning a *Taxi Driver* musical anytime soon (profuse apologies to anyone reading this who might be planning a *Taxi Driver* musical anytime soon).

So watch it. Then watch it again. And again. And again. And if this is your first time on the quest, don't blame us if you follow the path of your elders and end up quoting the lines ad infinitum. But most of all, please remember: it's only a model... TF

James White

APED CRUSADERS

The Pythons talk *Grail*...

GILLIAM ON THE STYLE
"We approached *Grail* as seriously as Pasolini did. We were watching the Pasolini films a lot at that time because he had to be able to capture a place and period in a very simple but really effective way."

JONES ON THE FANS
"I think very, very intelligent, beautiful people probably get it better. Hardcore fans are extremely intelligent and very, very beautiful."

CLEESE ON THE WORK
"Because we were shooting out of doors, we finished when it got dark. I used to go back, shower, go into this restaurant and eat really well."

PALIN ON HARDSHIPS
"I had this huge helmet on and I remember complaining that no one could see my face. I could barely see the camera."

IDLE ON THE FOLLOWING
"Ten- and 11-year-olds love *The Holy Grail*. I would have thought that you wouldn't get into that until you were 16 or 17."

38

NEED TO KNOW

Year 1973
Running time 94 mins
Director Terrence Malick
Stars Martin Sheen, Sissy Spacek, Warren Oates, Alan Vint
Buy it on Region 2
Tagline "In 1959, a lot of people were killing time. Kit and Holly were killing people..."
Best line "Before we left, he shot a football that he considered excess baggage." – Holly
Critic's view "Movies about banal people are often banal... *Badlands* does not escape this pitfall." – *San Francisco Examiner*
Best watched when Your girl's dad takes a dislike to you.

BADLANDS

Dream meets nightmare as homicidal kids go on the lam...

Two young lovers, armed and on the run. Been there, done that, from Fritz Lang's *You Only Live Once* through Nick Ray's *They Live By Night*, Arthur Penn's *Bonnie And Clyde* and Robert Altman's *Thieves Like Us*... What could a 30-year-old tyro director and ex-philosophy prof with a $335,000 budget do that those impressive forerunners hadn't?

Plenty, actually. Using the Starkweather-Fugate killings of the late '50s as his starting point, Terrence Malick takes his chosen genre off into dreamlike, uncharted territory, heightening the sense of unreality with gracenotes of surreal humour.

Kicking off in 1959 Nowheresville, South Dakota, where 25-year-old garbageman Kit Carruthers meets 15-year-old Holly Sargis and initiates her into sex ("What was everyone talkin' about?" is her underwhelmed reaction), the deluded pair take off northward, heading for the Canadian border where Kit reckons he'll be welcomed into the Mounties. En route, he guns down anyone who looks like impeding their progress, through landscapes of ethereal beauty that reflect the couple's dysfunctional amorality.

But Malick's stroke of genius is his use of voiceover. Events are presented to us from two counterpointed angles: what we see on screen and via Holly's ingenuous diary entries. Her flat, detached narration veers from *Huckleberry Finn* to *True Romance*, with the latter predominating. "Better to spend a week with one who loved me than years of loneliness," she notes, soon after Kit has shot her father (Warren Oates). "He wanted to die with me and I dreamed of being lost forever in his arms."

This straightfaced dissociation pervades the dialogue, with comments inadequate to events. At one point the pair hole up with Cato (Ramon Bieri), a colleague of Kit's. Suspecting Cato's planning to turn them in, Kit shoots him. "How's he doing?" enquires Holly. "I got him in the stomach." "Is he upset?" "He didn't say anything about it." Holly, wishing to make amends for any impoliteness, goes over and has a chat with the dying Cato about his pet spider.

Sissy Spacek plays the teenage Holly with wide-eyed, note-perfect blankness and Martin Sheen (then 33) gives a career-making performance as Kit, tirelessly back-combing his James Dean quiff and, when captured, posing for pictures as befits a true folk hero. Malick himself shows up in a tiny role as an inopportune caller. Not a Hitchcockian gesture, simply that "we didn't have enough money to fly someone in."

Never apologise, never explain. Malick gives us no hint of any psychological or sociological reason why these two kids are the way they are. Nothing so crude as a 'society is to blame' rant ruffles the ironic surface of *Badlands*. Erik Satie piano pieces and Carl Orff's music decorate the limpid soundtrack. Cool, coherent and utterly assured, this is a debut film of rare mastery.

Philip Kemp

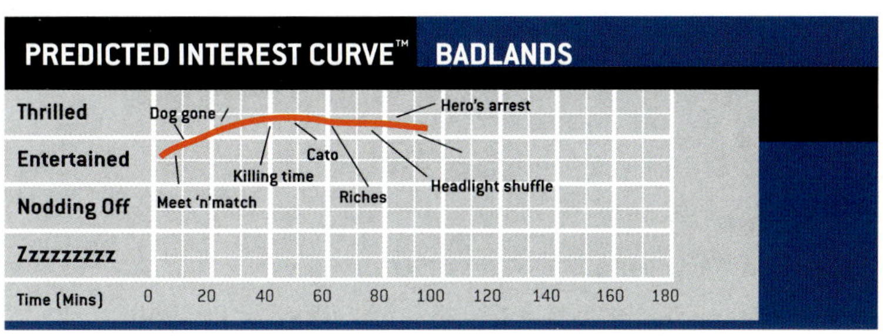

37

TOUCH OF EVIL

Orson Welles holds his hand over the flame for the classic noir era's curtain call...

There's more to *Touch Of Evil* than a three-minute tracking shot. But then, there's a lot more to *Evil*'s opening than a mere opening shot, too. In this sequence, Orson Welles condenses much about what is to come, about the between-states fever-dream we're about to dive into. In the Mexican border town of Los Robles, we switch between a honeymooning couple, Susan (Janet Leigh) and the Mexican cop Vargas (Charlton Heston), and the build-up to a car-bomb murder. The shot both maps out the lie of the land and cranks up the confusion. Welles uses a wide-angle lens to muddy clarity by emphasising every conflicting element in the frame, leading us to search for connections where there may not be any. Instead, it's fate that sucks Susan and Vargas into the murder investigation and links danger and eroticism via a kiss and an explosion. The shot is like a blueprint of the movie: bravura in the way that it eschews cause-and-effect information for something with a more dreamlike pull.

Dazzling as it has always been, the shot wasn't even seen in its full glory for many years. For *Evil*'s original release, against Welles' wishes, Universal laid the titles and Henry Mancini's score over Welles' orchestration of chaos. The director's disorienting, deep-focus photography and use of sound to evoke context were obscured. Sure, Welles described the film as "unimaginably pleasurable to make". Universal's input, though, left him "heartbroken", not least because *Evil* opened on the bottom half of a double bill. The film marked the end of the "classic noir" era, but it also marked the end of Welles' Hollywood career.

Little wonder, then, that Tim Burton's *Ed Wood* had a Welles imitator bemoaning his fate at the studios' hands. But Wood toys with the truth a tad. Burton's Welles said, "They want Charlton Heston as a Mexican." In fact, Heston starred in *Evil* because he wanted Welles (already cast as the grotesque 'tec Hank Quinlan) to direct and rewrite the script.

That might have been Chuck's best-ever move, even if Welles reworked Paul Monash's script without reading the Whit Masterson novel, *Badge Of Evil*, on which it is based. Arrogant? Sure, but *Evil* wouldn't be *Evil* without Welles's over-reaching direction. Nor would it be what it is without his over-reaching Quinlan, a US cop in Los Robles who tussles with Vargas about whose territory the murder took place in. Like Welles as a director, but with monstrous consequences, Quinlan takes risks: he gets his man by intuition and cooks evidence to do so. Vargas wants to go by the book, though, and quell Quinlan's corruption while he's at it...

"Touch Of Evil was unimaginably pleasurable to make..." Orson Welles

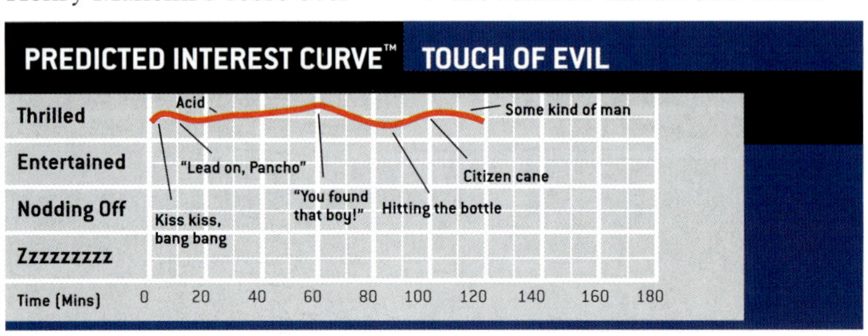

Welles works a devilish, dark character-study into this premise, one rank with themes of racism, corruption, perversity – and, possibly, pre-emptive autobiography. In a sense, Quinlan is no less a warped self-portrait than Welles' earlier Charles Foster Kane. All three (star and characters) are brilliant over-reachers; to paraphrase Marlene Dietrich's fortune-teller Tanya in *Evil*, all some kind of men.

A lot of men, in fact. Having lost his wife to a murderer ("The last killer who ever got out of my hands") years before the film, Quinlan has turned to alcohol and then food. "It's either the candy or the hooch," he says of his oral hits, which play like a man trying to replace something lost. Giving in to his lewd appetites, Welles sports padding to play the bloated, infantile, insolent Quinlan; the actor padded out for real later. When Tanya tells Quinlan that his future is used up, we wonder if Welles knew his Hollywood time was running out. A portrait of a character struggling to scrabble out of the hole he's in, *Evil* is the work of a director going for broke, gaining much of its standing by playing as a pulp tragedy on-screen and a great talent's last stand off-screen.

As Vargas' investigations plunge Quinlan into a dark downward spiral, he leaves Susan unprotected. Big mistake: Susan is attacked on Quinlan's orders and it's now that the rhyming scheme of fatalism set up between Quinlan and Vargas truly stings. Vicious machinations click into gear and find their parallel in Welles' stylisations. Echoing images suggest an entirely filmic world whose logic is all its own but no less palpably brutal for it.

You feel almost stained by *Evil* because Welles' wide-angle photography lures us in, makes us peer into the depths of the film's neo-gothic squalor. Its close, clammy heat of corruption and sadism becomes immersive, playing like a fever-dream as it builds the sense of a waking nightmare on its bordertown setting and chafing mix of good and evil, civilisation and animalism. Almost hot and heaving with night-sweats, you don't just see or hear *Evil*. It's so deeply felt, you can almost touch it.

Kevin Harley

NEED TO KNOW

Year 1958
Running time 112 mins
Director: Orson Welles
Stars Charlton Heston, Janet Leigh, Orson Welles, Joseph Calleia, Akim Tamiroff
Buy it on Region 2 SE
Tagline "The strangest vengeance ever planned!"
Best lines: "He was some kind of a man. What does it matter what you say about people? Adios!" – Tanya
Critic's view "A flat-out all-cylinders-running, eye-popping masterpiece, one of a few monumental '50s swan songs." – *Chicago Reader*
Best watched when... You're on honeymoon.

36

2001: A SPACE ODYSSEY

Stanley Kubrick tackles life, the universe – and an evil computer called HAL...

From flying femur to gliding spacecraft. It's all in that one infamous cut. Four million years of world history lost in the gap between two frames of celluloid. The most audacious edit in the history of cinema? Perhaps. We're nearly 30 minutes into *2001: A Space Odyssey* and visionary director Stanley Kubrick, in a cinematic sleight of hand worthy of Sergei Eisenstein himself, has delivered a brash match-cut that casually sandwiches an angry bone-swinging apeman with a slow-moving nuclear satellite. In doing so, he says more about the concurrent progress and symbiotic connections between civilisation, technology and violence than could be achieved in a hundred conventional narratives or a thousand academic treatises. "There is no document of civilisation that is not a document of barbarism," said the great German-Jewish post-modernist philosopher Walter Benjamin, just before he overdosed on morphine in 1940. "Too right!" says Kubrick's film.

Quite simply, the film that saved sci-fi from the annals of B-movie ignominy

The cut itself boldly sets the tone for the rest of the movie – which is all about inferring meaning and context, and teasing out subtext. Thus from the graceful satellite sequence we move to the moon, where a shiny black monolith is sending radio waves to Jupiter. There, 18 months later, mission commander Dave Bowman (Keir Dullea) will battle malfunctioning super-computer HAL (Douglas Rain), fly through a psychedelic interstellar wormhole and eventually land in a strange, white room, only to find his own ancient doppelgänger lying in bed in front of another large black monolith. Go figure...

"If you understood *2001* completely, we failed," said co-writer Arthur C Clarke at the time. "We wanted to raise far more questions than we answered." Which is precisely why the movie remains infuriatingly intriguing to this very day. For while other Kubrickian classics, like *Lolita* and *Barry Lyndon*, have not fared well with the passing of time (the former too tame, the latter too camp), *2001* is relentlessly renewable, as fresh and alarmingly recalcitrant as it was on 6 April 1968 – released, appropriately, on the eve of riots and revolutions. It's a film that refuses to give up its secrets, and instead somehow continues to engage with the ever-changing interests of the day.

Hence today, in our globally aware corporate-bashing age, it's impossible not to be struck by the amount of product placement in the movie. *2001* is the first example of mainstream studio-produced all-out branded entertainment. In 1965, in a ploy that would later be aped by Spielberg (*Minority Report*) and Michael Bay (*The Island*), Kubrick held

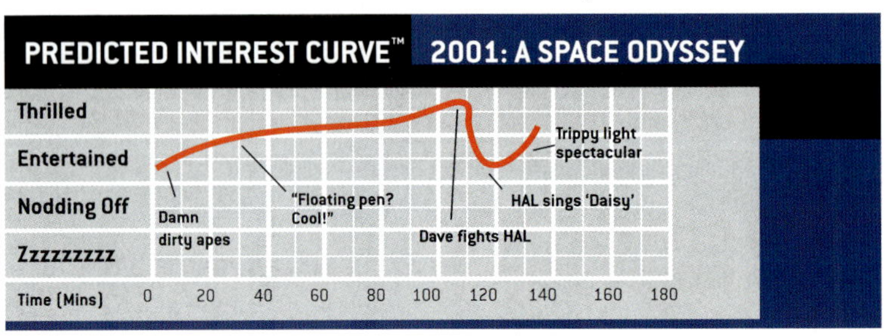

a pre-production meeting with the brightest forward thinkers form NASA, Pan Am, Whirlpool, RCA, Hilton Hotels and Bell (now AT&T) to brainstorm future concepts for his movie. This key meeting resulted in the movie's video phones, zero-gravity toilets and moon-based hotels, plus a wealth of lavish plugs for too many brands to mention here.

And yet, typically with Kubrick and especially with the mercurial reality of *2001*, there is always subtext. This is not branding for branding's sake. Instead, the concept of invasive corporate sponsorship further reinforces the movie's dominant thematic concern – that the messy business of human intimacy has been completely eradicated by technological advancement and the sterile tyranny of 'civilisation' (as epitomised in the banality of the conversations in the movie, the politeness of exchanges, and the supremely courteous HAL). As such, Kubrick is ahead of his time, at the forefront of an anti-corporate critique that pitches anonymous global companies against the emotional freedom of humankind.

Elsewhere, beyond narrative ambiguities and sprawling thematics, Kubrick's main concern is the movie's breathtaking visual style. For Kubrick and Clarke, this was to be the prestige production that saved sci-fi from the annals of B-movie ignominy. Consequently they had no qualms about spending $6.5 million of the movie's hefty $10 million price-tag, plus two long years of post-production time, on special effects. What they achieved was not just the salvation of a disreputable genre, but the beginnings of an entirely new perspective on special effects and sci-fi realism. No longer were spaceships condemned to look like yoghurt pots in tinfoil, no longer did special effects scenes have to occupy a subordinate position in movie narratives. Instead what Kubrick did – ironically, with this slow meditative movie on the mind-melding nature of human existence – was to usher in the age of thrilling visual spectacle and the era of the jaw-plummeting special effects movie. Step forward, *Star Wars*...

Patrick Donovan

NEED TO KNOW

Year 1968
Running time 149 mins
Director Stanley Kubrick
Stars Keir Dullea, Gary Lockwood, Daniel Richter, Leonard Rossiter, Margaret Tyzack
But it on Region 2 SE
Tagline "An epic drama of adventure and exploration."
Best line "Look Dave, I can see that you're really upset about this." – HAL
Critic's view "Will someone tell me what the hell this is about?" – Rock Hudson, at the premiere.
Best watched when... Experimenting with Class-A drugs (or if you're bored by *The Island*).

35

A MATTER OF LIFE AND DEATH

Powell and Pressburger's sublime fantasy climbs the stairway to Heaven...

At six decades removed, it seems the most unlikely way for any movie to get greenlit. In 1944, as World War Two lurched towards its atomic finale, Anglo-American relations were severely strained. The Ministry of Information thought a propaganda picture might help foster understanding. An unpromising beginning morphed into the most surprising outcome: the Ministry found themselves presented with an extravagant fantasy of love transcending the laws of the universe itself.

But what do you expect when you hand the job to the writing/directing/producing team of Michael Powell and Emeric Pressburger, then in the middle of an astonishing purple patch that also gave the world *Black Narcissus* and *The Red Shoes*?

Urbane Hungarian émigré Pressburger, the scribbler of the two, was fascinated by the true-life tale of an RAF airman falling from his plane without a parachute... and surviving. The story chimed strongly with his idea that a script "should have a little bit of magic". "Magic being untouchable and very difficult to cast, you can't deal with it at all," Pressburger later reflected. "You can only try to prepare some nests, hoping that a little bit of magic will slide into them."

"It was Michael's favourite film – he could be a magician with it" THELMA SCHOONMAKER

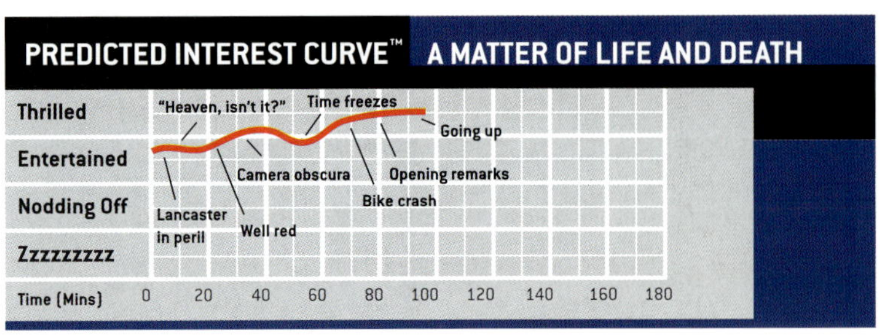

For *A Matter Of Life And Death*, Pressburger's nesting encompassed a giant staircase ascending to the stars, a trial in Heaven over whether a man might remain on Earth and the outrageous proposition that two souls – David Niven's RAF pilot Peter and Kim Hunter's American radio operator June – could find love together without even meeting in person. "I love you, June," says Peter over the air before he jumps to apparently certain death from his burning Lancaster. "You're life and I'm leaving you."

But even a writer who cultivated magic was positively restrained in comparison to his partner, director Michael Powell, a showman who revelled in any opportunity for big-screen visual trickery. *Life And Death* afforded ample chances for such flourishes. His cohort as cinematographer was the endlessly inventive Jack Cardiff, handed the break of his life when he was chosen.

At times in his career, Powell went over the top; in *Life And Death*, however, Powell gets the balance between ambition and excess just right, perhaps because he identified so closely with the material, subsequently claiming it was his favourite among his films.

Thelma Schoonmaker, Powell's widow and Martin Scorsese's film editor, has also said it was the movie that came closest to showing her husband's true personality. "Living with him," Schoonmaker reflected, "I found he had no fear of death. 'Love is sacrifice and sacrifice is love,' he used to

say. The real reason it was his favourite was he could be a magician with it. He could create Heaven and Earth and stop time."

And what a Heaven. The raw statistics of the trial scene alone show off the scale of the film. The backcloth of the court scene, suggesting a near-infinite number of spectators, measured 350 feet long and 40 feet high. More than 5,000 extras were employed. Elsewhere, the huge escalator linking Heaven and Earth, and built by engineers of the London Passenger Transport Board in the delightfully monikered Operation Ethel, had 106 steps, each 20 feet wide.

This was big-budget cinema in thrall to MGM-style spectacle, spectacular enough to be chosen for the inaugural Royal Film Command Performance. And yet, at a time when the studio system had still to buckle because of competition from television, it's impossible to imagine it having been made in Hollywood. It's too unsentimental, for all its boy-meets-girl central premise. Compare *Life And Death* to *It's A Wonderful Life*, also from 1946, and it's arguable that Frank Capra had to sugar the pill that little bit more to sneak through similar wit and invention.

Look again at the movie's opening scene, a glimpse at the vastness of space. A star explodes and the narrator makes a gag about the atomic bomb – used, remember, just the previous year against Japan. Throughout, Pressburger puts in dangerously barbed lines. "One is starved for Technicolor up there," sighs Conductor 71, the angel who failed to usher Peter into monochrome Heaven, a thinly veiled reference to post-war abstinence. It may have Tinseltown production values, but Pressburger's sensibilities subvert the surface gloss.

No wonder those movie brats of the '70s, Scorsese and Coppola, championed Powell and Pressburger. Trying to create a new kind of Hollywood cinema, they were instinctively drawn to a duo whose work referenced Tinseltown without being constrained by it. Or, maybe like the rest of us, they noticed all this later, long after they'd been captivated by a beautiful, beguiling love story conjured by men at the absolute peak of their creativity.

Jonathan Wright

NEED TO KNOW

Year 1946
Running time 104 mins
Directors Michael Powell and Emeric Pressburger
Stars David Niven, Kim Hunter, Roger Livesey
Buy it on Region 2
Tagline "The Greatest Adventure A Man Ever Lived!"
Best line "A weak mind isn't strong enough to hurt itself. Stupidity has saved many a man from going mad." – Doctor Frank Reeves
Critic's view "Like other P&P pictures, the striving to appear intellectual is much too apparent." – *Variety*
Best watched when... You think you'll never fly cos you'd die if something went wrong.

34

THE SEARCHERS

Savagery and salvation in Wayne's world: the most provocative Western ever made...

It's as significant as puberty – the moment you discovered ambiguity in film

From the thrilling pages of Life rides a man you must fear and respect, a man whose unconquerable will and boundless determination carved a lusty, rough and boisterous slice of history called *The Searchers*. It's John Wayne as Ethan Edwards, who had a rare kind of courage, the courage that simply keeps on and on, far beyond all reasonable endurance, never thinking of himself as martyred, never thinking of himself as brave. Here is the story of a man, hard and relentless, tender and passionate, a people who dared to challenge a hostile land. Here is drama of great love and aching loneliness."

The trailer for John Ford's 115th feature tries hard to make Wayne the hero. It has to. He may have been the biggest star in the world but it's hard to imagine an audience busting a block if the voiceover had intoned, "From the warped history of America rides a racist bigot, a bigot who desires his brother's wife, racially abuses his adopted nephew and plans to shoot his niece; a bigot whose thirst for revenge and boundless brutality carved a troubling slice of cinema called *The Searchers*." The trailer's real clue to the character of Ethan is "beyond all reasonable endurance". He can't stop: he is powered by hate.

If you're under 40, it's almost certain the first time you saw *The Searchers* was on television. Chances are you were young. Perhaps John Wayne was your favourite actor and watching the hard-but-fair hero of *Rio Bravo* or *Rio Grande* was a weekend or holiday regular; an entertainment which also played a part in divining your moral barometer and understanding what it meant to be a man (a more pertinent supposition if, of course, reading this, you *are* a man). The film would have been confusing – aren't we supposed to *like* John Wayne? Watch *The Searchers* early enough in life and it's an event as significant and mysterious as the stirrings of puberty. It's the moment you discover ambiguity in cinema. There's no going back.

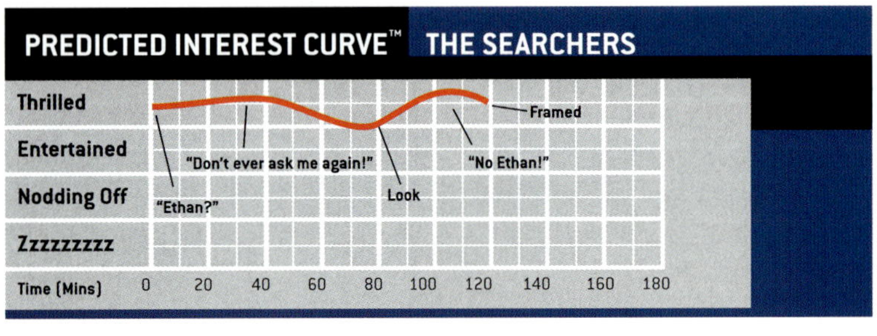

People struggle with ambiguity. American critic Roger Ebert, for one, is equivocal in his praise for Ford's greatest film, claiming "his glorification of Ethan's search invites admiration for a twisted man." There is the worry, expressed by Ebert again, that audiences in 1956 would not have recognised the film's implicit criticism of Ethan and others' racism, buying into the characters' point of view. Perhaps we should not allow films about racism or racists – the poor 'people' are so easily confused...

Put aside such nannying concerns. Save the patronising for the politicians. *The Searchers* is a masterpiece, one that grows only more rewarding with each viewing. (Naturally, it received no Oscar nominations. The Academy's snobbishness is

stubborn and long-standing. Ford won Best Director gongs for his 'serious' pictures *The Informer, The Grapes Of Wrath, How Green Was My Valley* and *The Quiet Man.*) Wayne is monumental: God's original lonely man. Monument Valley, where virtually all the film was shot in iris-stretching VistaVision, is beautiful, but Wayne's face is the landscape that tells the story and churns the emotions: when he gazes longingly after his brother's wife (Dorothy Jordan); when, stranded miles from the homestead, he realises the Comanche are killing his family; when after his five-year search he first confronts Debbie (Natalie Wood) and contorts with hatred for the niece who's been with "a buck".

You can thank Howard Hawks. Yes, Wayne's career was revitalised when Ford cast him in *Stagecoach* (1939) – a pure, archetypal Western that has a very good case for being on this list, too – but it was Hawks who gave him the chance to stretch: casting him as the bitter rancher in *Red River* (1948). "I never knew the son of a bitch could act," said Ford, who then cast him as a soldier on the verge of retirement in *She Wore A Yellow Ribbon* (1949) before going on to give him his finest role. It's a performance of such fearlessness, nuance and passion that it's staggering to think there are those who say Wayne could only play himself (just contrast the borderline-psychotic on show here with the principled professional of *Rio Bravo*). Everything flows from it, although there should be no underrating Jeffrey Hunter as the "half-breed" youngster who holds his own with Duke and the racism all around him to prove the film's conscience. Ultimately it is he who kills Ethan's alter ego, the Indian chief Scar (Henry Brandon) and rescues Debbie. Ethan only carries her to the Jorgensen's house, where – with his hatred and cruelty and racism and self-loathing – he is framed in the doorway, which closes into blackness as the Sons Of The Pioneers sing: "A man will search his heart and soul/Go searching way out there/His peace of mind he knows he'll find/But where, oh Lord, Lord where?"

Nev Pierce

NEED TO KNOW

Year 1956
Running time 119 mins
Director John Ford
Stars John Wayne, Jeffrey Hunter, Natalie Wood, Ward Bond, Henry Brandon
Buy it on Region 2
Tagline "He had to find her, he had to find her..."
Best line "That'll be the day." – Ethan Edwards
Critic's view "Undoubtedly one of the greatest Westerns ever made. For sheer scope, guts and beauty, I can think of no picture of the Indian wars of the Southwest to compare with it." – *The Hollywood Reporter*
Best watched when... You're wondering if revenge is really a good idea.

33

STAR WARS

Blockbusters make the jump to hyperspace with Lucas' space opera...

'Ultimately, Darth Vader's just a pathetic guy who's had a very sad life' GEORGE LUCAS

Close your eyes for a moment, as Ben Kenobi's ghostly voice instructs Luke Skywalker when he's making his final attempt to destroy the Death Star. Now imagine the first, startling fanfare burst of John Williams' beyond-iconic theme erupting in your head. Smiling yet? Chances are you will be... You will be. Because in your mind, the opening crash of music is already leading you to such highs as the Star Destroyer eclipsing the sky in the opening frames, the hum of lightsabers and the sheer thrill that grabs your heart when the "piece of junk!" better known as the Millennium Falcon makes its first jump beyond the light speed barrier.

Star Wars was, and is, despite any number of computer-spewed tweaks, still up there with the most impactful films ever made. Sure, it's been followed by the glorious *Empire Strikes Back*, a deeper, darker, more durable movie, and *Return Of The Jedi*, a lightweight-but-riveting end to the original trilogy, but its original lustre hasn't been tarnished. Hell, not even a trilogy of largely disappointing, effects-focused prequels managed to take the shine away.

Feeding off his own childhood dreams and square-eyed immersion in all things TV and film, George Lucas took just about every influence he could think of – myths and fairytales plus *Flash Gordon*, *The Searchers*, *Tarzan*, *Hidden Fortress* and *Metropolis* – and blended them into a special effects vehicle that was so high concept it touched the stars. And didn't worry too much about the science: "I just wanted to forget science, that would take care of itself. I wanted to make a space fantasy that was more in the genre of Edgar Rice Burroughs," recalls Lucas. It shows – and not in a negative sense. It's easy to lose yourself in the story.

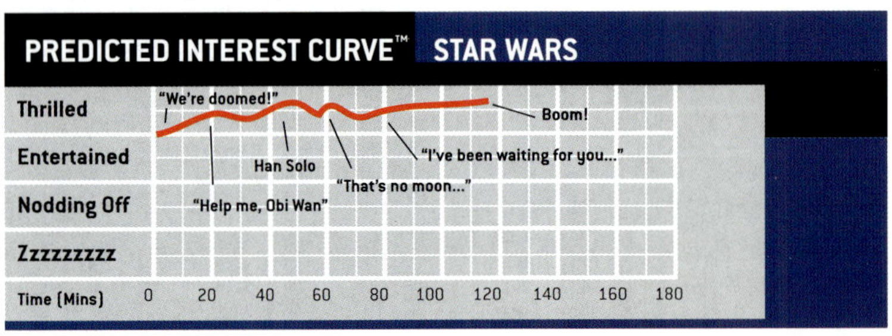

Most of all, though, it was a labour of love, Lucas and his team of technicians sweating blood and tears to bring new worlds to life at a time when it took far more than a few keyboard flourishes. If something wasn't possible during the making of *Star Wars*, he *made* it possible. He wasn't going to let such trifles as time, money and logistics get in his way, driving the effects crew at the expense of personal relationships. Watch any of the footage that shows the ILM team at work: it was a painstaking, slow process bringing the Falcon and co to life, not something to be taken lightly, and well worth the results.

Likewise with the aliens that populate his wholly realised universe. Glance around the Mos Eisley Cantina and you're immediately convinced that you're in another world, not a soundstage in Borehamwood. That hammer-headed creature

in the corner? He's some bloke in a suit, but you never look for the zip because you're caught up in the characters, the surroundings, and the adventure. You accept it all without question – the robots, the cyborgs, the starships... Besides, the movie sensibly moves at such clip that you're never given time to linger on the logistics. Instead you're right there in the trench of the Death Star, mouthing silent prayers as Luke closes his eyes and trusts in the Force. Ask any thirtysomething and they'll say the same thing: to turn on *Star Wars* is to turn back the years... back, back, back to a time when watching movies was an experience of wide-eyed wonder.

But while ream upon ream has been written about *Star Wars'* advances in technology and its cementing of the Blockbuster after *Jaws'* mighty bites at the box-office, not enough is made of the casting and characters. Harrison Ford might have said, "George, you can type this shit but you sure can't say it", but that doesn't stop us from falling in love with *Star Wars'* gallery of rogues and rebel heroes. Mark Hamill *is* Luke Skywalker, so much so that he never managed to escape the Jedi typecasting (despite a strong performance as a shattered grunt in Sam Fuller's blistering World War Two drama *The Big Red One*). Harrison Ford is the perfect counterbalance to Hamill's innocent, asexual dreamer. His Han Solo is rugged, charming, world-weary and sarcastic, a roguish smuggler who's struggling to live in a universe that no longer seems to tolerate him. Carrie Fisher's Princess Leia, meanwhile, survives the worst hairdo in cinema to win hearts with her fiery independence and sparky flirtatiousness. Fisher's problems during the making of the movie are well documented, from drugs to sheer discomfort. "I was at a surreal age, on a surreal set... For some reason there wasn't any lingerie in space, so I didn't wear a bra, and when there were running scenes, they bound my breasts with gaffer tape," she recalled. "*Star Wars* taught me everything – how to shoot a gun and how to have my breasts taped." But those various hardships, blended with her take-no-shit attitude, at least add fuel to Leia's impulsive streak.

NEED TO KNOW

Year 1977
Running time 120 mins
Director George Lucas
Stars Mark Hamill, Harrison Ford, Alec Guinness, Carrie Fisher, Peter Cushing
Buy it on R2 Star Wars Trilogy Box Set.
Tagline "A long time ago in a galaxy far, far away..."
Best line "That's no moon. It's a space station." – Obi-Wan
Critic's view "Here, all mixed together, were whimsy and fantasy, simple wonderment and quietly sophisticated storytelling." – *Chicago Sun-Times*
Best watched when... You're stuck on a boring farm job and need to escape the routine...

Around this central trio, Lucas builds a colourful cast of wizards and wonders, monsters and murderers. Special mention must go to Alec Guinness' sagacious mentor Obi-Wan Kenobi (Sir Alec didn't enjoy the filming experience and detested the fact that Obi-Wan won him screaming adoration from people who had never even heard of Ealing comedies, let alone seen one) and Peter Mayhew's Chewbacca, while Anthony Daniels and Kenny Baker excel at providing comedy and exposition as bickering 'bots C-3PO and R2-D2. All of them fade like a faltering hologram, however, when compared to the greatest villain ever to menace celluloid. Darth Vader, black-clad and remorseless, is more nightmarish than any Norman Bates, Hannibal Lecter or Ghostface.

Cold, metallic, ruthless, asthmatic and seemingly unstoppable, his single-minded goal is to crush the rebellion and make sure the Empire rules the galaxy. Yet there's more: "His character's got to go beyond that," says Lucas. "That's how we get his impersonal way of dealing with things. He's done a lot of horrible things in his life that he isn't particularly proud of. Ultimately, he's just a pathetic guy who's had a very sad life." The driving force (pun intended) behind the prequels is the director's desire to explore Vader's demons. But here, DV is the demon, watching him is like eyeing Freddy Krueger in the original *A Nightmare On Elm Street*: he's evil-concentrate, remorseless and terrifying.

Star Wars is the pinnacle of escapist entertainment, a movie that speeds along on heart, passion, wit, enterprise and thrilling set-piece after thrilling set-piece. It has left an indelible mark on more than one generation and continues to inspire debate, devotion and discussion (hello Kevin Smith), with every minutiae dissected. Like the Force, the legacy of *Star Wars* will be with us, always. TF

James White

THEY ALMOST SERVED

The near-miss Star Wars auditions...

KURT RUSSELL
Russell was up for the part of Han Solo. Lucas recalls it as being a decent audition, but Ford got the nod. No matter – Mr Kurt went on to play a similarly anti-(authoritarian) hero in *Escape From New York*.

TERI NUNN
The singer with the band Berlin auditioned to play Princess Leia. Alas, she never really enjoyed a stellar career – rather, she appeared in a few TV shows (*TJ Hooker*!) and, of course, became best known as the pipes behind *Top Gun* standard 'Take My Breath Away'.

ORSON WELLES
Citizen Kane's wünderkind was a serious consideration to voice Darth Vader, but George Lucas feared his voice would be too recognisable. Poor guy, he could have had a really great film career. Oh, wait...

BILLY DEE WILLIAMS
The future Lando was considered for Han when Lucas was thinking of making Solo black. Aretha Franklin's hubby-to-be Glynn Turman was also in the running – he was cast, then Lucas changed his mind and went for Ford instead.

The Earth's greatest SF and fantasy magazine

SFX

YOU ARE NOT ALONE

Beaming down to your newsagent every month

EXCLUSIVE NEWS, IN-DEPTH FEATURES, REVEALING INTERVIEWS AND DEFINITIVE REVIEWS!

"This *is* the magazine you're looking for..."

www.sfx.co.uk

32

LES ENFANTS DU PARADIS

A romantic tribute to the glories of Gallic culture...

The partnership was a bizarre one. Jacques Prévert: gregarious, committed, highly political, a great lover of women and one of the most popular French poets of the 20th century. And Marcel Carné: cool, withdrawn, apolitical, ultra-controlled, fastidiously gay. A union of complete opposites. "Carné never really believed in happiness," said their friend Ivo Jarosy. "Prévert believed in nothing else." Together, with Prévert writing the scripts and Carné behind the camera, they created seven films, including three of the all-time towering masterpieces of French cinema.

Les Enfants Du Paradis was the pinnacle of their teaming, and the supreme expression of the cinematic movement for which they're best known: 'poetic realism'. Although 'romantic pessimism' is a more apt description: movies suffused with a drifting, downbeat fatalism, heavy with slum-glamour, beached somewhere between existentialism and film noir. On the eve of the Second World War they made *Le Jour Se Lève*, starring Jean Gabin as a reluctant killer holed up in a tenement block as fate closes in. Some pundits actually accused its doom-laden mood of contributing to France's defeat at the hands of the Nazis.

Then in 1943, with the Gestapo jackboot still stamping on their occupied country and wartime restrictions on filmmaking at their tightest, the two decided to make the biggest, most expensive film in the history of France. It would be set 100 years earlier, during the reign of Louis Philippe (1830-1848), and it would celebrate the eternal, indomitable spirit of French culture. Just as cinema was the popular art form for the 20th century, theatre held the reins

In August 1943, construction began on the largest set ever built in a French studio

the century before. And its most faithful supporters were les enfants du paradis: the poor people who crammed the cheap seats up in the 'gods'.

In August 1943, construction began on the largest set ever built in a French studio: a quarter-mile of two-sided street frontage representing the 'Boulevard de crime' – the stretch of Paris's Boulevard du Temple where nearly all the popular theatres were sited, and also home to a turbulent streetlife of jugglers, hucksters, mimes, pickpockets, hookers, and other riff-raff. For his plot, Prévert aspired to create something that contained the richness and multi-personed complexity of a novel by Victor Hugo or Honore Balzac, weaving real-life figures in with fictional characters. The great mime Baptiste Debureau (a career-making role for Jean-Louis Barrault) really existed, as did the imperious actor-manager Frédérick Lemaître and the crook-turned-playwright

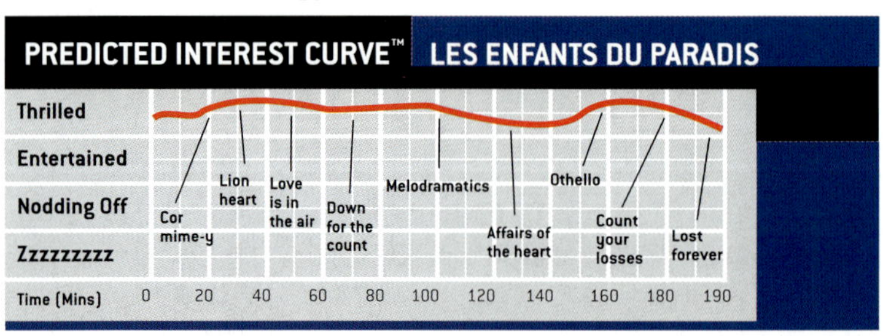

Lacenaire. But Garance, the woman who entrances them all (played with infinite cool by Arletty), is a fantasy, an embodiment of the unconquered spirit of France.

As you might imagine, shooting *Paradis* while a world war raged wasn't easy. And it's claimed that Carné and Prévert deliberately strung things out; the more people working on their movie, the fewer could be siphoned off for the German war effort. But plenty of the problems were genuine. Film stock was in short supply; props and materials had to be filched from scrapyards. The initial producer, André Paulvé, was forced to quit when he fell under Nazi scrutiny. The film's composer, Josef Kosma, and art director, Alexandre Trauner – whose contributions make such a staggering impact – were both Jewish and had to work on the film in hiding, transmitting their ideas through third parties. Meanwhile, Robert le Vigan, who was originally cast for a key villainous role, turned out to be a collaborator and prudently fled with the German army as it retreated. His scenes were reshot with Jean Renoir's brother Pierre. Since the Nazis banned production of any film longer than 90 minutes, Carné had to split it into two parts.

No hint of these trials tinge the final product. *Les Enfants Du Paradis* is expansive, opulent, stylish and lovingly detailed down to the last boutonnière. A sweeping meditation on the nature of performance, fantasy and illusion, it's defiantly stagey, with all performances heightened and impeccably enunciated in classic French. The climactic confrontation in a theatre foyer is a blatant coup de théâtre that must surely have lodged in Orson Welles' mind when he was making Othello.

Eighteen months in the making, *Les Enfants Du Paradis* finally opened in newly-liberated Paris in March 1945 and was instantly hailed as a defiant statement of the lasting values of French culture. Even the disgrace of Arletty, who, as the mistress of a German officer, had been arrested and jailed, couldn't dim the film's triumph, and, since then, its status as one of the supreme achievements of French cinema has never wavered.

Philip Kemp

NEED TO KNOW

Year 1945
Running time 190 mins
Director Marcel Carné
Stars Jean-Louis Barrault, Pierre Brasseur, Arletty, Marcel Herrand, Pierre Renoir
Buy it on Region 0 USA
Tagline N/A
Best line "Shut up! We can't hear the mime!" – Audience member
Critic's view "One sits watching these people for three hours fascinated by their three-fold remoteness, by their happy irresponsibility and complete detachment." – *Film Survey*
Best watched when... You're planning a romantic weekend in Paris.

31

PAT GARRETT AND BILLY THE KID

Peckinpah takes on the Western and the Hollywood studio system. And wins. Just...

Brutal, bizarre and sublime – a battered, hangdog masterpiece

Like a few select films in Hollywood history – *The Wizard Of Oz, The African Queen* or *Jaws*, perhaps – Sam Peckinpah's *Pat Garrett And Billy The Kid* is one of those movies that exist in a tangled state of cinematic suspension: part finished product, part scandalous production story, and part industry legend.

It's an elegiac picture about the end of the Old West that became the end of Peckinpah's career as a director of Westerns. It's a movie about betrayal and duplicity (between Kris Kristofferson's Billy and James Coburn's Garrett) that became Peckinpah's greatest professional betrayal (by scissor-handed MGM president James Aubrey). And it's a film that celebrated the lifestyles of no-nonsense hard-drinking men made by a director whose own conspicuous alcoholism had begun to infect the quality of his work.

"After four hours Sam was gone," said star Coburn, referring to the amount of time his booze-sodden 48-year-old director could retain his faculties on an average shooting day. "He was a genius for about four hours, then it was all downhill." And *Pat Garrett* is the first movie where it officially starts to show. From the film's opening prologue to Billy's capture and eventual shoot-out and escape from Lincoln County jail (including the spectacular slow-mo slaughter of psycho bible-bashing deputy Bob Ollinger), the movie seems to jerk reluctantly along with its own clunky rhythm. Action shots are mismatched, the dialogue cuts are often crude, and the tone veers sharply from brutality to elegy and back again. Meanwhile Coburn, in sharp black duds and still demeanour, gives a mesmerising essay in screen cool, while Kristofferson's Billy sways from blank, bloodthirsty cipher to romantic hero outlaw.

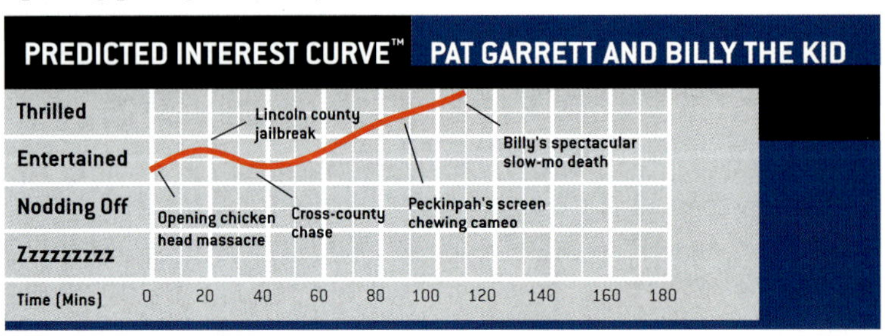

Peckinpah, in his defence, had plenty of reasons to want to be drunk. His movie had an impossibly tight schedule and thrifty budget (50 days shooting and a paltry three million dollars). His cast and crew went down with influenza, and he shot weeks of unusable footage with a busted camera lens.

When he eventually returned the completed footage to LA, studio head Aubrey announced that Peckinpah would only have three months to edit the movie (versus the whole year he had with *The Wild Bunch*). Naturally, Peckinpah's cut (124 minutes) was considered too long. His movie was taken away and chopped back to just over 100 minutes, "It was fucking terrible," said Coburn. Audiences were deprived of the full(ish)-length director's cut until 1989, five years after Peckinpah's death.

And yet, for all its many troubles and production agonies, there is genius at work

here. "How does it feel?" says Billy to Pat, in the movie's opening exchange. "It feels like times have changed," answers Pat, and in doing so he sets up the great Late Western theme of cowboys out of time, as explored by Ford in *The Man Who Shot Liberty Valance*, Leone in *Once Upon A Time In The West* and Peckinpah himself in *Ride The High Country*. Only this time, Peckinpah reinforces his theme with a roll-call of the greatest Western character actors then alive. Old, grizzled names like Jack Elam, Chill Wills, Katy Jurado and Slim Pickens being brought in to illustrate the end of an era.

He also makes sure that an explicit parallel to the sanctioned cynicism of the Watergate age is drawn, *Pat Garrett* demonstrating that it's the controlling interests of government and business (as seen in Jason Robards' Governor Wallace and Barry Sullivan's rancher Chisum) that conspire to rid the country of the Old Western ways these characters represent. Slim Pickens in particular has a devastatingly poignant death scene, limping with a bullet wound down to the river to die while Bob Dylan's 'Knocking On Heaven's Door' plays.

Of course, the casting of Dylan was yet another gesture to highlight that times were changing. Peckinpah and his writer Rudy Wurlitzer decided to pitch Billy and his gang (which includes Dylan and most of his band) as modern rock stars intruding onto the Old West. And certainly singer Kristofferson's energetic turn plus Dylan's stylised performance, make Coburn and his ilk seem even more dislocated than ever.

And then there's the final shoot-down. Not a shoot-out, more of a mercy killing. Pat sneaks into the darkened bedroom where Billy has just made love. Billy walks in bare-chested. Pat raises his gun. Billy opens his arms in wide cruciform pose, and Pat blows him clean across the room. The Christ-like self-sacrifice, the unflinching brutality and unbridled machismo: it's all very Peckinpah, and a suitably sublime ending to a bizarre and battered hangdog masterpiece. But a masterpiece nonetheless.
Patrick Donovan

NEED TO KNOW

Year 1973
Running time 122 mins
Director Sam Peckinpah
Stars James Coburn, Kris Kristofferson, Bob Dylan, Jack Elam, Slim Pickens
Buy it on N/A
Tagline "Best of enemies. Deadliest of friends."
Best line "You made me have a bowel movement in my britches. I ain't never gonna forgive you for that!" – Lemuel
Critic's view "Did the studio ruin an interesting film, or did it merely try to salvage a hopelessly muddled one?" – *Newsweek*
Best watched when... You've been forced to work to ridiculous time-restraints with no budget and need cheering up.

30

RESERVOIR DOGS

Quentin Tarantino storms on through in a hail of blood, guts, bullets and banter...

Unless you suffer from a delicate tummy, have a distaste for dapper crims or you're under 18, there's something for everyone in *Reservoir Dogs*. And that's the key to its appeal, both when it blasted into cinemas in 1992 and why it continues to resonate today: it's raw but multilayered. Brutal, chatty, sleek and indelibly acted by a wealth of quality thesps. What makes it work – and age – so damn well is the way it crams such rangey ingredients into a taut 99 minutes, making use of just a couple of locations and the minimum of props and costumes.

Raw, brutal, chatty, sleek and indelibly acted by a wealth of quality thesps

It's the little, almost throwaway, details that help make *Dogs* such a pedigree performer. The cringingly realistic depiction of gunshot wounds – normally shrugged off by heroes as trivial and cartoonish. Here, bullets hurt, and the injuries affect those who suffer them long after the uncinematic impact. No more heroes shrugging off those sucking shoulder wounds with a grizzled grimace. No more heroes at all, as it happens (maybe a few of the characters could be considered antiheroes).

Still, they're nothing without the central examples of *Dogs'* no-flab structure. Take the talk: a swirling clash of movie-chat taken from QT's early days as register-jockey at LA's Video Archives, and the only thing – aside from the blood – allowed to run free. The generous measures of pop culture have a smartypants sass all of their own, but they also add layer and bite to the storytelling. Take the drowsy drawl of cult comic Steven Wright as the K-Billy DJ, cueing up the soundtrack like Droopy on downers.

The dialogue is not only street-sharp and ear-catching, it's also beautifully tailored to tell us everything we need to know about the characters, ditching the need to resort to anything as tawdry as flashbacks. Mr Pink's notorious rant on selective tipping isn't just a throwaway piece of business to give Steve Buscemi the chance to riff on a real-life bugbear, it gives us genuine insight into Pink's weaselly psyche. And for a first-time director, Tarantino sure knows how to play to his actors' strengths. When Pink is briefly fingered as the "rat" who snitched to the cops and led to the heist's collapse, he's caught in angry crossfire with White (Keitel). "For all I know, *you're* the fuckin' rat!" snaps White. Pink's reaction is not anger ("See, now you're using your head!"). Buscemi perfectly nails the terminal twitch who sees traitors wherever he looks.

Back in 1991, armed with a 16mm camera and $30,000, Tarantino planned to make the film with a group of friends – including production partner Lawrence Bender. Then he got a call from Harvey Keitel, who

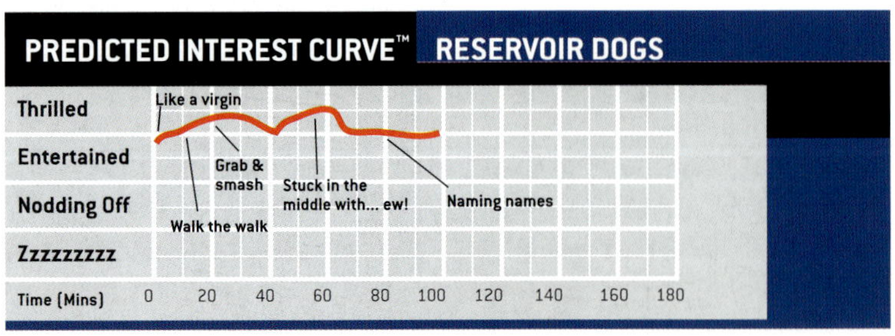

had heard of the script through Bender's acting class teacher. He offered to help produce and, with a name involved, the budget skipped up to $1.5m.

Buoyed by the endorsement of lo-fi Hollywood royalty like Keitel, Tarantino built up an audacious ensemble cast: Keitel, Steve Buscemi, Tim Roth, Michael Madsen... He even auditioned Samuel L Jackson but decided to save him for a more ambitious future project – just in case *Dogs* brought in enough money to get it made. He badgered James Woods' agent (reportedly for the role of Mr Orange) but Woods never received the message because the cash was nowhere near his going rate (Woods later learned this from Tarantino and fired his agent).

Keitel's granite-tough old mutt sets the acting standard for the other pups. As undercover cop Mr Orange, Roth (also *Pulp Fiction*-bound) makes a believable switch from subtle (early scenes) to manic (sucking chest wound). Chris Penn is slick and sleazy as not-really-very-Nice Guy Eddie. In smooth psycho Mr Blonde, Madsen creates one of cinema's most unpredictable, enduring monsters and Tarantino gifts him a scene (cop torture) of such casual brutality that it became a talking point outside of the film, even though the action happens mostly off-screen.

Just as Madsen plays with the idea of the unbalanced Blonde, so Tarantino messes with the structure. *Reservoir Dogs* jumps about in time, only briefly dropping into the frenzied crime scene as it all goes horribly wrong, and then pushing further back to witness the heist slowly coming together. Mostly though, we're living in the present, amid the paranoid fallout of the botched diamond-blag. We're always edgy and off-balance, second-guessing where the narrative might lurch next. To offset the temporal tweaking, QT keeps his camera solid, with nothing too gimmicky to further confuse.

If only Tarantino's army of imitators had spotted that what makes *Reservoir Dogs* great is the robust character construction and maturity of technique over the slo-mo, the style, the sharp suits, the smart mouths. *Dogs* is on this list because it's the greatest >>

NEED TO KNOW

Year 1992
Running time 99 mins
Director Quentin Tarantino
Starring Harvey Keitel, Tim Roth, Steve Buscemi, Quentin Tarantino, Michael Madsen
Buy it on Region 1 10th Anniversary Edition.
Tagline "Every dog has his day."
Best line "Let's go to work." – Joe Cabot
Critic's view "If this gritty, bone-chilling, powerfully violent new film, *Reservoir Dogs*, doesn't pin your ears back, nothing ever will." – *Washington Post*
Best watched when... You've just watched *Kill Bill: Vol. 2* and you need a fresh hit of early Tarantino aceness.

debut of modern times. It shook things up, launched a thousand parodies and homages and sent us away with heads full of killer lines and iconic imagery (witness the tiresome extent to which marketing monkeys aped the line-up of various 'Misters' in suits and shades).

It's also one of the most misunderstood films on our list. Censured for violence when the nastiest action happens off-screen. Responsible for spawning a mediocre litter of gangster-crim-heist films when it's really more about the characters and their clashing loyalties... Still, it launched Tarantino as the director of the '90s and although he happily believed his own hype, never forget he followed up with *Pulp Fiction*.

And the title? Taking one of his favourite films (*Straw Dogs*) as a jump-off point, the non-French speaking Tarantino worked in his shorthand-speak for *Au Revoir Les Enfants* ("That Reservoir movie"). Or so he says... TF

James White

MR MAGPIE

Where QT swiped his ideas for *Reservoir Dogs*...

The basic plot and several ideas for scenes are snatched straight from Ringo Lam's *Long hu feng yen*, aka *City On Fire*, starring Chow Yun-Fat.

A cool, original idea to name the criminals after colours, right? Try watching 1974's *The Taking Of Pelham One Two Three*, which features crooks with codenames including Mr Blue, Mr Green and Mr Brown.

The sleek, classy black-and-white suit look? A combo of Rat Pack cool and John Woo's *A Better Tomorrow II*.

Tarantino admits that Howard Hawks' *Rio Bravo* is one of his favourite films of all time. Mr Pink's constant exhortations for the others to be "professional" are a nod to Hawks' films.

Near the end of the film, Laurence Tierney says the words, "Dead as Dillinger". It's another loaded homage from QT, well aware that Tierney starred as John Dillinger in the 1945 gangster biopic *Dillinger*.

HUNDREDS OF GREAT MOVIES EVERY YEAR...

...ONLY ONE ESSENTIAL MOVIE MAGAZINE EVERY MONTH

TOTAL FILM

ON SALE EVERY FOURTH THURSDAY

29

LA REGLE DU JEU

Fun and games in Renoir's satirical masterpiece, rescued from oblivion...

La Règle Du Jeu is now accepted as one of the greatest films ever made. But for many years it was a virtually lost film, dismissed as a failure and available only in truncated versions.

Made at a crucial juncture in French history, as the country was teetering on the brink of World War Two, already soured by forebodings of defeat, it echoed Renoir's earlier masterpiece *La Grande Illusion* in that it used a microcosm to comment on the state of France as a whole. In this instance Renoir employed the events of a house-party at a country chateau. He described the film as, "a sort of reconstructed documentary... on the condition of society at a given moment... It is a war film, and yet there is no reference to the war. Beneath its seemingly innocuous appearance the story attacks the very structure of our society."

The film was attacked as frivolous, unpatriotic and incomprehensible

Originally Renoir had planned to make an adaptation of Musset's classic tragi-comedy of amorous intrigue, *Les Caprices De Marianne*. But as so often with Renoir, the project evolved as he worked on it. Sure, the film he ended up with owed something to Musset's play, but it was also indebted to a whole tradition of French theatre – Molière's comedies of obsession, Marivaux's master-servant erotic entanglements, Feydeau's bedroom fugues. And all of these artists, like Renoir, were creators of comedy with very dark undertones.

The plot revolves around three interlinked emotional triangles. André Jurieux, an aviator, loves Christine, wife of the Marquis de la Cheyniest. La Cheyniest, for his part, is having a covert affair with the socialite Geneviève. Cheyniest's gamekeeper, Schumacher, is violently jealous of his wife Lisette, Christine's maid, whom he suspects of dallying with poacher-turned-valet, Marceau. And around them all hovers the jocular, uneasy figure of Octave (Renoir himself): mediator, confidant and go-between, welcome everywhere and at home nowhere. During a weekend at La Cheyniest's chateau all these intrigues bubble over into confusion, chaos and tragedy.

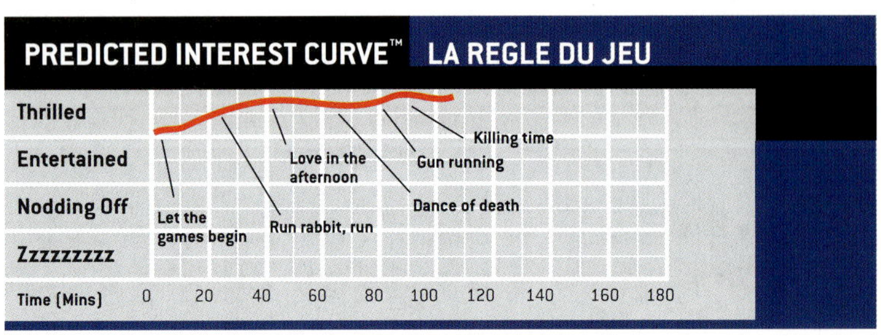

"Chacun a ses raisons" (everyone has their reasons), the line spoken by Octave, is often quoted as summing up the director's humanistic tolerance. But in its full form – "You know, in this world there's one thing that's terrible: that everyone has their reasons" – it's an insight into the awful incompatibility of human needs and desires. This seemingly elegant, old-world gathering is riven with rancour and hatreds, social, political and racial. The "rules of the game" are designed to exclude those who fail to grasp the unspoken assumptions behind them.

In *La Règle Du Jeu*, Renoir's camera virtually becomes one of

the characters — a roaming, inquisitive viewpoint constantly reframing the intricate flux of movements and events. The film swerves unpredictably between farce and tragedy, climaxing in the after-dinner sequence, a sustained tour de force of orchestrated chaos. Through the tattered remnants of amateur theatricals, with some guests clad as skeletons, others as Bavarian peasants, and Octave lumbering round seeking help in shedding his bear costume, there erupts the gun-wielding Schumacher, blasting in all directions while Lisette tries to restrain him and Marceau dodges behind furniture. La Cheyniest, proudly displaying his prized collection of mechanical toys, vaguely registers that some sort of disruption is in progress. "Stop this farce!" he orders his major-domo. "Which one, sir?" inquires the servant.

La Règle Du Jeu is a great film, but by no means a perfect one, flawed as it is by its casting. Dalio, Carette, Dubost and Modot are never less than superb, and Renoir himself turns his limitations as an actor to his advantage; but Gregor's Christine is too stiff and insipid to be, as she supposedly is, the object of every man's adoration.

Still, Gregor's banal turn was the least of the film's worries. Originally running to 113 minutes, it was trimmed to 100 upon the insistence of distributors Gaumont. The premiere was a disaster. The film was attacked as frivolous, unpatriotic, clumsy and incomprehensible. Devastated, Renoir agreed to further cuts, which only made things worse. And then, in October 1939, the film was suppressed by the French government as "demoralising". After the war the film received occasional showings in versions ranging from 80 to 90 minutes and was generally written off as a turkey. Not until 1956, when 200 cans of outtakes were discovered, could it be restored to very nearly its original form, the resurrected film premiering at Venice in 1959 where it was hailed as a lost masterpiece. It's reputation has continued to grow and it now stands as a film that often rivals *Citizen Kane* as the Greatest in the eyes of high-brow cineastes.

Philip Kemp

NEED TO KNOW

Year 1939
Running time 112 mins
Director Jean Renoir
Stars Marcel Dalio, Nora Gregor, Jean Renoir
Buy it on Region 1 Criterion Edition
Tagline N/A
Best line "I have no choice but to dismiss you. I can't expose my guests to your firearms. It may be wrong of them, but they value their lives." – Marquis de la Cheyniest
Critic's view "*La Règle Du Jeu* is a controversial pic bound to elicit comment but lacking marquee strength." – *Variety*
Best watched when... You've been invited for a weekend at a country house.

28

RAGING BULL

The consumate Method actor heads for fat city in the brutal boxing masterpiece.

The red, white and blue corner: *Rocky*. And in the black and white corner: *Raging Bull*. Two boxing Bildungsromans, made four years apart by the same studio, the same producer, that nail the difference between art and entertainment. "Hollywood films want to tell us truths we already know or falsehoods we want to believe in," veteran screenwriter William Goldman once opined. "In other words, they reinforce. Art films want to disturb us, to tell us truths we don't want to know. In other words, they unsettle." An oversimplification perhaps, but one that fits the contrast between Sly Stallone's go-the-distance American Dreamer and Robert De Niro's going-to-hell Neanderthal nightmare like an Everlast glove.

Look at the title sequence. Monochrome. Slow-motion. Opera music. Pretentious? *Bull*. The dusty, worthy connotations that 'art films' often carry don't apply here. *Raging Bull* doesn't view from a distance; it gives you an uncomfortably close ringside seat. It gives you the singular thrill of a master film-maker realising and revelling in his uncompromised vision.

Yet it took a while for him to get in the movie's corner. *Bull* began with De Niro, who, for years, couldn't convince Martin Scorsese to adapt the memoirs of '40s middleweight champ Jake LaMotta. It wasn't until 1978 that Scorsese found an affinity for LaMotta's self-destructive mindset. Ironically, it was *Rocky* that got the film greenlit: when United Artists demurred over the script (groundworked by Marty's pal Mardik Martin; rewritten by *Taxi Driver* scribe Paul Schrader), producer Irwin Winkler bartered a Balboa sequel in return for their backing.

We're repelled by Jake's wife-beating but compelled by Bobby's brilliance

UA's reservations are understandable. *Raging Bull* deals body blows to biopic convention. It doesn't root in its characters' backgrounds for specious motivation. It doesn't shoehorn in laboured parallels with historical events (the *Seabiscuit* syndrome). And the haymaker? Its 'hero' is a boorish, sadistic, self-loathing ogre. Good job, then, that De Niro gave the performance of his – or anyone's – career. It's a breathtaking balancing act: we're repelled by Jake's wife-, brother- and prison-wall-beating but compelled by Bobby's brilliance. The guilt, the fury, the paranoid possessiveness – De Niro doesn't impersonate, he incarnates. That's why it's so troubling, so powerful. What's more, both actor and film lay bare the essence of LaMotta's life – his purgatorial journey to a kind of bleary self-acceptance – without flogging facile moral judgements (hence the closing Bible quote, "Whether or not he is sinner, I do not know").

The 60-pound weight gain is at the forefront of the movie's legend ("We had to shut down

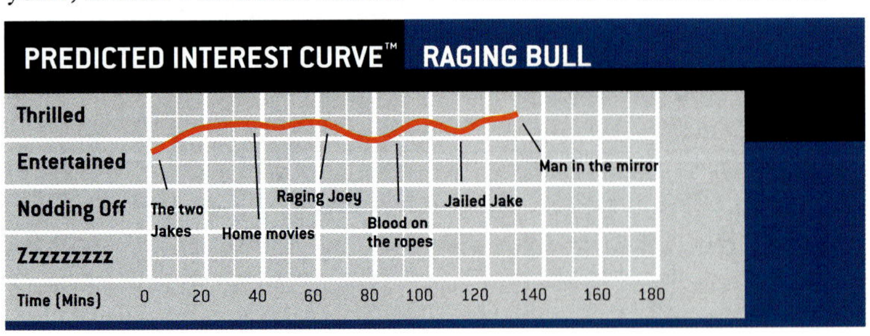

produced Michelangelo, Leonardo da Vinci and the Renaissance," he tells Martins, who is still reeling from the news that his friend has been peddling deadly penicillin. "In Switzerland they had brotherly love; they had 500 years of democracy and peace, and what did that produce? The cuckoo clock." The actor had devised the soliloquy as a jest, never assuming Reed would include it.

It was iconic moments such as this one that allowed him to resurrect the Harry Lime character on radio in the early '50s, enabling him to recoup some of the money he lost turning down a percentage of the profits in favour of a straight salary.

But *The Third Man* has more strong cards than its scene-stealing joker. It has Trevor Howard, deftly providing an unflappable English urbanity to offset Cotten's Yankee brashness. There's Bernard Lee as Sergeant Paine, a burly bruiser with a tender soul and a hilarious penchant for Martins' cheesy dime-store Westerns. There's Wilfred Hyde-White, delightfully dotty as the Foreign Office duffer who comes to regret his decision to invite Holly to speak at his literary evening. And above all there's Valli, still holding a torch for Welles' bad egg as she effortlessly rebuffs Cotten's clumsy advances.

For many, though, the biggest star of Reed's film is not seen but heard. Plucked from obscurity to supply its insistent, jaunty soundtrack, zitherist Anton Karas would become synonymous with *The Third Man*. He is Cotten's constant companion as he tries to solve the enigma of Lime's 'death', not realising he's being played for a fool. And he provides the accompaniment to a final act of conscience that costs Holly his friend, the girl and his peace of mind.

"At one time it was thought every picture must end with an embrace so the audience could go out happy," Reed said years later. "But a picture should end as it has to. I don't think anything in life ends right."

And no good deed goes unpunished in a downbeat classic that captures all the uncertainty and moral complexity of the postwar years.
Neil Smith

NEED TO KNOW

Year 1949
Running time 104 mins
Director Carol Reed
Stars Joseph Cotten, Orson Welles, Trevor Howard, Alida Valli, Bernard Lee
Buy it on Region 2 SE
Tagline "Hunted by men and sought by women!"
Best line "The dead are happier dead. They don't miss much here, poor devils." – Harry Lime
Critic's view "It combines superb artistry with 100 per cent entertainment value and a magnificent piece of screencraft." – *Daily Mirror*
Best watched when... You've been let down by a friend you thought you could trust.

25

SUNSET BOULEVARD

Billy Wilder's bracingly bilious tale of Tinseltown tragedy packs a cruel punch.

When Billy Wilder first previewed arguably the most brazen film he directed in a career full of boundary-pushing flicks, he was smart enough not to do it in Los Angeles. After all, the film anatomises the Dream Factory at its most fetid, dredges its surface to find washed-up lives, dreams decayed, ideals soured. When it did screen to industry types, MGM's head honcho, Louis B Mayer, flipped his lid, even accusing "this Wilder" of biting the hand that fed him.

The ageing fester, young talent is fast-tainted and the only way out is down

The nasty subtext was that the director, being an emigre, should have been more grateful. Wilder's response? "Fuck you," according to some, or, "Go shit in your hat."

Too right. Granted, *Sunset Boulevard* – or *Sunset Blvd*, as the name appears on a pavement during its cold, hard opening titles – offers a tatty-looking Tinseltown, where the ageing fester in mouldy old piles, young talent is fast-tainted and, once you're in, the only way out is down. But none of this would bite without teeth, which *Blvd* sharpens on its dense layers of allusion. At the film's neo-gothic core is a haunted hall of Hollywood mirrors, peopled by ghosts of a parade gone by.

As befits a film full of spooks, its narrator is a dead man. When preview audiences responded badly to a ghoulish but whimsical-sounding, morgue-set opening, Wilder shot an even more daring preface from the bottom of a pool, looking up at a dead man floating on the surface. From there, in flashback, we meet Joe Gillis (William Holden), a screenwriter over a barrel where work is concerned. Fleeing his creditors, he stumbles in twisted fairytale-style on the blighted mansion of a former silent-movie star, Norma Desmond (Gloria Swanson), and becomes ensnared in her plan for a comeback – or, as she insists, "return". She wants him to ghost-write a script for *Salome*; in return, he gets to be a kept man and more. But Norma is clearly 'cuckoo', Joe is out of his depth and La La Land won't let either go lightly...

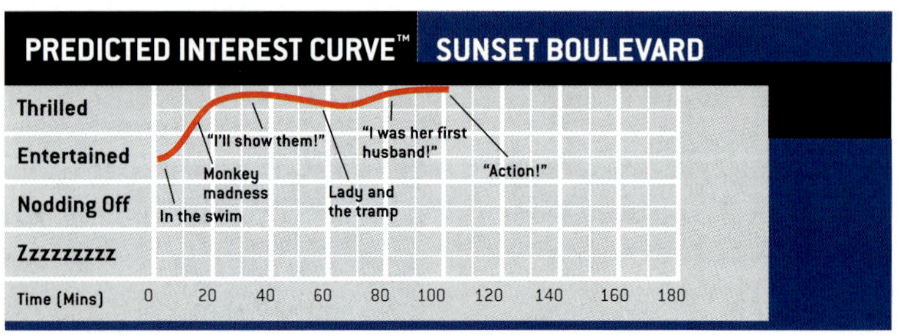

The flesh on this clammy set-up is, at least in part, the immensely resonant casting. Montgomery Clift was to play Gillis but backed out: having just made *The Heiress*, he didn't want another role involving a relationship with an older woman. So Wilder cast Holden, an actor who'd never fulfilled his own promise and therefore proved perfect for the on-his-uppers Gillis.

Swanson, though, being a former Silents star, was in early. She embodied '20s opulence, as noted by Wilder's co-writer, Charles Brackett: "We knew no time would be wasted getting into the story as soon as Swanson appeared... Youngsters who never saw her would accept

her as an old-time movie queen. Older fans would identify her with the characterisation and get a bigger emotional wallop from the story."

That wallop reverberates to the film's fringes. As well as peppering the film with real names such as Darryl F Zanuck and locations such as Schwab's Pharmacy, Wilder spiked it with familiar faces. At the bridge nights Desmond has with her old friends, Buster Keaton cameos. Not only was he a gone-to-seed star, he was also, Wilder said, an outstanding bridge player. Later, Cecil B DeMille appears when Desmond visits the studio on the mistaken belief that she is wanted on set.

But the cornerstone of this spider's web of allusions is a Teutonic titan – Erich von Stroheim as Desmond's creepy butler, Max von Mayerling. Late in the film, we learn he was Desmond's husband and that he directed her on screen. Von Stroheim directed Swanson, too, most notably in *Queen Kelly*, which proved so troublesome that it arguably stalled both their careers. And the film Desmond watches in her mansion, Gillis by her side, as she mourns the decline of the Silents? *Queen Kelly*, of course.

We get an extra sense of how thoroughly layered *Blvd*'s portrait of a life rooted in retrospective delusions really is when we learn that Max has been faking Desmond's fan mail. And whose idea was that? Erich von Stroheim's.

But it would be too easy to be merely cruel and caustic. Against Desmond, Wilder and Brackett set Nancy Olson's character, a script girl who wants to help Gillis. She isn't just a doting virgin: she's quick, clever, astute. What's more, there is a sadness in Desmond. Hollywood has used her up and spat her out, while she clings to the belief that she's still 'big'.

"I am big," she says. "It's the pictures that got small." Gillis' riposte? "I knew there was something wrong with them." What's great about *Blvd*'s convention-bucking, multi-layered tale is that it hits that "something wrong" square on the head. Biting the hand that fed it? In *Blvd*'s worldview, Hollywood didn't need teaching how to do that.

Kevin Harley

NEED TO KNOW

Year 1950
Running time 110 mins
Director Billy Wilder
Stars Gloria Swanson, William Holden
Buy it on Region 2
Tagline "A Hollywood Story"
Best line "There's nothing else – just us and the cameras and those wonderful people out there in the dark. All right, Mr DeMille, I'm ready for my close-up."
– Norma Desmond
Critic's view "Marvellous, satisfying, dramatically perfect and technically brilliant."
– *The Hollywood Reporter*
Best watched when... You need discouraging from whoring yourself.

24

REAR WINDOW

Hitchcock does voyeuristic murder mystery. You know you like to watch...

You're just as guilty, and you know it. That's the genius of *Rear Window*. Like James Stewart's wheelchair-bound photojournalist, the director drags the viewer into the role of accomplice voyeurs, the camera hungrily seeking out every morsel of plot development. So by the time Stewart's hero is menaced by the villain of the piece, you can't help but feel you're a part of it.

A rich psychological thriller that takes a cold, hard grip on your spine

Rear Window's key appeal is the simplicity of its set-up. Stewart is LB Jeffries, a photojournalist on sick leave after breaking his leg on assignment. He soon tires of the magazines and books he has for entertainment and longs to get busy again. So he does what... most of us would do. He picks up his telephoto lens and starts to spy on the activities in the next block of apartments. Soon, he's worked himself up into believing that a neighbour has killed his wife, hacked up her body and buried it in the garden. He involves girlfriend Lisa (Grace Kelly, in a luminous supporting role) and nurse Stella (the delightfully grouchy Thelma Ritter) in his sweet little mystery, which may well put them all in a lot more danger than they were in, originally – or at least land them in jail. As Stella helpfully reminds him, peeping toms used to have their eyes put out with red hot pokers.

Hitchcock builds and builds on his basic paranoid premise, cranking the tension tighter and tighter. At first, no one quite believes Jeffries when he tries to spin his theories. And when he does convince friends to help him investigate, he puts their lives at risk, becoming more and more frantic and obsessed with rooting out the 'truth'.

Stewart plays the lead with his usual easy charm, but piles on uncharacteristic layers of jittery frenzy as Jeffries becomes more and more driven by his (crazy?) beliefs. Initial ethical issues over the original act of voyeurism are quickly shoved aside in the quest for what the hell is actually going on. Hitchcock teases by hinting at the hidden – perhaps unpleasant – depths behind Stewart's everyman demeanour. At the same time, we're led to identify with our hero, since no one outside of his apartment is drawn with any real clarity. Raymond Burr plays Lars Thorwald, the character who both Jeffries and we suspect killed his wife. But he's kept just out of focus, as a vague, shadowy figure, a mystery personality, and Hitchcock retains his threatening nature by never allowing him to be dragged out into the light – at least not until the police arrive... (On the subject of shadowy threats, it's commonly assumed that Hitchcock cast Burr because of a physical resemblance to producer David O Selznick, who the director felt was interfering a little too much.)

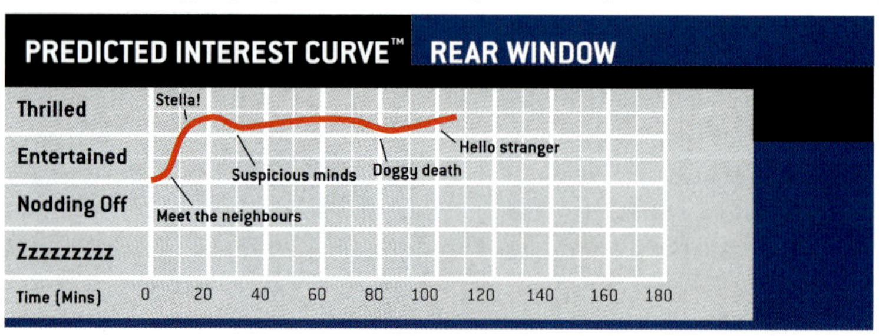

Like its set-up, *Rear Window* is fashioned from simple elements. The film effectively takes place on one giant set, with most of the running time dedicated to the intimate knowledge of Jeffries and his nosey pastime – though it never feels as studio-bound as it might have.

The production building was the largest indoor set ever created at the time, with the construction so vast that the soundstage floor had to be extensively excavated, meaning that Jeffries' apartment was, in reality, standing on street level. For authenticity's sake, every apartment set seen in the movie had running water and electricity despite the fact that we only ever see Jeffries' home in any real detail. (While shooting, Hitchcock worked only in Jeff's "apartment". The actors in the others wore flesh-coloured earpieces so that he could radio his directions to them.) No doubt Stewart got some inspiration for his character's obsessive nature from his director, but it's the attention to detail and drive for quality that helps claw you into the world. You believe what you're seeing.

And the craftsmanship shows. There's something new to glean from every new viewing. Whether it's spotting a tiny detail you didn't catch before – a character in one of the other apartments, a clue that your eye might have missed the last time – it's a film that always rewards revisits. Which is why it's become such an enduring classic. It's a rich, psychological thriller that takes a cold, hard grip on your spine and refuses to let go, without ever resorting to the shock tactics of so many modern mysteries.

Intelligent, accessible, finely constructed, with a crackling script that stays funny even as the suspense builds, it may be built on a tricksy gimmick, but it never feels mannered or forced, with Hitchcock at the helm, conducting and flowing every element perfectly into place. And while the DVD will do you just fine, *Rear Window*'s rangey, loaded visuals are gagging to be seen on the big screen, where you can peek and poke around to your dark heart's delight.

James White

NEED TO KNOW

Year 1954
Running time 112 mins
Director Alfred Hitchcock
Stars James Stewart, Grace Kelly, Wendell Corey, Raymond Burr, Judith Evelyn
Buy it on Region 1
Tagline "Suspense Of Screaming Proportions!"
Best line "Nobody ever invented a polite word for a killin' yet." – Stella
Critic's view "Not so much like watching a movie as like spying on your neighbours. Hitchcock traps us right from the first." – Roger Ebert, *Chicago Sun-Times*
Best watched when... You suspect your friends and neighbours.

23

THE GODFATHER

Francis Ford Coppola's epic enquiry into power, respect and family ties...

Of all the films in this Top 100, *The Godfather* is surely the most instantly familiar. The horse's head in the bed, the always misquoted, "*He made him an offer he couldn't refuse*", the gun in the khazi scene and that yearning, mournful score...

At first, Coppola thought The Godfather was an offer he should refuse

From Mario Puzo's 1969 pulp novel emerged an atypical, unremarkable modern-day gangster flick, directed by *On The Waterfront* helmer Elia Kazan, with Anthony Quinn as ageing mafia boss Don Corleone and his deceptively wholesome heir Michael – played by the all-American Robert Redford. Or rather that's just one of the numerous roads *The Godfather* might have ambled down, had fate and Coppola's sheer bloody-mindedness not prevailed.

Coppola was 31 years old when he got the opportunity to direct the adap of Puzo's best-selling book. But the then relatively unknown Italian-American was far from the producers' first choice, with a rack of other directors (Peter Yates, Sergio Leone, Otto Preminger...) also in line. Only after they'd all declined to take the reins, was an offer made to Coppola. And at first, he thought it was an offer he should certainly refuse...

Turned off by the material's emphasis on the Corleone empire's criminal element, Coppola was initially set to add his name to Paramount's lengthy rejection list. However, with his production arm Zoetrope in serious financial trouble, Coppola eventually realised that the work would offer him a means to an end: to keep alive the outlet of his more intimate, personal films. That was the intention, anyway. But once *The Godfather* had become a critically-acclaimed box-office behemoth, Coppola found himself in a similar situation as his close friend George Lucas, with the blockbuster tag irreversibly changing the direction of his career.

Despite his initial misgivings, Coppola set to work with the same unrelenting gusto which would see him suffer a nervous breakdown while tackling *Apocalypse Now*. He seemed to delight in making things difficult for himself. Instead of sticking to a more cost-effective '70s time-frame, Coppola insisted that the story should be set in the post-war period (Gordon Willis' bleached cinematography feels less lo-fi film stock, more time machine).

More drastically, he shifted Puzo's emphasis away from the mass of garrottings, bombings and betrayals to a subject closer to his heart: family. The focus on Puzo's Corleone family unit was also modified, with the emphasis shifting from leonine patriarch Don Vito to the college-educated youngest (of three) son Michael, and his ill-fated role as heir apparent to the family business. It was in

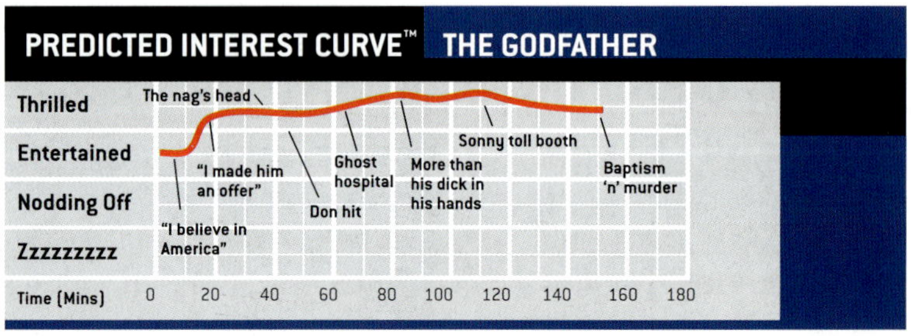

finding actors to fill the roles of father and son that the director found his biggest challenge outside the realm of the editing suite (where he'd be fired on no less than four occasions).

Having faded as Hollywood's brightest ever acting beacon, Marlon Brando had developed a well-earned reputation as a troublesome, not to mention costly, liability. Meaning that the Paramount executives wouldn't even entertain the proposal of employing the star. Coppola had other ideas. Despite all the studio pressure, the young upstart visited the former-heavyweight star to conduct a quick screentest in which Brando slicked back his hair, stuffed his jowls with tissue paper and instantly morphed into the powerful Sicilian Don. The execs were dazzled by the footage, some not even realising that they were applauding the very actor that they had so vehemently opposed.

It was a battle that was fought with Corleone incisiveness and cunning, and it was clearly a cause worth scrapping for. "If I've met three geniuses in my life," Coppola would later recall, "Marlon would have to be top of the list." The genius would eventually pick up an Oscar for his career-reigniting performance (or at least, notoriously, sent a faux-Native American woman to collect it and complain about her "people's" treatment by the US). Still, the award itself was hardly controversial. Brando's turn is majestic, casting Don Corleone as a king ruling his court, receiving the fawning well-wishers at his daughter's wedding with a kiss to the hand before judicially listening to their requests. Of course, the big man himself wasn't happy with his performance: "When I saw it for the first time, it made me sick," recalled Brando in his autobiography *Songs My Mother Taught Me*. "All I could see were my mistakes and I hated it."

While Brando's lively reputation as a handful had made him casting poison, it was Al Pacino's low profile that alienated the suits. They thought him an odd-looking, unattractive actor who surely wouldn't pull in the audiences as steadily as their preferred options of blue-eyed blond leading men Ryan O'Neal or

NEED TO KNOW

Year 1972
Running time 168 mins
Director Francis Ford Coppola
Stars Marlon Brando, Al Pacino, James Caan, Diane Keaton
Buy it on Region 1, for slightly better picture quality.
Tagline N/A
Best line "My father made him an offer he couldn't refuse." – Michael Corleone
Critic's view "Francis Ford Coppola has made one of the most brutal and moving chronicles of American life ever designed within the limits of popular entertainment." – *The New York Times*
Best watched when... You need a bit of family fortification in the run-up to Christmas.

Robert Redford. In contrast to the radiance of Redford's matinee idol glow, the young Pacino peers through sullen, dark brown hawk-eyes, looking both fearful and feral as he absorbs the reality of his family's 'business'. Slowly evolving from war hero to family foot soldier, up to assassin and eventual Don, his allegiance is no longer to the flag but to the immoral practices of the family he initially tries to distance himself from.

By the conclusion, with Michael as the new Don, the Corleone family ideal is almost eroded. His father is dead, his mother widowed – as is his sister Connie, thanks to Michael's swift and unrelenting vengeance – and the love between Michael and Kay is as hole-riddled as brother Sonny (James Caan). The film's opening, uncomplicated scenes of boisterous wedding celebrations seem to be of a different era. In a short period, the adopted country of the Sicilian immigrants has become a different, alien world. The film's opening line, in which Bonasera professes, "I believe in America," seems pale and distant. And Michael, always the black sheep of the family, has by the close become a more solitary and darker figure than anyone ever expected.

The lasting, classical appeal of the film is reflected best, though, in a letter sent to Coppola by another American-Sicilian immigrant: "It's the best film I've seen in the last 10 years. The acting was superb, the script one of the finest, and the directing? Out of this world. I cheered inwardly at scene after scene."

The author? *It's A Wonderful Life* director Frank Capra. TF

Scott Russon

BLOOD ORANGE

Think oranges are good for you? Not in *The Godfather* trilogy...

The Don suffers a heart attack after placing orange peel in his mouth and pretend-scaring his grandchild.

Vito is shopping for oranges when a would-be assassin tries to murder him. When he crumples to the ground, he sends a basket of oranges sprawling.

Sonny drives past a billboard advertising Florida oranges just prior to being gunned down at the toll booth.

In *The Godfather Part II* Hyman Roth gives messenger Johnny Ola a gift of an orange for Michael.

Don Fanucci, the crime boss, is shot dead by a young Vito (De Niro) after earlier helping himself to an orange from a fruit stall.

In *The Godfather Part III* an orange tumbles out of his hand when the old Michael Corleone dies.

22

NEED TO KNOW

Year 1927
Running time 95 mins
Director FW Murnau
Stars George O'Brien, Janet Gaynor, Margaret Livingston, Bodil Rosing, J Farrell MacDonald
Buy it on Region 2
Tagline "A song of two humans."
Best line N/A
Critic's view "Puts pep into pap... Simple, intense images of unequalled beauty."
– Time Out
Best watched when... You've just had a row with your partner and need to remember why you got together in the first place.

SUNRISE

All you need is love. And this...

Take your time. Spend what you have to. Make whatever film you like. That's the contract Hollywood slid German über-stylist FW Murnau. Fair to say, Orson Welles would have wept like an infant.

The David Fincher of '20s cinema, Murnau had already wowed with vampire chiller *Nosferatu* and bombastic drama *The Last Laugh*. Now he'd scored the kind of unfettered artistic control that Tinseltown would never grant again. The result? A masterpiece entranced with light, love and cinema itself.

The fable is simple: a farmer (George O'Brien), seduced by a shadowy urban vamp (Margaret Livingston), plots to murder his gentle wife (Janet Gaynor). Murnau's approach was anything but. Employing genius DoPs Charles Rosher and Karl Struss, the helmer shook every trick out of the cinematic grammar-book, blurring dreamy expressionism with Hollywood pep to conjure (and that's the only word for it) the most breathtaking silent ever.

We watch O'Brien, weighed down by guilt, trudge to his bed after an illicit rendezvous. Suddenly, water begins rippling into the frame: this is a man literally drowning in his own torment. Later, the vamp(ire)'s ghostly images surround him, lustful spectres caressing his weary soul. From snaking camera-dollies to fantasy flashbacks, Murnau marshals every frame, every shadow, every kiss of light. It's pure cinematic poetry: each shot physical and psychological.

The real wonder, though, is in the achingly vulnerable faces of O'Brien and Gaynor. His visual conceits astonish, but Murnau's affection for his actors is beyond heartbreaking. There's never been a more profound marriage of style and soul.

So, with the celluloid almost wrinkling in sorrow, the farmer's conscience shatters him and the couple flee to a glorious jazz-age city to fall in love all over again. In one mesmerising sequence, they cross a busy street, lost in each other's eyes as traffic rushes past. Slowly, the background dissolves into an idyllic pastoral garden. They kiss, reality returns and vehicles surround them in the middle of the street, honking their approval. It's True Love, styled to perfection. Joyous Chaplin-esque comedy follows (look out for the drunk piglet), but *Sunrise*'s stormy, heart-in-mouth finale reminds us that True Love is an infinitely delicate thing.

Released just days before *The Jazz Singer* gave cinema its first talkie, *Sunrise* crashed at the box-office only to grab a hattrick at the first Academy Awards. Seen now, it's a haunting reminder of what cinema lost when it disappeared into the chatter of a lairy new era.

Four years later, Murnau too was gone, killed in a car crash. His movie remains immortal, however, transcending a century in its lyrical simplicity, technical sophistication (everything from *Kane* to Cocteau owes it) and pure, shining emotion. As the opening titles read, "This song of the Man and his Wife is of no place and every place. You might hear it anywhere at any time..."
Jonathan Crocker

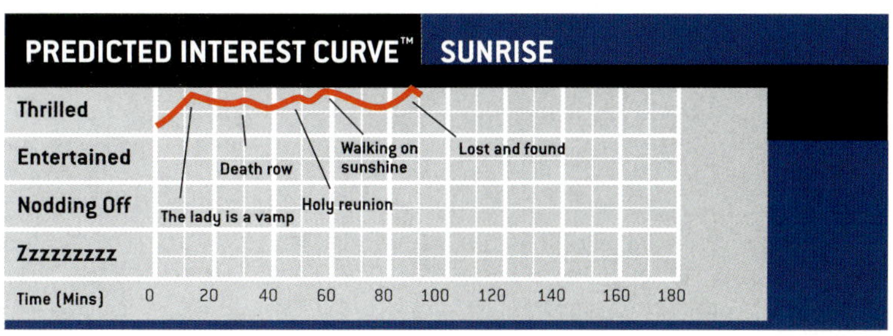

21

CRASH

Mangled metal and twisted sexuality. Buckle up, it's gonna be a bumpy ride...

"Don't make this movie. It will end your career." So came the advice of David Cronenberg's agent, who wanted the Canadian auteur to fortify his livelihood – go soft, take the easy buck – by seating himself at the Hollywood conveyor belt. Crank out *The Juror* instead.

The couple discover a world of semen, sump-oil and extreme S&M...

"Make the characters normal at the start so we can sympathise, see where they go wrong. Maybe a dog, a rabbit, two cats..." So came the (admittedly paraphrased) advice of potential distributors. They wanted *Fatal Attraction 2*, not some film about a disconnected couple who begin the movie by each fucking strangers before returning home to fuck each other, trading notes as they ogle gleaming cars racing along a multi-lane highway. If these characters really must explore a perverted sex'n'wrecks subculture under the dubious tutelage of a scarred freak in cum-stained leathers, at least let them set out from the right side of the picket fence.

Cronenberg, of course, was inflexible. Deciding to follow *Naked Lunch* and *M Butterfly* with his third literary adaptation on the bounce, he wasn't about to dilute JG Ballard's toxic 1973 novel. This was a book that he'd wanted to adapt for 25 years, waiting until he was ripe and the time was right. Ballard's literature shared strikingly similar philosophies to Cronenberg's movies ("We're amazingly in sync") and *Crash*, in particular, ran on Cronenbergian themes: transgressive sexuality, the melding of man and machine, pain and destruction embraced as positives. Glance in the rearview mirror and you'll spot the shimmering landscapes of *Shivers*, *Scanners* and *Videodrome*.

Back-to-basics Cronenberg, then? You bet, the writer/director working from a remarkably short 77-page script with a budget of under $10 million to ensure autonomy.

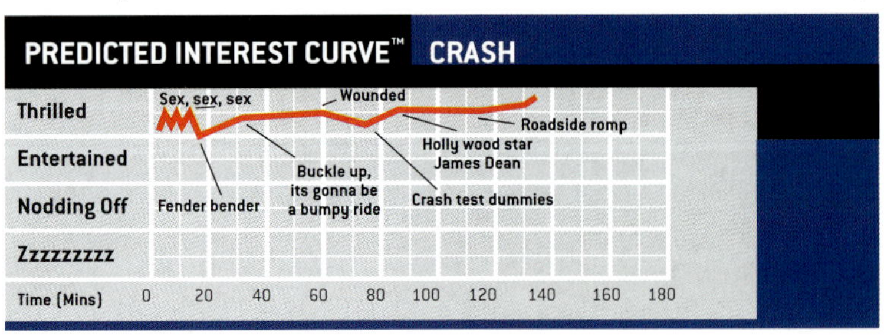

The shoot took place within half a mile of his house, Cronenberg transposing the novel's action from London to Toronto. It works, partly because it puts him firmly in the driver's seat, partly because Tornoto feels like a city located at the centre of Nowhere, No Time, and partly because the characters in the book drive American cars anyway. It is in the US of A, after all, that the car is not just a mode of transport but a status symbol, coming-of-age talisman and portable bedroom. "The first guy who had a convertible in high school was the first guy who had sex," said Cronenberg. "We've already incorporated the car into our understanding of sexuality. To want to merge with it in a more physical way seems a good metaphor."

So what of that merging? *Crash* follows advertising exec James Ballard (James Spader) and his wife Catherine (Deborah Unger) as their liberal-yet-

mechanical sex life is given new life by James' near-death collision with Dr Helen Remington (Holly Hunter). Gravitating towards scientist and serial crasher Vaughan (Elias Koteas), the couple discover a world of semen, sump-oil and extreme S&M: videos of crash-test dummies exploding through windscreens like cocks puncturing hymens; hazardous restagings of celebrity crashes; enforced prangs on choked highways, the smashed instrument panels acting as the Viagra by which to fuck freshly torn orifices.

Inevitably it all proved too much for some people. Respected critic Alexander Walker described the film as "beyond the bounds of depravity". *The Daily Mail* took up the baton, demanding it be banned. And Westminster Council consented, citing ridiculous fears that it might inspire incidents of road rage. Clearly none of them watched the film with open eyes and mind. *Crash* is a film of cool, calculated control, its uncluttered, unheated visuals (precise framing, muted colours) and equally minimalistic score (cold electric guitars and emotionless percussion) giving the movie a suitably metallic tone. Likewise its titular jolts: a world away from Hollywood's slo-mo, jazz'n'jizz spectacles, here the collisions are sudden, jarring and painful, more mundanity than money shot.

Some have called *Crash* European in sensibility but its from some place further, another world. Watching this film is like watching a pristine reflection in a mercury puddle on a blackened highway on a desolate star. It puts the alien in alienation, its characters seeking to end their disconnection (notice how all the sex is anal or rear entry, never face-to-face) and shatter sexual boundaries by attaining a new state of consciousness brought by the integration of mind, body and technology.

Cronenberg calls it the "psychology of the future" and it's this thrust towards the new millennium that makes *Crash* challenge *Fight Club* as the most potent film of the late '90s. As Scorsese succintly puts it: "Cronenberg is 20th century. *Late* 20th century."

Jamie Graham

NEED TO KNOW

Year 1996
Running time 100 mins
Director David Cronenberg
Stars James Spader, Holly Hunter, Deborah Kara Unger, Elias Koteas, Rosanna Arquette
Buy it on Region 2
Tagline "Love in the dying moments of the Twentieth Century"
Best line "The car crash is a fertilising rather than a destructive event." – Vaughan
Critic's view "Everyone whispers... because they are too embarrassed to have anyone hear the nonsense they're spewing."
– San Francisco Examiner
Best watched when... You've just seen *American Graffiti.*

THREE EASY WAYS TO ORDER

1. Subscribe online
at www.myfavouritemagazines.co.uk/TOF/2007

2. Call the hotline on 0870 837 4722
and quote code 2007

3. Return completed order form
to: Total Film Subscriptions, Future Publishing Ltd, FREEPOST RLSC-SXSE-SKKT, Unit 4, Tower House, Sovereign Park, Market Harborough, Leicestershire, LE16 9EF.

Terms and Conditions: This offer is for the UK only. For overseas offers visit www.myfavouritemagazines.co.uk

4 FREE ISSUES OF TOTAL FILM

Subscribe by direct debit for only £7.87 every 3 months – that's equivalent to 4 free issues over the next year!

❑ I would like to subscribe by Direct Debit for only £7.87 every 3 months. I will receive 13 issues during the next 12 months. If I am unhappy with my subscription I can cancel at any time and receive a refund on all unmailed issues.

Title................First name..Surname..

Address...

....Postcode...........................

Daytime tel no...

Your e-mail address...

We will use the contact details supplied to communicate with you about your *Total Film* subscription. We'd also like to keep you up to date with any special offers or new products/services that may be of interest. If you're happy for *Total Film*, Future Publishing and its sister companies to contact you by e-mail, indicate here: ❑ If you're also happy for us to pass your details on to carefully selected companies so they can send you relevant information about their products/services by e-mail, indicate here: ❑

Instruction to your Bank or Building Society to pay Direct Debits.

Future | DIRECT Debit

Originator's Identification Number

7	6	8	1	9	5

Future Publishing Ltd, Unit 4, Tower House, Sovereign Park, Market Harborough, Leicestershire LE16 9EF

Please send this form to address shown

1. Name and full postal address of your Bank or Building Society branch

To: The Manager

______________________________ Bank/Building Society

Address ______________________________

Postcode ______________________________

2. Name(s) of

3. Branch sort code

4. Bank or Building Society account number

5. Instruction to your Bank or Building Society

Please pay Future Publishing Direct Debits from the account detailed on this Instruction subject to the safeguards assured by the Direct Debit Guarantee. I understand that this instruction may remain with Future Publishing and if so, details will be passed electronically to my Bank or Building Society.

Signature ______________________________ Date ______________

Ref No (Office use only) ______________________________

Banks and Building Societies may not accept Direct Debit Instructions for some types of account.

Terms and conditions

*Money returned on unmailed issues. Copies of the DD guarantee are available on request. Your subscription will start with the next available issue. Thirteen issues are published in a year. Please indicate if you do NOT wish to receive relevant information about special offers or products/services from *Total Film*, Future Publishing or any of its sister companies by ❑ post or ❑ telephone. Please indicate if you do NOT wish us to pass your details on to other carefully selected companies to enable them to contact you about their products/services by ❑ post or ❑ telephone.

Order Code: 2007 **Offer ends:** 30 June 2006

20

APOCALYPSE NOW

Coppola's bold attempt to capture the first "rock'n'roll" war...

"There were too many of us... little by little, we went insane" FRANCIS FORD COPPOLA

To watch the hysterical, hazy, hallucinogenic *Apocalypse Now* without the *Hearts Of Darkness: A Filmmaker's Apocalypse* (1991) documentary is to experience only half of the horror. Using contemporary footage shot on the 228-day shoot, the doc fully supports Francis Ford Coppola's blunt assertion that "there were too many of us, we had access to too much equipment, too much money, and little by little we went insane". Much like the conflict it portrays, the filming ruined many of its warriors.

The calamities of the shoot are legend. Martin Sheen suffered a heart attack at the age of 36, civil unrest raged in its Philippines location and a typhoon caused a delay of several months. What began as an ostensibly simple story – Captain Willard (Sheen) is assigned to journey down the Nung River to "terminate" the "unsound" Colonel Kurtz (Marlon Brando) with "extreme prejudice" – on a modest budget of $12 million, mushroomed into a $38-million, debauched, yet monumentally impressive pilgrimage into the self. Long after filming, Coppola's wife Eleanor said her husband "made his journey and is still making it". With *Jack* now stinking up his CV and almost a decade gone since his last film (*The Rainmaker*), *Apocalypse* definitely took the oomph out of one of America's great filmmakers.

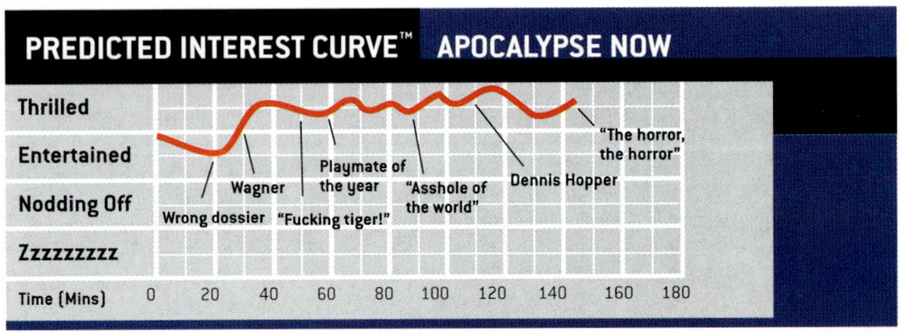

Still, what a way to be remembered. Experiencing the unfurling of his ambitious obsession for the first time is an unforgettable, incomparable, mind-ripping cinematic event.

At the time, *Variety* wrote "Coppola virtually recreates World War Three onscreen... the resulting footage outclasses any war pic made to date" and, more than 25 years and a *Saving Private Ryan* beach-storming later, the statement still rings true. The thrilling sequence cutting between the 'Ride Of The Valkyries'-scored chopper attack of Lieutenant Colonel Kilgore (Robert Duvall) and the soon-to-be-napalmed Vietnamese village, is an unsurpassed guilty kick. There's a reason why everyone can parrot "I love the smell of napalm in the morning". And that reason is in the iconographic images the line supports.

Apocalypse remains the most remarkable of war films because no one since has subjected themselves to the rigours, perils and lunacy of a shoot like that. Vehicles crash and burn, soldiers hurl themselves in front of camera, helicopters carry livestock overhead – oh, and everyone involved is smashed out of their minds on drugs. Rather than morphine to assuage wounded grunts, drugs here recall *The Onion*'s piss-take 1969 headline "US Soldiers Receive Badly Needed Heroin Airlift" – with both cast and crew mucking about with enough chemicals to accurately

represent what Vietnam correspondent Michael Herr (who also wrote Willard's narration) called "the first rock'n'roll war". From stoner band The Doors' 'The End', to the countless joints passed between soldiers, and the sudden, hallucinatory appearance of three Playmates at Hau Phat, drugs permeate *Apocalypse*'s jungle – creating a fog of war that's part napalm, part marijuana. Chef (Frederic Forrest) asks a supply lackey for Panama Red dope, Lance B Johnson (a speed, LSD and weed-tripping Sam Bottoms) drops acid at the Du Lung Bridge – a place where bedlam is calmed only by a soldier called Roach – and describes as "beautiful" a hole better christened the "asshole of the world". It's a murky, unredeemable war and with most soldiers and actors completely frazzled, it's a place no one's too likely to remember.

Coppola's mind, though, was agonisingly focused. Paranoid that he was making a pretentious movie – "My greatest fear is to make a really pompous film on an important subject" – he shot 370 hours for his "Idiodyssey" and spent almost three years splicing it together into something vaguely approaching coherence. His plan was to take John Milius' screenplay "and kind of mate it with whatever happened in the jungle". But, evidently not content with 1979's version, Coppola returned for a second go in 2001, with a *Redux* edition clocking in at a hope-you-brought-sandwiches 194 minutes. A new Playmates scene and an unnecessary French plantation foray that editor Walter Murch originally called an "indigestible lump of political information" later, and *Redux*'s main accomplishment is to jar an already peculiarly paced film. As a statement of what Coppola wanted to say, the original is, hard as it is to believe, far less pompous than his *Redux*.

Exactly what the helmer was trying to say is up for stoner debate. In dozens of comparisons between the screenplay and the stated influence of Joseph Conrad's *Heart Of Darkness* novella, much is made of how little the film resembles the text. Both deal with man's vulnerability and both are »

NEED TO KNOW

Year 1979
Running time 147 mins
Director Francis Ford Coppola
Stars Marlon Brando, Martin Sheen, Robert Duvall
But it on Region 2. Not *Redux*.
Tagline N/A
Best line "If that's how Kilgore fought the war, I began to wonder what they really had against Kurtz. It wasn't just insanity and murder. There was enough of that to go around for everyone." – Willard
Critic's view "Captures the genuine, sickening, orgiastic excitement of a licence to kill, with every GI his own 007." *– The Sunday Times*
Best watched when... You're thinking about signing up.

anchored in a primitive setting where the possibility for abuse of power by foreigners is endless. Sort of the antithesis to Crocodile Dundee's urban buffoonery, *Apocalypse* has members of a technologically superior culture coming into contact with supposed inferiors and enduring painful self-discovery. However, with at least two thirds of *Apocalypse* dedicated to 'Nam's "rock'n' rollers with one foot in their grave" before it arrives at Kurtz's Angkor Wat temple, the convergence of Conrad and Coppola hinged on Brando...

...and anyone with a sub-GCSE understanding of *Heart Of Darkness* can immediately spot one huge difference: Conrad's Kurtz is described as being "an animated image of death carved out of old ivory" while Coppola's Kurtz is fatso Brando. Forty kilos overweight, drunk and utterly unprepared, this was no happy *Godfather* reunion for director and star. The build-up for Kurtz's appearance though is monumental. We know about his excellent, tarnished military record and his succumbing to the "temptation to be God". However, we are not prepared for how his terrifyingly coherent speeches almost vindicate his actions – he has seen "the horror, the horror" and, well, fair cop, it would send anyone potty. Shot in half-darkness to disguise his obesity, Brando's Kurtz, as Dennis Hopper's speedy photojournalist gabbles, "enlarges minds" and spots the absurdities of war... "They train young men to drop fire on people. But their commanders won't allow them to write fuck on their airplanes because it's obscene!" His is perhaps the soundest mind of them all. And that is why he must die.

It may feel essentially '70s, but *Apocalypse Now* could be made today, for a post-Vietnam conflict, and still be relevant. With Iraq reeling from invasion, would it really be a great surprise if a Kurtz-a-like abandoned protocol somewhere up the Tigris River? But if one does show up, for God's sake persuade Francis Ford Coppola not to get involved. It may prove an apocalypse too far... TF

Jonathan Dean

CUTTING THE CRAP

Fanboys swooned over the much-discussed French plantation scene in the *Redux* version, but, frankly, it sucked. Here's why it should've stayed on the cutting-room floor...

MIST
The plantationers appear through the smoke like a gaggle of naff pantomime genies. It's not dreamy. It's a parody.

WAR?
Amid the clink, clink of cutlery there sits a uniformed bloke named Willard... is this some fancy-dress dinner party?

LONGEVITY
Playing like a '70s Jedi Council, the tone is politics, politics, politics. Oh look... your guests have quickly buggered off.

BREASTS
Some classic '70s mammaries and you overlook that Kurtz bloke completely... ah, he's the whole point of the film? We'd forgotten...

MIST
And that's that, the boat leaves in the same mist it arrived. What a complete and utter waste of everyone's time.

INT. ANGKOR WAT TEMPLE – NIGHT
Kurtz and Willard sit together.

WILLARD (VO)

On the river, I thought that the minute I looked at him, I'd know what to do, but it didn't happen. I was in there with him for days, not under guard – I was free – but he knew I wasn't going anywhere. He knew more about what I was going to do than I did. If the generals back in the Trang could see what I saw, would they still want me to kill him? More than ever, probably. And what would his people back home want if they ever learned just how far from them he'd really gone? He broke from them and then he broke from himself. I'd never seen a man so broken up and ripped apart...

KURTZ

Horror. Horror has a face... and you must make a friend of horror. Horror and moral terror are your friends. If they are not, then they are enemies to be feared. They are truly enemies. I remember when I was with Special Forces... seems a thousand centuries ago... we went into a camp to inoculate the children. We left the camp after we had inoculated the children for polio, and this old man came running after us and he was crying. He couldn't see. We went back there and they had come and hacked off every inoculated arm. There they were in a pile... a pile of little arms. And I remember... I... I... I cried... I wept like some grandmother. I wanted to tear my teeth out. I didn't know what I wanted to do. And I want to remember it. I never want to forget it. I never want to forget. And then I realised... like I was shot... like I was shot with a diamond... a diamond bullet right through my forehead... and I thought: 'My God... the genius of that. The genius. The will to do that. Perfect, genuine, complete, crystalline, pure.' And then I realised they were stronger than we. Because they could stand that these were not monsters... these were men... trained cadres... these men who fought with their hearts, who had families, who had children, who were filled with love... but they had the strength... the strength... to do that. If I had 10 divisions of those men, our troubles here would be over very quickly. You have to have men who are moral... and at the same time who are able to utilise their primordial instincts to kill without feeling... without passion... without judgement... without judgement. Because it's judgement that defeats us.

19

THE TEXAS CHAIN SAW MASSACRE

Five go missing (after being attacked with power tools)...

Mid-August, 1973. Eighteen-year-old drama student Marilyn Burns is trussed to a dining-room chair in a ramshackle farmhouse situated 20 miles outside Austin, Texas. On the table in front of her sits a rancid meat feast, sausages and chicken. It's been putrefying in the 120°F heat for 27 hours straight – the amount of time that a young, straggly-haired film crew has obsessed over the climactic scene of their guerilla horror movie. Burns is surrounded by four men playing a family of cannibals. She screams, they laugh. She cries, they laugh. She pleads, they laugh. The atmosphere is one of gleeful sadism... and the boundary between reality and fantasy has long since bled away.

"I was supposed to pretend to nick Marilyn's finger with a blade, squeezing a bulb in my palm to deposit a little fake blood," recalls Gunnar Hansen, the Icelandic-born carpenter who played masked killer Leatherface. "Well, the bulb kept clogging. I was sick of it. I turned away and stripped the tape off the knife's edge. That's really blood and she's really screaming."

This anecdote – one of many pertaining to the miserable conditions in which *The Texas Chain Saw Massacre* was made – is worth repeating because it perhaps explains why a $60,000 slasher shot on grainy 16mm is the greatest horror film of 'em all. Watch *Chain Saw* now and you can still feel the pain, taste the insanity. It burns out of the screen and microwaves your brain, scorching harrowing images on the mind's bulging eye. And it won't go away. Ever. "If we'd had a big budget and air-conditioned trailers, it wouldn't have been as good," explains Hansen. "You can't dismiss the talent of everyone involved, but the unexpected conditions meant there was a certain amount of serendipity to it, too."

Director Tobe Hooper has certainly never come close to matching his calling-card masterpiece, spending the last 30 years making genre flicks that range from the pretty good (*The Funhouse*) to the bad (*Spontaneous Combustion*) to the downright ugly (*The Mangler*). But *Chain Saw*? It cuts to the bone, its primitive terrors even eliciting respectful shudders from the most unlikely sources. *Evening Standard* critic Alexander Walker called it "the purest of all horror films". *Time* ranked it in the 10 most influential movies of the last 25 years. And the original print is part of the permanent collection in New York's Museum Of Modern Art.

The plot is one-third *Scooby-Doo*, two-thirds slasher cliché, a group of five kids running out of petrol in the sweltering Texan heat. A dilapidated farmhouse glowers on the

It unspools like your worst nightmare: illogical, amoral, devoid of resolution

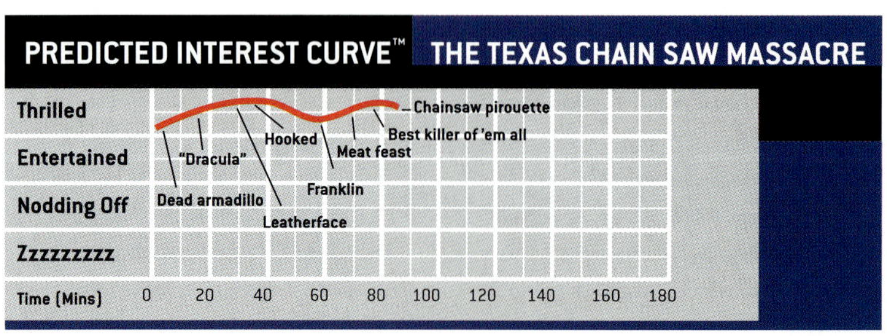

horizon. Inside its peeling walls lives a family of gurning flesh-eaters fronted by Leatherface, a 22-stone madman with a penchant for fleshy masks, blood-spattered aprons and unwieldy power tools. You can guess the rest.

Born out of the political angst of the time (Vietnam, Watergate, the oil embargo) and riding the (new) wave of terror visions spawned by 1968's *Night Of The Living Dead*, *The Texas Chain Saw Massacre* also owes something to Hooper's childhood. "I was about 11 and my Wisconsin relatives used to think it would be a great idea to scare the crap out of me with stories about Ed Gein [*the '50s serial killer who decorated his house with human artefacts*]," he says. "It tortured me. That stuff stays with you forever." It certainly stayed with him as he set out to make *Chain Saw* (or *Headcheese* as it was then monikered), the 30-year-old opting to stare down his demons by making a movie about "a whole family of Geins". The chainsaw angle, meanwhile, was hit upon as the fledgling director traipsed around Austin's Sears department store in the early '70s. "It was crowded and I started to have a panic attack. I was thinking, 'Please God, show me a way to get out of here...' And there, right in front of my eyes, was a big display of chainsaws."

Shot largely chronologically in 32 straight days, *The Texas Chain Saw Massacre* unspools like your worst nightmare: illogical, amoral, devoid of resolution. Its footage, overlaid by a soundtrack of sonic rumbles, clashing tambourines and shrill, shrill drills, plays with the raw immediacy of a low-budget documentary; its various death-rattles are fast, brutal and painfully real. Designed simply to "scare the shit out of someone", as writer Kim Henkel put it, Hooper's exploitation flick had many viewers motoring home from the drive-in theatre in a state of extreme shock, convinced they'd just seen a snuff movie.

What you won't find in *Texas Chain Saw Massacre*, however, is spurting blood – surprising given the fiendishly lurid title, sensational tagline ("Who will survive and what will be left of them?") and mythical reputation it's accrued over

NEED TO KNOW

Year 1974
Running time 80 mins
Director Tobe Hooper
Stars Marilyn Burns, Gunnar Hansen, Allen Danziger, Paul A Partain, Edwin Neal
Buy It On Region 2
Tagline "Who will survive and what will be left of them?"
Best line "My family's always been in meat."
– The Hitchhiker
Critic's view "It's really fucking scary."
– *Philadelphia City Paper*
Best watched when... The door is locked and the lights are on.

the past 30 years. Okay, so there's a fleeting shot of a chainsaw biting into Leatherface's leg – a teaspoon of grue – but Hooper's allegedly oh-so-sick-flick is otherwise not much different to Val Lewton's shadowy, suggestive pictures in the '40s and '50s. "One guy who saw the film recently told me, 'Your movie has the best special-effects I've ever seen. Why can't they do it so well now?'" says Hansen. "I said, 'There are no special-effects; we don't show anything.' He said, 'But I saw you slice that guy in half...'"

Perhaps it was this trick of convincing viewers they'd just witnessed the most unspeakable horrors in the annals of American cinema that caused BBFC President James Ferman to ban Hooper's movie. Labelling it "the pornography of terror", Ferman squatted on it until he retired in 1998. Ridiculous, but not half as ridiculous as his decision to lop off the c-word from all subsequent film titles, the innocuous *Hollywood Chainsaw Hookers* thus finding itself trimmed down to plain old *Hollywood Hookers*.

Finally revving into multiplexes in 1999, *The Texas Chain Saw Massacre* showed the *Scream* generation what real horror was all about. That it wiped the knowing smiles off their now-ashen faces is testament to its full-blooded integrity. Neither passing years nor increasingly silly sequels nor 2004's slick-but-pointless retooling can blunt its cutting, bleeding edge. To steal from *Driller Killer*'s infamous tagline as surely as that film ransacked *Chain Saw*, "...And the drill keeps tearing through flesh and bone!" TF

Jamie Graham

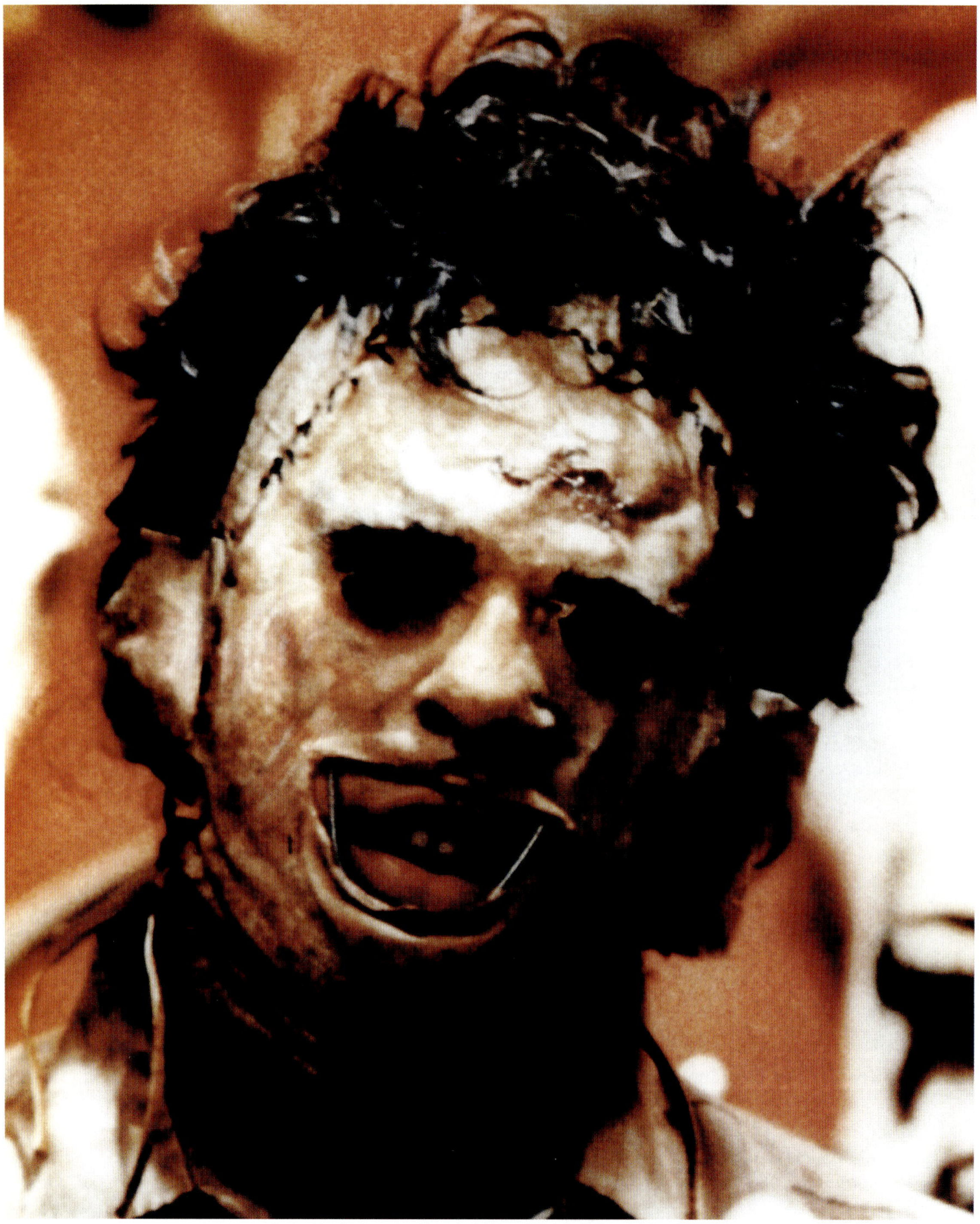

CUTTING DEEP

Rooting in Hooper's toolkit for hidden subtexts...

WARRING FACTION
Five blundering, arrogant kids in a foreign territory fighting a resolute foe who knows the lay of the land... Not hard to see why Hooper's slasher has been described as a Vietnam War allegory, but the director himself has always denied it: "You couldn't, in any sense, call it a political movie," he says.

VEGGIE DELIGHT
Leatherface's family used to work in the slaughterhouse. Now they're working from home, chopping up meat and hanging it on hooks. Why should we be unperturbed when the victims are cattle, but appalled when the flesh is human? "Yeah, I can see that," Gunnar Hansen tells *Total Film*. "For me, the most distressing image in the whole movie is the close-up of the cow drooling and panting."

FAMILY MISFORTUNES
No doubting that *Chain Saw* works as a satire on the traditional sitcom family, Hansen playing mom (wig, apron, lipstick-painted mask) to Siedow's dad and Edwin Neal's rebellious teenage son. "It succeeds as a parody of the nuclear family," concedes Hansen, "but I always tell people the same: first and foremost, we set out to scare people."

Classic Scene

EXT. FARMHOUSE – DAY
Kirk and Pam approach the farmhouse in search of help. Kirk raps at the door.

KIRK
Hello, is anyone home?

He raps again, stands back and steps on a tooth. He picks it up off the porch.

KIRK
Got something for you.

He puts the tooth in Pam's outstretched hand. She's appalled.

PAM
Eeugh!
(*storms off*)
Let's go!

Kirk raps at the door again.

KIRK
Hello... hello?

Pam sits on a garden swing.

KIRK
Hey Pam, come look at this...

PAM
What? No!

KIRK
Hello, anybody home? Hello!

He raps hard at door. It swings open onto a dank hallway. An open doorway at the end of the corridor reveals a red wall mounted with animal skulls. Pig squealing noises can be heard from somewhere in the house.

KIRK
Hey Pam!
(*Pause*)
Hello?

Kirk walks down the hallway, slips and stumbles forward as a huge aproned figure appears in front of him.

Close on: the blood-splattered apron. The camera rises to reveal a hideous fleshy mask and a powerful arm lofting a mallet.

The mallet descends, glancing off Kirk's skull with a sickening crunch. Kirk collapses, his body twitching, head thrashing, feet kicking.

The attacker deals another glancing blow, grabs Kirk under the shoulders and pulls him through the doorway. He slams a sliding steel door to block off our view. A headthrobbing sonic rumble rises on the soundtrack.

Outside, Pam sits on the swing, oblivious.

PAM
(*Annoyed*)
Kirk!

Machinery hums. Pam walks to the house, the camera sliding under the swing to follow her.

PAM
Kirk! Kirk? Kirk?

Pam enters the house. She takes in the corridor and steel door. She walks into a dark room off the hallway.

PAM
Kirk?

She yanks open a pair of curtains and falls through a doorway into into a room littered with bones and feathers.

A chicken clucks in a cage in the corner. Pam's wide eyes scan the room, taking in the horror – including a sofa fashioned from human bones. She wretches and stumbles into the hall.

The steel door crashes open and the killer lurches out, squealing. He picks Pam up and carries her thrashing body down the corridor.

In the backroom hangs a meathook. The attacker hoists Pam in the air. And hangs her on the hook.

Her flailing hands try to clutch behind her. There is a body on a table. The killer picks up a chainsaw.

He starts to cut up the body.

Pam screams in the background.

18

ALL ABOUT EVE

A venomous fable about art and celebrity that became Bette Davis' finest hour.

When a performer gets the part they were born to play, it's a wonderful sight – even more so when that part comes when they're considered over the hill. For proof, see Brando in *Last Tango In Paris*, Anna Magnani in *Mamma Roma*, Burt Lancaster in *Atlantic City* – or watch Bette Davis in *All About Eve*. That suggests that you have a choice in the matter. In fact, you can't do anything *but* watch Bette Davis in *All About Eve*: she commands the screen, rolling those expressive, marble-sized eyes, stalking the set like a hungry lioness where lesser actors merely try not to bump into the furniture, smacking her lips at each fizzy, crackling, poison-tipped line in Joseph L Mankiewicz's screenplay. She is defiance personified; could another actress have put as much panache into the moment when she toasts a despised adversary with a suggestively proffered stick of celery? (Or put as much vampiric bite into the act of chomping on it?)

Then there's the smoking. In our nearly nicotine-free times, Davis' on-screen chainsmoking becomes not just the expression of character and style that it was in the '50s, but an oddly incongruous symbol of transgression. Every sentence she delivers is chased out of her mouth by an alarming puff of smoke. And there's no smoke without fire...

The name Eve, suggesting the Garden of Eden, is a misnomer – she's all viper

As the actress Margo Channing, nudging 40 and fearing the steep decline of her career, Davis is red hot. In fact, the one serious flaw in the film's conception might be that we can never fully believe that the stalker-cum-wannabe Eve Harrington (Anne Baxter) poses as much of a threat to Margo as the script pretends. Baxter simply can't compete with Davis' ferocity, her relish for words and the menace they can convey. But that's a minor issue. Davis makes the battle as close to plausible as it can be, and Baxter is fine in Eve's more sinister moments – the scene, played with Davis in bed, when Margo first comprehends the extent of Eve's cunning, or the long, suspenseful passage later in the movie when Eve reveals her true nature to the playwright's wife (Celeste Holm). "You'd do all that for a part in a play?" she gasps when Eve has finished explaining how she plans to swipe a plum part from under Margo's nose. Eve's retort: "I'd do much more for a part that good."

The name Eve, suggesting the Garden of Eden, is a misnomer: she's all viper. That much becomes obvious as she progresses from being "the mousey one with the trenchcoat and the funny hat", as Margo describes her when she turns up in fan mode at her theatre dressing room, to ranking as a "killer", in the words of the acidic critic Addison DeWitt,

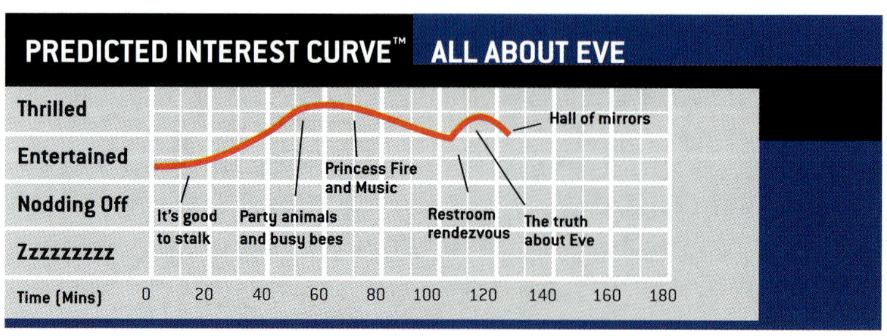

after she has shoved her way into being Margo's understudy and nemesis. Baxter was Oscar-nominated for Best Actress, as was Davis, and though both lost out to Judy Holliday (for *Born Yesterday*), the picture was nominated for 14 Oscars (a record unmatched until *Titanic*) and won six, including two for writer-director Mankiewicz.

Davis, though, was not even second choice for the part. After 20th Century Fox bought the rights to Mary Orr's story 'The Wisdom Of Eve', the producer Darryl F Zanuck announced he wanted Marlene Dietrich in the role. But Mankiewicz originally cast Claudette Colbert, who then had to pull out due to a back injury. Davis showed no mercy on set, apparently snarling at Celeste Holm when she tried to say "Good morning". The pair didn't speak after that. Davis' affection was reserved for another cast member; soon after shooting finished, she married her fourth husband, Gary Merrill, who plays Margo's director boyfriend.

Among the rest of the cast are three exquisite turns without which the picture would be noticeably less idiosyncratic. A certain Marilyn Monroe delivers a sparkling cameo as a budding starlet from "the Copacabana School of Acting". Thelma Ritter, as Margo's croaky-voiced, sarcastic assistant Birdie, is a scream, dispensing put-downs with vicious ease; she doesn't get more than a handful of screen time, but she's a straight-up tonic amidst all the clandestine scheming. George Sanders, as Addison DeWitt, is extraordinary, finding numerous ambiguities in a character who seems initially to be just a hissable twit. The Best Supporting Actor Oscar that Sanders received for his efforts was richly deserved. As were Mankiewicz's brace, particularly the screenplay award; the crackerjack dialogue is so satisfying that it's easy to take for granted the cleverness of Mankiewicz's structure, which hands the narration from character to character like a baton in a relay race. Then there's the subdued shock of the final scene, in which the narrative comes full circle, devastatingly so, and Eve finds herself saddled with an admiring fan/PA who is >>

NEED TO KNOW

Film 1950
Running time 138 mins
Director Joseph L Mankiewicz
Stars Bette Davis, Anne Baxter, George Sanders, Thelma Ritter, Marilyn Monroe
Buy it on Region 2
Tagline N/A
Best line "Fasten your seatbelts. It's going to be a bumpy night."
– Margo Channing
Critic's view "*All About Eve* is a withering satire: witty, mature, and worldly-wise."
– *The New York Times*
Best watched when... You're being hounded by a crazy-ass stalker who wants your job.

to her what she was to Margo so long ago.

Like many of Davis' best films – *Dark Victory, The Little Foxes, Now Voyager, Whatever Happened To Baby Jane?* – *All About Eve* quickly acquired the status of gay classic, helped no end by its swirling emotion, its glistening dialogue and Davis' own iconic performance. But unlike those other pictures, *All About Eve* has itself spawned or influenced a number of other key films in gay cinema, most notably *The Killing Of Sister George, Prick Up Your Ears* and Pedro Almodovar's *All About My Mother*, which features affectionate twists on several scenes in Mankiewicz's picture. It was also adapted into an underwhelming Broadway musical, *Applause*, which at one point featured Anne Baxter herself in Davis' old part. The blasphemy of it: what would Margo Channing have made of that? Through it all, the rumours that Margo was based on Tallulah Bankhead never went away, though Mankiewicz went on record to say that this wasn't so. Bankhead was not noticeably placated, and once promised that if she saw Davis she would, "tear every hair out of her moustache". TF

Ryan Gilbey

VOICES CARRY

Eve packs an acerbic wallop, but here are five more revolutionary voiceovers...

CITIZEN KANE (1941)
Orson Welles' masterpiece is an unsolvable puzzle, and though the voiceovers deliberately fail to illuminate Kane, Welles' skill at moving between perspectives is something to behold.

LONDON (1994)
This visionary pseudo-documentary by Patrick Keiller uses Paul Scofield's enigmatic narration to lend new magic and eeriness to images of a city crushed by Thatcherite Conservatism.

THE BIG LEBOWSKI (1998)
The Coen brothers' funniest picture has an air of stoned detachment that comes partly from Sam Elliott's narration: at one point he even forgets what he was saying. "Now, where was I?"

THE OPPOSITE OF SEX (1998)
Few voiceovers are as duplicitous as that of DeeDee Truitt (Ricci). Director Don Roos deploys his amoral heroine to smuggle taboo subjects under the radar of a mainstream audience.

THE THIN RED LINE (1998)
Terrence Malick is the master of the evocative voiceover (see also *Badlands*). But here, the narration is daringly mysterious: sometimes you don't even know who's speaking.

Classic Scene

INT. MARGO'S BEDROOM – DAY
Margo's assistant, Birdie, draws the curtains and presents her with a breakfast tray.

MARGO
Birdie.

BIRDIE
Hm?

MARGO
You don't like Eve, do you?

BIRDIE
You want an argument or an answer?

MARGO
An answer.

BIRDIE
No.

MARGO
Why not?

BIRDIE
Now you want an argument.

MARGO
She works hard.

BIRDIE
Night and day.

MARGO
She's loyal and efficient.

BIRDIE
Like an agent with only one client.

MARGO
She thinks only of me.

Birdie shoots her a doubtful sideways glance.

MARGO (CONT'D)
Doesn't she?

BIRDIE
Well. Let's say she thinks only *about* you anyway.

MARGO
How do you mean that?

BIRDIE
I'll tell you how. Like – like she's studying you. Like you was a play or a book or a set of blueprints. How you walk, talk, eat, sleep, think...

MARGO
(*interrupting*)
I'm sure that's very flattering, Birdie, I'm sure there's nothing wrong with it.

There's a knock at the door. Eve pokes her head into the room.

EVE
Good morning.
(*she walks in*)
Well, what do you think of my elegant new suit?

MARGO
Very becoming. It looks much better on you than it did on me.

EVE
I can imagine. You know, all it needed was a little taking in here and letting out there. Are you sure you won't want it yourself?

MARGO
Quite sure. I find it too seventeen-ish for me.

EVE
Oh come now, as though you're an old lady! I'm on my way; is there anything more you thought of?

MARGO
There's that script to take back to the Guild.

EVE
I've got it.

MARGO
And those cheques or whatever it is for the income tax man.

EVE
(*patting her case*)
Right here.

MARGO
It seems I can't think of a thing you haven't thought of.

EVE
That's my job. See you at teatime.

MARGO
(*sternly, as Eve reaches the door*)
Eve – by chance did you place a call from me to Bill, midnight California time?

EVE
Golly, I forgot to tell you.

MARGO
Yes, dear, you forgot all about it.

EVE
Well, I was sure you'd want to, of course, it being his birthday. You've been so busy these past few days and last night I meant to tell you before you went out with the Richards... I guess I was asleep when you got home.

MARGO
Yes, I guess you were. It was very thoughtful of you, Eve.

EVE
Mr Sampson's birthday – I couldn't forget that. You'd never forgive me. As a matter of fact, I sent him a telegram myself.

Eve waltzes off. Margo bristles and exchanges disapproving looks with Birdie, who leaves after delivering her own long, told-you-so look at Margo. We fade out on a sour-looking Margo.

17

ONCE UPON A TIME IN THE WEST

Sergio Leone saddles up to bid an epic farewell to the Old West...

While Sergio Leone's name will forever be linked with his Clint Eastwood-starring *Dollars* trilogy, it's his later *Once Upon A Time In The West* – the one where Charles Bronson's Harmonica usurps Clint's taciturn, no-name gunslinger – that's the Italian's greatest masterpiece. Produced on a grander scale and boasting a greater political complexity than Leone's previous efforts, it also works as a summation of the entire genre: the Monument Valley locations and the presence of Henry Fonda tie *West* to John Ford's traditional horse operas, while the stylised violence and unflinching revisionism show how the West was really won.

To fully understand *Once Upon A Time In The West*, however, it's vital to first go back to the *Dollars* trilogy: the spaghetti Western sub-genre, like Rome, was not build in a day. It started with Leone reworking Akira Kurosawa's wandering Samurai flicks *Yojimbo* and *Sanjuro* as *A Fistful Of Dollars* and *For A Few Dollars More*, pop cinema extravangzas packed with booming guns and looming close-ups. Heavily dubbed and featuring a TV cowboy who preferred to squint than talk, these cartoonish, kinetic and shockingly amoral movies offered US audiences a head-spinning reinvention of their beloved, home-grown genre. Somehow, the Italian Leone had managed to blend his Japanese source material with an American star and Spain's Almeira region (doubling for the desert land of Arizona, New Mexico and Utah) and not mix a Euro pudding. Anything but, in fact: his colourfully monikered spaghetti Westerns caused the desired stir, exhilarating audiences from Naples to New York. And the best was still to come, with Leone completing his trilogy with 1966's *The Good, The Bad And The Ugly*. Operating on a markedly larger scale that added a welcome grain of committed realism to the volatile mix by setting the action among the US Civil War, Leone's final chapter made his former tinkerings seem like trite play-things in comparison.

Don't expect honour and integrity. Do expect money, greed and blood

By 1968, Leone was poised to take another leap by making the last word on Westerns – an epic, sprawling, grandiose, down'n'dirty, exhilarating, tragic and plain vicious oater that would ride under the suitably bombastic title of *Once Upon A Time In The West*. Plot-wise, the Leone/Bernardo Bertolucci/Dario Argento-penned story appears simplistic, with a struggle over a patch of arid land the stimulus for the slaughter of a family and other personal confrontations. Brush away the surface dirt, however, and you'll find a movie that's concerned with a much bigger picture, systematically destroying Ford's creation myth (see *The Iron Horse*)

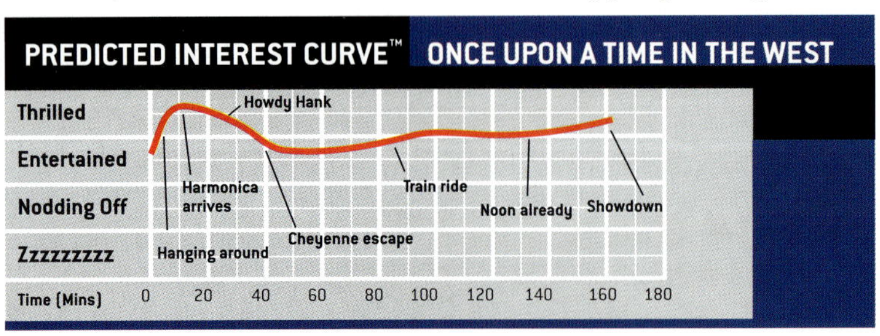

by foregrounding the various personal vendettas against a railroad magnate's bloody determination to shackle the West with tracks. Don't expect honour or integrity. Do expect money, greed and blood.

Not content to merely reference American Westerns, Leone originally planned to nod at his own *The Good, The Bad And The Ugly*, too. His idea to cast that film's titular trio as the gunmen in the audacious opening shoot-out (see classic scene) went awry, however, when Eastwood's schedule wouldn't permit such a cameo. Unsurprisingly, Leone had initially approached Clint to reprise his Man With No Name role, but was forced to look elsewhere when Eastwood said no – he'd had his fill of working on gruelling Western sets under the direction of the combustible Italian. Lee Coburn, the helmer's first-choice substitute, also passed. It would have been a nice fit given Coburn's appearance in John Sturges' *The Magnificent Seven*, a film which was itself inspired by a Kurosawa movie – *Seven Samurai*. Yes, it would have been a nice fit... so much so that Leone turned to Bronson, another of Sturges' magnificent septet, to play the tight-lipped Harmonica. An off-putting proposition? Don't be put off by his mahogany turns in the *Death Wish* series: here he's whittled from the same hardwood as Eastwood, his lifeless eyes intent on retribution. Notice how he's not tempted by the curves of Claudia Cardinale

NEED TO KNOW

Year 1968
Running time 165 mins
Director Sergio Leone
Stars Henry Ford, Charles Bronson, Jason Robards, Claudia Cardinale, Gabriele Ferzetti
Buy it on Region 1 Collector's Edition
Best line "How can you trust a man who wears both a belt and suspenders? The man can't even trust his own pants." – Frank
Critic's view "They walk. They wait. They circle. They stare. They squint. They spit. They take off their jackets. They wince. Why hurry a good shoot-out?" – *Chicago Sun-Times*
Best watched when... The TV's HUGE and the volume's LOUD.

or the financial gain that Sweetwater farm will offer: all he wants is revenge.

Revenge on whom? Frank, the ruthless leader of a posse of gunmen. Frank, the killer with the coldest eyes you'll ever see. Frank, the evil sonofabitch who once did something nasty, very nasty, which that Harmonica will never forget and that we learn of in the closing moments, the blood rushing to our temples as the adrenalin kicks in.

And who plays this cold-hearted bastard? Why, good ol' American icon Henry Fonda of course, his chilling portrayal making for the greatest image-trash you'll see on film.

Not that he wanted to do it at first. Put off by the shoddy script, he was swayed only » after watching the *Dollars* trilogy and talking to close friend and *The Good, The Bad And The Ugly* star Eli Wallach. "Pay no attention to the script," urged Wallach. "Just go – you'll have a marvellous time, believe me." Fonda did go, turning up on set with his trademark blue eyes covered by brown contact-lenses and his instantly-recognisable visage obscured by a bushy handle-bar 'tache. Leone wasted no time in getting back the Fonda that US viewers knew and loved. What better way to shock viewers than have those blue peepers icing over as he spits out cruel lines like: "People scare better when they're dying"?

A monumental triumph that simultaneously gunned down the genre and lofted it to the heavens in jubilant celebration, *Once Upon A Time In The West* bit the dust at the box office. Critics moaned that it was too long, too boring, while Paramount lopped off chunks to enable them to cram in an extra showing a night. More popcorn, less sense. But then, in 1984, it all became clear: *West* was finally released uncut, theatrically and on video. At last it was possible to witness Leone's greatest work in all its operatic glory, to revel in its rugged landscapes and weathered faces, dynamite set-pieces and lush, evocative score (Morricone's greatest), soiled politics and clean thrills. The greatest Western ever made? You'd better believe it. TF

Scott Russon

HONOURABLE HANK

The film roles that made Henry Fonda's casting as a sadistic killer so damn shocking...

YOUNG MR LINCOLN (1939)
John Ford's courtroom drama casts Fonda as a young Abe Lincoln, back when Presidents were revered. "For me, it was like playing Jesus Christ," murmured an awestruck Fonda.

THE GRAPES OF WRATH (1940)
Ford and Fonda again, Pete playing former-murderer-turned-man-of-the-people Tom Joad in a near-perfect adap of Steinbeck's novel.

THE OX-BOW INCIDENT (1943)
Mob violence gets a kicking in this wartime Western as Fonda sets out to prove the innocence of three drifters lynched for rustling cattle.

MY DARLING CLEMENTINE (1946)
Fonda as one of the nation's greatest lawmen, Wyatt Earp, in Ford's wondrous print-the-myth Western – still the best Earp movie ever. Only Fonda could make a trip to the barber's quite so meaningful.

12 ANGRY MEN (1957)
Sidney Lumet's courtroom drama sees eleven jurers convinced that a young defendant has murdered his father. One man disagrees. Guess who?

Classic Scene

EXT. TRAIN STATION – DAY
The elderly Station Master writes times to and from Flagstone on a chalkboard.

A cowboy enters, complete with long-barrel rifle and dust coat. The Station Master gives him a gummy smile. He turns to see a second and then a third cowboy enter what pass for doorways in the rickety station. No one says a word. Birds sing, crickets chirrup and there's a rhythmic squeaking from a nearby mechanical instrument.

STATION MASTER
Hey, hey, if you want any tickets you'll have to go around to the...

Cowboy One stares him down.

STATION MASTER
Oh, all right. I suppose it'll be all right. How am I supposed to...
(*mumbles and walks off*)

Cowboy Three makes aggressive tweeting noises with his cat-like face at a caged bird.

The Station Master returns with tickets in hand.

STATION MASTER
Let's see... Three.
(*holds out the tickets*)

Cowboy One stares at him, before eventually taking the tickets.

STATION MASTER
That'll be seven dollars...

Cowboy One releases the tickets from his grasp and they blow away in the wind

STATION MASTER (CONT'D)
...and 50 cents.

Cowboy One takes the Station Master by the scruff of the neck and throws him into a cupboard. He raises a finger to his lips and shushes him before slamming the metal door shut.

Cut to black. White titles trail across the screen and read, "A Sergio Leone Film".

Cowboy One adjusts his hat. The native American woman, who had been sweeping the station, flees – leaving a trail of dust behind her.

The cowboys take up various positions of comfort as the credits of the cast intermittently appear on screen.

The sound of the mechanical squeaking gets louder as a windmill is seen turning.

Cowboy Three takes water from a trough.

Cowboy Two gently rocks on a seat as an incoming message on the wire begins to tap rapidly. After a number of clickety-clicks, he yanks the machine apart.

Drips from the water tower fall on the head of Cowboy One. He puts his hat back on.

Cowboy Three cracks his knuckles at the water trough.

Cowboy One is harassed by a fly and tries, unsuccessfully, to blow the fly from his chin.

Cowboy Three continues to crack his knuckles.

The water still rhythmically drops on Cowboy One's hat. He traps the fly within the barrel of his six-shooter and listens to its buzz. A train's whistle is heard in the distance.

We watch from underneath as the clanking train passes overhead.

Cowboy One drinks the collected water from his hat. He releases the fly.

Cowboy Three turns to face the approaching train.

Cowboy One loads his sawn-off rifle.

The train comes to a halt, the steam engine breathing rhythmically.

A freight door slides open and a man throw's a case out before sliding the door shut again. The train slowly begins to pull out of the station. The cowboys walk back to the station and suddenly stop in their tracks as harmonica music is heard.

As the train pulls away, a solitary figure is revealed stood on the opposite side of the track. The trio turn back around, poised.

Harmonica finishes playing his wistful tune.

HARMONICA
Are you Frank?

COWBOY ONE
Frank sent us.

HARMONICA
Did you bring a horse for me?

COWBOY ONE
(*laughs*)
Looks like... looks like we're...
Looks like we're shy of one horse.

Off screen, Cowboy One laughs.

HARMONICA
(*shakes his head*)
You brought two too many.

The cowboys draw and fire; Harmonica shoots them all dead. The windmill turns.

16

THE APARTMENT

Billy Wilder's corporate America morality tale still tops the agenda, satire-wise.

Pimping, prostitution, bribery, blackmail, urban alienation, suicide – got to be a comedy, right? Well, a Billy Wilder comedy anyway. No one does the pitch-black flipside of funny like Wilder, and *The Apartment* is the darkest he ever made. Plus it's got Jack Lemmon – what more can you ask?

'Wilder knew all about Siggy's pet theory on wealth: money equals shit'

Wilder took US citizenship on his arrival in the States in 1935 but retained the quizzical scepticism and Mitteleuropean sophistication of his Viennese upbringing, turning on his adopted country the beady-eyed, disenchanted stare of the outsider. In fact it's astounding that he largely avoided trouble during the anti-commie witch-hunt years, because *The Apartment*'s take on Free-Market Enterprise and The American Way of Life would have had Marx dancing a jig.

In the offices of Consolidated Life, the gargantuan insurance company where much of the movie's action is played out, the workers sit at row upon endless row of identical desks in vast soulless hangars – processed slabs of wage-slavery straight out of *Metropolis*. The bosses, almost without exception, are greedy, treacherous, self-serving scumbags whose sole preoccupation – beyond upping their richly-undeserved salaries and doing each other down – is groping the arses, and whatever else they can gain access to, of any attractive young female employees unwary enough to pass within grabbing distance. (The boss class in this enlightened establishment, of course, is exclusively male – and presumably hetero.) And the ultimate coveted status-symbol in this capitalist heaven on earth? A lavatory key. That's right – the Key to the Executive Washroom. Wilder, born and brought up in Freud's Vienna, knew all about Uncle Siggy's pet theory on wealth: money equals shit.

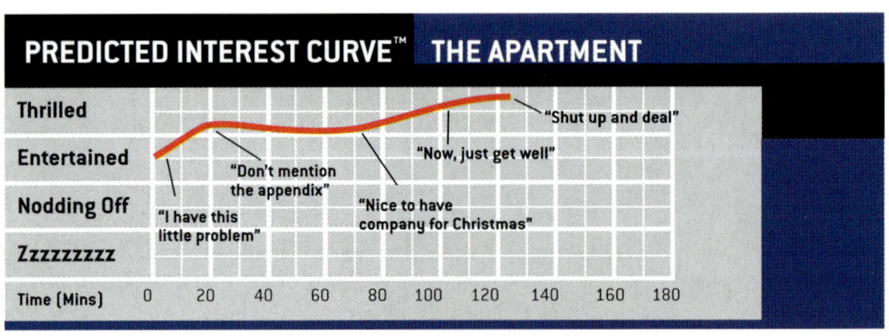

Almost without exception? Yes, there's one boss who isn't – not quite, not yet – an unregenerate louse. Which is strange, because he's JD Sheldrake, Consolidated's head of personnel, in theory the biggest, most powerful bastard of all. And the reason he isn't – and here we approach the heart of what makes *The Apartment* such a great film – is that he's played by Fred MacMurray.

Wilder liked to say, quoting his revered mentor Ernst Lubitsch, that "casting is 95 per cent of a film". An exaggeration, maybe – but not by much. As CC Baxter ("It stands for Calvin Clifford, but everyone calls me Buddy"), Lemmon is as good as he's ever been – which is saying a lot playing the twitchy, put-upon corporate Everyman who finally decides to become a mensch. Shirley MacLaine's gamine charm as funny, sweet, wounded Fran Kubelik marks a highpoint in her career. But

Wilder's masterstroke was in choosing MacMurray as Sheldrake – because he knew the actor would be fighting him all the way. He'd pulled just the same trick on him once before.

MacMurray had made a successful film career playing nice guys – solid, tweedy, pipe-smoking, maybe a bit dull but utterly dependable. Then in 1944 Wilder, who had spotted something in MacMurray's stolid screen persona no one else had noticed, talked him into playing Walter Neff, sleazy insurance salesman, adulterer and killer, in *Double Indemnity*. It was the finest work MacMurray had ever done, and the reviews were terrific but the actor hated the way he'd been made to look, and scuttled straight back to being Mr Tweedy-Pipe.

Now Wilder was at it again. And once more MacMurray felt deeply uncomfortable and kept trying to redeem his character. Which of course is just what the role needs. Because Fran Kubelik isn't stupid, or ditsy, or insensitive, and though she might fall for a total shit once she wouldn't be dumb enough to do it twice. So there has to be that small surviving core of genuine warmth, genuine tenderness in Sheldrake's character that she can respond to. Watch the scene with the two of them in the Chinese restaurant. Sheldrake's giving her the old line about divorcing his wife, and she's knows damn well it's bullshit. But then he starts reminiscing about a trip they took together and a rickety canoe they rented – and you see that this guy really still can be nice, and tender, and sexy, and that she's remembering the good times they had together, and that's what gets her back into bed with him at poor old Baxter's apartment. And as Sheldrake sweet-talks her over the cocktails you can't tell – and she can't, and probably even he can't – where the sincerity ends and the fake sincerity begins.

Okay, it's not just the casting. Of course it isn't. Wilder's script, in tandem with his regular collaborator Izzy Diamond, is a masterly piece of writing, treading that knife-edge balance between comedy and tragedy, deftly setting up what Alexander Mackendrick »

NEED TO KNOW

Year 1960
Running time 122 mins
Director Billy Wilder
Stars Jack Lemmon, Shirley MacLaine, Fred MacMurray, Ray Walston, Edie Adams
Buy it on Region 2
Tagline "Movie-wise, there has never been anything like it – laugh-wise, love-wise, or otherwise-wise!
Best line "Shut up and deal." – Fran
Critic's view "A gleeful, tender and even sentimental film." – *New York Times*
Best watched when... You just got back from the office party.

always liked to call 'depth-charges' – casual mentions and references that'll later explode at just the right moment. Look how many of them pop up in the final 10 minutes: the fruitcake, the champagne, the gin rummy, Baxter's botched suicide attempt, Fran's inability to spell, etc, etc. There's the work of the great French set designer Alexander Trauner – that monstrous office set with its forced perspectives and midgets at the furthest desks. There's Joseph LaShelle's noirish framing and lighting, making brilliant use of the bleak expanses of widescreen black-and–white, and Adolph Deutsch's score seamlessly ringing the changes from full-blown romantic to ironic to small-hours blackest melancholia.

And so, ultimately, *The Apartment* just has the edge over *Some Like It Hot* in the Wilder Masterpiece Stakes. *Hot* is sharp, fast, stylish, gloriously tasteless, fizzingly funny and has the greatest punchline ever. But its characters, though brilliantly drawn, are essentially caricatures with scant connection to real life. In *The Apartment* Wilder's got his usual crowd of blithely stereotyped support players – check out the warm-hearted, nosy Jewish couple in the next apartment, chicken-soup clichés piled high – but at its heart are three real people and it takes them (or two of them at least) right to the edge of the abyss of defeat and despair. In the Christmas Eve sequence that follows the office party we cut between Fran in Baxter's apartment after Sheldrake's left, realising he's treated her as a $100-a-trick hooker, her eyes lighting on a bottle of sleeping pills – and Baxter maudlin and pie-eyed in a downtown bar, knowing Sheldrake's bedding the girl he loves, being picked up by a woman as sad and lonely as he. (Another casting coup – Hope Holiday looks scarily like what Fran might become in 20 years if things went badly.) At this juncture *The Apartment* is just one thin chill whisker away from out-and-out tragedy. It's a rare, brave comedy that'll do that. TF

Philip Kemp

WORKING SCHMOES

CC 'Buddy' Baxter isn't the only number in the system...

Jonathan Pryce, Brazil
Sam Lowry battles against red-tape beaureacracy at the Ministry of Information. I wish I could fly.

Edward Norton, Fight Club
Our disillusioned, disintegrating narrator has had enough of punching time to punch faces instead.

Frank Whaley, Swimming With Sharks
Hollywood studio assistant Guy soaks up endless verbal abuse from his producer boss (Kevin Spacey): "If you were in my toilet, I wouldn't bother flushing you."

Stephen Root, Office Space
The beleagured mumbler Milton loses his stapler, his desk and, finally, his job before seeking revenge against obnoxious middle manager Bill Lumbergh (Gary Cole).

Jack Lemmon, Glengarry Glen Ross
Real estater Shelley Levene finds himself blasted by Alec Baldwin's foul-mouthed bigwig: "The fucking leads are weak? You're weak!"

INT. SHELDRAKE'S OFFICE – DAY
Sheldrake is having his shoes shined, flipping a coin in his hand with a slight air of impatience. Shoeshine Boy finishes. Sheldrake flips a switch on the desk intercom.

SHELDRAKE
Baxter, would you mind stepping in here a minute?
(*tosses coin to Shoeshine Boy*).
There y'are.

B'S VOICE
Yes, Mr Sheldrake.

SHOESHINE BOY
Much obliged.

The shoeshine 'boy' leaves and Baxter enters, talking fast.

BAXTER
Here's a breakdown of figures on personnel turnover. Thirty-seven per cent of our female employees leave to get married and twenty-two per cent...

SHELDRAKE
Baxter, you're working too hard. It's New Year's Eve. Relax!

BAXTER
Yes, sir.

SHELDRAKE
Well, I expect you'll be on the town celebrating?

BAXTER
Naturally.

SHELDRAKE
Me too. I'm taking Miss Kubelik out. Finally talked her into it.

BAXTER
I see.

SHELDRAKE
The only thing, Baxter, I'm staying at the Athletic Club and it's strictly stag. So, if you don't mind...?
(*holds out hand*)

BAXTER
Don't mind what?

SHELDRAKE
You know, the other key to your apartment. Well, when we had that little, er, scene about Miss Kubelik I thought I'd better get rid of it quick, so I threw it out the window of the commuter train.

BAXTER
Very clever.

SHELDRAKE
So, now I'll have to borrow your key.

BAXTER
Sorry, Mr Sheldrake. You're not going to bring anybody to my apartment.

SHELDRAKE
I'm not just bringing anybody – I'm bringing Miss Kubelik.

BAXTER
Especially not Miss Kubelik.

SHELDRAKE
How's that again?

BAXTER
No key.

SHELDRAKE
Baxter, I picked you for my team because I thought you were a bright young man. You realise what you're doing – not to me but to yourself? Normally it takes years to work your way up to the 27th floor – but it only takes 30 seconds to be out on the street again. You dig?

BAXTER
I dig.

SHELDRAKE
So what's it going to be?

Baxter takes out the key, looks at it and tosses it on the desk.

SHELDRAKE
Now you're being bright.

BAXTER
Thank you, sir.

Baxter leaves. In his office next door he takes a pen from his breast-pocket, tosses it on the desk and flips a folder closed. He glances sourly round his office. Sheldrake enters.

SHELDRAKE
Say, Baxter, you gave me the wrong key.

BAXTER
(putting on his coat)
No I didn't.

SHELDRAKE
But this is the key to the Executive Washroom.

BAXTER
That's right, Mr Sheldrake. I shalln't be needing it because I'm all washed up around here.

SHELDRAKE
What's gotten into you, Baxter?

BAXTER
Just following doctor's orders.
(*puts on bowler hat*)
I've decided to become a mensch. You know what that means? A human being.

SHELDRAKE
Now hold on!

BAXTER
Save it. The old payola won't work any more. Goodbye, Mr Sheldrake.

Cut to outside as Baxter walks through general office. A triumphal march theme starts quietly on the soundtrack. Reaching the lifts, Baxter removes bowler, pops it on head of the surprised shoeshine boy and exits into lift.

15

IT'S A WONDERFUL LIFE

War-weary James Stewart plumbs depths of despair to conjure life-affirming classic.

"Where's that money you silly stupid old fool? Where's that money? You realise what this means? It means bankruptcy and scandal and prison – that's what it means. One of us is going to jail; well it's not going to be me." James Stewart could do angry. Grabbing a whimpering Thomas Mitchell by the scruff – after the normally jolly codger Uncle Billy has mislaid a crucial eight grand – his George Bailey boasts a fearsome rage. Nearly 50 years later it's his voice that shocks, roaring with mania and unmistakable fury. He has his back to us – America's nice guy idol hiding his rage from the camera, reflected only in Mitchell's petrified doughy face.

Gloria Stewart said her husband had a temper, which he worked hard to keep. It's also said the picture of good-natured diffidence who left for World War Two came back a changed man. Years as a bomber squadron leader, seeing kids barely out of short trousers shot out of the sky, must do that to you. He came back decorated; but scarred. He came back bearing sorrow edged with darkness.

> **Capra said it was the lousiest piece of shit he'd heard and sent Stewart home**

An emotional rawness bordering on hysteria had always been his to explore – just look at his hoarse-throated idealist in *Mr Smith Goes To Washington* but now Stewart's axis had been tilted, his certainties tested. The Hollywood gadabout who won a Best Actor Oscar for frothy comedy *The Philadelphia Story* had spent nearly six years off-screen and wasn't sure he even wanted to act anymore. Never a particularly social animal on set, he was more introspective than usual during the shoot – lost in memories and shaken confidence. Anthony Mann would later exploit this older, more troubled Stewart in the magnificent series of psychological westerns the pair made in the '50s, culminating in *The Man From Laramie*. Alfred Hitchcock would unleash a figure tortured by doubt, pain, regret; and a kind of violent madness behind the eyes in *Vertigo*. But it started in Bedford Falls – no wonder the picture bombed.

"Now, Jimmy, it starts in heaven. It's all about this small-town family man who's in serious financial difficulty and thinks he's a failure. As he's getting ready to jump in the river on Christmas Eve, an angel named Clarence, who wants to earn his wings, jumps in first. Since Clarence can't swim, our hero has to save him. Then Clarence shows the man what a wonderful life he's had... Gee, Jimmy, it doesn't sound so good when I tell it, does it?" So Frank Capra "sold" *It's A Wonderful Life* to Stewart – right before saying it was "the lousiest piece of shit I've ever heard" and telling the actor to go home and forget about it. But the story

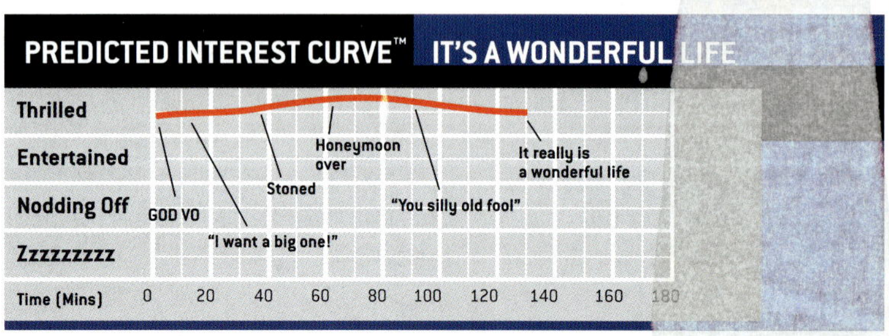

chimed with Stewart. He agreed to do the picture and Capra decided it was effluent worth the effort.

And it had already been quite an effort. Developed from a short story called *The Greatest Gift*, which writer Philip Van Doren Stern had sent to friends on Christmas cards (his agent was one such friend and sold the film rights), the script went through eight writers, including Clifford Odets and Dalton Trumbo (a member of the Hollywood Ten, it is tempting to attribute this with the film's thematic opposition to free market capitalism). It was originally intended as a vehicle for Cary Grant, but the studio put it in turnaround and Capra's production company Liberty Films bought it for the director.

It's not hard to see, though, why Stewart was attracted to the role. Like George Bailey, he was a small-town boy who originally had ambitions to be an architect and was continually urged by his father to take over the family store – just as George is urged by his dad to take over Bedford Falls' Building and Loan, the only means for the poor people of the town to buy their own homes and escape the slum dwellings owned by the unredeemed Scrooge Mr Potter (Lionel Barrymore). Just as George has to come to terms with his frustrated ambitions (to travel the world and design grand buildings) and settle down with a woman he wants, violently, *not* to love (the telephone scene seduction, when Stewart shakes Donna Reed to her core – "Now you listen to me. I don't want any plastics and I don't want any ground floors. And I don't want to get married ever to anyone! You understand that?" – remains passionate and disturbing), so Stewart was settling down in his own life and trying to find meaning in an arguably frivolous profession after the pain he had experienced during the war. Bailey could have been played as a smug goodie-two-shoes, but Stewart makes him a man at war with himself, whose better nature never begins to slide into piety.

The enduring image of *It's A Wonderful Life* is Stewart hugging his sprogs and grinning rheumy-eyed under the Christmas Tree. Enduring, but it shouldn't be considered »

NEED TO KNOW

Year 1946

Running time 130 mins

Director Frank Capra

Stars James Stewart, Donna Reed, Lionel Barrymore, Thomas Mitchell, Henry Travers

Buy it on Region 2 CE

Tagline "They're making memories tonight!"

Best line "Teacher says every time a bell rings an angel gets his wings." – Zuzu Bailey

Critic's view "The April-air wholesomeness and humanism remind us the screen best offers unselfconscious, forthright entertainment." – *Variety*

Best watched when... It's Christmas, stupid.

defining. Nor is it the whole story to emphasise, in contrast, how dark Capra's film is (although Bailey contemplating a swan dive and the cruel alternate reality of Pottersville are far from saccharine). *It's A Wonderful Life* has light and shade and throughout a playfulness and love of how cinema can tell a story. It's bold from the beginning – the stars pulsing in the sky as God and Joseph decide to send the bumbling Clarence (Henry Travers) to help – and structurally superb, with the divine powers showing selected highlights of his life and not afraid to interrupt when necessary (the freshness of the freeze frame on Bailey's exhortation about the size of his travelling trunk – "I want a BIG one!" – may have you checking the year of release the first time you see it. (Yes, 1946). It's about love and family, regret at the road not travelled – and finding the joys in where you've chosen to go or life has taken you. Watch it again. And again. And each time look at the people you love with eyes afresh... Anyone got a hanky? TF
Nev Pierce

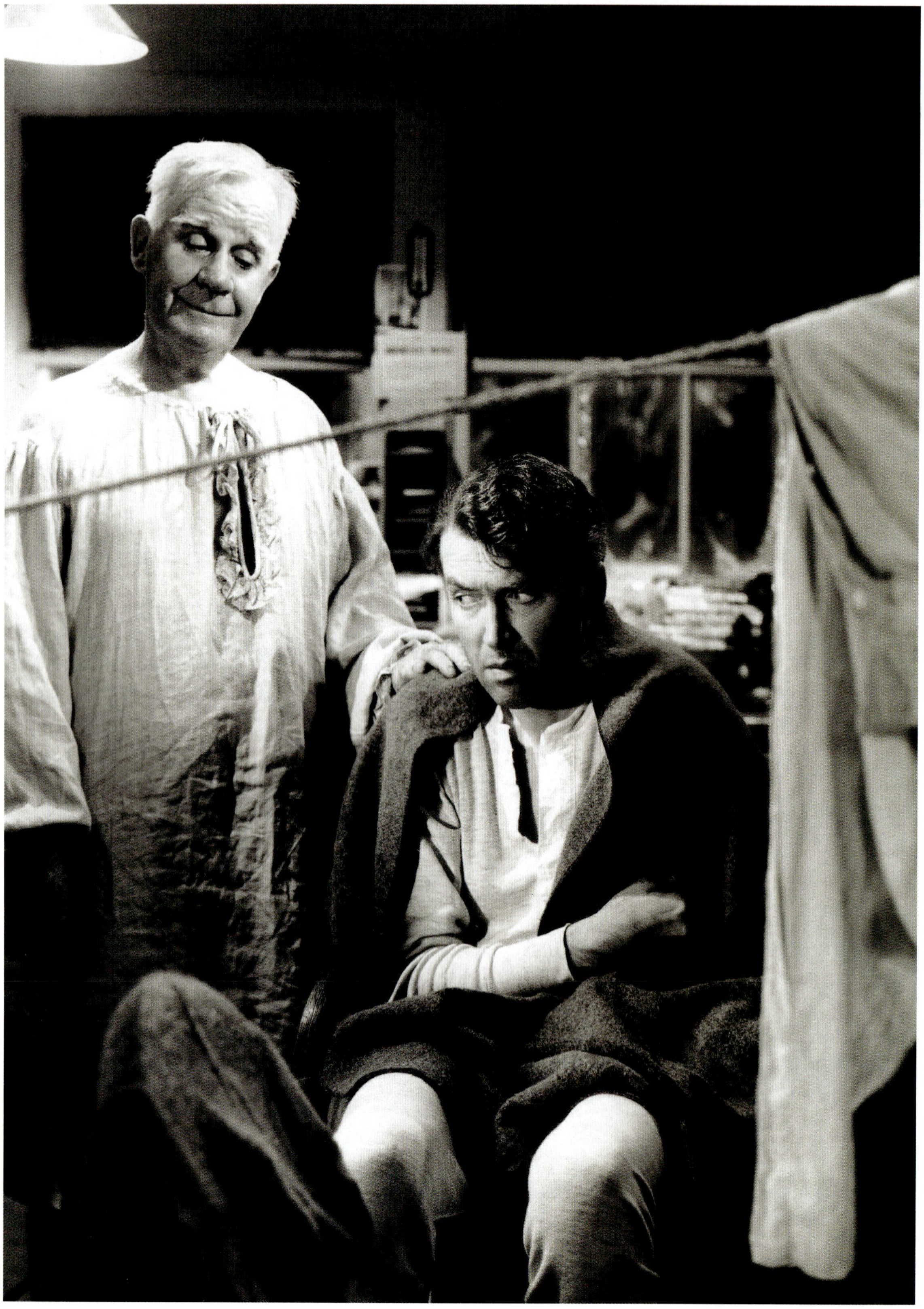

WITH OR WITHOUT YOU

George Bailey sees how life would unfold without him. And now so do these film characters...

JACK, TITANIC
Guardian angel St Patrick allows Leo DiCaprio's purdy Oirish stowaway to watch Kate Winslet doss about with her rich mates before being used as a lifeboat by cruel Billy Zane when the big boat sinks. Boo hoo.

NEMO, FINDING NEMO
With no Nemo to comfort Marlin after all his other kid clownfish are scoffed, the grieving father falls into a downward spiral of substance abuse: clams, plankton and pure-seed Thai heroin.

BALIAN, KINGDOM OF HEAVEN
No longer killed defending his wet-blanket son Liam Neeson's knight returns to Jerusalem, offs the warmongering French bastards, averts inter-faith catastrophe and saves tens of thousands of lives. Better film, too.

ET: THE EXTRA-TERRESTRIAL
ET watches from heaven-space as Elliot grows up in a broken home and becomes a beardy Oscar-winning film director who relentlessly fills his films with mawkish father-son relationships and won't just GET THE HELL OVER IT.

EXT. TREE-LINED RESIDENTIAL STREET – NIGHT
George and Mary stand outside the weather-beaten Granville House. George throws a rock and breaks a window – in order to make a wish.

MARY
What'd you wish, George?

GEORGE
Well, not just one wish. A whole hatful, Mary. I know what I'm going to do tomorrow and the next day and the next year and the year after that. I'm shaking the dust of this crummy little town off my feet and I'm going to see the world. Italy, Greece, the Parthenon, the Colosseum. Then I'm coming back here and go to college and see what they know... and then I'm going to build things. I'm gonna build air fields. I'm gonna build skyscrapers a hundred stories high. I'm gonna build bridges a mile long.

As he talks, Mary listens intently. She finally stoops down and picks up a rock, weighting it in her hand.

GEORGE
Are you gonna throw a rock?

Mary throws her rock and a window breaks.

GEORGE
Hey, that's pretty good.
What'd you wish, Mary?

Mary looks at him provocatively, then turns and shuffles off down the street, singing as she goes. George hurries after her.

MARY
(*sings*)
Buffalo gals, can't you come out tonight...

George joins her in the singing as they proceed down the street.

MARY AND GEORGE
(*sings*)
...can't you come out tonight, can't you come out tonight. Buffalo gals can't you come out tonight and dance by the light of the moon.

GEORGE
(*sings*)
What'd you wish when you threw that rock?

MARY
Oh, no.

GEORGE
Come on, tell me.

MARY
If I told you it might not come true.

GEORGE
What is it you want, Mary? What do you want? You want the moon? Just say the word and I'll throw a lasso around it and pull it down. Hey, that's a pretty good idea. I'll give you the moon, Mary.

MARY
I'll take it. And then what?

GEORGE
Well, then you could swallow it and it'd all dissolve, see? And the moonbeams'd shoot out of your fingers and your toes and the ends of your hair.

Am I talking too much?

An old man on a porch nearby jumps up and shouts.

MAN
Yes! Why don't you kiss her instead of talking her to death?

GEORGE
How's that?

MAN
Why don't you kiss her instead of talking her to death?

GEORGE
Want me to kiss her, huh?

MAN
Aw, youth is wasted on the wrong people.

GEORGE
Hey, hey, hold on. Hey, mister, come on back out here, and I'll show you some kissing that'll put hair back on your head.

Mary scurries off...

14

TAXI DRIVER

Who's gonna drive you home tonight? It's Scorsese's modern apocalypse...

Robert De Niro's Travis Bickle trying out his guns, a 12- to 13-year-old Jodie Foster as a prostitute, Harvey Keitel's hairy pimp, Martin Scorsese ranting from the back seat... *Taxi Driver*'s images have become frozen as icons now, in a way that runs the risk of diluting their power. On top of that, who didn't tire of the way that Bickle became the poster boy for a few thousand student-house walls? Even so, Scorsese's savage centrepiece of the '70s "cinema of loneliness" is still a film that begs to be experienced. You have to feel his vision of New York as an urban hell to get its complexities, all the way to Bickle's neo-Biblical blood-symphony of monstrous purgation.

Taxi Driver is a savage psycho-drama of sickness, alienation and loneliness

Try to imagine what it must have looked like in 1976. The bomb, at a guess. Of all of Scorsese's 'New Hollywood' contemporaries, even *Bonnie And Clyde*'s take on how the media represents violence couldn't prepare anyone for *Taxi Driver*. And what a response it got. At one extreme, its writer, Paul Schrader, arrived late for a midday screening at Cinema 1, New York, to find a line around the block. "Something's wrong," he thought, before realising that the queue was for the second screening. At another extreme, Columbia's David Begelman and Stanley Jaffe wanted Scorsese to trim the highbrow references (Bickle's Alka-Seltzer fizzing in the glass refers to Jean-Luc Godard's *Two Or Three Things I Know About Her*) and, inevitably, the violence. The film was rattling cages, pushing buttons and, for the most part, they were the right ones.

And it continued to do so. While Scorsese's vision of after-hours New York stems from German expressionism via film noir, it crystallised cinema's portraits of urban underbellies. Try to imagine *Se7en* or *Blade Runner* without it. The same goes for Bickle. Scorsese looked to the 19th-century Russian writer Dostoyevsky's short novel *Notes From Underground* for influence, but it's fair to say Bickle's insomnia was the key to the narrator in *Fight Club*, his romantic dysfunction to Morell in *A Room For Romeo Brass*. *Taxi Driver*'s influences outside of the cinema may have been less than happy (John Hinckley), granted, but Schrader had something to say about that, referring to the murderous character in Dostoyevsky's greatest novel: "I think that if you do get involved in this kind of censorship you'll end up having Raskolnikov; you just don't have *Crime And Punishment*."

Part of *Taxi Driver*'s potency lies in its coalescence of seemingly conflicting sources. In terms of creative input, the deeply troubled Schrader brought a strict Dutch Calvinist upbringing to the table, along with an interest in existentialism, guns and Arthur

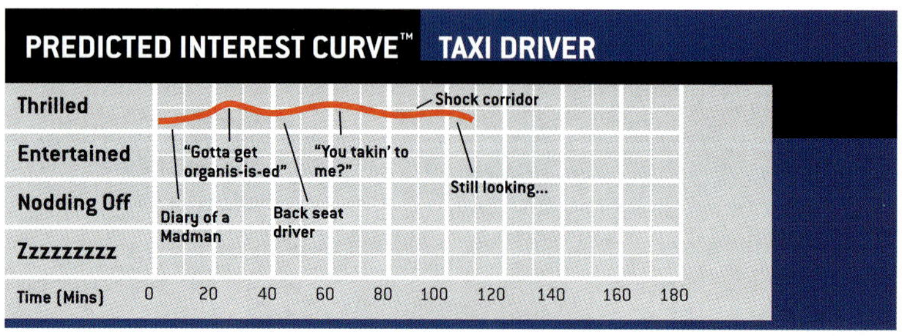

Bremer, a would-be political assassin. Little wonder that the script is intense, even on page: its opening description of Bickle partly succumbs to the hipster nihilism *Taxi Driver* has been accused of, but it also hums with white-heat chutzpah. "He has the smell of sex about him: sick sex, repressed sex, lonely sex, but sex nonetheless. He is a raw male force..."

More artfully, Bernard Herrmann's (last great) score is as central to *Taxi Driver* as Schrader's ragged Calvinism or Scorsese's baroque spectacle of expressionist excess and ritualised Italian-American Catholicism. Think of the opening, where music and direction converge in the emergence of Bickle's cab-cum-hearse from steam and sound, Herrmann's score brooding with repressed threat, swelling like something rising from underground. The other half of his score captures the flavour of Bickle's misguided stabs at romance with discomforting accuracy: part Gershwin-esque sentiment, but breaking down suggestively at key spots.

It's the man at the centre, though, that you can't tear your eyes off. Robert De Niro makes our watchfulness as intense as Bickle's, and one of the film's perverse triumphs is the intimacy it forges with his man on the edge. The film feels Bickle's suffering, albeit uncomfortably, without romanticising him. After he has taken Betsy (Cybill Shepherd) on a grotesque date to a porn film, his loneliness is suggested by the way the camera pans away from him, down a corridor, as he tries to talk her round on the phone. We know she won't budge. Who would? He's losing it, and we know he has appalling ideas about race and sexuality. Schrader and Scorsese don't stint when it comes to pathologising him, and De Niro's charisma can't candy-coat that. But just as Scorsese wanted us to feel something when Joe Pesci's psychopath in *Casino* met an open grave, he doesn't make Bickle a mere monster: he and Schrader humanise him, forcing us to think and preventing us from settling on simple, judgemental responses.

While Bickle is a conjunction of conflicting forces, so is the »

NEED TO KNOW

Year 1976
Running time 109 minutes
Director Martin Scorsese
Stars Robert De Niro, Cybill Shepherd, Jodie Foster
Buy it on Region 1 CE
Tagline "On every street in every city, there's a nobody who dreams of being a somebody."
Best line "Here is a man who would not take it any more." – Travis Bickle
Critic's view "A really intelligent appraisal of the fundamental ingredients of contemporary insanity." – *Time Out*
Best watched when... You're thinking of taking a date to a porn film. There's a lesson here.

film. Scorsese set out to mix gothic horror with *New York Daily News* sensibilities, new-wave naturalism with melodrama, outsiderhood with something wholly de-romanticised. Aesthetically, the film is a document of its time, in which raggedy-edged realism meets with homages to great American directors (in this case John Ford, via *The Searchers*) and the European innovations the '70s movie brats picked up in film school.

Historically, *Taxi Driver* picks up its era's garbage en route, too. In its references to political campaigning we see the post-Nixon era's uncertainty. We see the fallout of Vietnam – Bickle being an ex-Marine – combined with a reactionary take on the sexual revolution. Sure, Bickle is the US everyman become an outsider figure gone awry: an archetype. But he's also very much keyed into his historical moment.

In all this, does *Taxi Driver* exceed its hipster flash? Does it do more than create a poster boy for pseudo-nihilists? Of course. The film doesn't exactly validate Bickle's rage but it does refuse to provide a get-out clause, does refuse to nanny its audience. In doing so, it's a savagely felt psycho-drama of sickness, alienation and loneliness, which lays down a state-of-the-cinematic-art gauntlet to movies of surface and society's failure to answer the sicknesses it breeds. It doesn't deliver Band Aids or wash the muck off its back seat to make for a smooth, untroubled ride. Instead, it anatomises its world, its time and its place and its psychoses, with fierce, unblinking clarity and depth. TF

Kevin Harley

FROM THE UNDERBELLY

Five other severe social malcontents...

JOHNNY, NAKED
Mike Leigh's evisceration of post-Thatcher Britain, with David Thewlis as a manic misogynist on an odyssey through London's underbelly.

UNDERGROUND MAN, NOTES FROM UNDERGROUND
"I am a sick man... I am an angry man." The diarist sucks us into his sickness as he rails against his life, times and body.

MORELL, A ROOM FOR ROMEO BRASS
Shane Meadows' buddy movie has at its fringes Paddy Considine's Morell, whose woman problems make Bickle look like a charmer. And he only drives a three-wheel.

NARRATOR, FIGHT CLUB
"With insomnia, nothing's real..." Like Travis, Ed Norton's narrator can't get no sleep – and *Club*'s final twist takes the split psyche suggested by Travis' exchanges with his mirror to a logical conclusion.

SAM BICKE, THE ASSASSINATION OF RICHARD NIXON
Sean Penn amps up his De Niro-isms as a would-be political assassin who rants at the wall, bothers his ex and does a good job of imploding in slo-mo.

Classic Scene

INT. TRAVIS' CAB – DAY
Travis is brooding over his date with Betsy. Three men get into his cab. Travis turns on the meter and pulls off.

MAN'S VOICE
St Regis Hotel.

Travis checks the mirror.

Scanning across the back seat, he recognises the middle passenger. It is CHARLES PALANTINE, candidate for President. He must have left the hotel shortly after Betsy.

TOM, seated on the jump seat, checks his watch and speaks deferentially to Palantine.

TOM
It's 12:30 now. You'll have 15 minutes before the actual luncheon begins.

Palantine nods as his assistant picks up the thread of an earlier conversation.

ASSISTANT
I don't think we have to worry about anybody committing themselves until things start coming in from California.

Travis puts out his cigarette.

TRAVIS
(interrupting)
Say, aren't you Charles Palantine, the candidate?

PALANTINE
(mildly irritated)
Yes, I am.

TRAVIS
Well, I'm one of your biggest supporters. I tell everybody that comes in this cab that they should vote for you.

PALANTINE
(pleased; glances to check Travis' licence)
Why, thank you, Travis.

TRAVIS
I'm sure you'll win, sir. Everybody I know is going to vote for you. I was going to put one of your stickers on my taxi but the company said it was against their policy.

PALANTINE
(pleasant)
I'll tell you, Travis, I've learned more about this country sitting in taxi cabs than in the board room of General Motors.

TOM
(joking)
And in some other places, too...

Palantine, his Assistant and Tom all laugh. Palantine, quickly reassuming canditorial mien, speaks to Travis.

PALANTINE
Travis, what single thing would you want the next President of this country to do most?

TRAVIS
I don't know, sir. I don't follow political issues much.

PALANTINE
There must be something...

TRAVIS
Well, he should clean up this city here. It's full of filth and scum. Scum and filth. It's like an open sewer. I can hardly take it. Some days I go out and smell it then I get headaches that just stay and never go away. We need a President that would clean up this whole mess. Flush it out.

Palantine is not a professional bullshitter, and Travis' intense reply stops him dead in his tracks. He's forced to fall back on a stock answer but tries to give it some meaning.

PALANTINE
I know what you mean, Travis, and it's not going to be easy. We're going to have to make some radical changes.

TRAVIS
(turning the wheel)
Damn straight.

13

MANHATTAN

Woody Allen's ode to New York City is a film about love for love...

Woody Allen was in a strange place in 1979. Still only 43, winner of a brace of Oscars for writing and directing *Annie Hall*, his small but astonishing CV already included a pair of comedy classics: *Sleeper* and *Love And Death*. Yet *Interiors*, his first stab at "serious" cinema made the year before, had been welcomed with about as much warmth as a Chris Rock spot at a Ku Klux Klan rally. "That was a horrible experience for me," remembers Allen. "As a fan of Bergman and Fellini – although I'm nowhere near as gifted an artist as those gentlemen – I longed to make a movie of real worth. But the critics were horrible. So, yes, I went back to what I know best, which is comedy and New York." From the depths of despair came *Manhattan*, one of the most affecting and attractive love letters in the annals of cinema.

Opening with a gorgeous montage of New York City and signing off with a mad dash though its streets, every lovingly-crafted second of *Manhattan* is laced with Allen's infatuation for the city that never sleeps. At a time when Spielberg and Lucas were in the ascendancy and Hollywood was starting to clasp the blockbuster to its sweaty bosom, Allen opted to do something as simple as take his hat off to his hometown. "You know, this place really is a knockout," Allen's Isaac sighs to Diane Keaton's Mary as they watch the sun rise over the Brooklyn Bridge —a fairly audacious statement given that NYC in the '70s was widely regarded, unfairly or not, as a crime-ridden, urban battle zone, a real-life equivalent of Mos Eisley.

'I went back to what I know best, which is comedy and New York' WOODY ALLEN

"Of course, I'm aware of New York's failings," Allen would later say. "You only need to look at the guy at the side of the road begging for change to realise everything's far from wonderful. But other directors romanticise their hometowns – look at Fellini with Rome – and no-one complains, so why should I be pilloried for showing New York in a good light? At least the tourist industry people love me."

But if *Manhattan* is streaked through with unabashed sentimentality, Woody's exceptional sense of humour dispenses the spoonfuls of sugar to keep it from sticking in your throat. From Isaac's endorsement of monogamy ("I think people should mate for life, like pigeons or Catholics") to his advocacy of direct action in dealing with Nazis ("A satirical piece in the *Times* is one thing, but bricks and baseball bats really get right to the point"), *Manhattan* is more consistently funny than even the superb *Annie Hall*. Nonetheless, Allen, forever comparing his talents to cinema's greats and insisting he fell hideously short, was appalled at his first edit.

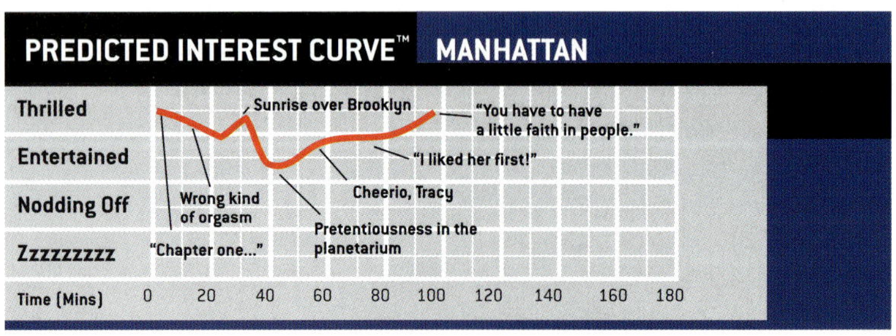

"I approached United Artists with an offer to direct another film for free providing they agreed never to release *Manhattan*," says Allen. "But they wouldn't have a bar of it, so the film came out, and, fortunately, people seemed to like it."

The fact that *Manhattan*'s smarts extend beyond a few decent jokes is a big reason behind its enduring appeal. "The line about gossip being the new pornography, hasn't that turned out to be the case!" smiles the writer-director. "At the time, you could see people were becoming increasingly interested in trivia. 'Oh, my God! Farrah Fawcett's broken up with Lee Majors. The bionic man and one of *Charlie's Angels* are getting divorced!' It's sad for the people going through it, but it's no one else's business."

As in all his films, the line between Allen and his on-screen persona is razor thin. In the case of Isaac Davis – a TV writer who longs for artistic success in spite of universal acclaim – you don't have to squint to see that Woody's working through personal issues. The casting of Diane Keaton as Mary Wilkie, with whom Isaac has an affair, is interesting given the actress went out with Allen for a few years (although they'd split by the time *Manhattan* was made). While other elements of the story seem to bear no relation to real life (Isaac's first wife – played by Meryl Streep – leaves him for another woman), others such as his infatuation with Mariel Hemingway's schoolgirl (inspired by Allen's relationship with the actress Stacy Nelkin, whom he dated when she was still in full-time education) and his separation from his young son would become aspects of his existence following his later estrangement from Mia Farrow and his settling down with her stepdaughter Soon-Yi Previn.

Providing the bridge between the "early, funny ones" and the "later, serious ones", *Manhattan* found Woody Allen taking full advantage of his unique relationship with veteran producers Charles Joffe and Jack Rollins. They were so enchanted with their discovery they let him do whatever he wished, not even flinching when Allen insisted on shooting his movie in black-and-white >>

NEED TO KNOW

Year 1979
Running time 96 mins
Director Woody Allen
Stars Woody Allen, Diane Keaton, Mariel Hemingway, Meryl Streep, Michael Murphy
Buy it on Region 2
Taglines N/A
Best Line "Not everybody gets corrupted. You have to have a little faith in people." – Tracy
Critic's View '.. both a grim dissection of perpetually dissatisfied New Yorkers and an ode to the city itself, filmed in glorious black-and-white.' – *The New York Times*
Best watched when... You're about to move out of your parents' house in Rochdale.

and in widescreen. Lucky for us they didn't, for while *Manhattan* would have also worked marvelously in colour, the high contrast visuals double as both the central motif and the key supporting character.

Like any over-indulged artist, Allen doesn't entirely benefit from getting his own way. *Manhattan* also illustrates a tendency towards snobbishness with obscure references that few would pick up on. But wandering through Allen's fantasy city 26 years later, the viewer is struck less by the picture's occasional pretension than by the fact that, although it's a fabulously romantic film, it's also far more interested in loss than love, with Isaac falling out of three relationships. But for Woody – a man who finds modern cinema baffling, who adores New Orleans jazz and hates most music post-Paul McCartney – the death of romantic love seems less significant than the death of a romanticised New York; the Kodachrome images and Gershwin-soaked soundtrack pointing to a place that no longer exists outside of old Hollywood movies and history books. In our post-9/11 world, old New York feels even more distant. "I can never bring myself to look at my pictures once they're released," Allen remarks solemnly. "But in the case of *Manhattan*, the process is doubly difficult." Yet whatever the future brings for New York, we'll always have *Manhattan*. TF

Richard Luck

THE (UN)REAL WORLD

Woody Allen isn't the only director to romanticise a place out of all proportion.

AMELIE (2001)
On the director's commentary on the DVD, Jean-Pierre Jeunet mentions that it took a helluva lot of effort to reclaim Montmartre from the countless little "messages" left by Paris' pooch population.

GARDEN STATE (2004)
Far from being the murder capital of the East Coast, Zach Braff portrays New Jersey as a place populated by ageing slackers and amiable eccentrics.

MARY POPPINS (1964)
Shot on the Disney lot, Uncle Walt's efforts to bring EL Travers' nanny to life might as well have taken place in London, Ontario, or East London, South Africa.

NOTTING HILL (1999)
Comic Junior Simpson joshed that Richard Curtis deserved a special effects Oscar for erasing all the black people from West London. Four years on, Simpson cameoed in Curtis' *Love Actually*.

THE QUIET MAN (1952)
Like many Irish-Americans before and after him, John Ford seemed convinced the Old Country was exclusively populated by drunken, brawling males and flame-haired, sharp-tongued maidens. If only.

Classic Scene

*Yes, this is the wrong picture. But we like it.

INT. ISAAC'S APARTMENT – DAY
Over a montage of both famous and unfamiliar New York views, Isaac dictates the opening of a new book.

ISAAC

Chapter One: 'He adored New York City. He idolised it all out of proportion.' No, make that: 'He romanticised it all out of proportion.' Yeah. 'To him, no matter what the season was, this was still a town that existed in black and white and pulsated to the great tunes of George Gershwin.' Ah, let me start this over. Chapter One: 'He was too romantic about Manhattan, as he was about everything else. He thrived on the hustle-bustle of the crowds and the traffic. To him, New York meant beautiful women and street-smart guys who seemed to know all the angles.' Nah, corny, too corny for my taste. Let me try and make it more profound. Chapter One: 'He adored New York City. To him, it was a metaphor for the decay of contemporary culture. The same lack of individual integrity to cause so many people to take the easy way out was rapidly turning the town of his dreams in...' It's going to be too preachy. I mean, let's face it, I want to sell some books here. Chapter One: 'He adored New York City. Although to him, it was a metaphor for the decay of contemporary culture. How hard it was to exist in a society desensitized by drugs, loud music, television, crime, garbage...' Too angry. I don't want to be angry. Chapter One: 'He was as tough and romantic as the city he loved. Behind his black-rimmed glasses was the coiled sexual power of a jungle cat.' I love this! 'New York was his town – and it always would be.'

12

CHINATOWN

Nicholson's finest hour. Polanski's finest hour. Dunaway's... Oh, you get it...

Easy to forget, in our auteur-obsessed age, that film is and always has been a collaborative medium. Like *Raging Bull* a decade later, *Chinatown* represents that rarest of moment in cinema history: a cosmic collision of ferocious talents simultaneously hitting peak. Born of perfect, poisonous alchemy, *Chinatown* became one of the greatest, bleakest epics in the history of American cinema: a ruthless tale of obliterated innocence.

It's a cosmic collision of ferocious talents simultaneously hitting peak

Doped-up on the brilliance of his Oscar-nommed screenplay for *The Last Detail*, Robert Towne wrote *Chinatown* specifically for his friend Jack Nicholson. A throwback to the Raymond Chandler detective mould, it sees LA private eye JJ Gittes hired by a mysterious woman (Faye Dunaway) to spy on her husband. But as Gittes digs deeper, he uncovers a shady plot to control the city's power by stealing its water supply. Blockbuster producer Robert Evans loved the script, loved the title. Didn't know what it meant, but loved it. He called director Roman Polanski, who, coming off shuddering psycho-horrors *Repulsion* and *Rosemary's Baby*, was the master of painting choked freefalls into hell.

Without Polanski, *Chinatown* simply wouldn't have been *Chinatown*. The product of 18 months' splashed ink, Towne's doorstop script was a raking homage to the classic 'tec tale that had Nicholson's wise-cracking, laconic gumshoe sniffing down clues and sticking it to The Man. Indeed, Gittes' edgy vulnerability is closer to Chandler's concept of Philip Marlowe than many screen incarnations.

But at Polanski's touch, this stylish evocation of lonely romanticism of Golden Era '30s noir became something more: the most searing revision of the genre ever made, gutting the Bogart myth with cruel cynicism. "I saw *Chinatown* not as a 'retro' piece or a conscious imitation of classic movies shot in black and white," said the director, "but as a film about the '30s seen through the camera eye of the '70s." Look closely at Gittes with that evil eye and we see exactly what he means. A schmuck down to his very name, Nicholson's private dick is a failed cop reduced to picking up sleazy chump-change in LA. He's less a hero than a man lost in a wasteland that he'll never figure out. Snooping futilely through the film with a garish white plaster taped across his nose, Gittes often seems just a small dry speck on the arid landscape, stranded in the margins of the frame by DoP John Alonzo's gorgeous widescreen compositions. *Chinatown* is a sunshine noir, transporting the smouldering hell's kitchen of black-and-white pulps to parched, sweating LA. And while the story's classical, mythical undertones – the

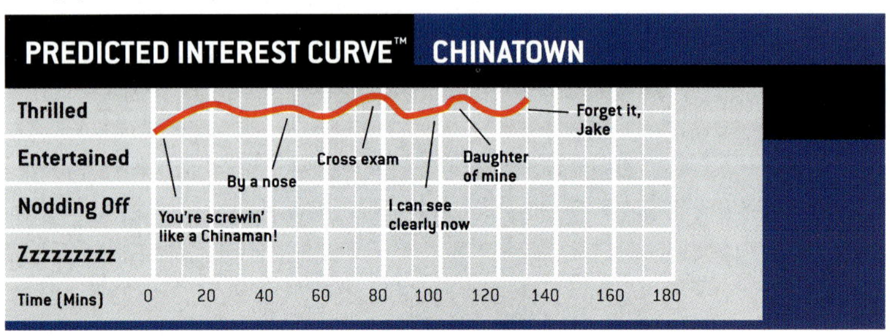

LA wasteland, the sterile kingdom, the dying King – all writhed in Towne's original script, the nihilistic fatalism was all Polanski's. He saw LA rotting in the hot sun.

Three years had passed since his pregnant wife Sharon Tate had been butchered by the Manson Family and Polanski still carried a pair of her panties in his pocket. For two long months at his house, the director battled with Towne over the script. "We fought every day, over everything," said Towne. "Over the script, over the teenyboppers Roman would take pictures of diving off the fucking diving board with no tops on..." "I went to art school in Poland!" yelled an exasperated Polanski at one point. "A Polish art school's a contradiction in terms, you fuckin' asshole," responded Towne. He wanted a redemptive ending. Polanski was having none of it, Evans backed him and the result was a shattering, horrific finale that finds Gittes reeling with the death of his love and his hope. "The tunnel at the end of the light," Towne called it. "Roman's argument was, 'That's life,'" he remembers. "Beautiful people die in LA. Sharon had."

Incidentally, Polanski's scalding intensity didn't let up on set. In the scene where Gittes' nostril is sliced by a thug, Polanski delighted in doing the job himself, terrifying Nicholson by using the blunt edge of a real pocket-knife. "It's a curious thing about that scene," Polanski said. "Many people have called the movie violent. But it actually has very little violence in it." His diva-ish lead actress might argue. Polanski referred to her as "the dreaded Dunaway" and their war of attrition ("Say the fucking words – your salary is your motivation!") culminated in Dunaway throwing a cupful of urine (possibly Nicholson's) into Polanski's face.

In any case, the director's dictatorial methods and the trauma of the shoot worked. These were the days before Nicholson retreated into gurning caricature and his "bedroom dick" is a magnificently understated lost soul. Eyed straining in veiled perplexity, his cocksure wryness slowly disintegrates in the face of confusion and, finally,

NEED TO KNOW

Year 1974
Running time 131 mins
Director Roman Polanski
Stars Jack Nicholson, Faye Dunaway, John Huston
Buy it on Region 2
Tagline N/A
Best line "You think you know what this is. But believe me, Mr Gits, you don't." – Noah Cross
Critic's view "*Chinatown* – with its beautifully structured script and draggy, over-deliberate direction – is something new: nostalgia for the '30s openly turned to rot and the celebration of rot." – Pauline Kael, *The New Yorker*
Best watched when... You start to fancy a member of your own family.

impotent horror. Nicholson's wounded, witty turn generated stinging chemistry with Dunaway's inverted femme fatale, whose birthmark ("a flaw in the iris") pinpoints the movie's heart of darkness. The film's gut-punch twist ("My sister! My daughter!" she screams as Nicholson smacks her face with ringing blows) reverberates like few others.

Many Hollywood epics are as sprawling and labyrinthine as *Chinatown*'s festering tangle of murders, lies and evil. Few can claim to be so controlled. Through twists, turns, red herrings and revelations, we stumble with Gittes towards *Chinatown*'s core. Waiting there, in all his sick charm, is monstrous tycoon Noah Cross (John Huston, director of '40s noir *The Maltese Falcon*). "Mr Gits," Cross drawls, ironically firstnamed after a man who saved humanity from the water (he never gets Gittes' name right), "most people never have to face the fact that, at the right time and the right place, they're capable of anything." Cross' words hang heavy with Polanski's knowledge of the darkness of the world. In fact, Cross is Polanski, his black power oozing unstoppably as he force-feeds us our deepest fears.

Almost certainly, Towne recognised this. And out of principle, hated the whole thing, even considered taking his name off it. But crucially, Robert Evans had seen it too. All ego and little talent, Evans was the glue holding *Chinatown*'s Towne/Polanski/Nicholson triumvirate together – it was he who allowed Polanski to deliver his vision. "I was protected," said Polanski later. "Robert gave me complete freedom. All my energy went into the right channels. It's not the way things are now..." Ironically, it was Towne who found himself taking home the film's only Academy Award, out of 11 noms, as *The Godfather II* mopped up. More than a decade later, after he and Nicholson had coughed up abortive sequel *The Two Jakes*, the writer finally admitted that *Chinatown* – a synonym for all the corruption and chaos of the human soul – owed its director rather a lot. "Roman was the best collaborator I ever had," he conceded. "The little fart." TF

Jonathan Crocker

WHAT'S IN A NAME?

Towne said 'Chinatown' referred to Gittes' "fucked-up state of mind". But what do these enigmatic titles mean?

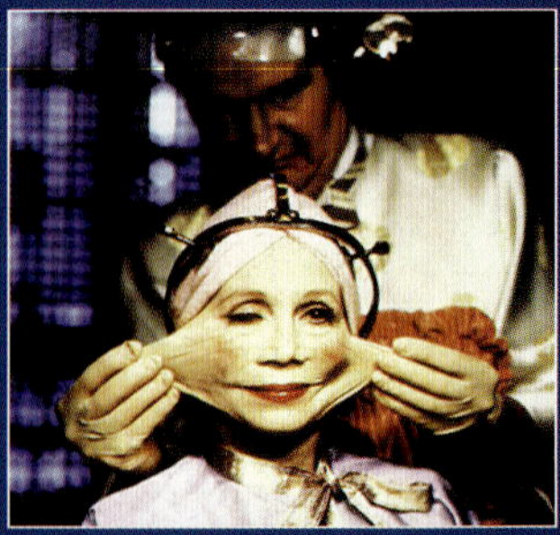

RESERVOIR DOGS (1992)
Rubbish at French, Tarantino always referred to Louis Malle's moving *Au Revoir Les Enfants* simply as "that *Reservoir* movie". He combined it with 'Bloody' Sam Peckinpah's long-banned *Straw Dogs* to make *Reservoir Dogs*.

BRAZIL (1985)
Refers to the popular Latin song from the late '30s crooned by Arry Barroso, often used as an escapist theme in the orchestral soundtrack.

DUCK SOUP (1933)
Director Leo McCarey nicked it from a two-reel Laurel and Hardy film he'd made. Groucho explained thusly: "Take two turkeys, one goose, four cabbages, but no duck, and mix them together. After one taste, you'll duck soup for the rest of your life."

TRAINSPOTTING (1996)
Describes: a) the obsessive, stupid, time-consuming behaviour of any nerd subculture; and: b) the search for a viable vein for drug-pumping. In Irvine Welsh's book, Begbie and Renton take a "pish" in Leith, Edinburgh's defunct Central Station. Welsh always joked that Leith hasn't had a rail link for decades.

Classic Scene

EXT. ALBACORE SOCIAL CLUB – DAY
Jake Gittes sits at a lunch table with Evelyn's father Noah Cross, who is picking apart a fish.

CROSS
Mr Gits.

GITTES
Gittes.

CROSS
Oh. How do you do? You've got a nasty reputation, Mr Gits. I like that.

GITTES
Thanks.

CROSS
If you were a bank president, that would be one thing. But in your business it's admirable and it's good advertising.

GITTES
It doesn't hurt.

Gittes peers down at a whole fish on his plate. The dead fish, way out of its element, stares helplessly back.

CROSS
It's, um, why you attracted a client like my daughter.

GITTES
Probably.

CROSS
Hmm. It disturbs me, making me think you take my daughter for a ride. Financially speaking, of course. What are you chargin' her?

GITTES
My usual fee plus a bonus if I get results.

CROSS
(*smirks lasciviously*)
Are you, uh, sleeping with her?

Gittes ignores this.

CROSS (CONT'D)
Come, come, Mr Gits. You don't have to think about that to remember, do you?

GITTES
(*gets to his feet.*)
If you want an answer to that question, Mr Cross, I'll put one of my men on the job. Good afternoon.

CROSS
Mr Gits.

GITTES
Git-tes.

CROSS
Gittes. You're dealing with a disturbed woman who's just lost her husband. I don't want her taken advantage of. Sit down.

GITTES
What for?

CROSS
You may think you know what you're dealing with but, believe me, you don't.
(*Gittes smiles.*)
Why is that funny?

GITTES
It's what the District Attorney used to tell me in Chinatown.

CROSS
Yeah? Was he right? Exactly what do you know about me? Sit down.

GITTES
Mainly that you're rich; too respectable to want your name in the papers.

CROSS
'Course I'm respectable. I'm old. Politicians, ugly buildings and whores all get respectable if they last long enough... I'll double whatever your fee is and pay you $10,000 if you find Hollis' girlfriend.

11

PERSONA

Sex, psychosis and symbiosis in Bergman's soul-searching masterwork...

Ingmar Bergman wasn't having the best of it when he set out to make *Persona*. His reputation as the daddy of European cinema, the ruler of the (art) house, had been unceremoniously stripped away by the upstarts of the French New Wave, their freewheeling cameras, jittery jump-cuts and warm, improvised dialogue robbing him of his alpha male status. Once praised for his rigorous composition, concentrated psychoanalysis and worrywart scrutinising of an empty sky, Bergman suddenly found his sombre, symbolic films greeted with rolled eyes and clucked tongues.

But that was just the start of his problems. Crushed by the savage reviews of *Now About These Women* (a rare and excruciatingly brittle comedy that mocked his own pretensions as an artist) and exhausted by his extra-curricular duties as MD of the Royal Dramatic Theatre in Stockholm, Bergman found himself hospitalised with double pneumonia and acute penicillin poisoning. Feverish, barely able to stand, he nonetheless felt duty bound to meet his commitment to the Svensk Filmindustri and crank out a movie. And so it was that he started penning *Persona* (or *Cinematography* as it was originally called) in April 1965, a dauntless masterpiece that would restore his reputation in 80 shattering minutes.

Shot "slowly and squeakingly", the sickly director asking his regular DoP Sven Nykvist to arrange take after take as he grappled to find the film's shape, *Persona*'s plot mirrored Bergman's own convalescence. Put simply, it sees famous actress Elisabeth Vogler (Liv Ullman) retire to an isolated coastal cottage in search of her health. Only that's not it. Elisabeth's actually "perfectly healthy, both mentally and physically", as a no-nonsense psychiatrist (Margaretha Krook) points out. What she's really in search of is her voice, her words having dried up as she performed *Electra* on stage.

Only that's not it, either. If Elisabeth wanted to speak, to fill the silence with click-clacking babble, she could do so – or at least that's the assumption. What she needs to discover is her *inner* voice: the one that's hidden beneath all the masks, rituals and lies; the one that's loaded with truth and meaning; the one that doesn't sound petty when played alongside the silent screams emitting from her TV as protestors torch their own bodies to shed a terrible light on the Vietnam War. "Don't you think I understand?" says the psychiatrist before Vogler leaves for the cottage. "This hopeless dream of being. Not seeming, but being... Every tone of voice a lie, every gesture a falsehood, every smile a grimace."

Nurse Alma (Bibi Andersson) is Elisabeth's constant

A dauntless masterpiece that would restore Bergman's reputation

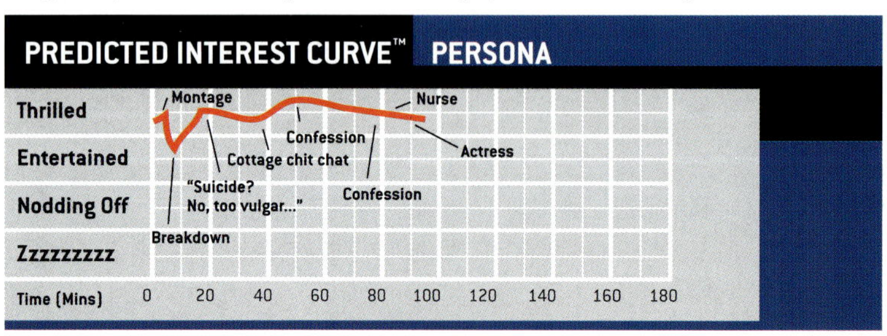

companion at the seaside retreat. Twenty-five years old, contentedly engaged and two years into her secure job, her future is "nothing to ponder over". She happily fills Elisabeth's self-imposed silence with inane chatter, culminating in a drunken sexual confession (see classic scene, overleaf) delivered deep into the night – the hour of the wolf.

For her part, Elisabeth soaks up the words and gestures being thrown at her. Is she simply a good listener, the caring sister that Alma's always craved? Does she find her carer's trust and compassion a soothing balm, a remedy for her ailing faith in humanity? Are there hints of a sexual attraction? Is she appalled or perhaps saddened by Alma's gushed trivialities? Or is the actress readying a new role, scrutinising and absorbing?

But there's yet another reading: the two women are consuming each other's identities, slurping, sucking and assimilating until, in one incredible shot, they literally become one. Which in turn leads to more questions. Does their communion signal a moment of true understanding, of grace? Is it an act of vampiric aggression, as suggested by the (fantasy?) sequence where Elisabeth hungrily feeds from Alma's open wrist? Has one or both of the women slipped into madness?

It's this refusal to be pinned down that allows *Persona* to reward unlimited viewings, each fresh pass throwing up five new answers, 20 more questions.

NEED TO KNOW

Year 1966
Running time 83 mins
Director Ingmar Bergman
Stars Bibi Andersson, Liv Ullmann, Margaretha Krook, Gunnar Björnstrand
Buy it on Region 2
Tagline N/A
Best line "Suicide? No, too vulgar. But you can refuse to move, refuse to talk, so that you don't have to lie." – The Doctor
Critic's view "Not an easy film, but an infinitely rewarding one." – *Time Out*
Best watched when... You feel on the edge of a nervous breakdown or you're about to vacation at a seaside cottage.

Trust us, the last 30 minutes of *Mulholland Dr.* have nothing on this. What we do know is that *Persona* grapples with two of the director's favourite themes: the impossibility of true communication and the artist's place in society. And while one or other, or sometimes both, can be found in just about any Bergman film you care to mention – *Autumn Sonata, Shame, The Rite, Scenes From A Marriage* and *The Magician*, which also features an artist/charlatan named Vogler – they're here taken to thrilling extremes. Hell, it's not just the words that fail but the images too, the film breaking down halfway through. Art is artifice, Bergman is hollering, incapable of distracting let alone impacting. Likewise, >>

Persona opens with a strip of celluloid shuddering through sprockets. It then leaps into a wild montage: cartoons, slapstick comedies, a tarantula, an erect penis (banned on release but restored in 2001) and a nail hammered through a palm as fingers flex and curl. Modern viewers seeing the film for the first time might think of *Fight Club*, which gleefully breaks the fourth wall in much the same way, subliminal cock'n'all. Bergman connoisseurs, meanwhile, will be reminded of God being envisaged as a spider in 1961's *Through A Glass Darkly*. No matter – the effect is the same. Expert or novice, you're left in no doubt that you're watching a movie, just a movie. The real world is outside the window, as broken and bleeding now as it was in 1966.

Persona ends with Alma back in her nurse's uniform, catching a bus towards her pre-packaged life, while a made-up Elisabeth gets ready for her close-up. Fantasy? Reality? Either way, Bergman seems to be saying that little has changed. His film has failed to make a dent.

Or maybe not. As Elisabeth's husband states towards the end of the picture, "It's the effort that's most important, not what we achieve." And *Persona* is some effort, an alchemy of phenomenal acting, searing images, unsettling score (harsh percussion, wailing strings), slippery subtexts and bewitching, amorphous patterns, both visual and aural. As Bergman himself would later write in *Images*, a painfully honest reflection on his life and career: "Today I feel that in *Persona*... I had gone as far as I could go. I touched wordless secrets that only cinema could discover." TF

Jamie Graham

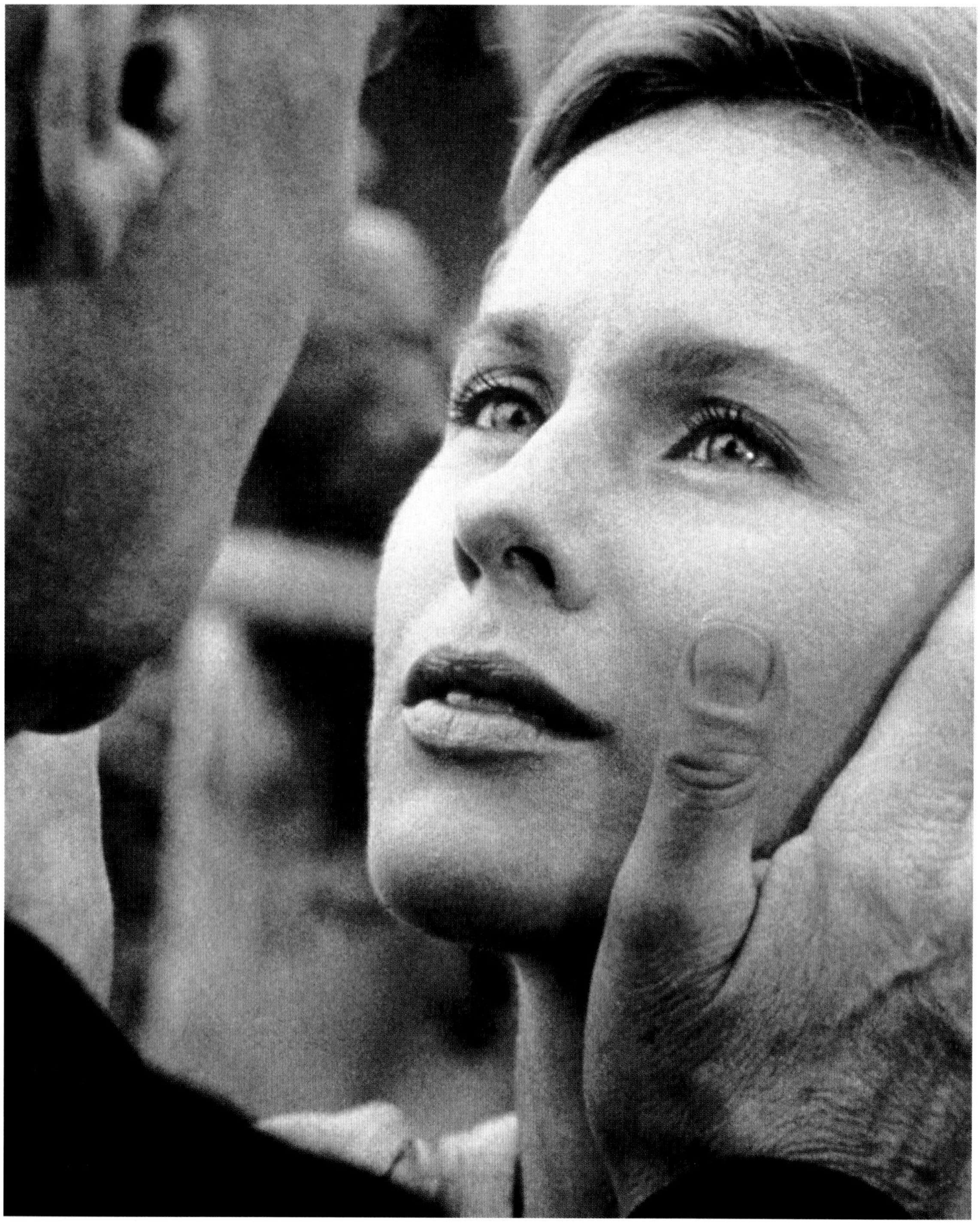

BLUFFER'S GUIDE

How to know you're watching an Ingmar Bergman film...

It stars at least three of the following: Liv Ullmann, Max Von Sydow, Bibi Andersson, Gunnar Björnstrand, Ingrid Thulin and Erland Josephson.

It's about the fragility of young love, the sham of marriage, the impossibility of true communication, the absence of God or the artist's place in society.

The words "shabby" and "shame" pop up at some point or other.

Everyone looks glum as hell and incessantly picks at their psychological wounds until a faint echo of hope resounds at the very end of the movie.

It's set on a near-desolate island or at least by the sea. No water, no Bergman.

The camera rarely moves and records much of the characters' relentless yakking in close-up.

There's little or no music, Bergman favouring silence or the odd wail of cello over jukebox hits. Rumours that ABBA were set to score *Scenes From A Marriage* remain unsubstantiated.

Classic Scene

EXT. ELISABETH'S BEDROOM – NIGHT
Elisabeth sits up in bed smoking as Nurse Alma huddles in an armchair by the window, looking away from her patient.

ALMA
One day when Karl-Henrik had gone into town, I went to the beach alone. It was really nice and warm. There was another girl there. She lived on an island nearby but had come over as our beach lay to the south and was more relaxed. So we lay beside one another completely naked and sunbathed. We slept a little, woke up, put on some oil. We wore these hats on our heads, you know, those cheap straw hats. I had a blue ribbon around my hat. I lay looking out from under the hat – glanced out at the landscape, the sea and the sun. It was so curious. Suddenly I saw two figures jumping about on the rocks above us. They hid and peeped out occasionally. "There are two boys looking at us," I said to her. Her name was Katarina. "Well, let them look," she said, and turned on her back. It was such a strange feeling. I wanted to run and put on my costume, but I just lay still. On my belly with my bum in the air, totally unembarrassed, totally calm.

We watch Elisabeth, as Alma continues to talk out of frame.

ALMA (CONT'D)
All the time I had Katarina beside me with her breasts and thick thighs. She just lay there giggling a little to herself. Then I saw the boys had come nearer. They just stood looking at us.

We return our gaze to Alma.

ALMA (CONT'D)
I saw that they were terribly young. Then one of them, the bravest one, he came to us and squatted down beside Katarina. He pretended to be busy with his foot and sat poking between his toes. I felt totally strange. Suddenly I heard Katarina say: "Aren't you going to come over here?" Then she took his hand and helped him take his jeans and shirt off. Suddenly he was over her and she helped him in and held his behind. The other boy just sat on the slope and watched. I heard Katarina whisper in his ear and laugh. I had his face right next to me. It was all red and swollen. Suddenly I turned over and said, "Aren't you going to come to me too?" Katarina said, "Go to her now." And he pulled out of her and he fell over me, completely hard. He took hold of one breast. God, it hurt so much. I was all ready somehow – I came at once. Can you understand that?
I was just going to tell him, "Be careful so I don't get pregnant" when he came. I felt it like I'd never felt it before, how he sprayed his seed into me.

We look back at Elisabeth, who is smoking and listening.

ALMA
He gripped my shoulders and bent backwards. I came over and over. Katarina lay on her side. She held him from behind. When he came she embraced him and made herself come with his hand. And when she came she screamed really loud. Then all three of us started laughing...

Alma reaches for her cigarettes. She gets up from the chair and walks to the window.

10

HIS GIRL FRIDAY

The fastest, funniest, sharpest 'comedy' you've ever seen. Thank goodness it's *Friday*...

"The reason people don't think about Howard Hawks is that he's invisible..." John Carpenter once said in an interview. "You know, Hitchcock's easy to copy because he wears his style like loud clothes. You can see how he did *Psycho* and the shower scene. I can do that. But how do you do something like *His Girl Friday*?" So how *do* you do something like *His Girl Friday*? How do you make the fastest, funniest movie in cinema history?

"They're called moving pictures. So let's make 'em move!" HOWARD HAWKS

Well, if you believe Hawks, all you ever need to make a great film are three good scenes and no bad ones. "As long as you make good scenes," said the legendary Hollywood filmmaker, "you have a good picture." But Hawks knew he had a movie packed with them in Ben Hecht and Charles MacArthur's salty 1928 play *The Front Page*, already adapted for film once in 1931. Gliding on some of the briskest, wittiest dialogue of the time, it followed ruthless newspaper editor Walter Burns as he schemes to persuade his want-away star reporter Hildy Johnson to cover a huge breaking story: a loser everyman who shot a black policeman is to be hanged to garner re-election votes for the crooked Mayor.

Now Hawks thought *The Front Page* had the best modern dialogue ever written. And to prove it, he'd been auditioning actors using his secretary to recite Hildy's lines. Suddenly, the idea hit him like a freight train. "It's even better this way!" he exclaimed. He wasn't wrong – the gender-twist turned *The Front Page* inside-out. Hildy now became Walter's recently divorced ex-wife, meaning Walter must keep his ace "newspaperman" on his staff and dispose of her mummy's boy fiancé Bruce (Ralph Bellamy). Thus, unlike previous versions, *His Girl Friday* became a screwball rom-com – the burgeoning '30s genre Hawks had pioneered with *Twentieth Century*, *Bringing Up Baby* and *Only Angels Have Wings*. Wisecracking improv-master Cary Grant had wowed in all three and Hawks wasted no time in casting him as Walt. Amazingly, Katharine Hepburn, Jean Arthur, Ginger Rogers and Claudette Colbert all passed on Hildy, leaving Rosalind Russell one of the juiciest roles ever written for a woman.

"They're moving pictures," Hawks loved to proclaim. "Let's make 'em move!" And boy, does *His Girl Friday* move. Faster than a speeding bullet. Faster than Carl Lewis on crack. Faster than a pensioner's bowels after a steam-curried vindaloo. *Fast*. Burning up the 191-page script in 92 frantic minutes, Grant and Russell lock their jaws on full-auto to motormouth through a riotous, overlapping avalanche of in-jokes, word gags, plot twists, mugging sarcasm and fizzing witticisms. It's a supersonic babble-of-the-sexes that crams every second with talk and

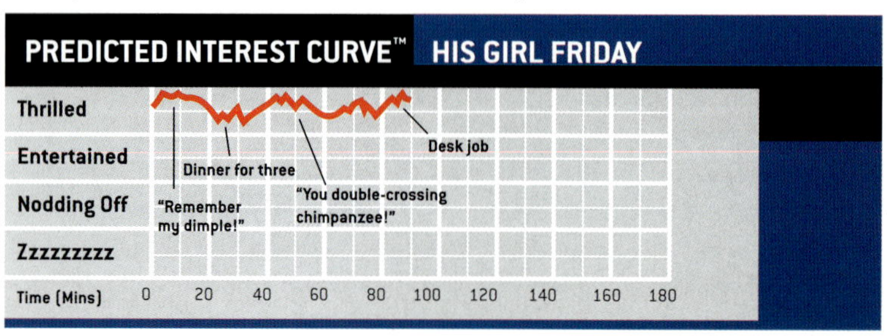

torque. "I'd noticed that people talk over one another," Hawks told longtime admirer Peter Bogdanovich. "Especially people who talk fast or who are arguing or describing something. So we made the beginnings and ends of sentences unnecessary – they were there for overlapping." This constant war of overlap and interruption between Walt and Hildy gives *Friday* a gasping forward propulsion. Forget pauses. Hawks just rams them with more chat, often staging conversations two at a time. It's less dialogue than dualogue. With an astonishing average talk-rate of 4.3 words per second, *Friday*'s fastest scenes ratchet up to five, six, even *seven* words per second. As the film storms into its finale, Hawks turbocharges the action further still, gatecrashing all the main characters into the press room for four simultaneous conversations: Walt on the phone to his copy-man Duffy; Bruce pleading with Hildy; Walt trying to jettison Bruce; and all the while, Walt heckling Hildy to finish her story. It's hilarious, miraculous, breakneck stuff.

You see, Hawks' cinema really does begin with the Word. Until the final scene, there's no music eating up *Friday*'s airtime. Language is the soundtrack, the sonic rhythm. This is the "invisibility" that John Carpenter was talking about: Hawks' style is nestled deep inside dialogue and gesture. He zeroes his camera squarely on the actors, framing Walt and Hildy together, while his editing lashes conversations off each other like shards of shrapnel. And, like Hawks' direction, Grant and Russell's physical turns are curved intimately around their lines. They're constantly full of hustle and haste – checking a tie-knot, putting on lipstick, pointing, grabbing and gesticulating... Watch the way Grant and Russell subtly lean towards each other, magnetised even when at blows. For grace, timing, speed and snap, it's performance of breathtaking sophistication, naturalistic and stylised.

Hawks saw flirtation as nothing less than an art form. He pulled the same trick backwards in *To Have And Have Not*, slowing down the smoky groove between Bogie and Bacall to max up the sex factor. But here, it's lethal love, love that »

NEED TO KNOW

Year 1939
Running time 92 mins
Director Howard Hawks
Stars Cary Grant, Rosalind Russell, Ralph Bellamy
Buy it on Region 2
Tagline "She learned about men from him!"
Best line "Listen, the last man who said that to me was Archie Leach, just a week before he cut his throat." – Walt (Archie Leach, of course, being a young Bristolian who grew up to be one Cary Grant.)
Critic's view "Explodes into the decorous quiet of the cinema like a high-powered shrieking bomb." – *The Times*
Best watched when... You've just finished a vow of silence.

works only on the brink of disaster. Walt and Hildy are constantly circling each other, like sharks gnashing their razor grins. Settling down means death for both of them. And, under *His Girl Friday*'s screwball skin, death and darkness bleed heavily. Look closer: this is a "comedy" of political corruption, murder, attempted suicide, fraud, kidnap, entrapment, communism, media sensationalism and execution. "There's action only if there's danger," Hawks used to say and, indeed, *Friday*'s moral apathy adds yet another level of urgency. Walt and Hildy need horror and crisis to sell papers. Ethics are for the other guy. Maybe it's this that makes a 67-year-old movie so savagely modern.

John Ford called Hawks "the Grey Fox" for his womanising ways, but the nickname's keenly appropriate for an independent force who squirmed free inside the might of the Hollywood studio system. Howard Hawks *was* invisible, a ghost in the machine, smuggling his own darkness and smarts into commercial genre convention. And in Grant, the director had a perfect partner in crime. Just as Hawks showed Ford that John Wayne knew how to act, he showed Hitchcock the slick, Satanic harm in Cary Grant's charm way before *Notorious* and *Suspicion*. "No, no, never mind the Chinese earthquake for heaven's sake," Walt barks joyously. "Look, I don't care if there's a million dead. No, junk the Polish Corridor. Take Hitler and stick him on the funny page... No, no, leave the rooster story alone – that's human interest."

In *Bringing Up Baby*, Grant is a bumbling victim of women and society. Here he's the dark lord of both. Roaring, cartoonish, ironic, maniacal, devious, seductive, elegant... devilish. Yes, that's the word.

And maybe that's what scared off the Academy. Cary Grant wasn't nominated, nor was *Friday*, nor was Hawks (he never won a Best Director Oscar in five decades of moviemaking).

So behind all its furious chatter, what is Hawks' career masterpiece really saying? As critic David Thomson notes, "It means you shouldn't trust the paper you read or the person you wake up with. But you knew those things already, deep down. You just need an old-fashioned movie to admit them." TF

Jonathan Crocker

A COPY OF A COPY OF A COPY OF A...

Hollywood just won't let a good idea go...

The Front Page (1931)
His Girl Friday (1939)
The Front Page (1974)
Switching Channels (1988)

Seven Samurai (1954)
The Magnificent Seven (1960)
Battle Beyond The Stars (1980)
The Seven Magnificent Gladiators (1983)

Rio Bravo (1959)
El Dorado (1966)
Rio Lobo (1970)
Assault On Precinct 13 (1976)
Assault On Precinct 13 (2005)

Roadhouse Nights (1930)
Yojimbo (1961)
Fistful Of Dollars (1964)
Django (1966)
Last Man Standing (1996)
Miller's Crossing (1990)

Classic Scene

INT. WALT'S OFFICE – DAY
Hildy has only just revealed she is quitting the newspaper game to marry insurance salesman Bruce Baldwin. This is goodbye...

Walt is stunned – if only for a split second. His mischievous mind is already working overtime to find a way to send Bruce packing. Hildy's husband-to-be is waiting outside the door and Walt really wants to meet him...

WALT
Oh, now you're not afraid, are ya? Come on, let's see this paragon. Is he as good as you say?

Walt bursts out of his office in front of Hildy and firmly marches ahead of her through the paper's work area to confront Bruce. An elderly gentleman is sitting in the waiting area – Walt shakes his hand with gusto as Bruce looks on with bafflement...

WALT
Well, I can see right away my wife picked out the right husband for herself. How do you do, sir?

DAVIS
Must be some mistake. I'm already married...

WALT
Already married? Tsk, tsk, tsk. Oh Hildy, you should have told me.

BRUCE
Mr Burns...

WALT
Well, congratulations again, Mr Baldwin.

BRUCE
Mr Burns...

DAVIS
Oh no, my name is...

WALT
Excuse me will you, I'm terribly busy. Just leave your card with the boy. What did you just say, Mr Baldwin?

DAVIS
My name is...

BRUCE
Mr Burns? Mr Burns?

WALT
Some other time, I'm busy with Mr Bruce Baldwin here. I didn't hear what you said, Mr Baldwin.

BRUCE
But you see, there's some sort of confusion, Mr Burns, you see.

DAVIS
I was going to say that my name...

WALT
Now what is it with you? Can't you see that...

BRUCE
I'm Bruce Baldwin.

Having cheekily undermined him, Walt shakes hands with Bruce's wooden umbrella handle instead of his right mitt.

WALT
Hildy, you led me to expect you were marrying a much older man... I realise you didn't mean old in years.

He looks at Bruce's stuffy, uptight attire – he's carrying an umbrella and is clad in raincoat and rubbers.

WALT
A man ought to be prepared for any emergency...

HILDY
You're wasting your time, Walt. It won't do you a bit of good...

9

THE LORD OF THE RINGS TRILOGY

Peter Jackson crashes the top 10 with one film in three volumes... Sneaky hobbitses!

It is, it must be said, better than *Krull*. "You can't imagine what you'll experience when you see the pages of *The Lord Of The Rings* come to life," said Ian McKellen upon *The Fellowship Of The Ring's* release, coming over quite the Selznick-ian showman. The actor proved an insightful guide to the expectation-laden adaptation of JRR Tolkien's seminal book. He only read the novels when he was offered the role of über-wizard Gandalf and provided a non-fanatic window into the world of Middle-earth through his online journal. And his hyperbolic statement proved entirely justified. We were about to see part one of the most completely realised, astonishingly ambitious fantasy film of all time.

Film? Oh yes. For just as Tolkien's epic was one novel split into three volumes, so *The Lord Of The Rings* is best considered one film split into three parts – conceptually whole, filmed concurrently and telling an over-arching story of near biblical proportions. Audiences and critics alike couldn't avoid the *Star Wars* comparisons – particularly between *The Two Towers* and *The Empire Strikes Back* – but Lucas' overall story was loosely considered, with years between movies. Cut *The Fellowship Of The Ring, The Two Towers* and *The Return Of The King* together, in contrast, and you've a perfectly unified tapestry: a 558-minute long masterwork (682 mins in its extended DVD edition – our recommendation) that virtually redefines epic.

Unlike the Star Wars saga, it's a perfectly unified tapestry... a masterwork

With hobbits Frodo (Elijah Wood), Sam (Sean Astin) and co embarking on a quest to Mordor to destroy the world-threatening One Ring, it is the ultimate road movie.

Looking back to *Fellowship*'s 2001 release, it's hard to remember what a risk *Rings* was, how the $270-million production was branded, in the more breathless corners of LA, "Hollywood's biggest gamble". Ralph Bashki's 1978 animation had cult appeal, but money trouble meant it was released with only a half-finished third act and what there was never truly captured Tolkien's magic. There were big question marks over whether CGI had evolved enough to make Middle-earth a credible creation and few believed a fantasy film could ever triumph at the Oscars.

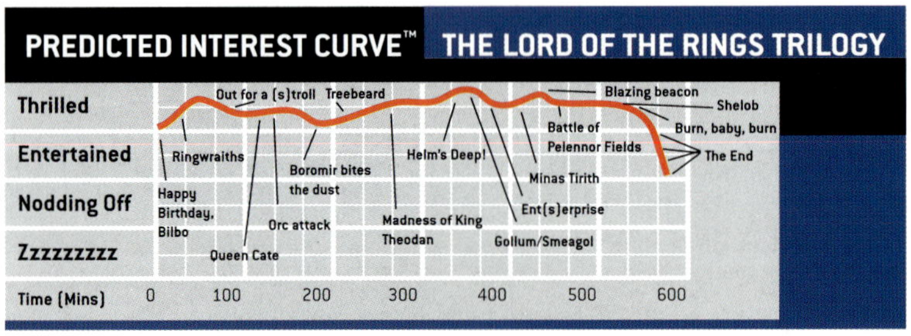

Even harder to credit now, the jury was out on Peter Jackson. Like a pre-*Rings* Bashki, whose *Heavy Traffic* and *Coonskin* had caused controversy, the director was best known for films in questionable taste: sick-trigger 'classics' *Bad Taste* and *Braindead*. *The Frighteners* was a diverting failure, struggling to convincingly blend effects and emotion, although it was enough to convince New Line that *The Lord Of The Rings* could be done. But it was 1994's

Heavenly Creatures that had *Total Film* holding its breath. Could he manage such a delicate balance of love and despair, fantasy and heart-squeezing reality, on a much grander scale?

'Course he could. Well, it seemed that obvious five minutes into *Fellowship*, with the haunting gravitas of Cate Blanchett's prologue giving way to a vividly realised Shire, McKellen's sage magic-monger and Elijah Wood as pint-sized hero Frodo. They'd had desperate trouble casting the role of the questing, furry-footed hobbit, until a tape arrived of the American actor, stood in a park dressed in a homemade costume reciting lines from the book. Jackson had never heard of him, "But the minute I saw those luminous blue eyes and heard his voice, I knew we had our Frodo."

Those luminous eyes would brim with enough tears and longing gazes over the nine-hour journey to make Wood appear like a Labrador (for goodness sake, give him a biscuit), but the star has steel, too – particularly evident in *King*'s journey into the heart of darkness, where he goes a bit Kurtz: "No Sam. I can't recall the taste of food... nor the sound of water... nor the touch of grass. I'm... naked in the dark. There's... There's nothing. No veil between me and the wheel of fire. I can see him... with my waking eyes." The acting in *Rings* was underrated by the Academy (who granted a single nomination, for McKellen in *Fellowship*), but it's hugely

NEED TO KNOW

Year 2001-03
Running time 558 mins
Director Peter Jackson
Stars Elijah Wood, Andy Serkis, Viggo Mortensen, Ian McKellen, Sean Astin, Christopher Lee
Buy it on Region Two 12-disc Special Extended DVD Edition box set.
Tagline "There can be no triumph without loss. No victory without suffering. No freedom without sacrifice."
Best line "Stupid, fat hobbit." – Gollum
Critic's view "With spectacular scenery, stupefying effects and epic scope, is a dream come true." – *Washington Post*
Best watched when... Off work with the flu.

accomplished – all the more impressive given the scale of what the performers have to compete with. Viggo Mortensen is a brooding, charismatic king-in-waiting, McKellen brings screen subtlety to a warm stage presence, Astin ensures what could have been the Fat Sidekick role is instead an equal partner in a touching platonic love story. But there's no doubting *Rings'* leader: precious little Gollum (Andy Serkis). Looking like the bastard offspring of a newt and a weasel (or Ken Livingston and Peter Mandelson), Gollum was realised through ground-breaking technology too involved and, frankly, boring to go into here (computers, Lycra suit, blah, blah, blah). What's important is Serkis' soul » behind the CG mask. The 'Classic Scene' excerpted here is more than just an example of brilliant editing, it is astonishing acting. Serkis projects a tortured soul at war with himself, played – in the actor's own words – "like an addict who will go to any lengths to get his fix. He's not just a Machiavellian villain, but someone going through absolute hell." Oscar should have been bold and given another little bald fella a break.

The Academy did eventually fully credit Jackson's achievement, with 11 Oscars for *King*, to add to *Towers'* two and *Fellowship's* four. Perhaps the most richly deserved was Jackson, Fran Walsh and Philippa Boyens' gong for Best Adapted Screenplay. Anyone who's read *Rings* knows there's an extraordinary amount to distil and what an achievement it is to retain Tolkien's sense of a history born and bled over. On the script's structure the trilogy builds a staggering amount of spectacle, while never losing its essential humanity – or hobbit-anity, at any rate. As the journey progresses, we're treated to ever more jaw-shattering visions of this awesome world, from a characterful cave troll to the huge battle at Helm's Deep and the engulfing conflict at Pelennor Fields. It's a picture of rich, invigorating majesty...

The End.

Oh, and it'll probably be higher next time...

And we forgot to mention the other hobbits, who are pretty good, too...

And yes, it does go on a bit at the end...

Er, that's it. Really. You can go. Group hug. Roll credits. TF

James White

LORD OF THE THINGS

Facts. To bore people with in pubs. For hours.

The Elve's eyes are different colours depending on where they hail from. Rivendell Elves (such as Hugo Weaving's Elrond) have dark blue peepers. Lothlorien Elves (Galadriel and co) have light blue windows to the soul.

Bilbo's birthday cake in the party scene near the start of *Fellowship* has 111 real candles on it. It ended up catching fire mid-take, though Ian Holm gamely finished his scene.

Wondering who the portraits are hanging in Bag End? That would be Peter Jackson and Fran Walsh as hobbits. And their kids appear in all three films – at the birthday party (*Fellowship*), Helm's Deep (*Towers*) and Minas Tirith (*King*).

To achieve their inky black mouths, the Orc performers swilled a liquorice-based mouthwash.

All the Uruk'hai Orcs were supposed to be six-feet-tall, but the production couldn't find enough lofty stuntmen or actors. The five-footers were labelled the "Uruk'Low". No wonder they look angry on screen.

Classic Scene

EXT. ROAD TO MORDOR - NIGHT
Sam and Frodo are asleep after a long day's travelling. Frodo sleeps restlessly, clutching the ring.

Gollum observes them from a short distance away, enviously.

GOLLUM
We wants it. We wants it. Must have the precious. They stole it from us. Sneaky little hobbitses. Wicked! Tricksy! False!

As he turns, it's clear that the Smeagol side of his personality is also present. The argument is played out using camera angles.

SMEAGOL
No! Not master!

GOLLUM
Yes, precious! False! They will cheat you, hurt you, lie!

SMEAGOL
Master's my friend!

GOLLUM
You don't have any friends! Nobody likes you!

SMEAGOL
(*horrified, clutching his ears*)
Not listening! Not listening!

GOLLUM
(*smug, pushing his advantage*)
You're a liar! And a thief!

SMEAGOL
No!

GOLLUM
Murderer!

SMEAGOL
(*on the verge of tears*)
Go away!

GOLLUM
(*laughs*)
Go away?

SMEAGOL
I hate you! I hate you!

GOLLUM
Where would you be without me?
(*coughs*)
I saved us! It was me! We survived because of me!

SMEAGOL
(*suddenly seeming resolved*)
Not any more.

GOLLUM
What did you say?

SMEAGOL
Master looks after us now. We don't need you.

GOLLUM
(*angry*)
What?

SMEAGOL
Leave now, and never come back!

GOLLUM
No!
(*Smeagol is getting stronger and happier*)

SMEAGOL
Leave now and never come back!

GOLLUM
(*straining with the effort of holding on*)
Aaaaarrrrggggh!

It's like Smeagol is trying to expel a demon from his body. Which in a way, he is.

SMEAGOL
Leave! NOW! AND NEVER COME BACK!

He pants with the exhaustion of the verbal conflict, but looks around. Gollum no longer answers. Smeagol is visibly delighted.

SMEAGOL
Heh! Heh! We told him to go away! And away he goes, precious!

Overjoyed to be free, Smeagol begins leaping about like a gangly frog, dancing with joy and relief.

SMEAGOL
Gone! Gone! Gone! Smeagol is freeeee!

8

THE EMPIRE STRIKES BACK

Adventure. Excitement. Paternity issues. A Darth night of the soul...

No Jedi mind tricks are needed to make you suspend your disbelief here...

So just how do you follow up one of the most popular hits of the '70s? With a complete dud, as it happens. "I did *More American Graffiti* [1979], it made 10 cents, it failed miserably," said George Lucas of his first foray into sequeldom. That film's inability to recapture the imaginations stirred by its 1973 forebear didn't bode well for Lucas' next project. Would *The Empire Strikes Back* turn out to be simply *More Star Wars*, another pale imitation of a dazzling original? Emphatically, no. It turned out to be a different beast entirely. Oh, and the defining chapter of the greatest space story ever told, too.

Lucas' refusal to rehash was underwritten by the financial independence – and, by extension, creative freedom – that *Episode IV*'s seminal success had brought him. "This film was not a traditional sequel," he says. "It didn't have a beginning and an end. It had a unique structure where a lot of the big action sequences are early on in the movie and it ends on a personal note. These are things I'm not sure a studio would have gone along with, if they'd had their say about what was going to happen."

George was calling the shots – figuratively if not literally, having decided to put down the megaphone, and executive produce instead.

So who'd direct? Step forward Irvin Kershner, Lucas' former film-school tutor. It was an off-the-wall but inspired choice: Kersh didn't have blockbuster credentials (he'd just come off the thriller *Eyes Of Laura Mars*), but was determined to put a human face on this far-away galaxy. "My main concern was how to characterise the people you'd already met in *Star Wars*," he reflects. "I wanted humour. I wanted emotion. I wanted the people to be interesting." And boy, did he reward his ex-pupil's faith. Look at *Empire Strikes Back* and you don't see sorry evidence of a production that went over-budget and over-schedule; where the original screenwriter (*Big Sleep* scribe Leigh Brackett) died, rows erupted over the first rough cut and the film stock snapped in the camera – the latter during the Hoth shoot, in coldest Norway.

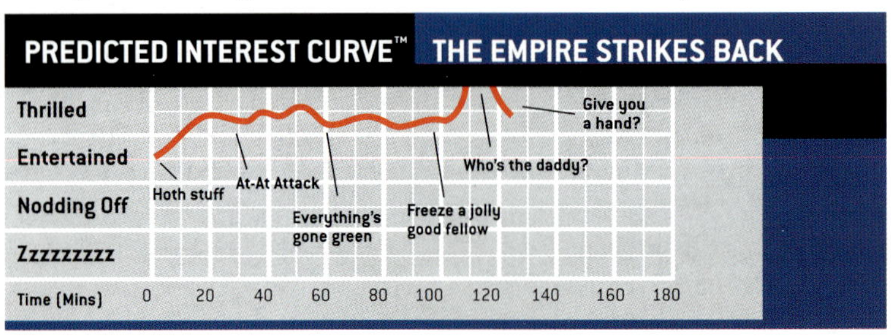

No. None of that. What you see, instead, is a film that's brimful of confidence, risk, vision. It sparkles with laughs (Yoda squabbling with R2-D2; C-3PO's fussbudget prattlings) and smoulders with feeling (the classic Leia-Han "I love you"/ "I know" exchange; even Chewie's mournful Hoth howl). And yes, the people are interesting. *A New Hope* zaps you into euphoria, but emotionally it's as callow as its farmboy hero. Here, the characters are more complex. Take Luke, neck-deep in a moral quandary over the fate of his friends; or Leia, torn between princessly propriety and a hankering for a bit of

rough. Okay, so not everyone's a cauldron of contradictions, but there's no denying that scripter Lawrence Kasdan, Kersh and the cast brought fresh shading to these creations.

And there's the new intake: duplicitous smoothie Lando Calrissian (the series' answer to accusations that it was set in an all-white universe); bounty hunter Boba Fett (an instant icon despite doing and saying next to nothing); and perhaps *Episode V*'s biggest gamble, Einstein-eyed Force wrangler Yoda. "If that puppet had not worked, the whole film would have been down the tubes," Lucas reckons. The puppet worked, wonderfully. Thanks to Frank Oz's ultra-expressive performance, no Jedi mind tricks are needed to make you suspend your disbelief when lil' green's on screen. Nor, indeed, when ILM are in full flight, the FX johnnies upping their own ante with quadruped war machines, treacherous asteroid fields and the daddy of all space wagons, Darth Vader's Star Destroyer (introduced to the rhythms of John Williams' 'Imperial March', surely the saga's top tune). And did we mention the pin-sharp photography by Cronenberg regular Peter Suschitzky? (Compare with *Return Of The Jedi*'s lack of lustre, or the chintzy look of some of the prequels' digi-visuals.)

But it's the darkness that defines *Empire Strikes Back*: the betrayals, the tortures and, of course, That Moment. No, not Vader's fatherly revelation – earth-shattering though it is – but Luke's suicidal fall, his choice of death over Darth. Gives you a bigger chill than a Wampa's freezer. Lucas' concerns over the ending's bleakness – symbolic hand loss and all – were so grave that he even spoke to psychologists about whether the younglings could handle it. ("These are the things you consider when going through a story like this – what is the potential to cause damage?") But he bit the bullet and the rest is box-office history: the film was one of the '80s' biggest winners. (Although, worldwide, it's the lowest-grossing *Star Wars* movie, top dog being *The Phantom Menace*. Wrong with this picture, something is...)

And of course, it gained swift recognition as the most divine of the Holy Trilogy... didn't it? "It's funny, people always »

NEED TO KNOW

Year 1980
Running time 122 mins
Director Irvin Kershner
Stars Mark Hamill, Harrison Ford, Carrie Fisher, Billy Dee Williams, Anthony Daniels
Buy it on Region 2 box set
Tagline "The Star Wars saga continues."
Best line "No. I am your father." – Darth Vader
Critic's view "A visual extravaganza from beginning to end, one of the most visionary and inventive of all films." – *Chicago Sun-Times*
Best watched when... You feel like a walk on the Dark Side.

talk about *Empire Strikes Back* being their favourite," says sound-effects supremo Ben Burtt. "Yet at the time, it was not considered as such. It leaves things undone, and when it came out there was a lot of disappointment. It was a success and it was respected, but there wasn't this judgement that it was the best of the three films." Time's been on its side, though. In 1997, *Empire Strikes Back* got the lightest Special Edition facelift of the trio (a Cloud City wide shot here; a *Return Of The Jedi* outtake there), which spoke volumes. And today, with the Skywalker circle completed by *Revenge Of The Sith* – close, but no cigar to *Empire Strikes Back*'s intensity – it's as plain as Dagobah that the Force was strongest in this one.

You can count on one hand the sequels that have surpassed their predecessors – *Bride Of Frankenstein* (1935); *The Godfather Part II* (1974); maybe *Aliens* (1986). And *Empire Strikes Back* was a fat middle-finger to industry wisdom that says a follow-up shouldn't fuck with formula. It paid for Skywalker Ranch, the post-production facility used by the movie-making world and its wife. More importantly, it gave audiences a childhood classic that's stayed with them as adults; a grown-up fairytale minus a sappy ending. Unlike *Star Wars*, this second-act stunner can't stand on its own. But in the Lucas firmament, its the one that stands tallest. TF

Matthew Leyland

EXTENDED UNIVERSE

1. CLONE WARS
Prequel-bridging 'toon series charting epochal Lucas-verse conflict in handy bite-sized pieces. Heavy on action, light on dialogue, no Jar Jar. If only the new movies had been the same...

2. THE STAR WARS HOLIDAY SPECIAL
Mesmerisingly dismal TV cash-in, shown once and then buried forever (unless you can get hold of a bootleg). Introduced Boba Fett to the *SW* universe. As well as Jefferson Airplane.

3. EWOK MOVIES
Two post-*Return Of The Jedi* telemovies based around everyone's least favourite furballs. Second one (*The Battle For Endor*) was scripted by David and Jim Wheat, who went on to ink *Pitch Black*.

4. DROIDS TV SERIES
Short-lived cartoon outing for the Laurel and Hardy of the robot world, with Anthony Daniels once more lending his larynx to C-3PO.

5. WILLOW
Flop-tastic fantasy adventure involving a trainee sorcerer, a rougish mercenary and a skull-faced baddie. And a skip-load of original ideas, obviously.

Classic Scene

EXT. DAGOBAH SWAMP – DAY
In the midst of Jedi training, Luke stands on his hands, with Yoda perched on his feet.

YODA
Use the Force. Yes...

Yoda taps Luke's leg – he lifts one hand from the ground.

YODA
Now the stone. Feel it.

A large rock floats off the ground, resting on top of another one. R2-D2 bleeps in alarm. Luke's X-Wing is sinking into the lagoon. Luke loses concentration and drops Yoda.

LUKE
(*walking over to the water*)
Oh, no. We'll never get it out now.

YODA
So certain are you. Always with you it cannot be done. Hear you nothing that I say?

LUKE
Master, moving stones around is one thing. This is totally different.

YODA
(*stamping cane*)
No! No different! Only different in your mind. You must unlearn what you have learned.

LUKE
All right, I'll give it a try.

YODA
No! Try not. Do. Or do not. There is no try.

Luke stretches out his arm.

Slowly, the X-Wing's nose starts to lift out of the water. Yoda's eyes widen in anticipation, and then... the ship drops back beneath the surface.

LUKE
I can't. It's too big.

Drained, Luke sits beside Yoda.

YODA
Size matters not. Look at me. Judge me by my size, do you?
(*Luke shakes his head*)
And well you should not. For my ally is the Force. And a powerful ally it is. Life creates it, makes it grow. Its energy surrounds us and binds us. Luminous beings are we...
(*he pinches Luke's shoulder*)
...not this crude matter.
(*gesturing*)
You must feel the Force around you. Here between you... me... the tree... the rock... everywhere! Yes, even between this land and that ship!

LUKE
(*standing up*)
You want the impossible.

Luke walks away and sits in a huff. Yoda closes his eyes and points his arm at the ship. Gracefully, the ship climbs out of the water and floats safely onto the shore.

Luke looks on in astonishment. R2 almost explodes.

LUKE
I don't... I don't believe it.

YODA
That is why you fail.

7

TOKYO STORY

Soft as a smile, sad as a sigh: Ozu's haunting tale of life, death and disappointment...

At first glance, Yasujiro Ozu's films seem subtle to the point of being invisible. But if you think *American Beauty* is the last word in emotionally shattering studies of family life, take its advice: look closer. Ozu's 46th film, *Tokyo Story*, is gentle but its quiet power and precision takes you unawares. It seeps into you, taking its careful time to emerge as a study in life, death and the gap in between. What more do you want?

Tokyo Story is gentle – but its quiet power and precision takes you unawares

Tokyo wasn't released in America until 1972, almost a decade after Ozu's death at 60 in 1963. But that neglect has been slowly rectified, so that *Halliwell's* recently voted *Tokyo Story* the best film *ever*. Better than the razzle-dazzle of *Citizen Kane* – which Ozu admired when he watched it while waiting out the war in Singapore in 1945 – and *Vertigo*? Better than other key '50s Japanese films, such as *Ugetsu Monogatari* (also 1953) and *Rashômon* (1951)? In terms of recent Japanese cinema, better than the recent, post-Takashi Miike, post-Manga flurries of exuberant excess? There's a lot to be said for these films, but *Tokyo* is no less powerful for being pitched at another register.

The simple premise is at once context-specific and universal. The fact that Ozu's writer, Kôgo Noda, took influence from the American film *Make Way For Tomorrow* (1937) while Ozu didn't watch it suggests how expansive the film's questions are. As parents age, how does their relationship with their children change? Plot-wise, an elderly couple, Tomi (Chieko Higashiyama) and Shukishi (Chishu Ryu), visit their children in Tokyo. The young set are too busy to spend time on the oldsters; only their daughter-in-law, Noriko (Setsuko Hara, the "eternal virgin" of Japanese cinema, who devoted her late career to Ozu's films), has time for them, despite having lost her husband in the war. Instead of looking after their parents, the children send them to a spa, where young people carouse. Outside the old couple's door, we see one of the most famously potent and simple shots in cinema: two pairs of shoes, neatly placed. The next day, as Tomi and Shukishi sit on a sea wall, Tomi feels faintly dizzy and we realise all is not well. No histrionics follow. Instead, the film's wallop is slowly accrued in the insecurities beneath smiles, sighs, stoicism. When Tomi asks her grandson if he wants to be a doctor when he grows up, she adds, "I wonder if I'll still be here when you are," registering the gentlest breeze of unease and revealing an interior world with the greatest of restraint.

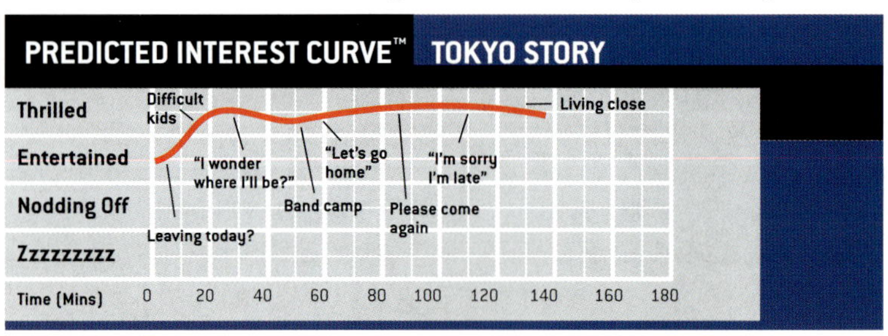

The cast don't 'emote'. No one gets their 'close-up' moment. But as we watch, the Ozu regulars Higashiyama and Ryu talk about going home on the

seafront and we realise how acutely they suggest a lifetime spent together as they gently chide each other while saying little, as long-term partners do.

Nor does Ozu judge the children: he observes their behaviour and persuades us that this is true of people. The children are afraid of death because they're human. When Shukishi points out to Noriko how strange it is that she has been more generous than his children, it isn't a judgement but an observation. Some critics have seen this aspect of Ozu as 'Zen'-like, which the director had this thought on: "Whenever Westerners don't understand something they simply think it's Zen." Better to say that his films are "humanist", in that they tease out human consistencies from beneath surface conventions.

His style is just as understated and exact, matching content and theme head-on. After the war, Ozu rarified his approach after his bawdier silents ("Obvious plots bore me now," he once said), while maintaining the lessons he learned on the silents in a willingness to embrace silence and an emphasis on composition over style. Ozu didn't made his first talkie until 1936 and his style is quiet in itself, abandoning fades and the like because, he said, "dissolves and fades are not part of cinematic grammar. They are only attributes of the camera."

He was after something purer, more exacting. As Ryu noted after Ozu's death, "Mr Ozu looked happiest when he was engaged in writing a scenario with Mr Kôgo Noda, at the latter's cottage... by the time he finished writing a script, after about four months' effort, he had already made up every image in every shot, so that he never changed the scenario after we went on the set."

The result is art drained of mannerism, a portrait of people and their quiet struggles rather than a display in style. Ozu excels at shooting people, often sat together in profile, as if we are watching life over someone's shoulder rather than being led by the hand. The camera nearly always observes the protagonists from the low "tatami-mat" position, in that its three-feet height is supposedly the height of someone sat on a tatami mat. »

NEED TO KNOW

Year 1953
Running time 135 mins
Director Yasujiro Ozu
Stars Chishu Ryu, Chieko Higashiyama, Setsuko Hara
Buy it on Region 1
Tagline N/A
Best line "I feel the days have got longer, living alone." – Shukishi
Critic's view "What we have here is a work that expresses in every image a whole attitude to living, an attitude that comprehends the painful necessities as well as the joys of existence." – *Sight & Sound*
Best watched when... You resent your parents for coming to visit. You may cut them some slack...

One story suggests Ozu adopted that position to make a film about children but liked it so much he stuck with it; at any rate, it worked for him, giving the screen room to breathe.

In scenes where someone goes upstairs to do something, we wait until they come back. Ozu doesn't cut in time to usher them back: things take as long as they take. A film obsessed with time, *Tokyo* acutely registers what the passage of it feels like. In keeping, Ozu's camera rarely moves, often beginning a scene by taking in the shape of a room and ending it by lingering long after the people have left, taking in every tiny detail. It's a faintly haunting technique: in a film about mortality, we get a simple, clear sense of what its world looks like after people have left it.

Tokyo Story ends on just such a plaintive note, with Shukishi alone at his seaside home, contemplating the years ahead without his wife as a boat slowly passes him by. People die, life continues. *Tokyo Story* might very well teach us to appreciate these people while they're around, although it doesn't lecture us, doesn't proffer homilies, doesn't rail against inevitability. What it can change, though, is the way we watch films. TF

Kevin Harley

THE ETERNAL VIRGIN

The other five films Masae Aida, aka Setsuko Hara, made with Ozu...

LATE SPRING (1949)
Hara remained unmarried and childless throughout her life, and her films with Ozu seem to play out her life-long theme of the pressure to pair off. Here, Hara plays Noriko (her namesake in *Tokyo Story*), a grown-up woman living with her father (Chishu Ryu), who insists she marry.

EARLY SUMMER (1951)
Hara's Noriko is Ryu's sister here, again pushed into marriage: this time, to help out her family financially during the tough post-war years.

TOKYO TWILIGHT (1957)
Another daughter: Hara's Takako is again Ryu's child, this time a single mother separated from her abusive husband. Darker than the average Ozu.

LATE AUTUMN (1960)
Still in relationship crises, Hara plays a widow, Akiko, whose family and friends struggle to hunt down a suitable fella for her.

EARLY AUTUMN / THE END OF SUMMER (1961)
Another study in family and the individual, with Hara as a widow torn between what she and her family want as they try to find her a partner.

EXT. ATAMI RESORT – DAY
As maids go about cleaning the hotel rooms, Tomi and Shukishi sit on a seaside wall, fanning themselves. Neither of them has slept well due to the loud music playing in the hotel all night.

TOMI
What's the matter?

SHUKISHI
Well...

TOMI
It's because you didn't sleep well, isn't it?

SHUKISHI
Well... But you did.

SHUKISHI
That's not true. I didn't sleep a wink...

TOMI
Yes, you did! You even snored.

SHUKISHI
Anyway, this is a place for the younger generation.

TOMI
That's true.

Cut to the maids talking as they continue to clean the living quarters.

MAID
How were the newlyweds last night?

SECOND MAID
They were rude, weren't they?

MAID
I doubt they were really newlyweds. She kept smoking in bed even after the husband got up. He is really spoiling her. I overheard him saying to her, "Your eyes, mouth, all of you belong to me." That woman must sleep with anyone!

Cut back to Tomi and Shukishi

TOMI
I wonder what Kyoko is doing back at home?

SHUKISHI
Well... shall we go back home?

TOMI
You must be homesick already!

SHUKISHI
It's you who's homesick. You want to go home, don't you? We saw Tokyo... we saw Atami... so let's go home.

TOMI
Shall we? Shall we go home?

SHUKISHI
Yes...

They slowly get up and walk off. Tomi, however, crawls, in an early intimation that she is weakening.

SHUKISHI
What's the matter?

TOMI
I felt a bit dizzy... I'm alright now.

SHUKISHI
You didn't sleep well. That's why.

TOMI
Let's go.

SHUKISHI
Yes.

We watch them slowly walking along the wall, Tomi just behind Shukishi. The camera caresses the surrounding setting: the resort, the seaside wall – all of which will be empty without them.

6

CITIZEN KANE

We may not think it's The Greatest. But it's still pretty damn good.

Orson Welles loved villains. He usually played them, too. In the 11 of his own movies that he starred in, he played the baddie in all but four – and in those four he was nothing if not morally ambiguous. And in other people's movies he was rarely anything but the heavy.

He never denied that affinity with the dark side, either, acknowledging a feeling "of human sympathy for these different characters I have created, though morally I find them detestable". Which is maybe why it's so difficult to loathe a Welles villain. His own sympathy for them makes them perversely sympathetic to us. Think of his greatest role outside his own movies, in *The Third Man*. Do we really want to see Harry Lime die? For all the horrible, despicable, cynical things he's done, don't we keep hoping, right to the very end, that the desperately clutching fingers will push up the manhole cover and Lime's distorted shadow will skitter off round the next corner of those darkened, insanely-skewed Vienna streets?

'I have sympathy for these characters, though I find them detestable' ORSON WELLES

Of course it's there, that love-hate passion, isn't it, right from the very start of his film career? Welles, the left-wing maverick, detested everything that Charles Foster Kane stood for – detested even more Kane's original: the all-powerful, ruthless press baron William Randolph Hearst. And the way Kane's written, he's fit to be abominated by any right-thinking person. In one of the movie's most famous scenes, hoping to boost the circulation of his struggling paper, he sends a reporter off to Cuba to foment a war. "Could send you prose poems about scenery, but don't feel right spending your money. There is no war in Cuba," wires the hack. "Dear Wheeler," responds Kane, "You provide the prose poems. I'll provide the war." And he does. Thousands die and his circulation rockets. What's more, those are virtually the exact words used by Hearst in a telegram as he kick-started the 1898 Spanish-American War that launched the USA on its career as an imperial power. And look what that led to...

So we should hate Kane. But we don't. There's too much of Welles in him. Welles, too, could treat people abominably. Throughout his life friends and colleagues were abused, cheated, lied to and conned, yet time after time they came back for more, just as Kane's closest friend and associate, Jedediah Leland (Joseph Cotten), can never quite bring himself to quit, right to the end speaking of him with compassion and regret. Did Welles know how closely he was portraying himself in Charles Foster Kane, with his arrogance and ruthlessness, his deviousness and gnawing insecurity? Surely he must have done; he was an intelligent and painfully self-aware man. But what he can't

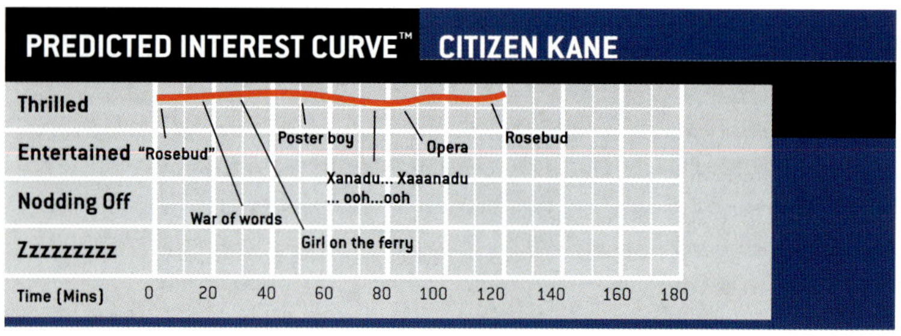

have known – and what gives the film a poignancy that grows stronger with each passing year – is how much he was foretelling his own life, the long, slow, sad decline of that dazzling early promise.

True, Kane takes far longer to fall, and at the end he's still an unimaginably rich and powerful man. Welles ended up making ads for third-rate sherry and frozen peas, surrounded by the fragments of his half-finished projects, a bloated parody of his youthful good looks. ("Orson grew fat spreading himself thin," noted his waspish friend Kenneth Tynan). But watching him as the aged Kane, alone in his grotesque Gothic monstrosity of a castle stuffed with broken, disassembled artefacts from all corners of the globe, babbling "Rosebud" ("Dollar-book Freud," mocked Welles in later years) to no one with his dying lips, it's impossible to suppress the shudder of unwitting premonition. How could he have known? Yet there it is on screen, clear as doom – Orson Welles: this is your life.

So maybe that's why, over the years, *Citizen Kane* has steadily expanded its reputation from the debacle of its original release to being often hailed The Greatest Film Ever Made. (but not by us). It's vital, in saying that, to remember it wasn't initially dismissed as a failure, despite the myth. Most critics raved about it – the *Time* review quoted in the Need To Know box is typical, while many other influential voices – Bosley Crowther in the *New York Times*, John O'Hara in *Newsweek* – were just as enthusiastic. Even so, the movie's release was sabotaged. While making the film Welles had kept its subject matter closely under wraps, rightly fearing repercussions from the Hearst press. But his screenwriter Herman J Mankiewicz, a brilliantly witty yet hopeless lush, couldn't resist showing off his great work by giving a copy of the script to his pal Charles Lederer. Lederer's aunt, whom he adored, was the actress Marion Davies, Hearst's mistress. Davies was a lively, intelligent woman and a gifted actress, and her portrayal in Kane as the talentless Susan Alexander >>

NEED TO KNOW

Year 1941
Running time 114 mins
Director Orson Welles
Stars Orson Welles, Joseph Cotton, Agnes Moorehead
Buy it on Region Two, Classic Collection Box Set
Tagline "It's Terrific!"
Best line "Maybe Rosebud was something he couldn't get or something he lost. Anyway, it wouldn't have explained anything. I don't think any word can explain a man's life." – Thompson, the reporter.
Critic's view "A work of art created by grown people for grown people." – *Time*
Best watched when... You think the press can't sink any lower.

was a far crueller libel than any perpetrated on Hearst. Lederer was outraged. In no time the whole crushing weight of Hearst's press machine went into action against Welles' movie, ensuring it never got a decent release.

A lot of the commonly-accepted guff about *Kane* is misleading, if not downright false. Welles wasn't the first to use deep-focus photography – plenty of others, such as Jean Renoir and William Wyler, were there before him. The same goes for ceilinged sets, sound montage, jump cuts, overlapping dialogue, chiaoscuro lighting, the device of revealing a man's life through multiple-narrator viewpoints – although probably no previous director had dared sling them all together with such gusto and visual inventiveness as Welles. The film's underlying message is staggeringly conventional for such a ground-breaking work: the sentimental Capra-esque thesis is that the rich and powerful shouldn't be envied since they've forfeited the simple pleasures of true love and happiness. (A deeply conservative doctrine, and highly comforting to the rich and powerful). Yet Kane does deserve its status. First, because Welles' personal signature is so compelling, so powerful and so unmistakably inscribed in every frame. Second because through the baroque showmanship and look-at-me technique, dazzling though they are, the howl of Welles' future pain, frustration and blocked genius sounds ever louder in our ears. TF

Philip Kemp

AWESOME WAILS

Welles often complained that critics and colleagues singled him out with particular venom. He wasn't wrong...

"There, but for the grace of God, goes God."
– Herman J Mankiewicz

"Orson Welles treating himself to broad, operatic sculpturings of body, cloak and diction, his eyes glinting in the Rembrandt gloom like side orders of jelly."
– James Agee, on Welles as Mr Rochester

"I just can't stand that man's genius." – Rita Hayworth, his ex-wife

"Pure Orson Welles and impure balderdash, which may be the same thing."
– Gerald Weales reviewing *Touch Of Evil*

Welles had a bite of his own, however. Once on a TV chat-show, a nervous young host floundered into a introduction that ran on far too long, with Welles glowered in impatience.

"Mr Welles, could I ask –"

Welles (interrupting): "You may have three questions."

Host: "Oh, er, ha-ha, couldn't we have–"

Welles: "No. And now you have two questions."

Classic Scene

Welles' origins in radio left him knowing more about sound technique than most people in Hollywood. In this sequence he makes masterly use of sound editing. Dissatisfied in his marriage, he has just met Susan Alexander (Dorothy Comingore), a pretty young would-be singer.

INT. SUSAN'S APARTMENT – NIGHT
Susan sits at the piano, playing and singing badly. Kane sits, legs crossed, smiling. As she ends, he applauds.

Dissolve to: Susan, still at piano, now singing in Italian. Badly. As she ends Kane applauds more warmly.

Applause intensifies as we dissolve to street political meeting. Small crowd listening to Leland.

Posters: KANE FOR GOVERNOR.

LELAND
There is only one man who can rid the politics of this state of the evil domination of Boss Jim Gettys...

BYSTANDERS
Hooray! Shh! Shh!

LELAND
I am speaking of Charles Foster Kane – the fighting liberal, the friend of the working man, the next Governor of this state, who entered upon this campaign...

Dissolve to huge meeting hall. Kane speaking in front of enormous poster of himself, inscribed KANE FOR GOVERNOR.

KANE
...with one purpose only: to point out and make public the dishonesty, the downright villainy, of Boss Jim W Gettys' political machine...

The timbre of Kane's voice changes, as heard through the sound system. We track in towards Kane over the audience and his timbre returns to normal.

KANE
...now in complete control of the government of this state. I made no promises...
(*spreads arms wide*)
...because until a few weeks ago I had no hope of being elected!
(*grins, laughter, applause.*)
Now, however, I have something more than a hope...
(*more laughter and applause*)
...and Jim Gettys – Jim Gettys has less than a chance!

Emily and Charles Jr watch Kane – Emily impassive, son beaming, standing up. Emily shushes him.

KANE
Every straw vote, every independent poll, shows that I'll be elected.
(*thunderous applause*).
Very well then – I can afford to make some promises!

Charles Jr waves enthusiastically.

KANE
(*waves back*)
The working man – the working man and the slum child know they can expect my best efforts in their interests.

Leland listening, sceptical.

KANE
The decent, ordinary citizens know that I'll do everything in my power to protect the underprivileged...
(*he strides forward to front of platform, pulling back jacket, aggressive pose*)
...the underpaid and the underfed!

Furious applause. Bernstein, watching, claps. Charles Jr looks at his mother.

CHARLES JR
Mother, is pop Governor yet?

EMILY
Not yet, junior.

KANE
Well, I'd make my promises now if I weren't too busy arranging to keep them!

Applause, cheers. Now Leland is applauding and laughing.

KANE
But here's one promise I'll make and Boss Jim Gettys knows I'll keep it. My first official act as Governor of the State will be to appoint a special District Attorney to arrange for the indictment, prosecution and conviction of Boss Jim W Gettys!

Kane sticks out his chin. Deafening applause. A brass band starts to play. High in the upper balcony a thickset man rises, puts on his hat and quietly exits with an air of purpose. This is Boss Jim Gettys.

5

THE GODFATHER PART II

Francis Ford Coppola keeps it in the family to deliver cinema's greatest sequel...

Honour, death, tradition... Francis Ford Coppola's return to the world of the Corleone family thumps each of them home but none more than family. It's family that Michael battles to protect in the '50s against the government, other Mobsters and traitors within his own men. It's family that his father Vito struggles to revenge in Sicily and establish anew in America at the start of the 20th century. And it's the Corleone family that emerges both stronger and ironically weaker, by the time the screen finally goes black again.

The Godfather we see here is a ferocious figure, mericless and deadly

Part I was all about Michael attaining power; *Part II* is about him using it to ruthless and devastating effect. The Godfather we see here is a ferocious figure, merciless and deadly. Whether it's facing down senators, ordering deaths or simply seeing the pattern of the course of events faster and more accurately than anyone else – witness the shot of him leaving a plush Havana building alone minutes before anyone else even realises that Cuba's revolution has arrived – Michael is a king at the height of his power.

But that power comes at a price. Michael's not just merciless with others, he's merciless with himself. He makes the decisions that have to be made, regardless of the cost. Vengeance could be passed over, but then those forgiven could come back to haunt the family. Those who oppose him have to be stamped out. "I don't feel I have to wipe everybody out, Tom," he says to consigliere Tom Hagen (Robert Duvall). "Just my enemies." The trouble is, anyone who's a threat to the family is an enemy of Michael's, regardless of how close they are to him.

He starts the film with a wife, a mother, a brother, a sister and an adopted brother. By the end, haven taken the decisions he felt had to be made, by doing what is right for the family, he's kept the family secure from crooks and lawmakers alike but he's alone. The wife's left him, the mother's dead, the sister is a ruthless manipulator, the adopted brother's been hurt and pushed aside and the brother Fredo? He's been assassinated. On Michael's orders.

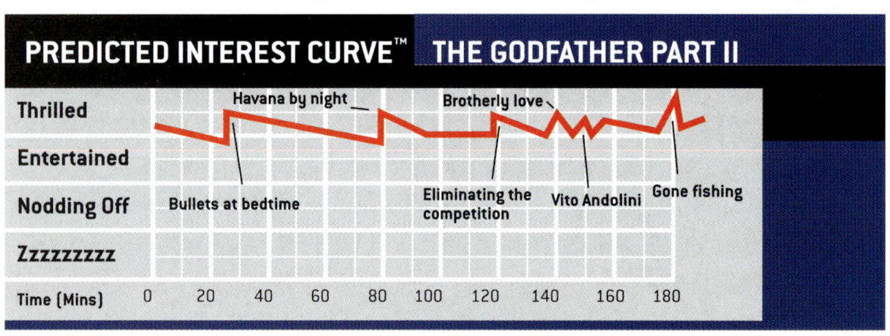

The final shot of Pacino's face is a masterclass in restrained acting. Watch the Pacino of today, with the shouty "Hoo-aah!" flourishes, and it's almost impossible to believe the same man gave such a performance of brutally tied-down restraint. The script doesn't give Michael many words to express his deep-buried regret for some of his actions – it doesn't need to. The tension in his frame, the set of his lips and the very smallest flickers around those deep, tired, dark eyes say all that you need to know.

But Michael's story isn't the only one *Part II* tells. Interwoven with it is an account of the rise to power of the young Vito

Corleone, from his forced departure from Sicily to his transition from penniless immigrant to criminal man of respect among New York's Italian population.

Apparently, Coppola toyed with the idea that he could cast Marlon Brando to play the young Vito Corleone in the backstory section of the film. After all, Brando had aged up to play the old Don, so why couldn't he age down a little to play the younger version? Then he remembered a vicious, brilliant screentest given for the part of Sonny by a young actor named Robert De Niro. All thoughts of Brando vanished from his mind.

In its own way, De Niro's performance is as buttoned down as Pacino's. It's all about stillness, about silence, the moments when Vito erupts into violence given added punch by their rareness. Performing the role almost entirely in Italian, this is De Niro at his chameleonic Method best. With echoes of both Pacino and Brando in his performance, he all but vanishes into Vito.

It's tempting to treat the two time periods as separate tales. After all, Coppola did when he assembled the all-in-one TV cut of the *Godfather* saga. Rearranging all the backstory about the reasons why little Vito had to leave Sicily – a local capo had killed his parents and wanted him dead too in order to avoid a blood feud – it runs everything in chronological order. In purely narrative terms, it works, but you lose so much else. Even Coppola admits that "these stories are nowhere near as good alone as when they're told in parallel."

It's not just the way that the sepia tones of the past and the gorgeous yellow warmth of Sicily play off the blue coldness of Michael's lakeside home and the marble courtrooms he fights the Mafia-hunting government in. The plots of both stories complement and counterpoint each other with such poignant brilliance. The fade from "present day" Michael talking to his son after the attempted assassination to Vito picking up his first born boy Sonny from his crib... Michael learning that Kay had a miscarriage to Vito watching his sick baby being looked after... Vito finally slaughtering the man who killed his parents as Michael's orders lead to the death of his »

NEED TO KNOW

Year 1974
Running time 192 mins
Director Francis Ford Coppola
Stars Al PAcino, Robert De Niro, Robert Duvall, Diane Keaton, Talia Shire, John Cazale
Buy it on Region 2 Box Set
Tagline "The Legacy Continues"
Best line "If anything in life is certain, if history teaches us anything, it's that you can kill anyone." – Michael Corleone
Critic's view "The daring of *Part II* is that it enlarges the scope and deepens the meaning of the first film... It's an epic vision of the corruption of America." – Pauline Kael, *The New Yorker*
Best watched when... Someone needs a favour.

own brother... The links, the similarities and the gaping differences between the father and son are stapled to the front of the audiences mind by Coppola's judicious intercutting.

"It was a film I really never wanted to do," remembers Coppola. "I didn't love the experience of working on the first *Godfather* and the idea of doing it again... was too much to even think of." But Paramount were so desperate for a sequel and so determined that he should direct it – they turned down his suggestion that Martin Scorsese should wrestle the reins – that Coppola negotiated an interference-free deal. Forgive him the deeply flawed *Godfather Part III*, the ostentatious tomfoolery of Bram Stoker's *Dracula* and – heaven forfend – the idiocy of *Jack*. *The Godfather Part II* is the work of a great filmmaker at his very peak.

Mixing Byzantine Mafia politics with lightning fast shoot-outs, rampant nostalgia with hardnosed cynicism, tricksy narrative time jumps with actor-loving cut-free scenes, Coppola creates a movie that offers so much more than the original in almost all departments. Don't get us wrong – *The Godfather* is a great movie, as its placing at number 23 on this list shows. But *Godfather Part II* is something else again, the kind of film that invites breathless superlatives. Awesome. TF

Ceri Thomas

THE DYING GAME

Death in *The Godfather Part II* – the five greatest hits...

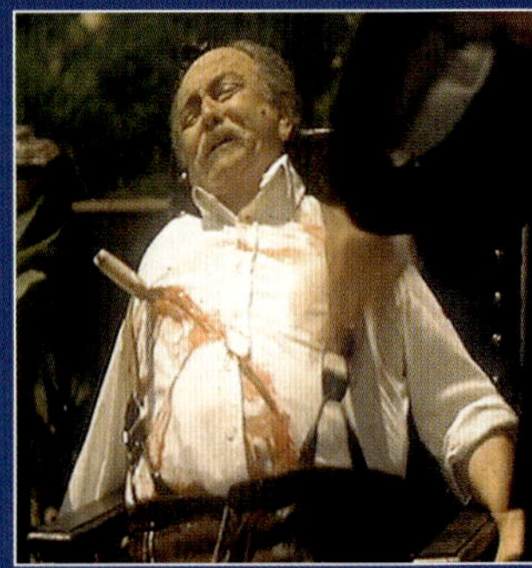

DON CICCIO
Revenging his parent's murder decades earlier, Vito guts the old don on his own porch with a butcher's knife from right to left across the belly.

FREDO
Fooled into believing Michael's forgiven him, Fredo goes fishing with a Corleone henchman. One bullet to the head later and he's sleeping with the fishes. Literally.

DON FANUCCI
After a walk home through a festival, the old don meets wannabe don Vito on a stairwell. A bullet through the cheek, one through the stomach and a third up through the roof of the mouth and there's a new godfather in town.

FRANKIE PENTANGELI
Not strictly a hit as Frankie commits suicide in his bathtub, but it's Tom Hagen who persuades the old man that it's the only way he can keep the rest of his family safe.

HYMAN ROTH
Apparently out of reach, Mafia financier Roth finally gets his – after surviving an attempt to strangle him in Havana – when Michael has someone gun him down at close range in an airport. Anyone can be killed...

Classic Scene

INT. LAKE TAHOE HOUSE – DAY
Silhouetted by the light from tall floor-to-ceiling windows, Michael Corleone walks across to where his brother Fredo is slumped back in a chair.

Outside the windows, snow is falling on the lake. Michael sits, silhouetted in profile, and stares at Fredo.

FREDO
(*without looking up at his brother*)
I haven't got a lot to say, Mike.

MICHAEL
We have time.

FREDO
(*still not looking up*)
I was kept pretty much in the dark.I didn't know all that much.

MICHAEL
What about now? Is there anything you can help me out with? Anything you can tell me now?

Fredo slumps in the chair.

FREDO
They got Pentangeli. That's all I know.

Fredo stands, walks over to the window and looks out.

FREDO
I didn't know it was going to be a hit, Mike. I swear to God, I didn't know it was going to be a hit. Johnny Ola bumped into me in Beverly Hills. He said that he wanted to talk. He said that you and Roth were in on a big deal together and that there was something in it for me if I could help them out. He said you were being tough on the negotiations. That if they could get a little help they could close the deal fast. It would be good for the family.

MICHAEL
(*turning from the window*)
And you believed that story? You believed that?

FREDO
He said there was something in it for me! On my own!

MICHAEL
I've always taken care of you, Fredo.

FREDO
Taken care of me! You're my kid brother! You take care of me! You ever think about that, eh? You ever once think about that?

Michael looks away and turns back to the window.

FREDO
Send Fredo off to do this! Send Fredo off to do that! Let Fredo take care of some Mickey Mouse nightclub somewhere! Send Fredo to pick somebody up at the airport! I'm your older brother Mike and I was stepped over!

MICHAEL
That's the way Pop wanted it.

FREDO
It ain't the way I wanted it! I can handle things! I'm smart! Not like everybody says! Like dumb! I'm smart and I want respect!

MICHAEL
Is there anything you can tell me about this investigation? Anything more?

FREDO
(*slumps back in his seat*)
The senate lawyer, Questadt. He belongs to Roth.

MICHAEL
Fredo, you're nothing to me now. You're not a brother, you're not a friend. I don't want to know you or what you do. I don't want to see you at the hotels, I don't want you near my house. When you see our mother, I want to know a day in advance, so I won't be there. You understand?

Michael walks out slowly.

FREDO
Mikey...!

INT. ANOTHER ROOM – DAY
Michael talks to one of the Corleone family's soldiers.

MICHAEL
I don't want anything to happen to him while my mother is still alive.

4

FIGHT CLUB

A generation-defining tussle with identity, loneliness and the primal need for love...

Everyone talked about the violence. And there's no point pretending that on theatrical release the joint-jolting scraps weren't the most obviously impactful element of David Fincher's tale of pre-millennial tension. They were certainly what the marketing department clung to, pushing the film as an amped-up ride for adrenaline junkies: an MTV actioner as slick as Brad Pitt's marble, sweat-flecked six-pack. Critics both enraged and befuddled queued up to completely confuse picture with poster and give it a kicking for macho posturing and teenage nihilism. The film has both in spades, so it wasn't simply a case of hacks judging adverts, not product, but there was a need to "look closer" – as suggested by the tagline of 1999's other exploration of the modern male, *American Beauty*.

Many viewers were enthralled by the idea of fight clubs, as well as the Project Mayhem prankster-terrorists (anarchic in intent; fascist in iconography) and the towering, too-cool-for-school figure of Tyler Durden, as embodied in Pitt's perfection (as he tells Edward Norton's Narrator, "All the ways you wish you could be, that's me. I look like you want to look, I fuck like you want to fuck, I am smart, capable and most importantly, I am free in all the ways that you are not"). There were largely two outward workings of this fascination: devotion or repulsion. An audience of (primarily, though not exclusively) young men embraced Tyler Durden's smart-mouth, straight-edge, thrift-store chic rebellion and made the film a cult. Certain prominent critics – the *Chicago Sun-Times*' Roger Ebert, the *London Evening Standard*'s Alexander Walker – appeared scared by how the movie made them feel, by the power of Tyler's message. They labelled it "cheerfully fascist" and "an inadmissible assault on personal decency".

As the years go by, Fight Club only looks more prescient, powerful and rewarding

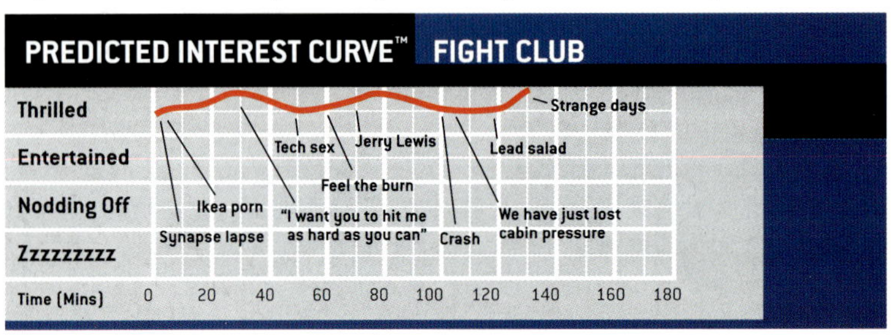

But neither adoration nor disgust fully appreciated the (bigger) picture. Yes, *Fight Club* wows with the glamorous Tyler, his mordant anti-lifestyle slogans and uncanny grasp of 21st century ennui; with the allure of violence and the promised pleasure of giving and receiving pain (yes, men *like* fighting). But that's not the end-all. Tyler is, after all, an idea: a figment of the Narrator's insomniac imagination. It's both wonderful and frightening that his grandstanding monologues – "our Great Depression is our lives" – chimed to such an extent with generations hexed by the failure of idealism embodied by the Baby Boomers; that the film turns on that generation, in Norton's words, "and says, 'Fuck you for the world you made.'"

But Tyler is defeated. Pitt's casting is so perfect (you can't fake the cult of personality) as to be bewildering for some: his cocky, charismatic, sexy swagger

blinds them to the real story of *Fight Club*; the journey of the Narrator out of despair. It's about Man working through materialism and nihilism, about Generation X growing up and living with scepticism but not helplessness. For it is the hollowed out everyman of Norton – subtle, touching and hilarious – who ultimately flips his id and clings to a kind of hope. It's just that Fincher doesn't hold your hand or underline any message.

"I remember when Fincher sent me the book," Norton told *Total Film* when we declared *Fight Club* the greatest film of the magazine's lifetime, "I thought, just off having seen *Se7en*, 'This is such a great guy to make this movie because he is completely comfortable posing questions and refusing to give you the answer. That's the kind of courage needed to make *Fight Club*.'"

It's the kind of courage that makes the film scabrous but never glib. You glimpse its soul in the final hand-hold between The Narrator and Marla (the exquisite Helena Bonham Carter) as the towers come tumbling and The Pixies kick in with 'Where Is My Mind' (possibly the greatest marriage of music and moving image since Scorsese used The Ronettes' 'Be My Baby' in *Mean Streets*): it's about the need to connect; the need to love. But its conclusion can only be sincerely reached if Tyler's vision is presented in as exciting and seductive a manner as possible: if it's tried on and then rejected. *Fight Club* is so committed – and so far from mawkish or moralistic – that certain critics can't cope, but you need to have seen the appeal in brutality, tasted the testosterone and nearly been swallowed by Tyler's whole absurd scheme to realise that he isn't the messiah; he's a very naughty boy. As Fincher has it, "It was more deeply rooted in Monty Python than it was in, you know, Fail-Safe." And it is very, very funny: "Chloe looked the way Meryl Streep's skeleton would look if you made it smile and walk around the party being extra nice to everybody"... "Candy stripe a cancer ward. It's not my problem"... "Emergency water landing – 600 miles-an-hour. Blank faces: calm as Hindu cows." And not just »

NEED TO KNOW

Year 1999
Running time 133 mins
Director David Fincher
Stars Brad Pitt, Edward Norton, Helena Bonham Carter
Buy it on The two-disc Region 1 Special Edition. If you can find it.
Tagline "Mischief. Mayhem. Soap."
Best line "Our Great Depression is our lives." – Tyler Durden
Critic's view "The most frankly and cheerfully fascist big-star movie since *Death Wish*, a celebration of violence in which the heroes write themselves a license to drink, smoke, screw and beat one another up." – Roger Ebert, *Chicago Sun-Times*
Best watched when... You think you've lost faith in everything.

the dialogue. There's priceless physical comedy, from slapstick (Tyler's beating at the hands of Lou; The Narrator assaulting himself; Tyler falling off the bike), to situational (The Narrator enfolded in Meat Loaf's pendulous breasts; the minister hitting the mechanic; Marla stealing clothes from the launderette). And where most comedies look like tarted-up sit-coms, *Fight Club* looks like a million (well, 67 million) dollars – which is probably why it's often filed under Thriller. It's Fincher's blessing and curse to make blockbusters for people on the fringe: films that require big budgets but risk limited appeal (although both *Se7en* and *Panic Room* were big hits). Visually, *Fight Club* is extraordinary: all shimmering darkness and envelope-pushing verve (the subliminals; the frame rattling). It tanked, but you don't measure greatness in dollars and cents. There are few, very few, films that provoke and entertain in vast and equal measure. It's taken some time – having been dubbed a failure on release – but as the years go by *Fight Club* only looks more prescient and powerful, more rewarding. It morphs and challenges and thrills with each fresh viewing. We'll be rolling around in it for decades to come, revisiting it as we do *Taxi Driver* and *Citizen Kane*. It's a masterpiece and it will endure: a hilarious comedy, a scream and a prayer. Join the club. TF

Nev Pierce

MR ED

Edward Norton talks critical pounding...

***Fight Club* is generation defining...**

Yeah. I think that we all had that sense of it when we were doing it. Not that you ever know what other people's response is going to be, but that was our response to the material.

It irritated some people...

They can hammer at it all they want, but the bottom line is it goes out and forms a direct conversation with people, whispering in their ears. Slowly, that becomes something and so eventually one day Roger Ebert walks up to you and apologises for the review he wrote because he's realised that everyone around him is saying something else about it and he might have missed it.

Roger Ebert said the movie was "cheerfully fascist"...

Yeah. I remember thinking like, "What fucking movie was he watching?" The irony being the people who are always decrying the lack of bold filmmaking are the first to beat a film into submission for stepping out of the box. These days, if the movie doesn't spoon-feed them a theme at the ending, it's just too much work to write the fuckin' review. I'm still amazed by the threat it was to some people. But they can't make it go away.

Classic Scene

INT. KITCHEN – LATE NIGHT
The Narrator watches as Tyler picks up a jar.

TYLER
Now, ancient peoples found that clothes got cleaner when they washed them at a certain point in the river. You know why?

NARRATOR
No.

Tyler beckons the Narrator over and pulls on black rubber gloves.

TYLER
Because human sacrifices were once made on the hills above this river. Bodies burned. Water seeped into the wood and ashes to create lye.

Tyler puts on protective goggles and holds up the jar.

TYLER (CONT'D)
This is lye, the crucial ingredient. Once it mixed with the melted fat of bodies, a thick, white, soapy discharge crept into the river. May I see your hand, please?

Tyler licks his lips until they're gleaming wet. He kisses the Narrator's hand.

NARRATOR
What is this?

TYLER
This...
is a chemical burn.

Tyler sprinkles lye over the Narrator's hand. The Narrator shouts in agony.

TYLER (CONT'D)
It'll hurt more than you've ever been burned and you will have a scar.

NARRATOR (VO)
If guided meditation worked for cancer, it could work for this.

The Narrator pictures a forest.

TYLER
Stay with the pain. Don't shut this out.

NARRATOR
No, no! Oh, God!

TYLER
Look at your hand! The first soap was made from the ashes of heroes, like the first monkey shot into space. Without pain, without sacrifice, we'd have nothing.

NARRATOR (VO)
I tried not to think of the words "sear" or "flesh".

The Narrator pictures a forest; pages in a dictionary.

TYLER
Stop it! This is your pain. This is your burning hand. It's right here.

NARRATOR
I'm going to my cave. I'm going to my cave, I'm going to find my power animal.

The Narrator, in an icy cave. With Marla.

TYLER
No! Don't deal with it the way those dead people do! Come on!

NARRATOR
I get the point. Okay, please!

TYLER
No. What you're feeling is premature enlightenment. This is the greatest moment of your life and you're off somewhere missing it.

NARRATOR
I'm not!

TYLER
Shut up! Our fathers were our models for God. If our fathers bailed, what does that tell you about God?

NARRATOR
No, no!

TYLER
(*slaps him*)
Listen to me. You have to consider the possibility that God does not like you, he never wanted you. In all probability he hates you. This is not the worst thing that can happen?

NARRATOR
It isn't?

TYLER
We don't need him.

NARRATOR
We don't! I agree.

TYLER
Fuck damnation, man. Fuck redemption. We are God's unwanted children? So be it!

The Narrator struggles to get away.

TYLER
Listen! You can run water over your hand to make it worse or – look at me – you can use vinegar to neutralise the burn.

NARRATOR
Please let me have some, please!

TYLER
First, you have to give up. First you have to know, not fear, know that someday you're going to die.

NARRATOR
You don't know how this feels!

Tyler shows a burnt kiss on his own hand.

TYLER
It's only after we've lost everything that we're free to do anything.

Tyler lets go of the Narrator, who holds his smouldering hand out and bears the pain. Tyler douses it in vinegar and the Narrator slumps to the floor.

TYLER
Congratulations. You're one step closer to hitting bottom.

3

JAWS

Spielberg's proto-blockbuster. It will never be safe to go back in the water...

Everyone knows the story of Bruce, the little robot shark that couldn't. "It was like a wake," was how Steven Spielberg's director buddy Brian De Palma described watching the first rushes of the mechanical fish in almost-action. "Bruce's eyes crossed and his jaws wouldn't close right." And those were the takes where it moved at all, rather than simply sinking. After a long silence in the screening room, actor Richard Dreyfuss was first to speak: "If any of us had any sense, we'd all bail out now."

Bruce wasn't the only problem the *Jaws* shoot faced and Dreyfuss wasn't alone in worrying that this could just be "the turkey of the year". The producers might have splashed the cash to buy up the rights to Peter Benchley's fishy bestseller, but by mid-shoot, nobody would have bet a chocolate dubloon on *Jaws* being a hit.

Co-star Robert Shaw thought the novel was "a piece of shit" and only took the part because his missus liked the script. The crew were constantly being badgered by unhappy Martha's Vineyard locals. Yachts kept wrecking takes by drifting into shot. The boat playing Quint's Orca barely stayed afloat. Everything cost three times as much as expected and took twice as long to shoot. Spielberg was petrified by how badly things were going. Explaining why, unlike the rest of the crew, he didn't take even a day of holiday during shooting at Martha's Vineyard, he said, "I was afraid if I left, I'd never have gone back." He was only half-joking.

Somehow, though, the boy wonder overcame it all. He took that Martha's Vineyard footage, additional takes shot in the Pacific and even a few reshoots done in editor Verna Field's swimming pool (the head popping out of the bottom of the boat was redone there because SS wanted audiences to "scream louder") and did more than just make it work. He assembled it into a genre-defining shocker.

How? Well, part of it's clearly down to the the decision forced upon him by the twitchy "Bruce" (there were actually three models depending on what kind of movement was needed). With John Williams' primal, pulsing music slathered over the top – and Spielberg wasn't sure about that at first either, famously asking Williams if the theme was a joke the first time he heard it – a disaster became a nerve-shredding triumph. As copycat filmmakers the world over have realised in the years since, not seeing the damn shark and letting audience imaginations thrash rampantly about on their seats turns out to be so much more effective.

Another part of it is undoubtedly down to the way his leads interracted. We'll

Showcases the skill and innate feel Spielberg has had from the start...

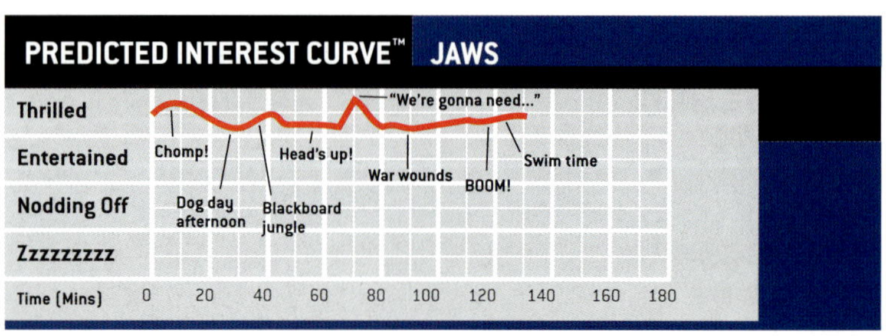

never know for sure, but you can't help having a sneaking suspicion that literally being stuck together on an island may have helped, not hindered performances. Dreyfuss and Shaw weren't keen on each other to start with, and Scheider really was nervy about being out on a boat (he hid emergency axes around the ship in case he got trapped for real during the sinking sequence). Throw in days turning into weeks turning into months bobbing, swimming and sinking on the ocean blue together, and suddenly the muttering tension of the early scenes and the scowling one-upmanship on the shark hunt seem as much to do with the arduous conditions as painstaking rehearsal or thespy skill.

But – and this is a huge, shark-sized 'but' – the biggest reason that *Jaws* works and works so damn brilliantly is Spielberg himself. At the time, critics struggled to accept that someone as young as Stevie – 26 when he was hired and doing only his second cinematic feature, after all – could possibly have orchestrated that opening shark attack on the swimmer with such tidal force. Surely a relative beginner couldn't have pulled off the audacious reverse dolly zoom (the bullet-time of its day)? Or balanced the humour with the horror so effectively that you almost forget this is a film about a flesh-mangling monster of the deep?

He did, though. Fields was certainly a huge help (she along with John Williams and the sound crew bagged the film's only Oscars), but, as the three decades since show only too clearly, *Jaws* has Spielberg's stamp all over it. His innate feel for pacing a story, his skill at judging the climax of a scene, his unerring ability to know how long to stretch out his hold over an audience but still shock them when he snaps away... those are skills he's had since the very beginning and *Jaws* showcases them to perfection.

Of course, it also boasts signs of what's gone on to become his weaker side: his love of sentiment, his desire to shape everything into a happy ending, his overreliance on the cash-heavy "big shot" – but crucially in *Jaws* they're still a part of the overall package, bits of his game that feed into the film but »

NEED TO KNOW

Year 1975
Running time 119 minutes
Director Steven Spielberg
Stars Roy Scheider, Richard Dreyfuss, Robert Shaw
Buy it on Region 2
Tagline "You'll never go in the water again."
Best line "The thing about a shark, it's got lifeless eyes, black eyes, like a doll's eyes. When it comes at you it doesn't seem to be livin'... until he bites you, and those black eyes roll over white." – Quint
Critic's view "An $8 million film of consummate suspense, tension and terror." – *Variety*
Best watched... After you've just gone paddling. Not before. Definitely not before...

don't ever capsize it. Think about it; no one ever questions Dreyfuss' survival at the end in the way they do the son in *War Of The Worlds*. It's a moment to cheer, not jeer.

Universal tried everything to get Spielberg to cut spiralling costs during filming, including asking him not to reshoot shots where you could see leisure craft in the background ("We couldn't do it," Spielberg said. "You have three guys out in a rickety boat hunting a killer shark. What kind of menace is there going to be if there is a family of four only 50 feet away, having a picnic on their sailboat?"). Then, thinking it was a guaranteed stinker, they threw Spielberg's movie into more than 400 theatres simultaneously. The theory was that it would make good money on the opening weekend and then die. They were half right.

"My secretary handed me this piece of paper and said, 'Here's the opening figures.' And I just stared at this number," remembers Spielberg. "Then I kept waiting for the next weekend to drop off and it didn't; it went up and it went up." *Jaws* eventually took $129 million in the US, a record that was only beaten when *Star Wars* came along two years later. Before *Jaws*, the good films were drip-fed out on a small number of prints to "build a platform". After *Jaws*, they all got huge TV and marketing pushes and came out in as many theatres at once as possible. It was the film that taught studios that a mass opening might save shoddy movies from themselves, but it can turn the great films into blockbusters. It's the lesson that's shaped the Hollywood summer ever since.

These days, Spielberg still maintains that *Schindler's List* is his best film. He's wrong. *Jaws* is a decapitated head and shoulders above everything else he has ever produced. It's as slick as *Raiders Of The Lost Ark*, does shocks better than *Jurassic Park*, marries the domestic to the dramatic with as much elegance as *Close Encounters* and pulls you, kicking and screaming, into its world from the moment that... well, someone first starts kicking and screaming. All together now: dur-dum, dur-dum, dur-dum... TF

Ceri Thomas

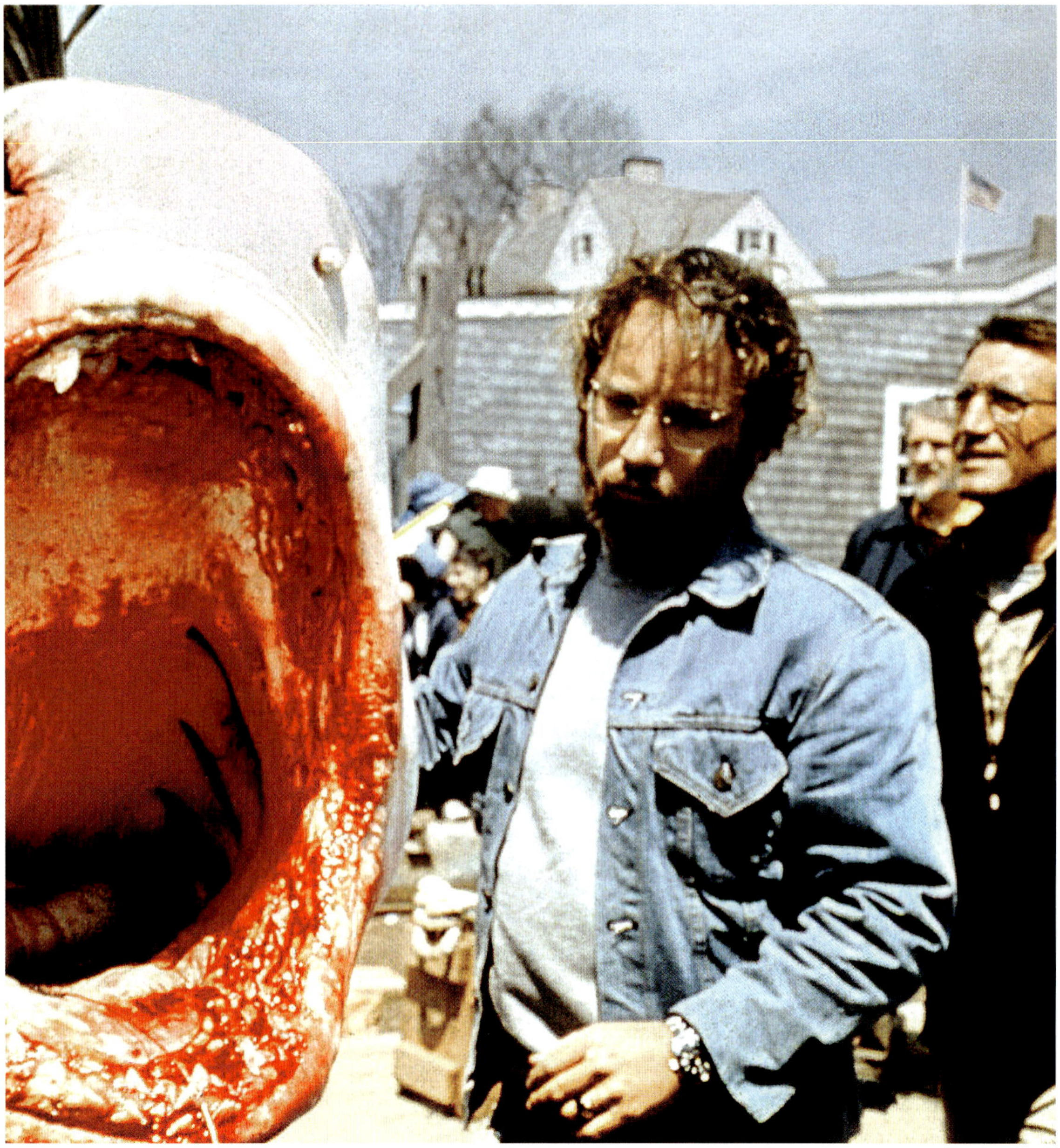

BITE ME

Jaws takes a bite out of Hollywood as other movies "pay homage"...

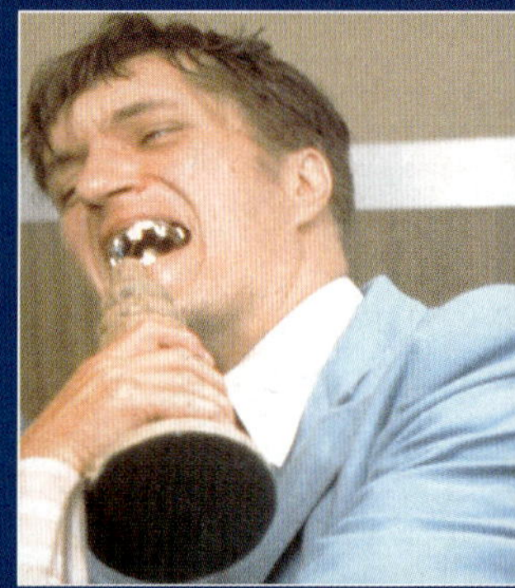

THE SPY WHO LOVED ME (1977)
Jaws – the giant with the steel choppers, that is – survives a final explosion and faces a long swim to shore. Coincidence? We think not...

AIRPLANE! (1980)
The Zucker boys fin-in-cheek shot of a plane's tail cutting through the clouds accompanied by John Williams' music.

MOUNTAINS OF THE MOON (1990)
Bob Rafelson's underrated Victorian adventure movie isn't where you'd expect to see a *Jaws* tribute, but how else do you explain the scene where explorers Burton and Livingstone start comparing scars?

THE USUAL SUSPECTS (1995)
The title may be a homage to *Casablanca*, but Bad Hat Harry, Bryan Singer's production company, is a reference to a line from *Jaws*. "That's some bad hat, Harry," Brody deadpans to a fella wearing a bathing hat.

GODZILLA (1998)
Unseen monster, two old men sitting fishing on a pier, "We're going to need a bigger gun": the list goes on. There's even a reverse dolly zoom thrown in for good measure.

Classic Scene

INT. ORCA CABIN – NIGHT
After the first day of the hunt, Quint, Hooper and Chief Brody sit around drinking.

Brody gingerly feels the cut on his head.

QUINT
Don't you worry about it, Chief, it won't be permanent. Wanna see somethin' permanent, ba-ba-boom?

Quint pulls out a false front tooth and cackles.

QUINT
Hey Hoop! You wanna feel something permanent? You just put your hand underneath my cap. You feel a little lump? Knockalorum. St Paddy's Day. Boston.

HOOPER
(*to Quint*)
I got that beat.
(*to Brody*)
I got that beat.

Rolls up his sleeve and shows Quint a scar.

HOOPER
That's a moray eel. Bit right through my wetsuit.

QUINT
(*leaning forward and putting him arm on the table like an arm wrestler*)
Well, Hoop, now listen – I don't know about that, but I entered an arm wrestling contest in an Okie bar in San Francisco and you see this? I can't extend it and you want to know why? I got to the semi-final celebrating my third wife's demise and a big Chinese fella pulled me right over!

Hooper shuffles along the bench, puts his leg up on the table and rolls up his trousers.

HOOPER
I got a... It's a bull shark. Scraped me when I was taking samples.

Quint rolls up his trouser leg and plonks it on top of Hooper's.

QUINT
I got something for ya. That's a thresher. You see that, Chief? Thresher's tail.

BRODY
Thresher?

HOOPER
It's a shark.

QUINT
(*laughing, to Hooper*)
You want a drink? Drink to your leg.

HOOPER
I'll drink to your leg.

They swig down booze from tea cups.

QUINT
Okay, so we'll drink to our legs!

They drink, they laugh. Brody sheepishly pulls up his shirt to look at a scar, then thinks better of it.

HOOPER
(*unbuttoning his shirt*)
I've got the creme de la creme! Right here. Now you see that?
(*points to a scar-free chest*)

BRODY
You're wearing a sweater.

HOOPER
Right there. Mary Ellen Moffat.
(*giggles*)
She broke my heart!

BRODY
(*nods towards Quint*)
What's that one?

QUINT
What?

BRODY
That one. There. On your arm.

QUINT
Oh, that. That's a tattoo. I got that removed.

HOOPER
Don't tell me! Don't tell me. "Mother"!

QUINT
(*with a tight smile*)
Hooper, that's the US *Indianapolis*.

HOOPER
(*serious*)
You were on the *Indianapolis*?

BRODY
What happened...?

2

VERTIGO

Deeper into you: James Stewart takes a tumble in Hitchcock's finest fancy...

Like its heroine to the hero, *Vertigo* is an elusive film. Reams of papers have been written on Hitchcock's adaptation of Pierre Boileau and Thomas Narcejac's darkly dream-like novel, trying to get a fix on it yet often having to settle for articulating how slippery it is. Taken as a meditation on cinema or sexuality, psychosis or seduction, it offers pleasures; yet stays tantalisingly out of reach. It is acutely attuned to cinema's ability to pull us in yet leave us craving further clues.

Weaves disbelief into a psycho-drama of guilt, obsession and paranoia

Granted, the film didn't seem so alluring to critics in 1958. "Far-fetched," sniffed the *The New Yorker*. "Hitch-poppycock," sneered *The Daily Mail*.

Prior to the shoot, when Columbia's Harry Cohn loaned Kim Novak to MGM to star, he told her: "It's a lousy script, just lousy. I'm going to loan you out to Paramount because it's Alfred Hitchcock."

Possession, sickness, obsession, psychosis, doomed love... What wasn't to like? Well, quite a lot actually, given the havoc *Vertigo* plays with thriller and romance conventions. The plot isn't exactly simple. James Stewart's Scottie is a former detective suffering from acrophobia after a rooftop chase in which a colleague fell to his death while trying to rescue him. Now retired, Scottie is employed as a private detective by an old schoolfriend-turned-businessman, Gavin Elster. Elster wants Scottie to trail his wife, Madeleine (Kim Novak), who seems possessed by a dead woman in a portrait. Scottie becomes enthralled by Madeleine, only to lose her in a seemingly fatal fall. After suffering a breakdown, he meets Judy, a woman resembling her (also Novak) and vigorously makes her over in Madeleine's image...

Complications accumulate from the off. For starters, Hitch doesn't tell us how Scottie survived what looked likely to be a fall to certain death, dangling from a drainpipe several floors up. How could he get down? How could he be rescued? Questions such as these are our lifelines to naturalism. *Vertigo* severs these ties, weaving in a dangling of disbelief into a psycho-drama of guilt, obsession, manipulation and paranoia that could well be the dreams of a dying man.

Taken as such, *Vertigo* becomes a freefall tumble into Scottie's psyche. Its masterful architecture of rhyming ideas and images become keys to his sickness: his ex-partner, Midge, talks about basing the design of a bra on a cantilever bridge; later Scottie rescues Madeleine from the churning waters below a cantilever bridge.

Elster and Pop Leibel, a bookstore owner, seem to taunt Scottie with talk of the "power" and "freedom" men enjoyed in days gone by, making it seem as if it isn't Madeleine who is in

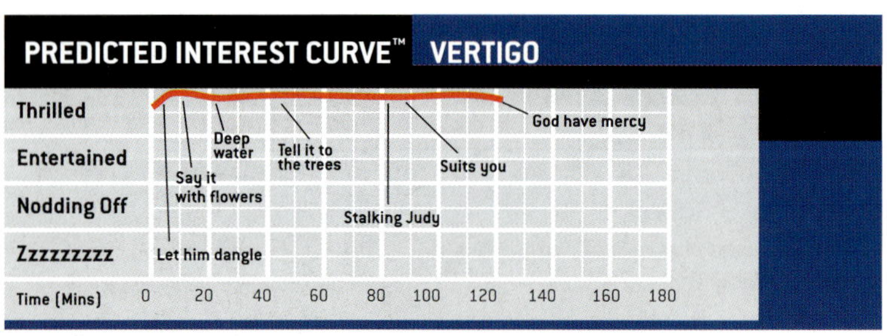

thrall to a potent past, but Scottie. What kind of man is he, anyway, trussed up in a corset, far from empowered? In the context of the story told, Scottie is a passive, beaten lead. Leading men did not act like this. Seen as the unwitting author of the film's world, too, he's obsessional, fixated; and caught in something deeper than a mere mid-life crisis.

Even if we do choose to take *Vertigo* at face value, Hitch and his screenwriters pull off a daring stunt by refusing to withhold the extent to which Scottie is manipulated by Madeleine and Elster. Instead, a scene is inserted in which Madeleine pens and tears up a confessional letter. This shifts the emphasis from the 'what next?' questions of plot to psychology and subtext, enriching the film - even if, for critics at the time, it may just have been bad timing.

That twist is complicated still further by Madeleine. Given her deceit of Scottie, there's a temptation to tar her with the tag of the wicked woman. But doesn't she seem to love him? What do we make of Scottie then, as he drives her to her death, in pursuit of an emotional shock to shake off his acrophobia? Everywhere we look, there are layers on layers, questions inside questions. As Scottie nurses Madeleine after her first faux-suicide attempt, how deep does the play-acting go? Where does performance dovetail into desire? As Madeleine disappears after she enters her hotel, where does she go? Even when we learn that the possession story is just a front, why does the film sustain its eeriness?

These ambiguities accumulate resonantly because the film is so sure of itself. In this sense, *Vertigo*'s conviction is often viewed in terms of the extent to which it is a confessional, Hitch being a man who knew about obsession and once talked about choosing "the kind of girl I can mould into the heroine of my imagination". Surely, though, on closer examination, many of *Vertigo*'s strengths are symptoms of the extent to which it exceeds Hitchcock. It's a test-case in collaboration, where the parts click with force. How persuasive would it be without Stewart's restraint? Bernard Herrmann's score? >>

NEED TO KNOW

Year 1958
Running time 128 minutes
Director Alfred Hitchcock
Stars James Stewart, Kim Novak, Barbara Bel Geddes, Tom Helmore, Henry Jones
Buy it on Recently re-released Region 2.
Tagline "Alfred Hitchcock engulfs you in a whirlpool of terror and tension!"
Best line "You remind me of someone..." – Scottie
Critic's view "The old master has turned out another story in which the mystery is not so much who done it as who cares." – *Time*
Best watched when... Hospitalised in the aftermath of a crippling obsession.

Robert Burk's woozy cinematography? Even the city is a collaborator, San Francisco a character unto itself, meticulously researched and exquisitely directed.

And Kim Novak's glacial cool? Interesting to note that Hitch didn't want Novak for the role: he wanted Vera Miles. Later, he would talk as if the film were fundamentally flawed by Novak. That isn't true: Hitch may have drawn out Novak's best performance, but it's still her delivery, and a great one in its mixture of chic and sexuality. Try to imagine it without Midge (Barbara Bel Geddes), too, who endears us to Scottie, a man who might otherwise seem crackers. Midge wasn't Hitch's innovation but the creation of one of the film's screenwriters, Samuel A Taylor.

As such, *Vertigo* exceeds the sum of its parts to exist in and of itself, occupy its own world, untethered from mere naturalism or auteurism. In that, it's close to pure cinema and endlessly analysable.

It makes us look and look again, even teaches us how to look, in that we emerge from it not knowing quite how to read or trust what we've seen.

Seen umpteen times, its mystique remains. Why? Because *Vertigo* helped us recognise the dark magic and mellifluous mechanisms of that look and that mystique in the first place. TF

Kevin Harley

YOU GOT THE LOOK

Hitch's close interest in his leading ladies' clobber...

GRACE KELLY
What did Hitch talk to Kelly about when they first met? "We talked," she said, "about clothes..." He obsessed over her shoes for *Rear Window*. "Haven't you heard," he told his AD, "of the shoe fetish?"

VERA MILES
"The first thing I did when I hired Vera Miles," Hitch said, "was to have Edith Head design a complete wardrobe..."

KIM NOVAK
Vera Miles' replacement in *Vertigo* didn't want to wear grey. Hitch made it clear that she would dress as dictated, although he didn't protest at her refusal to wear a bra.

EVA MARIE SAINT
"I supervised the choice of her wardrobe in every detail," said Hitch, "just as Stewart did with Novak in *Vertigo*."

TIPPI HEDREN
Hitch had Edith Head devised an on- and off-screen wardrobe for the *Marnie* and *The Birds* star. "He spent as much money," Hedren said, "on an outright gift of a personal wardrobe as he did on my year's salary."

INT. RANSOHOFF'S – DAY
Judy and Scottie are being waited on by a saleswoman.

A girl assistant stands nearby. Scottie looks tense. Judy looks at him wonderingly. A model enters wearing a grey tweed suit.

SCOTTIE
No, that's not it. Nothing like it.

SALESWOMAN
But you said grey, sir.

SCOTTIE
Now look, I just want an ordinary simple grey suit.

He puts his hands to his waist.

JUDY
But I like that one, Scottie.

SCOTTIE
No, no, it's not right.

SALESWOMAN
The gentleman seems to know what he wants. All right. We'll find it.

JUDY
(*apprehensive*)
Scottie, what are you doing?

SCOTTIE
I'm trying to buy you a suit.

JUDY
But I loved the second one she wore. And this one is beautiful.

SCOTTIE
No, no, they're none of them right.

JUDY
But why?

SALESWOMAN
Oh! I think I know the suit you mean! We had it sometime ago! Let me go see. We may still have the model.

SCOTTIE
Thank you.

Judy looks at Scottie with understanding.

JUDY
You're looking for the suit that she wore! For me?

Scottie looks at her anxiously.

JUDY
You want me to be dressed like her?!

SCOTTIE
Judy, I just want you to look nice. And I know what kind of suit would look well on you.

JUDY
(*walks off*)
No, I won't do it!

SCOTTIE
(*pleading*)
Judy, it can't make that much difference to you, I just want to see what you look...

JUDY
(*burying her head in the mirror*)
No, I don't want any clothes, I don't want anything, I want to get out of here...

SCOTTIE
Judy, do this for me.

She looks up at him, frightened. The model enters, wearing the grey suit.

SALESWOMAN
Here we are.

SCOTTIE
Yes! That's it!

SALESWOMAN
I thought so!

JUDY
I don't like it!

SCOTTIE
We'll take it! Will the thing fit?

SALESWOMAN
Well, yes! It may need some slight alterations, but it is madam's size.
(*to the model*)
All right, dear.
(*to Judy*)
We'll have it for you to try in a moment.

SCOTTIE
How long will the alterations take?

SALESWOMAN
Well...

SCOTTIE
May we have it by tonight?

SALESWOMAN
Well, if it's absolutely necessary...

SCOTTIE
Yes, it is. Now, we'd like to look at an evening dress, a dinner dress, black, short, long sleeves... and a kind of a square neck...

JUDY
(*pleading*)
Scottie...

Scottie whirls on her with blazing eyes.

SALESWOMAN
(*laughs*)
My, you certainly do know what you want, sir...

1

GOODFELLAS

Scorsese's Mob classic takes the number one spot. You know why? Respect.

Driving.
Thud, thud thud thud.
"What the fuck is that?"

Pull over. Standing behind car, bathed in red. Tailights. Hell.

Trunk, open, bleeding body. Knife, stab stab stab, fast.

Swishpan, face, frozen, voiceover: "As far back as I can remember, I always wanted to be a gangster."

Has Martin Scorsese got your attention? Good, that's the point. One of them. There are two others. Open with the murder of made-man Billy Batts and you're starting in the middle of the story, giving what is essentially a traditional rise-and-fall-of-the-American-gangster movie a neck-snapping twist. Open with the murder of made-man Billy Batts and you also pinpoint the moment when our fellas' lives pivot from good to bad: from pasta, weddings, drinking, anniversaries, bustin' balls and Christenings to fear, loathing, paranoia, betrayal and death, death, death. *GoodFellas* is slick, arguably the slickest film ever made. But it's also considered, layered and freighted with meaning.

'I wanted to make it as primitive as possible. Want. Take. Simple' MARTIN SCORSESE

Scorsese was making studio pic *The Color Of Money* when he was told about an excerpt from Nicholas Pileggi's *Wiseguy* in *The New Yorker* magazine. Pileggi's book recounted 25 years in the Mob (1955 to 1980) from the viewpoint of Brooklyn-born Irish-Italian hoodlum Henry Hill, gopher turned snitch. "There had been several books about Mob bosses, but it was like getting hold of a soldier in Napoleon's army," explained Pileggi. "I wanted to know how it worked on the inside... the minutiae of how to live as a wiseguy." Scorsese wasn't interested – "What's the point of making another gangster picture?" – until colleagues persuaded him to read the damn book. Then, impressed by the "free-flowing arrogance" of the prose, he phoned Pileggi. "I've been looking for this book for years," he said. "I've been waiting for this phonecall my whole life," came the response. Together they raced through 12 drafts of the script, Pileggi typing and Scorsese scratching shot lists and music cues in the margin. Title: *Wiseguy*. Not an option – bagged by a TV show and Brian De Palma's feature comedy. Switch. *GoodFellas*.

Casting De Niro as bagman/killer Jimmy Conway was a cinch. He was too old to play 28 at the start of the film, but try to imagine any other actor pitching those sideways glances at the bar as the camera glides in to Cream's 'Sunshine Of Your Love'. Pesci as raging bull Tommy DeVito was another no-brainer. Finding Henry and Karen Hill was harder. Nine months later, Ray Liotta and Lorraine Bracco were in place. "We were the new kids on the block," says Bracco. "Marty always referred to us as 'the kids'. Y'know, like, 'Bring out the kids.'" Thirty-three-year-old

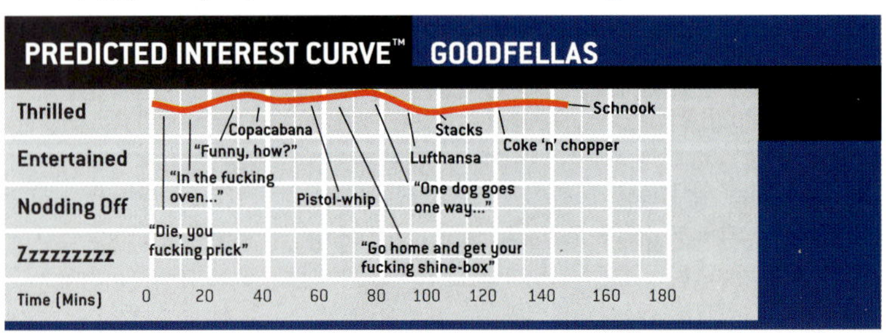

"kid" Liotta makes for an incredulous 21 in his opening sequences, but what's a few wrinkles in the face of such energy – such innocence clashed with experience? Bracco plays it similarly tough yet tender, seizing the chance to give a female voice to a testosterone-soaked genre – literally, her voiceover breaking into Henry's rich, incessant patter. Bracco works hard to make Karen strong. A survivor. She finishes the movie with her stuffing flushed down the toilet, finally quashed by drugs and Henry's addiction to wiseguys and "ready-made whores". But she's gone the distance.

GoodFellas has it all: story, dialogue, performances, music, technique. Most of all technique, Scorsese capturing the breakneck lifestyle ("If we wanted something, we took it...") and illicit glamour ("We were treated like movie stars with muscle") in an avalanche of whip-pans, crash zooms, jump cuts, time-lapse, slo-mo, freeze frames, voiceover and improv ("Funny how?"). Characters talk straight to camera. Continuity's all over the place. Peripheral figures disappear for years at a time then pop up with no explanation. Watch the film 50 times and you still can't take it all in: the extended families, marching foot soldiers, back-door scams (cigarettes, whiskey, shrimps, furs), heists, protection rackets, firebombed restaurants, pinkie rings, initialled shirts, racks of suits, rolls of cash, $100 tips and gleaming pink cadillacs; the doors sweeping

NEED TO KNOW

Year 1990
Running time 145 mins
Director Martin Scorsese
Stars Ray Liotta, Robert De Niro, Joe Pesci, Lorraine Bracco, Paul Sorvino
Buy it on Region 2 SE
Tagline "As far back as I can remember, I always wanted to be a gangster"
Best line "Fuck him in the ear, fuck him in the other ear" – Morrie
Critic's view "America's finest filmmaker at the peak of his form" – *Chicago Sun-Times*
Best watched when... You're dragging home your groceries and wish someone would do it for you.

open at the Copacabana for Henry and Karen to glide through corridors and kitchens, past tables and chairs, 'til they emerge front and centre like "king and queen" (Scorsese). Karen says it best: "By the time I'd finished meeting everyone, I thought I was drunk."

Overwhelming or just plain overwrought? Such exuberant style certainly doesn't please all. Esteemed critic David Thomson argues that Scorsese uses music, camera movement and décor to create "an imprint of feelings". Others have queried Marty's motives, tagging *GoodFellas* as the irresponsible wide-eyed wonderings of an arrested adolescent. Where's the psychological depth?

"Basically, I'm interested in what they do," retorts »

Scorsese. "You know, they don't think about it a lot. They don't sit around and ponder, 'Gee, what are we doing here?' The answer is to eat a lot and make a lot of money and do the least amount of work as possible. I wanted to make it as practical and primitive as possible. Want. Take. Simple."

In *GoodFellas*, life really is that basic. All these guys want is the money and the suits, the women and the "respect". The *Godfather* movies gave us a different take on the Mob – mythic, operatic – and posited the Mafia as family. Marty's wiseguys are the grunts in the New York boroughs; they don't give a shit about anything past the hustle. Wives? Saturday nights. Girlfriends? Friday nights. Kids? We're not even told Karen's pregnant – that's how important it is to Henry. Colleagues? Murderers come with smiles. Religion? Henry wears a Star of David *and* a crucifix. These 'good' fellas have no morality, no emotion, no desire to grapple souls... and they receive no redemption come the end, everyone either dead or in prison.

Henry's cell is suburbia, the Witness Protection Scheme shrinking him from somebody to nobody – a "schnook". It's his own private purgatory and it's been coming since the hit on Billy Batts, Henry's journey matching that of America's as his idealism in the '60s gives way to disillusionment in the '70s. Watch closely and you'll see the sickness set in: the glitzy home furnishings; the brutal whacking of just about everyone involved in the Lufthansa heist; the lines of coke that cut the third act into jagged shards; even the soundtrack's degeneration from the romance of The Harptones' 'Life Is But A Dream' to the toxicity of Sid Vicious snarling 'My Way' via the decadence of Italian doo-wop. The characters may not have religion, but Marty does: "If you live for a certain kind of value... you're gonna come smack up against a brick wall. It's materialism versus a spiritual life."

Wide-eyed wonderings? Think again. Scorsese makes the way of a GoodFella a rush to watch, but he, like us, knows the awful truth: it would be hell to live. TF

Jamie Graham

FAMILY TREE

GoodFellas **thrums with a love of cinema... and gives plenty back.**

Before...

THE GREAT TRAIN ROBBERY
Scorsese salutes the first ever Western/gangster movie (1903) by resurrecting its most famous shot: a ghostly Tommy DeVito (Pesci) fires a gun straight to camera to close the movie.

THIRTIES GANGSTER MOVIES
A big fan of *Public Enemy* and *Scarface*, Scorsese set out to mimic the Warner Bros gangster cycle through frenetic pacing, ferocious violence and a rise-and-tumble structure.

And after...

MENACE II SOCIETY, TRAINSPOTTING, BOOGIE NIGHTS, BLOW, THE BUSINESS
Makeshift family, drugs, wall-to-wall tunes, relentless technical flourishes... these dramas owe more than a little something to Marty's masterpiece.

THE SOPRANOS
Telly's Tony Soprano and his mob wouldn't exist without a certain wiseguy movie. Scorsese gave his blessing with a cameo, while half of *GoodFellas'* supporting cast make up the leads.

Classic Scene

*Yes, this is the wrong fuckin' picture, but none exist from the correct scene. You got a fuckin' problem with that?

INT. BAMBOO LOUNGE – NIGHT
Tommy is holding court at a table of wiseguys, having just finished a raucous tale involving telling a cop to go fuck his mother.

HENRY
(*chuckles*)
You're a pisser, you know? Really funny. Really funny.

TOMMY
What do you mean I'm funny?

HENRY
(*laughs*)
It's funny, you know. You're... it's a good story. It's funny. You're a funny guy.

TOMMY
(*chuckles*)
What do you mean, you mean the way I talk? What?

HENRY
It's just, you know, you're – it's – you're just funny. It's... it's funny, you know, the way you tell the story and everything.

TOMMY
Funny how? I mean, what's funny about it?

The atmosphere is becoming tense.

STABILE
Hey, Tommy, you got it all wrong...

TOMMY
Whoa, whoa, whoa, Anthony. He's a big boy. He knows what he said. What'd you say?

STABILE
You're right.

TOMMY
Funny, how?

HENRY
Just...

TOMMY
What?

HENRY
Just... you know, you're – you're funny.
(*chuckles*)
So?

TOMMY
You mean, let me understand this, cos I like... you know, maybe it's me, I'm a little fucked up, maybe. But, I'm funny, how? I mean, funny like I'm a clown? I amuse you? I make you laugh? I'm here to fucking amuse you? What do you mean funny? Funny, how? How am I funny?

HENRY
Come on, just... you know, how you tell a story. What?

TOMMY
No, I don't know. You said it. How do I know? You said I'm funny. How the fuck am I funny? What the fuck is so funny about me? Tell me what's so funny.

Henry is very uncertain what to say.

HENRY
Get the fuck outta here, Tommy.

Everyone laughs. The tension is diffused.

TOMMY
You motherfucker! I almost had him. I almost had him. Ya stuttering prick, ya. Frankie, was he shaking? Huh? I wonder about you sometimes, Henry. You may fold under questioning.

Editor-in-Chief Aubrey Ganguly
Editors Jamie Graham, Matt Mueller, Nev Pierce
Picture Editor Sarah Tully
Art Paul Sinclair, David Hicks
Production Alex Burrows, Nick Judd, Stuart McGirk, Scott Russon, Cassie Whittell
Contributors Dennis Brabham, Jonathan Crocker, Jane Crowther, Jonathan Dean, Patrick Donovan, Ryan Gilbey, Kevin Harley, Philip Kemp, Matthew Leyland, Andy Lowe, Richard Luck, Scott Russon, Mark Salisbury, Neil Smith, Ceri Thomas, James White, Jonathan Wright
Photo credits All Star, Aquarius, Album, LFI, Moviestore, Rex, Ronald Grant Archive
Publisher Simon Maxwell
Total Film Editor Mark Dinning

Published by **Future, 99 Baker Street, London W1U 6FP** Tel: 0207 317 2600
www.futurenet.co.uk
Entire contents ©2005 Future Publishing Limited. All rights reserved

SUBSCRIPTIONS AND BACK ISSUES
A 12-month subscription to *Total Film* costs £34 (UK) To subscribe call **0870 837 4722**
Or e-mail **totalfilm@subscriptions.co.uk**
For overseas orders call **+44 (0) 1858 438 794** For customer queries call **0870 8337 4773**
For overseas queries call **+44 (0) 1858 438 795**